Socialist Economic Development and Reforms

By the same author

The Economics and Politics of East–West Trade
The Economics of Socialism

Socialist Economic Development and Reforms

FROM EXTENSIVE TO INTENSIVE
GROWTH UNDER CENTRAL PLANNING
IN THE USSR,
EASTERN EUROPE, AND
YUGOSLAVIA

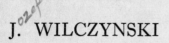

J. WILCZYNSKI

PRAEGER PUBLISHERS
New York · Washington

BOOKS THAT MATTER

Published in the United States of America in 1972
by Praeger Publishers, Inc., 111 Fourth Avenue,
New York, N.Y. 10003

Library of Congress Catalog Card Number: 73–165528

Printed in Great Britain

To Janet,
with an appreciation of her patience and understanding

Contents

Tables

Preface

'If Liberman did not exist it would be necessary to create him.'
We can thus paraphrase Voltaire's maxim if we take E. G. Liberman, the Soviet economist well publicized in the West, as a symbol
of economic revisionism under modern Socialism. The theme of this
book is twofold. Firstly, a systematic treatment is presented of
economic reforms in the eight European Socialist countries –
Bulgaria, Czechoslovakia, the German Democratic Republic,
Hungary, Poland, Romania, the USSR and Yugoslavia. Secondly,
it is demonstrated that the reforms have not been an accidental
by-product of political de-Stalinization or a 'return to Capitalism',
but a logical and necessary evolutionary process to meet the needs
of higher stages of economic development.

Economic growth is derived from two sources – extensive and
intensive. Extensive growth is based on increases in the volume
of the factors of production, especially labour and capital. On
the other hand, intensive growth consists in the increases in
productivity. Before the economic reforms, the Socialist countries
overwhelmingly relied on extensive sources of growth, but by the
early 1960s these sources were becoming rapidly exhausted. It
became obvious not only to theoretical writers but also to planners
and the Party leaders that to support continued rapid economic
development, particularly in these days of technological revolution, it was imperative to activate the reserves of intensive growth.
In this context, centralized, directive planning and management
proved wasteful and anachronistic and it had to be replaced by a
system more conducive to the growth of productivity.

Before the reforms, the economic systems in the eight Socialist
countries were virtually identical. They were all imitations of the
Soviet model with hardly any national originality, and thus the
study of each economy was in this sense monotonous and un-
rewarding. However, since the reforms that uniformity has been

broken up. This, as the author has found, makes writing a book on modern Socialist economies more arduous than before because exceptions can be cited to almost any generalization.

Each country has in fact been developing its own model to suit its stage of economic development, available resources and national peculiarities and ambitions. The region has become a manifold and dynamic economic laboratory where new principles are being tested and better solutions evolved. Theoretical discussions and empirical evidence in these countries are introducing new dimensions into the strategy of economic development.

The study of economics in Socialist countries, for a long time reduced to the regurgitation and reinterpretation of Marxian ideas, is being rejuvenated. Instead of providing apologia and justification for arbitrary ('voluntaristic') policies, economics is evolving into a creative science where economic common sense has a better chance of prevailing over doctrinaire orthodoxy. Many contributions being made by Socialist economists, as in the fields of accelerated growth in different stages of economic development, the interaction between planning and the market, optimal planning, cybernetics and economic forecasting, are obviously significant landmarks in the history of world economic thought.

A study of the reforms in the European Socialist countries is obviously of interest and value to the outside world. These countries represent one-tenth of world population, one-fifth of world area and of national income and nearly one-third of the world's industrial output. An examination of the reforms provides insight into the past and present working of their economies and a better understanding of their changing relations with the Capitalist world.

But probably the greatest value consists in the lessons that can be provided by Socialist experience to other countries which have adopted some elements of Socialism, such as nationalization, economic planning and welfare programmes, and which have embarked upon accelerated industrialization. Socialist ideas, success and mistakes can provide guidance for choosing growth strategies best suited to the different stages of economic development – particularly in the developing nations determined to speed up their economic growth. In fact in several respects, conditions in underdeveloped non-Socialist countries relevant to economic growth are similar to those which prevailed under Socialism in the past – although for different reasons – such as substantial labour reserves in agriculture, a small pool of competent managers and skilled workers, no, or imperfect, markets for the factors of production, and an institutional set-up not conducive to rational economic accounting.

J. WILCZYNSKI

Royal Military College of Australia,
Duntroon, University of New South Wales

1 Economic Development and Growth under Socialism

THE postulate of rapid economic development has dominated Socialist thinking, policies and national life in general ever since the formation of the first Socialist State in 1917, certainly much more than in Capitalist countries. As viewed by the Party leadership, such development promotes the industrial and social processes conducive to the consolidation and perpetuation of Communist power, it offers the hope of a Communist cornucopia for the masses and it provides a solid basis for military strength. But above all, it has been regarded as a chariot for winning the economic race with the most advanced Western countries and thus as evidence of the superiority of Socialism over Capitalism as an economic and social system. 'Socialism must prove', it was emphasized in a Polish study on the subject, 'that it can be a superior system to Capitalism not only from the standpoint of social justice (which is obvious) but also as a more progressive and dynamic system in respect of the growth of labour productivity, the efficiency of resources in general and of national income. . . . This rivalry represents the basic phenomenon of our era and it is likely to decide the fate of mankind.'[1] Preoccupation with the maximum possible economic growth has overshadowed the national scene so much that it has sometimes been identified with an end in itself.

However, the most obvious recent evidence of the weight attached to high rates of growth is afforded by the far-reaching economic reforms. It has been so compulsive that, in spite of triumphant I-told-you-so's from Washington and continual diatribes from Peking, not to mention the opposition of recusant Stalinist diehards at home, these countries[2] have decided to adopt

---

[1] J. Kleer, J. Zawadzki and J. Górski, *Socjalizm–Kapitalizm* (Socialism v. Capitalism), Warsaw, KiW, 1967, pp. 81, 85.

[2] The countries considered in this study are the European Socialist countries, except Albania (which still adheres to the old economic system), including

several elements peculiar to the Capitalist economy – features for which traditionally they have had only ideological contempt. In this chapter, we shall review the Socialist road to economic development, the official rates of growth since 1950 and their appraisal and the question of optimum growth.

A. THE SOCIALIST ROAD TO ECONOMIC DEVELOPMENT

There are two basic characteristics of the Socialist economies relevant to economic development: the social ownership of the means of production and central planning. Practically all mining, manufacturing, transport, communications, trading and financial enterprises and other entities are socially owned and operated, i.e. by the State or by co-operatives (collectively). Taking the eight countries as a whole, the socialized sector embraces 92 per cent of agricultural land and is responsible for 99 per cent of industrial output, 98 per cent of retail sales (100 per cent of wholesale turnover) and for 95 per cent of the national income produced. The proportions for individual countries are shown in Table 1.

Economic processes are subject to central planning which is exercised in each Socialist country by the State Planning Commission (or Office). Although the extent and methods of planning and administration have changed considerably as a result of economic reforms, the major proportions in the economy strategic to development are still centrally determined. These determinations include the proportion between consumption and saving, between productive and non-productive investment, investment amongst the major divisions of the economy (such as industry, agriculture, trade) and amongst the branches of industry (e.g. heavy, chemical, light industries).

The effectiveness of economic planning is enhanced by the

Bulgaria, Czechoslovakia, the German Democratic Republic (East Germany), Hungary, Poland, Romania, the USSR (including Soviet Asia) and Yugoslavia. The first seven countries (plus Mongolia) are members of the Council for Mutual Economic Assistance and are known as CMEA (or Comecon) countries. Yugoslavia is only an associate, not a full, member of CMEA.

social ownership of the means of production. Private enterprise is not in a position to undermine centrally laid-down directions of development as it is tolerated only in the less dynamic or minor spheres of economic activity (agriculture, handicrafts, catering and retailing).

TABLE I   THE SHARE OF THE SOCIALIZED SECTOR IN AGRICUL-
TURAL LAND, INDUSTRIAL OUTPUT, RETAIL SALES AND
NATIONAL INCOME IN 1967

COUNTRY	PERCENTAGE SHARE REPRESENTED BY THE SOCIALIZED SECTOR			
	Agricultural Land	Industrial Output	Retail Sales	NATIONAL INCOME
Bulgaria	99	99	100	95
Czechoslovakia	90	100	100	95
GDR	95	88	79	94
Hungary	94	99	99	96
Poland	15	100	99	76
Romania	91	100	100	95
USSR	100	100	100	96
Yugoslavia	16	98	n.a.	77
AVERAGE (weighted)	92	99	98	95

n.a. = not available.

Sources. Based on: Central Statistical Office of Poland, Rozwój gospodarczy krajów RWPG 1950–1968 (Economic Development of CMEA Countries 1950–1968), Warsaw, 1969, pp. 66, 84, 125; Federal Institute for Statistics, Statistički godišnjak Jugoslavije 1969 (Statistical Yearbook of Yugoslavia for 1969), Belgrade, 1969, p. 110.

In contrast to Capitalism, the macroeconomic constraint on economic development is normally not a lack of effective demand but rather limits to the availability of resources. The most distinctive features of Socialist developmental strategy are two: first, the process of capital formation which, together with its efficiency, determines the rate of economic growth; and second, the industrialization drive, to the neglect of agriculture, domestic trade and services, with further priorities being assigned to iron and steel, machine building, and more recently to chemical, electronic and power-producing industries (see Chapters 11 A and 13 B, pp. 192–97, 239–40).

It is worth pointing out that in Socialist countries a good deal of significance is attached to the distinction between 'development' and 'growth'. Development is a broad concept signifying progressive changes involving resources, institutions and methods of production, leading to changing production relations and social transformation in general. As such, it is regarded as an evolutionary process towards the Marxian ideal of Full (the 'second stage' of) Communism.

Whilst economic development consists in continuous structural and qualitative transformation, economic growth is a narrower concept denoting changes in quantitatively measurable magnitudes, such as national income, industrial output, investment, consumption. The rate of growth naturally depends on economic development, and in turn economic development itself changes in response to economic growth. In Capitalist economies the preoccupation of theoreticians and policy-makers is with 'growth' whilst 'development' is ignored or neglected, which is indicated by the fact that the two concepts are often used interchangeably.

B. OFFICIAL RATES OF GROWTH

(a) National Income

The scope of national income accounting in Socialist countries is limited to the material production sphere, i.e. services (unless they are rendered directly to enterprises engaged in material production) are not included.[1] The official Socialist rates of growth are normally given at constant prices in which the Laspeyres (as

---

[1] Consequently the following services, although constituting part of production by the Western method, are excluded from the Socialist national income: public administration and justice, education, science and culture, health and social welfare, finance and insurance, local government and housing administration, defence, entertainment, personal postal services, private travel and

opposed to the Paasche or Fisher) index is applied, i.e. the price relations in the base period are taken for value aggregation in subsequent years.

Table 2 shows the annual rates of growth of national income in the eight Socialist countries over the period 1951–69. The highest rates, of on the average 8–9 per cent p.a., were attained by the USSR, Bulgaria and Romania. Of these countries, the USSR has the advantage of ample resources and of the economies of scale; in the case of Bulgaria and Romania the high rates can be partly explained by the relatively early stage of their economic development, where given increases in production yield high percentage increases. On the other hand, the more developed countries, Hungary and Czechoslovakia, exhibited lower average rates (5–6 per cent p.a.) than average for the region.

The widest fluctuations in the rates are evident in the case of the smaller Socialist countries – Bulgaria, Czechoslovakia, Hungary and Yugoslavia – in which bottlenecks are more likely to appear; all these countries experienced negative rates in at least one year over the period. In the case of the USSR, growth has been more even, largely due to the advantages already mentioned above (for further discussion, see section D of this chapter).

Taking the eight countries as a whole, we can distinguish three stages in their growth since 1950. Up to the late 1950s high rates prevailed, averaging 11 per cent annually. From the late 1950s to the early 1960s there was a gradual decline reaching 4 per cent in 1963. Since that time the overall rate has improved to an average of 7 per cent in the late 1960s. The overall rates are represented in Table 3 where, for comparison, the rates for the European Economic Community, Japan, the United Kingdom, the United States and the world are also given.

---

domestic service. Socialist national income is calculated on a *net* basis (as by the Western method), i.e. depreciation is deducted, but it is valued at *realized* prices, i.e. including sales ('turnover') taxes (which contrasts with the Western valuation 'at factor cost'). If brought to the Western basis the Socialist national income may be up to 40% higher (although in extreme cases it could be lower) than the official figure. As a very rough approximation, to bring the official Socialist national income figure to the Western basis, add one-quarter (and to bring the Western national income figure to the socialist basis, reduce it by one-fifth).

TABLE 2 RATES OF GROWTH OF NATIONAL INCOME* IN THE
EUROPEAN SOCIALIST COUNTRIES, 1951–1969

YEAR	BULGARIA	CZECHOSLOVAKIA	GDR	HUNGARY	POLAND	ROMANIA	USSR	YUGOSLAVIA
1951	41	10		16	8		12	10
1952	—1	10		—2	6		11	—8
1953	21	7	13†	12	10	14	9	12
1954	0	4		—5	11		12	3
1955	5	11		8	8		12	13
1956	1	5		—11	7	—7	11	—4
1957	13	7		23	11	16	7	23
1958	7	8	7†	6	6	4	12	3
1959	22	6		7	5	12	8	17
1960	7	8		9	4	11	8	6
1961	3	7	4	6	8	11	7	6
1962	6	1	2	5	2	4	6	4
1963	7	—2	3	6	7	10	4	12
1964	10	1	5	5	7	12	9	13
1965	7	3	5	1	7	10	7	2
1966	11	10	6	8	7	8	8	9
1967	9	7	5	9	6	8	9	2
1968	6	8	5	5	9	7	8	5
1969‡	8	6	5	5	3	7	5	9
1951–69§	8	6	7	5	7	8	9	7

* Official rates at constant prices. The comparability of the rates between the countries and especially between the years is questionable.

† At current prices.

‡ Subject to revisions.

§ The averages are based on the calculations carried out by the United Nations (United Nations, *Yearbook of National Accounts Statistics 1968*, vol. II, p. 112) and supplemented by the author.

Sources. Based on: Central Statistical Office of Poland, *Rozwój gospodarczy krajów RWPG 1950–1968* (Economic Development of the CMEA Countries 1950–1968), Warsaw, 1969, pp. 16–44; *Gospodarka planowa* (Planned Economy), Warsaw, 4/1970, pp. 6–11.

The factors which have contributed to these trends in Socialist growth are the subject of analysis in the following chapters of this study, but we may briefly highlight the main reasons at this stage. The high rates up to the late 1950s can be explained by the utilization of existing capacities made possible by the previously completed post-war reconstruction, large increases in employment and investment, the emphasis on the sheer volume of production (usually to the detriment of the quality and suitability of the articles turned out) and by the low absolute starting level of national income.

The following years, roughly covering the period 1958–63, witnessed a decline in the rates of increase of labour and capital, the inadequacy of incentives, widespread agricultural failures, growing waste, the preparation for reforms and the initiation of several changes,[1] all of which – to varying degrees in different countries – adversely affected the growth of production. The recovery since 1963 has been aided by major reforms, already producing benefits in the form of higher efficiency. However, the improvement has been slow so far, the overall annual rate of growth having oscillated around 7 per cent in the late 1960s. It is generally maintained in Socialist countries that the recent modest growth of production is temporary, owing to the inevitably disturbing effects associated with the changeover to the new economic system, after which the rates will improve further. A Polish expert on growth pointed out:

> The recent slow growth of production in the USSR and other Socialist countries does not provide a sound basis for assuming that these rates will tend to fall or become stabilized at low levels. The point is that Socialist economies are changing over to the intensive stage of development (with an emphasis on labour productivity and the effectiveness of investment) and are departing from extensive growth (based mostly on increases in employment and investment). This transition necessitates fundamental changes in the methods of planning administration and the management of the national economy.[2]

[1] Yugoslavia, of course, embarked on reforms much earlier, viz. during 1950–52, which also produced disruption to growth (see Table 2, p. 6).

[2] I. Timofiejuk, *Mierniki wzrostu gospodarczego* (Indicators of Economic Growth), Warsaw, PWE, 1968, pp. 124–5.

TABLE 3 ANNUAL RATES OF GROWTH OF NATIONAL INCOME*
IN SELECTED SOCIALIST AND CAPITALIST COUNTRIES,
1951–1969

YEARS	The 8 Socialist Countries†	EEC‡	Japan	UK	USA	World §
1951–69	8	5	10	3	4	5
1951–55	11	6	10	3	4	6
1956–60	8	5	10	2	2	5
1961	7	6	16	4	2	4
1962	5	6	7	1	7	6
1963	4	5	8	4	4	4
1964	7	5	14	6	5	7
1965	6	5	4	3	6	6
1966	8	4	10	1	6	6
1967	8	4	13	1	3	4
1968	8	5	16	4	5	5
1969 ¶	5	7	12	2	3	5

* At constant prices. The Socialist national income includes material production only, whilst in Capitalist national income services are included. The
comparability of the rates between the years and especially between the countries
is limited (see section C of this chapter).

† Bulgaria, Czechoslovakia, the GDR, Hungary, Poland, Romania, the
USSR and Yugoslavia.

‡ Belgium, France, the FRG, Italy, Luxembourg and the Netherlands
throughout.

§ Excluding the Asian Socialist countries (China, DPR of Korea, Mongolia
and DR of Vietnam).

¶ Partly based on estimates, subject to revision.

Sources. Based on: *Rozwój gospodarczy krajów RWPG 1950–1968*, op. cit., pp. 4,
16–43; United Nations, *Yearbook of National Accounts Statistics, Monthly
Bulletin of Statistics* and *OECD Economic Outlook.*

(b) Industrial Output

The Socialist concept of industrial output is much broader than the Western one. It covers the output contributed by the manu-facturing industry (including the processing of agricultural pro-ducts), mining, quarrying, timber cutting and processing, and fishing, but it does not include building and construction. The total is arrived at by adding up the output of all enterprises in these branches of 'industry', even if it consists of non-finished products, which gives a hybrid sum embodying a good deal of double-counting.[1] Consequently, the Socialist growth rates of industrial output are even less reliable indicators than those of national income. On the other hand, the Capitalist rates refer to manu-facturing *production* (i.e. value added only) which often includes building and construction.

The pace of industrial growth in the Socialist countries under consideration is shown in Table 4. The Socialist industrialization drive is clearly reflected in the high rates of growth throughout the period. If comparison is made with Table 2, p. 6, it is evident that consistently in all these countries, and in almost all years, the in-dexes of growth of industrial output exceeded the growth of national income, which means that other branches of the Socialist economies have been developing at much slower rates.

The relatively rapid industrial growth in Socialist economies is evident if comparisons are made with Capitalist countries. This is done in Table 5.

(c) Agricultural Output

The figures of agricultural output also embody double-counting, and moreover the valuation, even for the same product, usually differs according to the type of producer (State, collective, private) and the basis on which transactions are made (compulsory deliveries to the State, above-compulsory deliveries, private sales).

---

[1] In Socialist calculations of national income this double-counting is of course removed, but with the exception of Hungary and Yugoslavia, no Socialist country publishes figures of industrial production on the value-added basis.

TABLE 4 RATES OF GROWTH OF INDUSTRIAL OUTPUT,*
1951–1969

	BULGARIA	CZECHOSLOVAKIA	GDR†	HUNGARY	POLAND	ROMANIA	USSR	YUGOSLAVIA
1951	19	14	23	24	22	24	16	−7
1952	16	18	16	21	19	17	12	−2
1953	15	9	12	12	17	15	12	13
1954	11	4	10	2	11	6	13	15
1955	8	11	8	9	11	14	12	15
1956	15	9	6	−8	9	11	11	9
1957	16	10	8	16	10	8	10	17
1958	15	11	11	11	10	10	10	11
1959	20	11	12	10	9	10	11	13
1960	12	12	8	12	11	16	10	15
1961	11	9	6	10	10	15	9	7
1962	10	6	6	8	8	14	10	7
1963	10	−1	4	7	5	12	8	16
1964	10	4	6	9	9	14	7	16
1965	15	8	6	5	9	13	9	8
1966	12	7	6	7	7	11	9	5
1967	13	7	7	9	8	14	10	0
1968	12	5	7	5	9	12	8	6
1969‡	11	5	8	3	9	11	7	11
1951–69§	13	7	9	7	9	13	10	9

* Official rates at current prices. The comparability of the figures between different years and particularly between different countries is limited.

† At current prices.

‡ Subject to revisions.

§ See note § to Table 2, p. 6.

Sources. As for Table 2, p. 6.

TABLE 5 ANNUAL RATES OF GROWTH OF INDUSTRIAL OUTPUT*
IN SELECTED SOCIALIST AND CAPITALIST COUNTRIES, 1951–1969

YEARS	The 8 Socialist Countries	EEC	Japan	UK	USA	World†
1951–69	10	6	16	3	4	6
1951–55	14	9	18	4	5	7
1956–60	10	7	17	3	2	6
1961	9	7	20	1	1	5
1962	9	4	8	1	8	8
1963	7	5	10	3	5	7
1964	7	7	18	8	6	7
1965	9	4	5	3	8	8
1966	8	5	13	1	9	7
1967	9	1	20	0	1	2
1968	8	9	17	5	5	7
1969‡	7	13	16	3	5	6

* At constant prices. The Socialist industrial output includes manufacturing, mining, quarrying, timber exploitation and fisheries, whilst the Capitalist totals usually include manufacturing only. The comparability of the rates between different years and especially between different countries is limited (see section C of this chapter).
† Without the four Asian countries.
‡ Subject to revision.

Sources. As for Table 3, p. 8.

Thus these rates of growth can only have an approximate comparative value.

The growth rates for agricultural output in the individual Socialist countries are set out in Table 6. As one would expect, fluctuations from year to year are considerable. Although obscured by these fluctuations, it is evident that the average rates in each country over the period are low – only about one-half of those of national income, and even lower in comparison with industrial growth. The overall rates for the eight countries over the 1951–69

TABLE 6 RATES OF GROWTH OF AGRICULTURAL OUTPUT,*
1951–1969

	BULGARIA	CZECHOSLOVAKIA	GDR	HUNGARY	POLAND	ROMANIA	USSR	YUGOSLAVIA
1951	40	1	19	n.a.	—7	25	—7	45
1952	—16	—3	3	n.a.	2	—7	9	—34
1953	22	0	8	18	3	17	3	44
1954	—12	—1	4	2	6	1	5	—12
1955	9	11	1	13	3	18	11	14
1956	—7	4	—3	—12	7	—19	13	—13
1957	17	—1	7	13	4	24	3	14
1958	—1	3	4	4	3	—13	11	—18
1959	18	—1	—3	5	—1	19	0	33
1960	3	6	9	—6	5	2	2	—12
1961	—3	0	—11	0	10	5	3	—6
1962	4	—7	—1	3	—8	—8	1	5
1963	2	7	8	5	4	4	—7	10
1964	12	3	4	4	1	6	14	3
1965	2	—4	8	—4	8	6	2	—6
1966	15	11	3	8	5	14	9	24
1967	3	5	5	4	3	1	1	—5
1968	—8	6	1	1	4	—3	5	—4
1969†	2	1	—7	6	—5	5	—3	10
1951–69‡	6	2	4	4	3	5	5	5

n.a. = not available.
  * Official rates at constant prices. The comparability of the figures between different years and especially between different countries is limited.
  † Subject to revisions.
  ‡ See note § to Table 2, p. 6.

Sources. As for Table 2, p. 6.

period compare as follows (world averages are also given):

	The Eight Socialist Countries	The World
National income	8% p.a.	5% p.a.
Industrial output	10% p.a.	6% p.a.
Agricultural output	4% p.a.	4% p.a.

C. AN APPRAISAL OF SOCIALIST GROWTH RATES

For a long time, it was widely believed in the West that Socialist statistics, particularly those related to economic achievements, were deliberately falsified by Communist regimes for propaganda purposes. There is now sufficient evidence to prove that this belief was ill-founded, and it is now generally agreed amongst the experts on the subject that the Socialist statistical returns are genuine and do reflect the economic facts.

However, many Socialist economic concepts, procedures for collecting data and methods of valuation differ from those accepted in Capitalist countries, so that Socialist rates of growth may be misleading if not correctly interpreted. The superiority of the Socialist road to development, as frequently claimed by Socialist leaders, is indicated by both faster and more stable growth than in the case of Capitalist countries. We shall now briefly examine the extent to which these two claims are justified.

The Socialist rates of growth of national income tend to contain an upward bias or otherwise appear unduly high, particularly when compared with Capitalist rates. This conclusion can be supported by the following considerations. First, owing to the institutional set-up and the system of incentives traditionally based on fulfilled and exceeded targets, enterprises have tended to overstate their production achievements whenever they could get away with it. Second, the quality of Socialist production has on the whole been lower than in Capitalist countries. This was particularly the case until recently when targets were defined in quantitative terms and incentives were payable irrespective of the quality and use of the articles statistically recorded.

Third, in relation to developed Capitalist countries of comparable size, Socialist absolute production levels are lower so that absolute increases produce high percentage increases. This was particularly the case in the 1950s. Fourth, Socialist countries apply different criteria to the pricing of articles produced in different branches of the economy. Thus many industrial products carry heavy turnover taxes in contrast to other products. This makes the proportion of industrial production in national income unduly high.[1] As industrial production grows faster than production in other branches of the economy, in effect the national income rates are disproportionately pushed upwards.

Fifth, non-productive services, which grow very slowly in Socialist countries,[2] are excluded from national income accounts. This exclusion prevents their retarding effect being reflected in the growth rates of national income. Finally, Socialist countries for practical considerations find it expedient to apply the Laspeyres formula for calculating the total values of national income. This tends to produce higher rates if the structure of production is rapidly changing, as it is in these countries, in favour of industrial articles. In addition, new articles are normally priced higher than is justified by the price level of the initial base year owing to rising prices in general and the fact that new products embody a novelty mark-up.[3]

Some of the above considerations have been taken into account by a number of Western economists, mostly in the United States, who have carried out studies on Socialist growth rates in terms of Western concepts and methodology. A sample of such rates, compared with the official Socialist rates, is given in Table 7.

In evidence presented to the US Congress by a group of experts, the following rates of growth of the Soviet GNP at factor cost

[1] In 1967 the share at officially given prices ranged from 51% in Romania to 62% in Czechoslovakia. *Rozwój gospodarczy krajów RWPG 1950–1968* (Economic Development of the CMEA countries, 1950–1968), Warsaw, 1969, p. 61. However, if factor cost were applied to the valuation of all material production, the range would be closer to 35–50%.

[2] Compared with Capitalist countries where services generally contribute from 15 to 35% of national income.

[3] An extreme illustration is afforded by calculations made by Bergson to estimate the Soviet rates of growth of Gross National Product at factor cost for the period 1928–37. Using the 1928 price weights the average annual rate of 11·9 was obtained, but when he applied the 1937 price weights he produced the rate of only 5·5. A. Bergson, *The Real National Income of Soviet Russia since 1928*, Cambridge, Mass., Harvard UP, 1961, p. 217.

(1959 value-added weights) were given for the critical decade 1958–67 (the official Soviet growth rates for national income are given in brackets):

1958	9·4	(12·4)
1959	4·9	(7·5)
1960	5·2	(7·7)
1961	7·0	(6·8)
1962	4·2	(5·7)
1963	2·8	(4·0)
1964	7·9	(9·3)
1965	6·2	(6·9)
1966	7·1	(8·1)
1967	4·3	(8·6)
Annual Average	5·9	(7·7)

Sources. US Congress, JEC, *Soviet Economic Performance 1966–67*, Washington, GPO, 1968, p. 11; *Narodnoe khoziaistvo SSSR v 1969 g.*, p. 43.

It may be added that in some US estimates the rates for 1962 and 1963 were even lower. According to the Central Intelligence Agency the average for the two years was 2·5, and even less according to G. W. Nutter.[1]

Thus it may be concluded that the rates produced by the US economists are lower than the official Socialist rates by roughly one-third. However, it must be pointed out that the adoption of the Western basis for comparative calculations favours Capitalist (especially developed) countries. In these economies, services represent a high proportion of national income (roughly one-quarter) and they grow faster than material production, thus enhancing the total rate of growth. Yet Socialist countries do not regard most services as part of production.

It is interesting to register Socialist reaction to the Western estimates. Most Socialist economists are naturally highly critical

---

[1] For an objective discussion of this controversy, see A. Nove, '2½ Per Cent and All That', *Soviet Studies*, July 1964, pp. 17–21.

B

TABLE 7 WESTERN ESTIMATES OF SOCIALIST RATES OF GROWTH

AUTHOR	Basis of Estimate	Period	Average Annual Rate	Official Socialist Rate*	% by which Socialist Rate is Higher
Bergson	Soviet GNP at rouble factor cost of 1937	1950–60	7·0	10·3	47%
Bergson	Soviet GNP at rouble factor cost of 1950	1950–55	7·6	11·4	50%
Bornstein	Soviet GNP at 1955 factor cost weights	1950–58	6·5–7·5	10·9	45–68%
Campbell	Soviet GNP at 1958 non-agricultural sectors weights	1950–58 1958–63	7·0 5·5	10·9 6·3	56% 16%
Cohn	Soviet GNP at 1959 factor cost weights	1950–58 1958–64	7·1 5·3	10·9 6·7	53% 26%
Greenslade and Wallace	Soviet industrial production at 1955 value-added weights	1950–55 1955–61	10·1 8·7	13·2 10·1	31% 16%
Noren	Soviet ind. prod. at 1960 value-added weights	1951–55 1956–61 1962–65	11·3 9·0 7·3	13·2 10·1 8·4	12% 11% 15%
Nutter	Soviet ind. prod. with moving weights	1950–55	9·6	13·2	37%
Diamond	Soviet net agric. prod. at 1958 full-cost price weights	1951–64	3·8	4·1	8%
Willet	Soviet agric. prod. at 1958 price weights	1950–61	4·3	5·0	16%
Ernst	Eastern European GNP at 1956 factor cost weights†	1951–55 1956–60 1961–64	5·7 5·2 3·6	[8·5] [6·5] [4·5]	49% 25% 25%
Ernst	E.E. ind. prod. at 1956 factor cost weights† ‡	1951–55 1956–60 1961–64	8·5 8·1 5·8	[13·0] [10·0] [8·0]	52% 23% 37%
Ernst	E.E. agric. prod. at 1956 factor cost weights† ‡	1950–63	[about 1·5]	[2·5]	67%

* National income, industrial production, agricultural production according to Socialist definitions. The bracketed rates for the six Eastern European countries are this writer's rough estimates based on official returns.

† The countries included are: Bulgaria, Czechoslovakia, the GDR, Hungary, Poland and Romania. The price weights applicable to the GDR are the German 1936 weights (equivalent to the East German 1950 weights) and to Hungary of the year 1955.

‡ The industrial production of Bulgaria, Czechoslovakia, Hungary and Poland includes construction.

Sources. A. Bergson, *The Economics of Soviet Planning*, Yale UP, 1964, p. 306, and *The Real National Income of Soviet Russia since 1928*, Harvard UP, 1961, p. 217. M. Bornstein and D. R. Fusfeld (eds), *The Soviet Economy*, Homewood, Irwin, rev. ed., 1966, pp. 287–8. R. W. Campbell, 'The Post-War Growth of the Soviet Economy', *Soviet Studies*, July 1964, p. 3. S. H. Cohn, 'Soviet Growth Retardation: Trends in Resource Availability', in US Congress, Joint Economic Committee, *New Directions in the Soviet Economy*, Washington GPO, 1966, Part II-A, p. 105. R. W. Greenslade and Phyllis Wallace, 'Industrial Production in the USSR', in US Congress, JEC, *Dimensions of Soviet Economic Power*, Washington, GPO, 1962, Part II, p. 125. J. H. Noren, 'Soviet Industry Trends in Output, Inputs, and Productivity', in *New Directions in the Soviet Economy*, Part II-A, pp. 280, 282. G. W. Nutter, *Growth of Industrial Production in the Soviet Union*, Princeton UP, 1962, p. 163. D. B. Diamond, 'Trends in Output, Inputs and Factor Productivity in Soviet Agriculture', in *New Directions in the Soviet Economy*, Part II-B, p. 346. J. W. Willet, 'The Recent Record in Agricultural Production', in *Dimensions of Soviet Economic Power*, Part II, p. 98. M. Ernst, 'Postwar Economic Growth in Eastern Europe', in *New Directions in the Soviet Economy*, Part IV, pp. 880, 883–4, 913–14. Central Statistical Office attached to the Council of Ministers of the USSR, *Narodnoe khoziaistvo SSSR v 1967g* (The National Economy of the USSR in 1967), Moscow, Statistika, 1968, p. 59; Central Statistical Office of Poland, *Rozwój gospodarczy krajów RWPG 1950–1968* (The Economic Development of CMEA Countries), Warsaw, 1969, pp. 16–43.

of these estimates and they view them as malicious misrepresentations, calculated to underrate Socialist achievements.[1] On the other hand, some of the younger econometricians appear to be less critical. Of considerable interest is a study carried out by two Soviet economists, Mikhalevskii and Solovev, *and published* in 1966. They criticized the inconsistency of aggregation in Soviet national income statistics, and instead they employed the mathematical production function in their calculations. By their method, they arrived at an average annual rate of increase of 7·0 in the Soviet national income for the period 1951–63. Their rate is much lower than the official rate of 9·1 for the same period, but still

[1] e.g. a Soviet economist, I. Kotkovskii, writing in *Voprosy ekonomiki* (Problems of Economics), 4/1967, pp. 71–84, attacked Cohn's calculations for the USSR over the period 1959–64. Kotkovskii argued that over the period the Soviet GNP, or national income, increased by 48 %, not by 36 % as would appear from Cohn's figures.

slightly higher than the rate of 6·4 produced by Cohn.[1]* A Polish expert on growth, in a recently published book on the Socialist rates of growth, when discussing Soviet rates deemed it reasonable to quote some estimates by Western writers as well.[2]

From the preceding discussion it may be concluded that, on the whole, the Socialist rates of growth are certainly higher than those attained in the Capitalist world, even if the lower Western estimates are accepted as correct. What can be disputed is only the degree of the gap. Thus Cohn's average annual rate of increase of 6·4 in the Soviet GNP at factor cost for 1950–64 is still higher than the corresponding rates of 2·8 for the United Kingdom, 3·6 for the United States and about 5·0 for the Capitalist world as a whole. However, a few economically less mature Capitalist nations achieved rates comparable with those claimed by Socialist countries, viz. Israel, Japan and Taiwan, each of whom scored 9·0 over the same period.[3]

With regard to fluctuations in the rates of growth, one would expect smaller variations from year to year in Socialist than in Capitalist countries, owing to the centrally planned nature of development and practically continuous full employment in Socialist countries.[4] However, to make comparisons of the degree of fluctuations is not a grateful task. In the official Socialist growth rates of national income, fluctuations are partly hidden due to the peculiarities of national income accounting and pricing. In Capitalist market economies, services are usually the most sensitive element of economic fluctuations, but these are almost wholly excluded from Socialist national income accounts.

Furthermore, compared with prices prevailing in market

[1] B. N. Mikhalevskii and Yu. P. Solovev, ('The Growth Function in the Soviet Economy over the Years 1951–1963'), *Ekonomika i matematicheskie metody* (Economics and Mathematical Methods), 6/1966, pp. 823–40.

* If an article appeared in a foreign language, its title translated into English is shown *in parentheses*.

[2] I. Timofiejuk, op. cit., pp. 122–4.

[3] Based on United Nations *Yearbook of National Accounts Statistics* (different years).

[4] Yugoslavia being a notable exception. In the 1950s unemployment reached up to 5% of the working population; in the 1960s it ranged from 5 to 10% or more, averaging 250,000 persons. Based on: Federal Institue of Statistics, *Statistički godišnjak Jugoslavije 1969* (Statistical Yearbook of Yugoslavia for 1969), Belgrade, 1969, p. 104.

economies, Socialist prices are distorted because different criteria of valuation are applied to different types of articles. By market economy standards, prices of agricultural products are unduly depressed in relation to those in other branches of the economy. In effect, changes in agricultural production are 'underweighted' in Socialist national income figures.[1] Yet Socialist agriculture is noted for very wide fluctuations in output (see Table 6, p. 12).

Thus, for the ten-year period 1958–67, if we take the official Soviet rates for national income the average annual standard deviation works out to be 4·3, but if Western-estimated rates for the Soviet GNP are taken (see p. 15) the deviation is much greater, viz. 7·7. However, even the latter deviation is lower than in the case of the three leading Western countries for the same period, viz. the United Kingdom, 8·9; the United States, 10·8; and Japan: 16·9.[2]

From these calculations it is evident that even during the period noted for the greatest ups and downs in the USSR in the plan era (since 1928), the degree of fluctuation in Soviet rates of growth was lower than in the three important Capitalist countries. No GNP rates are available for other Socialist countries (covering long enough periods) to make comparative calculations of deviations. Upon examination of their official rates for national income, it is apparent that fluctuations in these countries in the past were greater than in the USSR (see Table 2, p. 6), although they do not seem to have been as pronounced as in most Capitalist countries. There are certainly no trade cycles, and those fluctuations that do occur do not significantly affect the level of employment (except in Yugoslavia) and the welfare of the population (however, see Chapter 10, p. 167n, and Chapter 15, p. 326).

[1] e.g., according to the official price structure, the share of agricultural production in the Czechoslovak national income in 1966 was 12%, but if a uniform pricing criterion were applied, then the share would be 24%. The respective proportions applicable to the Hungarian agricultural output in 1963 were 20 and 35%. Reported in: *Zemedelske noviny* (Agricultural News), Prague, 17/10/1968, p. 5; *Gospodarka planowa* (Planned Economy), Warsaw, 6/1969, p. 26.
[2] Adjustments were made for the differences in these countries' average annual rate of growth of GNP from the Western estimated average rate of 5·9 for the Soviet GNP. The rates for Japan, the UK and the USA were taken from the United Nations *Yearbook of National Accounts Statistics.*

D. THE PROBLEM OF THE OPTIMUM RATES OF GROWTH

There is little doubt that, on the whole, Socialist economic growth in the past was remarkably high, especially in the 1950s, and industrial development can be described as spectacular. The question that has naturally been asked frequently in the Capitalist world, and sometimes in the Socialist countries, is whether the results have been warranted by the cost of attaining them. We shall now examine this proposition.

On the one hand, it must be remembered that the Eastern European countries (with the partial exception of Czechoslovakia and the German Democratic Republic), even after the post-war reconstruction of the late 1940s, still had fresh memories of their economic plight under Capitalist regimes: backward economies overwhelmingly dependent on agriculture, low income levels, unemployment, instability, a handy reservoir of cheap food and raw materials for the industrialized Western nations and a dumping-ground for their manufactures. National pride simply could not allow the repetition of that state of affairs. Even the USSR was still a backward country by Western standards. After 1947 all these countries were faced with the Western embargo on exports of not only military items but also of advanced industrial equipment. The Communist regimes, of course, regarded rapid economic development as the only way out of these predicaments, and it appears that they had widespread popular support in this respect.

In a relatively short period of time, these countries have been transformed into progressive economies, with a solid and viable industrial base and with practically no help from Capitalist nations. In the two decades 1950–70, the national income of the eight Socialist countries more than quadrupled. During the same period, their industrial output increased seven times and their share in the world's industrial production rose from less than 18 to over 30 per cent.[1]

On the other hand, the accelerated growth has been attained at

[1] The proportion claimed by Socialist economists for the late 1960s was 31–33%. See, e.g., *Vop. ekon.*, 1/1969, p. 48; *Vunshna turgoviya* (Foreign Trade), Sofia, 4/1969, p. 13; *Życie gospodarcze* (Economic Life), Warsaw, 5/10/1969, p. 10.

tremendous costs, both to individual people as well as to society in general. These costs fall into three categories:

(i) *Depressed standards of living* – relatively small proportions of national income allowed for current consumption, a small range and poor quality of consumer goods including housing, shortages and even rationing, poor sales service and limited personal freedom.

(ii) *Prodigious expenditure of labour* – the virtual compulsion to work (including cases of the direction of labour), a high proportion of working females (including mothers), long working hours, extra 'voluntary' labour extracted from workers without remuneration and in some countries (especially in the USSR up to the late 1950s) forced labour.

(iii) *Extravagant use of the means of production* – little economy exercised in the consumption of materials and components in the process of production, extravagance in the use of capital equipment, land and other natural resources (which until recently were allocated to users free of charge).

Socialist leaders were naturally aware of these sacrifices, but in their wisdom they considered them to be justified in the context of long-run objectives. Those who bore the main brunt of the burden of rapid growth had little chance of influencing the priorities laid down by the Party.

The regimes in Socialist countries are in a position to set high rates of growth and then to proceed to find ways and means of achieving them – simply putting the cart before the horse. In this pursuit to realize the postulated rates there is a danger of either costs being ignored or otherwise of targets being assigned an inordinately high 'social' value.

But, of course, there is a number of constraints imposing upper limits on the rates. In the Stalinist era it was largely the verge of human endurance, at times pushed to extremes. But since the late 1950s, more serious barriers have begun to appear, especially in the more developed Socialist countries. It became obvious that to maintain the rates of growth, increasing outlays of resources were essential. This became most obvious in Czechoslovakia, where to support one koruna's increase in national income the following investment expenditures were necessary: in 1950, 1·33; in 1955, 1·27; in 1960, 2·41; and in 1963, 18·22 korunas![1] (For further details see Chapter 2 B, esp. Table 10, p. 36.)

In addition, the growing liberalization since the late 1950s has revealed other limits. Consumers, for a long time silenced by fear on the one hand and by promises on the other, began to reassert themselves. The authorities could no longer disregard what has come to be known as 'consumerism'. The successful operation of material incentives, a cornerstone of the new economic model, naturally depends on more and a wider range of consumer goods. Decentralization of planning and management have further limited the arbitrary power of central planners. There is also evidence suggesting that Socialist regimes are becoming more sensitive to the social cost involved in super-growth and that they may be reconciled with pursuing lower rates in the future (see Chapter 15 D, pp. 327–30).

Some Western economists have endeavoured to evaluate the costs and benefits of the high Socialist growth, particularly in the Soviet Union. According to J. P. Hardt, the sacrifices borne in the USSR were justified in the context of the aims adopted.[2] A. Nove came to the conclusion that, considering the backwardness of the Soviet economy and the objectives postulated, the austerity and coercion under Stalin were 'necessary' but not 'inevitable'.[3] On the other hand, G. W. Nutter thought that even in the context of the ambitious objectives adopted, the ruthless course and the great privations to the public were not justified.[4] In fact he went further by pointing out that '. . . the economy [of the USSR] would have grown at least as rapidly as it was while providing more welfare for the masses if the revolution of 1917 had resulted

---

[1] Both national income and investment being valued at constant prices (of 1963). See Ota Šik, *Plan and Market under Socialism*, Prague, Czechoslovak Academy of Sciences, 1967, p. 62.

[2] J. P. Hardt, 'Soviet Economic Development and Policy Alternatives', *Studies on the Soviet Union*, vol. VI, no. 4, 1966, pp. 1–25.

[3] A. Nove, *Was Stalin Really Necessary? Some Problems of Soviet Political Economy*, London, Allen & Unwin, 1964; and his 'Some Random Thoughts on Irrationality and Waste', *Survey*, July 1967, pp. 143–58.

[4] G. W. Nutter, 'Some Reflections on the Growth of the Soviet Economy', *Studies on the Soviet Union*, vol. VII, no. 4, 1967. pp. 144–50.

in the establishment of a constitutional government and a private enterprise economy along Western lines'.[1] Another American economist, M. Boretsky, in a comprehensive report presented to the US Congress in 1966, evaluated the Soviet growth performance over the period 1950–62 in comparison with that of the USA in the following words:

> . . . the whole secret of higher overall growth of the Soviet economy than in the United States . . . between 1950 and 1962 . . . is fully explainable by higher growth of physical inputs. Moreover, . . . the disparity between the Soviet and the United States growth in fixed business capital stock alone was more than sufficient to produce the difference between the GNP growths that actually occurred. Indeed, these data indicate that in those periods capital investment was used in the Soviet economy not only to produce the net excess in the overall growth over the United States, but also to cover the lag in the growth of productivity. That this could be done in the conditions of as low standard of living as prevailed in the USSR throughout the period must obviously be attributed to the dictatorial power rather than to the economic virtues of the system.[2]

In backward countries, with low income levels and the unsophisticated qualitative requirements of their economies, a maximum rise in production may be more beneficial than fine choice, quality and the immediate welfare of the population – if solid foundations are to be laid for further development. The experience of many Capitalist countries since the Second World War shows that a half-hearted humane approach may not lead to take-off and sustained growth. However, if the developmental strategy is unduly concentrated on quantitative increases for a long period, the Socialist experience indicates that much of the production may be unsuitable or of too low quality, impeding progress to more advanced stages of development. Yet it is a poor economy that can least afford waste, which in turn reduces its potential for further growth.

[1] Ibid., pp. 149–50.
[2] M. Boretsky, 'Comparative Progress in Technology, Productivity and Economic Efficiency: USSR versus USA', in US Congress, Joint Economic Committee, *New Directions in the Soviet Economy*, Washington, GPO, 1966, Part II-A, pp. 202–3.

It may be concluded that maximum growth is not necessarily optimum growth. High rates of growth may not be indicative of economic progress if – like a Pyrrhic victory – cost exceeds benefit. The ultimate goal of economic activity is not merely the maximum rates of growth of production but the maximization of social welfare – i.e. consumption and leisure. But there is little doubt that for a given country, the optimum rate is likely to be higher in the early phase of economic development than in the mature stage. Economic reforms in Socialist countries are conducive to creating conditions for the rates of growth to settle at levels closer to the social optimum than was possible in the past.

2 Extensive and Intensive Growth

THE concepts of extensive and intensive growth in Socialist thought were first introduced, in a crude form, by Marx when he distinguished between extensive and intensive extended reproduction.[1] But this problem did not receive much attention from later Socialist writers until the mid-1950s and from policy-makers some ten years later.[2] Extensive growth in its pure form is based on quantitative increases in labour, capital and land, whereas intensive growth is derived from gains in overall productivity, i.e. increasing efficiency of labour and a better utilization of capital and other means of production.[3]

Economic growth is usually supported by both extensive and intensive factors but, of course, during a particular period either extensive or intensive sources predominate. It may be observed that whilst extensive growth can occur in a pure form, intensive growth normally cannot because more effective methods of production (new processes, labour-saving devices, better factory layout, an improved quality of products) are usually possible only

[1] K. Marx, *Capital*, Moscow, FLPH, 1957, vol. II, chap. XVII, esp. p. 320.

[2] The first major study known to the author appeared in Bulgaria: E. Matiev, *Proizvoditielnostia na truda pri sotsializma i narodnostopanskogo planirovanie* (Productivity of Labour under Socialist Central Planning), Sofia, BCP, 1956. The problem was subsequently considered by such well-known economists as G. Kohlmey of the German Democratic Republic, A. Notkin of the USSR, K. Secomski of Poland, Ota Šik of Czechoslovakia and G. Varga of Hungary. Today, the question of the intensification of growth is the main theme in the Socialist literature on economic development.

[3] Socialist literature is quite confusing on the criterion of distinction. Many Socialist writers, steeped in the labour theory of value, reduce the basis of comparison only to labour. According to this view, extensive growth takes place whenever changes in employment produce corresponding proportional changes in national income, whilst the rate of growth of national income exceeding that of employment denotes intensive growth. See, e.g., M. Syrek, *Wpływ substytucyjnego i niezależnego postępu technicznego na wydajność pracy* (The Influence of Capital-Using and Neutral Technical Progress on Labour Productivity), Katowice, Śląsk, 1967, p. 7.

with additional capital outlays. Intensive growth is generally
identified with technological progress (see Chapter 13).

As a general background for the book, we shall demonstrate in
this chapter that in the case of the European Socialist countries up
to about the mid-1960s the extensive component of economic
growth was not only dominant but in fact on the whole relatively
increasing. The economic reforms, particularly those since the
early 1960s, have been largely designed to steer these economies
towards predominantly intensive growth.

A. EXTENSIVE SOURCES OF GROWTH

Pure extensive growth can be based either on more labour being
combined with the existing stock of the means of production
(capital, land), or on more means of production combined with
unchanged employment, or on an increase in both labour and the
means of production. In each case the consequent increase in
national income is proportional. In the Socialist countries up to
about the mid-1960s there was a large expansion in both labour
and the means of production (especially capital). In this section
we shall briefly examine the conditions responsible for this expansion, both on the supply and demand sides, and some general
features of the Socialist road to extensive development.

(a) Labour

All Socialist countries (with the exception of Yugoslavia)[1] have
consistently pursued the policy of full employment as a postulate of
social ethics. Maximum employment has been traditionally considered to be optimum employment, and the institutional set-up
in the past was such that the demand for labour tended strongly
to exceed supply.

There has been a continuous increase not only in the number but
also in the proportion of women going to work, owing to continued low levels of personal income, the provision of social
amenities for child care, the development of domestic labour-
saving devices and the expansion of facilities for the vocational
training of women. They now constitute from 40 to 50 per cent

[1] See Chapter 1 C, note 4, p. 18.

of the working population, compared with 25 to 35 per cent in most Western countries. This, together with the fact that one's own labour is practically the only source of personal income, explains the fact that in Socialist countries a much higher proportion of the able-bodied population is at work.[1] Moreover, with the exception of Yugoslavia,[2] no emigration of labour has been allowed.

All the European Socialist countries, except the German Democratic Republic,[3] have experienced high rates of natural increase since the Second World War, and an even faster growth in the working-age group. Thus over the period 1950–68, the total population in the CMEA countries[4] rose by 27 per cent (from 271m. to 343m.), whilst employment increased by 33 per cent (from 108m. to 143m.).[5] The effective supply of labour has been further kept increasing or maintained at high levels by long working hours, transfers of manpower away from the branches of the economy with labour reserves (mostly from agriculture and domestic service to industry) and by controlling the growth of the non-productive sphere (services). Up to the early 1960s only 15 per cent or less of the working population was engaged in 'non-productive' services (including defence), compared with about 33 per cent common in the West. All these countries have been lagging behind the West in shortening the standard hours of work (especially up to the mid-1960s). Moreover, a good deal of over-time was worked in the past owing to centrally depressed income levels, the system of material incentives and public appeals for more effort.

[1] e.g., according to a Soviet economist, K. Plotnikov, 82% in the USSR, compared with 70% in the USA. E. A. G. Robinson (ed.), *Problems in Economic Development*, London, Macmillan, 1965, pp. 62–3.

[2] By 1970 over 300,000 Yugoslavs were working in Western Europe.

[3] In the GDR the population gradually declined (owing to the low birth rate and escapes to West Germany) from 18,388,000 in 1950 to 17,028,000 in 1965, but it increased to 17,095,000 in 1968. Central Statistical Office of Poland, *Rozwój gospodarczy krajów RWPG 1950–1968* (Economic Development of the CMEA Countries, 1950–1968), Warsaw, 1969, p. 50.

[4] The countries belonging to the Council for Mutual Economic Assistance (established in 1949): Bulgaria, Czechoslovakia, the GDR, Hungary, Poland, Romania, the USSR and Mongolia. (Mongolia's population is very small – it increased by 0·4m. to 1·2m. in 1968; Yugoslavia's population increased by 3·8m. to 20·1m. in 1968.)

[5] Based on: *Rozwój gospodarczy . . .*, op. cit., pp. 16–43, 56.

Thus industry, which has exhibited the fastest growth of production,[1] has benefited most from increases in manpower, not only in absolute numbers but also in relation to other branches of the economy. Taking the CMEA countries as a whole, employment in industry rose from less than 24m. in 1950 to over 34m. by 1968, whilst that in agriculture declined from 53m. to 47m. The proportion of the working population now employed in industry ranges from 20 per cent in Romania to 42 per cent in the German Democratic Republic.[2]

A noteworthy feature of the Socialist labour market in the past was that, in spite of the high and rapidly rising supply, the demand tended to exceed the available manpower so that labour shortages were prevalent (except in Yugoslavia). Several factors were contributing to the abnormal demand. Production targets set by planners were frequently above the enterprises' capacities and employment of extra labour seemed to be the obvious way to reach such targets to qualify for bonuses. Shortages of capital and uncertainties of allocations accentuated the demand. The industrialization drive naturally created rapidly expanding requirements for skilled labour which, however, could not be trained fast enough. As an expedient, enterprises simply endeavoured to hire more unskilled workers wherever they could be found. This process magnified the demand for labour because it takes more unskilled workers to match a given number of skilled ones.

The cost of labour was of lesser concern. Either enterprises' total wage funds (in contrast to standard wage rates) were not strictly controlled by the State, especially when production targets were exceeded, or, where they were, enterprises tended to employ more unskilled (rather than fewer skilled) workers. Enterprise success was judged not by efficiency but by total output, and under this set-up 'it was easier to reach targets by expanding employment than by increasing labour productivity'.[3]

The abnormal demand for labour can be well illustrated by

[1] Taking the eight countries as a whole, according to official returns, the average annual rate of growth of industrial output over the period 1950–68 works out at 10, whereas that of national income is 8 and that of agricultural output is 4. Author's estimates based on *Rozwój gospodarczy* . . ., loc. cit.

[2] Author's estimates based on *Rozwój gospodarczy* . . ., loc. cit.

[3] M. Syrek, op. cit., p. 259.

TABLE 8 INDEX NUMBERS OF INVESTMENT, CONSUMPTION
AND NATIONAL INCOME IN THE EUROPEAN SOCIALIST
COUNTRIES, 1950–1959*
(1950 = 100)

COUNTRY	Investment	Consumption	NATIONAL INCOME
Bulgaria	367	183	264
Czechoslovakia	262	161	192
GDR†	414	160‡	242
Hungary	170	159	162
Poland	244	n.a.	199
Romania	336	n.a.	241
USSR	307	173	246
Yugoslavia§	212	n.a.	197

n.a. = not available.
* At constant prices.
† At current prices.
‡ Author's rough estimate.
§ 1952 = 100.

Sources. Based on: *Rozwój gospodarczy krajów RWPG 1950–1968*, op. cit.,
pp. 16–43; Central Statistical Office of Yugoslavia, *Statistički godišnjak Jugoslavije 1969* (Statistical Yearbook of Yugoslavia for 1969), Belgrade, 1969, p. 121.

Polish experience. The population growth in Poland over the
period 1950–65 was so rapid that the authorities were faced with
the problem of unemployment (more so than in any other CMEA
country). During that period the labour force increased by 4m.,
but the number of registered vacancies exceeded 22m., i.e. for
each person entering the labour market there were more than five
vacant jobs.[1] This tendency continued in the latter 1960s even
though the increase in manpower during that five-year period was
the greatest ever (by 1·5m.).

(b) Capital

Capital formation increased most rapidly in the 1950s. During
that period, the growth of investment dramatically outpaced the

[1] S. Góra, *Warunki produkcji a działanie bodźców* (Conditions of Production
and the Operation of Incentives), Warsaw, PWE, 1967, p. 89.

growth of national income. This is brought out in Table 8. By comparison, the adverse effect on the growth of consumption is conspicuous. Moreover, although there were wide fluctuations from year to year, the rates of increase in investment were rising up to 1958–59. Having reached this turning-point, the rates began to decline until 1964, since when they have recovered but, on the whole, not to the previous high levels (see Table 22, p. 168).

In consequence, the proportion of national income diverted to capital formation was gradually increased (see Table 21, p. 166). Although there was a setback in the early 1960s, the rate of growth of accumulation was stepped up later so that by 1968 in all these countries, with the exception of Yugoslavia, accumulation reached higher proportions of national income than before. The higher rate of growth of accumulation than of investment (cf. Tables 21 and 22, pp. 166 and 168) can be explained mainly by the embarrassing growth of stocks of partly unsaleable goods – a new form of waste (for further details, see Chapter 10 B, pp. 170–73).

The effective supply of capital to the material production sphere (which alone is reflected in the rates of growth) has been enhanced by the priority allocation of investment at the expense of the 'non-productive' service sector. Moreover, the proportion of 'productive' investment tended to increase in most of these countries (with the exception of the USSR) in the past – from less than 75 to about 80 per cent of total investment (however, see Chapter 11 D, pp. 210–11).

At the same time, enterprises' demand for capital was extraordinary. It was officially accepted, on ideological grounds, that only labour can represent cost, and consequently up to the mid-1960s State allocations of capital to enterprises were free.[1]

(c) Land

In contrast to labour and capital, land is virtually in fixed supply. Nevertheless it may be shown that land played a role in extensive growth in at least two respects. First, in some countries attempts

[1] Up to 1953 in Yugoslavia; at the time of writing capital charges did not apply in Romania.

were made to expand agricultural production, not so much by increasing productivity in agriculture but by extending the culti- vated area at the expense of pastures, steppes and wasteland. This was possible only in the less densely populated countries, viz. in the USSR, and to a lesser extent in Czechoslovakia, Romania and Bulgaria.

Thus in the USSR between 1950 and 1967, agricultural land was increased by 16 per cent (from 463·4m. to 545·1m. hectares); the Virgin Lands scheme, so enthusiastically pursued by Khrusch- chev in the late 1950s, was the most publicized evidence of the drive. In Czechoslovakia agricultural land was increased by 25 per cent (from 5·7m. to 7·1m. hectares), in Romania by 4 per cent (from 14·3m. to 14·8m. hectares) and in Bulgaria by 3 per cent (from 5·7m. to 5·9m. hectares).[1] Second, in industrial develop- ment often unnecessarily large sites were allocated for factories, warehouses and transport.

The lavish allocation of land was well matched by the extrava- gant demands made by farms and enterprises. Taking the region as a whole, most of the land since 1950 has been socially owned – over 90 per cent of agricultural land (see Table 1, p. 3). According to traditional Marxist thinking, land – not being a product of labour – has no value, and consequently socialized land has been allocated free to users. Thus with minor exceptions (see section C of this chapter) neither central planners nor farms and enterprises have considered the use of socialized land as cost.

Extensive-based growth is not atypical of the early stages of economic development under any social system. In the Socialist countries it was pushed to extremes by the excessive targets that were being imposed by central planners, by the system of moral and material incentives based on the volume of output (as distinct from the value of production) to reach and exceed such goals, and the prevalent disregard of the quality and efficiency of production. There was a strong tendency for the demand for resources to exceed their supply, with consequent tight balances, rationing, shortages and even frequent bottlenecks. This produced sellers' markets, not only for the factors of production but also for con- sumer goods, which plagued the Socialist countries well into the

[1] *Rozwój gospodarczy* . . ., p. 84.

late 1960s and are still largely in existence today (see Chapter 12 D, pp. 230–31).

The growth of production was, of course, partly attained by increasing productivity. But taking the region as a whole, extensive growth was prevalent at least up to the late 1960s, and up to the mid-1960s in some of these countries it was in fact in relative terms increasing. This became most obvious in Czechoslovakia – economically the most mature Socialist country (apart from the German Democratic Republic in recent years).

TABLE 9 THE SHARE OF EXTENSIVE AND INTENSIVE SOURCES OF GROWTH IN CZECHOSLOVAKIA'S NATIONAL INCOME, 1949–1964

YEARS	EXTENSIVE SOURCES	INTENSIVE SOURCES			TOTAL NATIONAL INCOME
		Total	Growth of Productivity	Savings in the Consumption of Raw Materials and Components	
1949–50	51·5	48·5	67·7	−19·2	100·0
1951–53	55·0	45·0	35·3	9·7	100·0
1954–55	68·4	31·6	38·5	−6·9	100·0
1956–58	74·1	25·9	35·0	−9·1	100·0
1959–60	84·7	15·3	30·1	−14·8	100·0
1961–64	320·7	−220·7	−133·2	−87·5	100·0

Source. Czechoslovak Economic Papers, no. 9, 1967, p. 33.

Over the sixteen-year period 1949–64, Czechoslovakia's national income grew on the average (at constant prices) by 6·4 per cent annually; in this rate the growth of resources (labour and capital) represented 5·5 per cent p.a. and the rise in total productivity only 0·9 per cent p.a., i.e. extensive factors were responsible for more than three-quarters of total growth.[1] The role of extensive and intensive factors for different periods in Czechoslovakia is shown in Table 9. Complete data for other Socialist countries are

[1] V. Nachtigal, 'Extensity and Efficiency of Economic Growth in Czechoslovakia', Czechoslovak Economic Papers, Prague, no. 9, 1967, p. 29.

not easily available.[1] According to an American study, more than two-thirds of growth in the USSR during the period 1950–62 was derived from increases in employment and capital.[2] It is also known that in Poland, even over the relatively recent period 1960–67 nearly nine-tenths of total growth was due to extensive factors.[3] In Yugoslavia during 1949–59, extensive sources contributed over two-fifths of total growth.[4]

B. WASTE AND STAGNATION

The economic losses associated with Socialist extensive growth were largely the consequence of faulty systems of information, target setting and incentives which tended to produce a self-justifying process with secondary waste effects. It was a common practice for enterprises to understate their production capacities when sending their returns to the State Planning Commission. They did this for two reasons: to qualify for the highest possible allocations of resources and in order to be awarded the lowest possible targets.

Central planners, aware of these practices, were imposing higher targets than the declared enterprise capacities would warrant.[5] But targets were in fact arbitrary because the degree of dishonesty amongst enterprises differed and the increasing complexity of the

[1] No Socialist country officially publishes figures on the composition of growth in our sense. As was indicated in note 2, p. 25, an extensive source is usually identified in these countries with increasing employment, whilst intensive growth is associated with rising labour productivity, for both of which official statistical returns are available. This approach has a greater propaganda value, but of course it conceals the sacrifice of materialized labour (capital) which usually makes such a rise possible. Thus in Czechoslovakia over the period 1949–64, officially the extensive source of growth (employment) constituted only 28%, but if increases in capital are included in extensive sources the proportion becomes about 80%. See V. Nachtigal, op. cit., pp. 28–9.
[2] M. Boretsky, 'Comparative Progress in Technology, Productivity and Economic Efficiency: USSR versus USA', in US Congress, Joint Economic Committee, *New Directions in the Soviet Economy*, Washington, GPO, 1966, Part II-A, p. 212.
[3] See Table 31, p. 238.
[4] *Gospodarka planowa* (planned Economy), Warsaw, 4/1970, p. 53.
[5] For further details, see, for example, S. Procherov, ('The Rights and Responsibility of Enterprises'), *Planovoe khoziaistvo* (Planned Economy), Moscow, 1/1966, pp. 62–6.

economy made detection more and more difficult. The prestige of enterprises and the bonuses payable to the personnel were made dependent not on the efficiency of production but on the quantitative fulfilment and over-fulfilment of targets where costs were of remote concern. This led to the following specific forms of waste.

The prevalent shortages of labour and the ease of finding employment led to a deterioration of work discipline, absenteeism, poaching of workers and a high labour turnover. At the same time, enterprises were hoarding labour not only because discharged workers could not easily be replaced when needed but also because, owing to unreliable supplies of raw materials and equipment, it was often necessary to catch up in production by using large numbers of workers.[1]

But the most spectacular waste occurred in respect of capital. The decision on the level of capital formation was made at the top political level, without any consistent economic analysis of investment efficiency. Allocations of fixed equipment to enterprises were free,[2] and similarly no charges were made for the stocks of raw materials and final products held.[3] Enterprises, in turn, were applying for the largest possible allocations, where the limit was not their ability to utilize the capital effectively but the planners' spurious cornucopia and gullibility – in a sense, Parkinson's law operating in a Socialist setting.

Hoarding ('Socialist speculation') was prevalent because not only did it hardly cost enterprises anything but also under the existing system of deliveries it was a logical precaution. Owing to priority allocations of investment to selected industries, differences in the effectiveness of management in different enterprises and unforeseen setbacks (caused, for example, by weather, or foreign trade), the degree of plan fulfilment amongst suppliers varied widely. Thus bottlenecks and the consequent uncertainty of receiving materials and equipment were the daily facts of economic

[1] M. Syrek, op. cit., pp. 259–60.

[2] i.e. it was merely transferred by the State to socialized entities free and no capital charges were payable for its use or possession (up to about the mid-1960s). There were, of course, depreciation charges, but the rates were low. See section C of this chapter.

[3] Only low interest rates (1–3% p.a.) were charged on bank credits to finance working capital.

life. As a result, concealed surplus capacities existed side by side with widespread shortages of both producer and consumer goods, and in effect further aggravated existing shortages.

There was also the prevalent practice of starting a large number of badly conceived, documented and distributed investment projects, some of which had to be abandoned and others completed over increasingly longer periods, with consequent losses and excessively long freezing of resources.[1] No depreciation (and, of course, no capital) charges were applied to investment projects until they were fully operative. Associated with this waste was gigantomania, as exemplified by vast State farms, unwieldy industrial *kombinats*, imposing factory buildings ('palaces of labour') and various show projects of dubious economic soundness.

Consequently, to achieve a given growth of national income it was essential to sacrifice an increasing volume of investment. This became most pronounced in the more developed Socialist countries, especially in Czechoslovakia, the German Democratic Republic, Poland and the USSR. It is illustrated in Table 10. But even in Romania, where the adverse effects of extensive growth were for long least apparent, the deterioration in the growth of investment efficiency began to appear after the mid-1950s, as is indicated by the declining increases in the productivity of fixed assets:[2]

1950–55	by +35 per cent
1956–60	by +9 per cent
1960–65	by +7 per cent
1966	by 0 per cent
1967	by −3 per cent

Another form of the waste of capital was the extravagant use of raw materials and components in the process of production. For example, in Czechoslovakia between 1957 and 1963 the outlays on

---

[1] e.g. the actual periods of the completion of production facilities in the USSR even over the period 1962–68 consistently exceeded those provided for in the plans; in 1962: actual, 5·4 years (planned, 5·2 years); in 1963: 4·8 (5·1); in 1964: 4·8 (4·6); 1965: 5·1 (4·8); in 1966: 5·4 (5·1); in 1967: 5·7 (5·6); and in 1968: 6·5 (6·2). *Finansy SSSR* (Soviet Finance), Moscow, 1/1969, p. 55.

[2] C. Mandescu and G. Pfrfianu, ('The Structure and Utilization of the Accumulation Fund'), *Probleme economice* (Problems of Economics), Bucharest, 10/1968, pp. 18–19.

TABLE 10 INCREASING INVESTMENT COST OF EXTENSIVE
GROWTH IN SELECTED SOCIALIST COUNTRIES, 1950–1963

*Investment Outlay Necessary to Attain
One Unit of Increase in National Income**

YEARS	Czechoslovakia (Korunas)	GDR (Marks)	Poland (Złotys)	USSR (Roubles)
1950–55	1·33†	1·52	2·72	1·52
1956–60	2·01‡	3·00	4·70	2·00
1961–63	11·72	6·17	5·13	3·67

* Both expressed in national currency at constant prices as annual averages.
The comparability of the figures between the countries is limited.
† For 1950.
‡ For 1958.

Sources. Based on: Ota Šik, *Plan and Market under Socialism*, Prague, Czechoslovak Academy of Sciences, 1967, p. 62; Z. Lewandowicz and M. Misiak (eds),
Reformy gospodarcze w krajach socjalistycznych (Economic Reforms in Socialist
Countries), Warsaw, PWE, 1967, p. 222; Central Statistical Office of Poland,
Rocznik statystyczny 1965 (Statistical Yearbook 1965), Warsaw, 1965, pp. 71,
85; Ia. B. Kvasha, 'Capital Intensity', *Problems of Economics*, Jan–Feb–Mar
1967, p. 67.

raw materials and components per one koruna of gross industrial
output increased from 0·582 in 1957 to 0·602 koruna by 1963;[1] in
the German Democratic Republic such outlays per one mark of the
value of total output increased from 0·47 in 1961 to 0·52 mark by
1966;[2] and in the USSR the value of circulating assets per one
rouble of the increase in national income rose from 0·25 in 1950 to
0·76 rouble by 1964.[3] There was hardly any incentive to economize. In fact at one stage, in some industries the *value of output*
was used as a basis for incentive payments. As a result, it was in the
interest of enterprises to use the most expensive materials in production. But even in the late 1960s it was reported that the material

[1] Z. Lewandowicz and M. Misiak (eds), *Reformy gospodarcze w krajach
socjalistycznych* (Economic Reforms in Socialist Countries), Warsaw, PWE,
1967, p. 168.
[2] *Wiadomości Narodowego Banku Polskiego* (Communications of the National
Bank of Poland), Warsaw, 10/1968, p. 423.
[3] B. Kvasha, 'Capital Intensity', *Problems of Economics*, Jan–Feb–Mar 1967,
p. 67.

intensity of production in the Socialist countries was about one-third higher than in the West.[1]

A good deal of waste also occurred in the use of land. As socialized land carried no explicit price or differential rent, farms, enterprises and other entities were not particularly interested in economizing and devoting different grades of land (with regard to fertility, location, physiography) to their most effective uses. Factories, trading enterprises and the entities concerned with urban development, water resources, mining and transport occupied unjustifiably large areas of land, with hardly any consideration given to the social cost of forgone alternatives.

It is virtually impossible to estimate the total amount of waste that arose in the use of land in Socialist countries, but according to calculations made by Soviet economists the annual losses caused by the maldistribution of buildings alone in the USSR amounted to 1,000m. roubles in the early 1960s (over 0·5 per cent of national income).[2] The cumulative effect of the mismanagement of resources in agriculture (coupled with adverse weather conditions) appeared most dramatically over the period 1962–67 when these countries (except Romania) – traditionally exporters of food – had to import huge quantities of grain.[3]

The repercussions of the growth strategy based on predominantly extensive sources on the overall performance of the Socialist economies are well known. Waste and stagnation were most pronounced in the early 1960s in the more developed Socialist countries – Czechoslovakia, the German Democratic Republic, Hungary, Poland and the USSR. The adverse effects were not as widespread in Bulgaria and Romania, which were still in the relatively early stages of economic development. Taking the eight European Socialist countries as a whole, the annual rate of growth of national income – even as officially published – gradually

---

[1] See, e.g., *Czechoslovak Economic Papers*, no. 9, 1969, p. 25; *Scinteia*, Bucharest, 12/6/1969, p. 4; *Życie gospodarcze*, 11/11/1969, p. 11.

[2] H. Chołaj, *Cena ziemi w rachunku ekonomicznym* (Pricing of Land in Economic Calculation), Warsaw, PWE, 1966, p. 158.

[3] Over the period, these countries imported 43m. tons of wheat and flour alone worth $4,000m., mostly from industrial Capitalist nations, and paid in valuable hard currencies which the Socialist industrialization drive could ill afford. The figures are based on: International Wheat Council, *World Wheat Statistics 1967*, pp. 40–3, and *1968*, pp. 33–5.

declined from 11 per cent in the mid-1950s to 4 per cent by 1964 (the rate subsequently recovered to about 7 per cent in the late 1960s).[1]

But even the declining growth was being attained at an increasingly higher social cost. A Czechoslovak economist attempted to estimate the gap quantitatively, and he demonstrated that in Czechoslovakia over the period 1954–64 social product (gross material product) increased by 94·1 per cent, but what he called the 'social reproduction cost' by 105·4 per cent.[2] According to M. Boretsky,[3] if the USSR had followed the Italian growth strategy over the period 1950–62 she would have achieved the rate of growth she did (of 6·3 of GNP) and have saved 116,000m. roubles in capital outlays,[4] equivalent to $190,000m. (in purchasing power of the US dollar of 1958).[5] The blind reliance on extensive sources of growth also resulted in a sub-optimal structure of production and poor quality, and in indifference and even opposition to technological progress. The growth of employment was not always associated with corresponding increases in production, which added to the already strong inflationary pressures (however well suppressed).

In an endeavour to pinpoint the causes responsible for this waste and stagnation, V. Nachtigal concluded: 'It is the result of a whole number of factors which cannot be considered a summation of isolated factors, but which acted in a complex way and in which the influences of the respective factors crossed, and mutually multiplied their effect.'[6] It is worth emphasizing that when stagnation first occurred in the more developed Socialist countries, the authorities were taken completely by surprise, hence the duration of the relapses was longer than otherwise would be necessary. Growth processes were not thoroughly understood at

---

[1] See Tables 2 and 3, pp. 6 and 8.

[2] V. Nachtigal, op. cit., pp. 33–6.

[3] Boretsky chose Italy, because she was at about the same stage of economic development and was similar to the USSR in several other respects. See M. Boretsky, op. cit., p. 214.

[4] This figure was nearly as high as the Soviet total national income produced in 1958 (127,700m. roubles). Central Statistical Office of the USSR, *Narodnoe khoziaistvo SSSR v 1963 g.* (National Economy of the USSR in 1963), Moscow, 1965, p. 501.

[5] M. Boretsky, loc. cit.   [6] V. Nachtigal, op. cit., p. 43.

that time, and even today not enough is known about them under the changing Socialist conditions.

C. THE TURN TO INTENSIVE GROWTH

The waste and stagnation that prevailed in the early 1960s convinced Socialist economists and political leaders of the need for activating intensive sources of growth. Their determination has been further strengthened by the fact that the reservoirs of labour and land were drying up and are certain to continue to do so in the future. Owing to the declining birth rate and death rate, the proportion of the population in the working-age group (16–60 years) in the region is expected to be decreasing (to about 57 per cent by 1980, compared with 59 per cent in the mid-1960s).[1] The reserves of labour in agriculture are no longer as abundant, which, together with the inevitable rehabilitation of the neglected 'nonproductive' sphere (services), will tend to curb the flow of labour to other 'productive' industries.

The possibilities of increasing agricultural production by bringing additional land under cultivation are practically nil. In fact agriculture is faced with decreasing acreage owing to the increasing requirements for land for industrial purposes, urban developments, transport and communications, water and power projects and mining. Although it may be assumed that the supply of capital will continue at high levels in the future, the pressure of the public for better living may be less easily withstood by the authorities than in the past, and higher proportions of national income may have to be devoted to consumption, at least in the more developed Socialist countries.

The recent Socialist preoccupation with the creation of conditions for intensive growth was clearly described by a Polish economist:

Economic developments make it crystal-clear that a determined shift to intensive sources of growth has become an absolute necessity. We must bear this in mind at all levels of economic

[1] K. Mikulskii, ('Urgent Problems Facing the CMEA Countries in the Distribution of Manpower'), *Voprosy ekonomiki* (Problems of Economics), Moscow, 7/1969, pp. 131–40; *Rozwój gospodarczy* . . ., pp. 51–3.

administration . . . A radical mobilization of intensive growth
factors is a means of not only overcoming strained balances in
the economy and accelerating the pace of social development,
but also an indispensable method of preventing bottlenecks and
a decline in the rate of growth of national income and consumption.[1]

According to a Soviet economist, the volume of output in the
USSR can be increased by about 50 per cent merely by improving
the technology of production.[2] A well-known Soviet authority on
growth pointed out that intensive growth is an indispensable stage
in the development of the Socialist society towards Full Communism.[3] A Bulgarian economist concluded that with the aid of
the intensive strategy of growth Bulgaria can start entering the
phase of Full Communism in about 1995.[4]

The economic reforms, particularly those since the early 1960s,
creating general conditions favourable to intensive growth, include
decentralization, profit, the commercialization of economic relations and specialization. In addition, there has been a revision of
policies and practices specifically designed to ensure a more intensive utilization of labour, capital and land. We shall briefly bring out
their relevance to the intensification of economic growth.

The abandonment of directive and detailed centralized planning
and management in favour of a greater independence of enterprises promotes local responsibility and initiative. Central planning authorities now concentrate on macroeconomic proportions
and overall co-ordination. Of particular relevance is their work on
programming prices, established on the basis of a comprehensive
system of information and electronic data-processing, which are
employed to achieve the most efficient allocation of resources
amongst different branches of the economy (see Chapters 4 D and
5 A, pp. 71–4, 78, 82). At the industry and enterprise levels,

---

[1] G. Pisarski, ('The Need for Intensification'), *Życie gospodarcze*, 14/9/1969,
pp. 1, 9.
[2] I. Kotkovskii, 'Present Conditions of the Economic Competition between
the USSR and the USA'),*Voprosy ekonomiki*, 4/1967, pp. 74–5.
[3] A. Notkin, *Tempo i proporcje reprodukcji socjalistycznej* (The Rate and Proportions of the Socialist Economic Growth), Polish translation from the Russian,
Warsaw, PWE, 1962, pp. 166–7.
[4] T. Yordanov, ('Intensive Development – A Natural Consequence of
Socialist Industrialization'), *Novo vreme* (New Times), Sofia, 7/1969, p. 43.

organization and time-and-motion studies, previously neglected, have been placed on a new footing, whilst Western management techniques and production methods are carefully examined with a view to local adaptations. The duality of the new approach – centralized and decentralized – is not necessarily incompatible but in fact is proving complementary, and is likely to promote a more efficient utilization of resources at the microeconomic level with the optimum broad allocation from the macroeconomic standpoint.

The acceptance of profit as the main or only criterion of enterprise performance and as a basis for material incentives to the personnel promotes the minimization of costs and the maximization of the value and quality of production. It also stimulates enterprises to adopt better and better technology. Subsidies have been drastically pruned and many loss-incurring enterprises are transferred to more efficient forms of production. Research institutes, design offices and experimental establishments have been placed on a commercial accounting basis, i.e. their source of income now consists wholly (or mainly) of charges made for the work commissioned by enterprises and other entities. Consequently their work is now more directly related to the needs of the economy. Rationalization and innovations are accepted as an indispensable, and the most dynamic, element of economic growth. Special incentive mark-ups on prices are payable to enterprises for novelty and improved quality of products (see Chapter 13 C, pp. 251–2).

Critical importance is now attached to concentration and specialization, and the prevalent emphasis is on capital-deepening rather than capital-widening. Resources, instead of being scattered on an excessively large number of projects, are carefully allocated, priorities being assigned to the technologically most dynamic branches, especially power-producing, machine-building, electronic and chemical industries. By a combination of direction and inducement, efforts are made to extend specialization and co-operation amongst enterprises to utilize the economies of scale and improve quality. This drive on the domestic scale is paralleled by similar efforts on the international scale.

Autarkic policies, obstinately pursued up to the mid-1950s, have been gradually abandoned in favour of a greater participation in the international division of labour, and this has been done not only within CMEA but also in relation to Capitalist countries.[1] Moreover, in contrast to the previous practice, special attention has been given to increasing the efficiency of foreign trade, at first by applying specially devised indexes of the effectiveness of exports and of imports, and more recently by reducing the degree of insulation from world markets and exposing domestic enterprises to foreign competition (for further details, see Chapter 14).

There have been several specific measures introduced since the early 1960s to promote a more economical utilization of labour. The profit criterion of enterprise performance has made the hoarding of workers no longer as attractive as in the past. In fact, some Socialist economists openly advocate employment 'up to the point where increase in net production is not smaller than the cost of labour'[2]. Several countries have introduced a greater differentiation of standard pay rates, and piece-work wages have been largely replaced by time rates – evidence of the official preoccupation with quality and efficiency, rather than mere quantity of production.

Determined efforts have been made to ensure a more intensive use of capital. There is a trend, notably in Czechoslovakia, Hungary and Yugoslavia, to reduce investment to 'realistic' levels in order to induce the maximum utilization of existing capacities. The most important step to prevent enterprises from demanding excessive allocations of capital and then hoarding it has consisted in the introduction of capital charges averaging about 5 per cent p.a. (Chapter 10 C, pp. 176–9).

Furthermore, most investments are now financed out of the enterprises' own liquid resources and by bank credits (instead of free allocations by the State, common in the past). Highly

[1] Between 1960 and 1970, the foreign trade turnover of the USSR was rising about 50%, and of the other European Socialist countries about 100%, faster than their national income. Compared with 1950, the share of foreign trade in these countries' net material product nearly doubled by 1970 (in the latter year the share ranged from 7% in the USSR to 75% in Bulgaria). In the past decade, these countries' total foreign trade was rising nearly as fast as that of the Capitalist countries (8 and 9% respectively, at current prices). Based on: S. Albinowski, *Handel między krajami o różnych ustrojach* (Trade between Countries with Different Social Systems), Warsaw, KiW, 1968, pp. 273–8; and United Nations sources: *Monthly Bulletin of Statistics, Yearbook of International Trade Statistics* and *Yearbook of National Accounts Statistics*.

[2] M. Syrek, op. cit., p. 108.

differentiated interest rates, especially heavy penalty rates, have been introduced to speed up the turnover of working capital and to shorten the duration of the construction of investment projects (see Chapter 9 C, pp. 156–7). Depreciation charges now apply to the projects as soon as they are completed, not when they are fully operative. Since the early 1960s improved investment efficiency formulae have been commonly applied to select the most efficient projects, and industrial associations and banks have been made co-responsible with enterprises for ensuring the most effective investment policy. Larger proportions of investment are spent on working equipment rather than on the construction of buildings and new projects (for details, Chapter 10 B, pp. 173–5).

There have also been several steps taken to promote a more rational use of land. Some Socialist countries, such as Czecho-slovakia in 1964 and the German Democratic Republic in 1968, have introduced laws specifying the compensation payable by non-agricultural occupiers of land. Others, such as the USSR in 1969, passed new land codes strictly regulating the use of land for non-agricultural purposes. The existence of differential rent under Socialism has been acknowledged officially by the differentiation of land taxes reflecting the quality of land, which spurs the occupants to devoting land to the most effective uses.[1] All the European Socialist countries (except Albania) now, at least partly, include land in the evaluation of investment efficiency.[2] A Polish supporter of land valuation under Socialism aptly remarked: 'The concept of the ''price of land'' need not cause any embarrassment to us. After all, it is certainly not a bit dirtier than profit.'[3]

[1] e.g., according to a Soviet source, published in 1966, the USSR was divided into six regions according to the quality of land, and the rent payable to the State in kopecks per square metre was: 0·4, 0·6, 0·9, 1·2, 1·5 and 1·8. In Czecho-slovakia, the differential land tax, introduced in 1967, on land occupied – whether used or not – ranges from 0 to 930 korunas per hectare. In Hungary, in addition to agricultural land tax there is differential rent on non-agricultural land ranging from 0·80 to 16·50 forints per sq. metre. In Bulgaria, as in Hungary, land occupied by enterprises is subject to capital charges (3% and 5% a year respectively). See D. Allakhverdyan et al., Soviet Financial System, Moscow, Progress Publishers, 1966, p. 222; Finanse (Finance), Warsaw, 12/1967, pp. 64–5, and 4/1970, p. 54; Ekonomista (The Economist), Warsaw, no. 6, 1969, p. 1400.

[2] Further details can be found in J. Wilczynski, 'Towards Rationality in Land Economics under Central Planning,' Economic Journal, Sep 1969. pp. 540–59.

[3] P. G. Ołdak, Produkcja a spożycie (Production and Consumption), Warsaw, PWE, 1967, p. 101.

The evidence of the official determination to turn to intensive sources of growth was first obvious in the 1966–70 five-year plans, especially in Czechoslovakia, the German Democratic Republic, Hungary and Yugoslavia.[1] However, during that period in all European Socialist countries (except Albania), major reforms were still being implemented, and in some of them (especially in Poland, Bulgaria and Romania) extensive tendencies reasserted themselves, so that in fact it was a period of transition. But a good deal of preparatory work was done in the late 1960s in search of 'hidden reserves' to place the 1971–75 plans on a substantially intensive basis of continuous growth.

D. IS THE SOCIALIST EXPERIENCE AN INEVITABLE PATTERN?

The prevailing view amongst Western specialists on economic development is that Socialist strategy is dominated by growth, i.e. quantity, in contrast to Capitalist development marked by choice, i.e. quality. This simplified generalization, which emerged in the late 1950s,[2] was based on the observation of the relatively undeveloped Socialist countries up to that time. Recent developments indicate that in advanced Socialist countries qualitative growth is likely to predominate, too.

There is obviously a relation of substitutability between quantitative and qualitative growth because each competes for limited resources. For a particular economy one could work out a transformation map where extensive–intensive growth possibility curves and long-run social benefit lines would indicate the optimum combination at different stages of economic development. But extensive growth can be pushed to greater extremes under Socialism because the authorities are likely to attach greater importance to accelerated growth than to current sacrifices, and because the State is in a position to determine major proportions in the economy and to direct resources to the required growth points.

---

[1] Earlier in Yugoslavia, significantly, in spite of the existence of substantial labour reserves.

[2] See especially P. Wiles, 'Growth versus Choice', *Economic Journal*, June 1956, pp. 244–55.

To identify extensive growth with 'inefficient' and intensive with 'efficient' would be an over-simplification. There is a stage in the economic development of a country when extensive growth is not necessarily inefficacious. This was on the whole the case in Czechoslovakia up to 1954, in Hungary up to 1958, in the USSR up to 1959 and in Bulgaria and Romania up to 1966–67. Even pure extensive growth may produce increasing *per capita* income. This can occur when employment rises faster than population (when there are labour reserves or when the population bulge passes through the working-age range), as historical experience shows is likely to be the case.

Several forms of the waste of extensive growth that occurred in the Socialist countries are not inevitably inherent in the Socialist road to development, and they need not be repeated in the future. The hoarding of labour, capital and land could have been largely avoided by the early adoption of the profit criterion, capital charges and differential rent. Material incentives to labour should have been based on enterprise performance and enterprises should have been given greater freedom to choose and substitute inputs and, within reason, outputs. Targets should have been subjected to strict quality control and, at least some of them, defined in broad value terms.

But the most important warning that must be heeded by any country adopting the Socialist road to economic development is not to repeat the thought orthodoxy and institutional inertia that may force the economy to continue relying on extensive sources well beyond the critical stage. The challenge to economic policy in choosing growth strategies is to know when, and to be able, to make the changeover. Once the reserves of labour and land begin to dry up and the productivity of capital to decline, the economy should be steered towards predominantly intensive sources of growth.

In a higher stage of development, an economy has a better system of information, a larger pool of experienced administrators, managers and technical and scientific workers, and a greater capacity for technological progress and the elimination of waste. A study of mature, progressive Capitalist economies shows that from one-half to four-fifths of growth is derived from intensive sources. Although intensive growth is usually not possible without some extension of resources, only predominantly intensive growth factors can ensure substantial and lasting increases in *per capita* income.[1]

If new Socialist countries were established in the future, would they repeat the Eastern European extensive growth pattern? This question was examined by an East German economist, G. Kohlmey. In his view no clear-cut answer is possible, as the actual course would depend on the initial situation inherited from the preceding system: '... if the revolution is victorious in a developed industrial country,' he concluded, 'it will be possible to do without some economic measures of an extensive nature. On the other hand, in less developed countries with an extremely large population and mass unemployment, the first task will consist in finding full employment for the working people. This automatically involves an extensive process of growth. ... Whatever the industrial set-up may be, in any case, the period of extensive growth, if needed at all, will not last as long as it did in the Socialist countries and need not produce the harsh bureaucratic forms of the past.'[2]

---

[1] Non-Socialist theoretical writers on growth differ as to the role of extensive and intensive factors in economic development. Some of them, such as W. A. Lewis, R. Nurkse and W. W. Rostow, attach great importance to the quantitative increase in resources (especially capital), whilst others, such as A. Cairncross, K. S. Krishnaswamy and R. M. Solow, emphasize qualitative factors. These models of growth are not in fact contradictory, but rather each is more appropriate to a different stage of economic development.

[2] G. Kohlmey, 'From Extensive to Intensive Growth', *Czech. Econ. Papers*, no. 6, 1966, pp. 25-6.

3 Economic Reforms

A. THE HISTORY AND EXTENT OF REFORMS

IF we disregard the pre-1950 period, the earliest reformist attempts can be traced back to the early 1950s – first in Yugoslavia (1950–52), then in Hungary (1953–54), Czechoslovakia (1953–54) and the German Democratic Republic (1954–55). However, only in Yugoslavia did they result in departures from command central planning and management, viz. directive annual plans were largely discontinued, the price mechanism was partly restored, workers' self-management was introduced and the de-collectivization of land followed.

The next wave of reformist ferment appeared in the period 1956–60. Very ambitious programmes of reforms were formulated by liberally inclined economists in Poland and in Hungary, but due to the overwhelming political opposition led by Stalinist hardliners few proposals were actually put into practice. In Poland workers' councils were legalized in 1956, industrial associations were formed to participate in economic administration and management, a good deal of land was de-collectivized (1956–57) and several experiments with market instruments were introduced. A half-hearted regional decentralization of economic administration was carried out in the USSR (1957) and some decentralization of planning and of price fixing was introduced in Hungary (1957–59). There were also periodical price revisions and other routine readjustments in all these countries, but strictly speaking they cannot be regarded as reforms. Yugoslavia was again an exception, where further progress was made in the decentralization of planning, management and financing of investment (1958).

However, with the exception of Yugoslavia, the modifications carried out did not change the economic system in any European Socialist country. They were all of the command bureaucratic type

limited to the mitigation of the most intolerable symptoms, so that
centralized and directive planning and management were essentially retained. But the reforms since that time have produced
fundamental transformations of the Socialist economies. As G.
Varga, a Hungarian economist, observed, '. . . the reforms have not
been aimed at tinkering with the old system. The *sine qua non* of
further rapid development in the long run is a comprehensive
overhaul of the previous system, going far beyond merely removing its obvious failings.'[1]

The driving force behind the reforms has been the determination
to restore and maintain high rates of growth of national income by
evolving favourable conditions for a rapid improvement in productivity, i.e. for the tapping of intensive sources of growth. These
general conditions include decentralization, flexibility and adaptability of the structure of production to demand, strengthened
incentives based on efficiency, competition and, in general, the
operation of the market mechanism where it is considered to be
desirable.

A summary of the reforms in each Socialist country under consideration over the period 1956–70 is presented in Table 11. The
new system was first applied to industrial enterprises, but soon it
had been extended in varying degrees to trade, transport, agriculture and even research establishments. We shall now briefly
bring out the spheres in which the new methods have been put into
operation (further details can be found in appropriate chapters).

1. *Planning.* Directive and detailed planning has been replaced
by broad indicative plans in which the number of compulsory
targets has been greatly reduced or completely abolished. Plans are
expressed, at least partly, in value terms (instead of exclusively in
physical targets) and with the participation of branch associations
and enterprises. The emphasis is on medium (five-year) and
perspective (15–20-year) periods.

2. *Economic Administration and Management.* Instead of the
rigid, hierarchical system of commands and detailed administrative
instructions handed down the line from above, central planners

---

[1] Z. Lewandowicz and M. Misiak (eds), *Reformy gospodarcze w krajach
socjalistycznych* (Economic Reforms in Socialist Countries), Warsaw. PWE,
1967, p. 336.

now leave a good deal of independence to enterprises, branch associations and other bodies. The role of the central authorities is confined to overall co-ordination and this is done mostly, not by handing out directives, but by operating 'economic levers' (as they are now described) in the form of incentives and disincentives. Enterprises are encouraged to exercise their own initiative and they have a greater freedom in dealing directly ('horizontally') with other enterprises, instead of having to deal via the central authorities.

3. *Pricing.* Prices payable to producing enterprises have been readjusted to reflect social costs and to reduce the need for subsidies. The level of agricultural prices, for long artificially depressed in relation to industrial prices, has been increased to bring it into closer correspondence with other prices. Most of these countries have introduced 'flexible' price systems whereby prices are largely determined by current market conditions, and some of these countries have linked their prices to those prevailing in world markets.

4. *Profit.* To promote efficiency, profit has been adopted as the main (or only) indicator of enterprise success. It is now in the enterprises' own interest to minimize costs and to maximize output for which there is demand. Profit is calculated on the basis of the output actually sold, not merely produced.

5. *Material Incentives to Labour.* There has been a tendency in several countries to introduce a wider differentiation of standard pay to give a greater recognition of responsibility and to further encourage the acquisition of skills. Bonuses to the personnel are now based on enterprise profits.

6. *Financial Instruments.* Credit, highly differentiated interest rates (including concession and penalty rates), depreciation charges and allowances, and innovation mark-ups and mark-downs on obsolete products are used flexibly. The authorities' attitude is that enterprises should be induced or deterred, rather than compelled by directives, so that the course of action is determined by enterprises themselves according to circumstances.

7. *Investment.* Free budgetary allocations of capital to enterprises have been greatly reduced and increasing proportions of investment are financed out of enterprises' liquid resources and

TABLE 11 MAIN ECONOMIC REFORMS I:

BULGARIA	CZECHOSLOVAKIA	GDR	HUNGARY
			1957 – some decentralization of planning and price setting; profit sharing introduced
			1959 – price mark-up to promote technical progress
		1961 – State National Economic Council replaced ind. ministries	
1964 – capital charges introduced		1963 – greater role to be played by ind. assns 1964 – reform of planning, management, price fixing and incentives	1963 – some decentralization in industry 1964 – capital charge introduced
	1965 – ind. assns to play greater role	1965 – SNEC abolished; increased self-financing of enterprises	1965 – increase in agricultural prices
		1966 – further reform of industrial prices	1966 – substantial decentralization of planning and management; reform of incentives
1967 – reform of producers' prices	1967 – decentralization of planning and management, flexible price system; strengthening of economic levers		
1968 – decentralization of planning and management; strengthening of economic levers 1968–69 – banking and credit reforms	1968 – second stage of the price reforms	1968 – banking and credit reform; strengthening of financial levers and controls	1968 – flexible price system; extension of material incentives in agriculture
	1969 – banking and credit reform	1969–70 – reform of industrial prices	

* Major reforms are indicated by the years shown in **bold** type (e.g. **1964**).

Sources. Daily and periodical literature of the countries concerned.

POLAND	ROMANIA	USSR	YUGOSLAVIA†
956 – workers' councils galized			
957 – decollectivization		1957 – most industrial ministries replaced by regional economic councils	
		1959 – greater centralization of banking	1958 – further decentralization of planning, management and financing
960 – major revision of holesale prices		1961 – domestic revaluation of the rouble	1960 – greater role of tariffs
			1961 – devaluation of the dinar
963 – some centralization in dustry	1963 – major revision of wholesale prices	1963 – savings banks taken over by the State Bank	
			1964–65 – banking reform
66 – strengthening of ancial levers		1965 – official acceptance of the profit criterion; greater independence of enterprises and farms; regional econ. councils replaced by centralized econ. ministries	1965 – further substantial decentralization; strengthening of fiscal and monetary instruments; closer orientation to foreign trade
67 – reform of factory ices	1967– branch assns set up	1967 – reform of producers' prices; extension of commercial accounting in agriculture	1967 – anti-dumping duties introduced
	1968–69 – some decentralization in industry and foreign trade; strengthening of economic levers and financial controls; diversification of banking		
69–70 – banking and edit reform	1970–71 – reform of producers' prices	1969–70 – rationalization of land use; increased commercialization of collective farming	
71 – reform of oducers' prices			

† The reforms over the period 1949–55: 1949 – workers' councils introduced; 1952 – decentralization planning and management; flexible prices; decollectivization; 1953 – capital charges introduced; 54 – repayable credits to finance investment.

by repayable bank credits. Capital charges and other financial instruments promote the maximum economy in the use of capital. The role of banks has been greatly enhanced to ensure a greater effectiveness of investment and to regulate economic activity in general.

8. *Agriculture.* In some countries (Poland and Yugoslavia) farming land has been largely de-collectivized (in the 1950s) and in all of them the former restrictions on private plots have been relaxed. Compulsory deliveries to the State have been reduced or abolished, and instead more reliance is placed on price incentives to promote agricultural production. Detailed administrative interference from above has been largely replaced by the extension of economic accounting on farms.

9. *Private Enterprise.* Although the private sector continues to be small (see Table 1, p. 3), in selected fields private enterprise has received a new lease of life under the stimulus of the reforms. Restrictive legislation has been liberalized in some respects and several forms of discrimination have been lifted (with the exception of Romania and the USSR). Private enterprise has become particularly active in retailing (grocery and fashion shops, children's footwear and clothing, florists, kiosks, petrol stations), catering (restaurants, hotels, guesthouses, boarding schools), laundering, private house construction, and passenger and odd-freight transport. There is a good deal of sub-contracting by State enterprises to small private producers (especially in the German Democratic Republic and Poland).[1]

[1] The private sector is more important than its contribution to national income would suggest, because it operates mostly in the service, 'nonproductive', sphere (and consequently does not form part of material production). Now to quote a few figures compiled from national statistical yearbooks and journals, illustrating the extent of private enterprise in specific fields. In Poland, employment in the private non-agricultural sector more than doubled between 1960 and 1970 to 400,000 persons, of whom nearly one-half are hired labour; there are 150,000 artisan workshops, 25,000 transport enterprises, 15,000 retail shops, 8,000 kiosks, 5,000 laundries and agencies and 1,000 restaurants, all privately operated. In Yugoslavia there are at least 185,000 privately owned enterprises; one-third of the value of art and craft objects is produced in private workshops; of the total number of dwellings constructed in 1967, more than one-half was privately undertaken and since 1967 the regulations regarding the opening of private retail shops have been considerably liberalized. In the GDR, there are 4,000 private industrial enterprises employing 100,000 persons and 20% of retail sales is handled by private shops. In Hungary, there

10. *Foreign Trade*. Foreign trade plans are less detailed and directive, allowing greater freedom to trading entities. The foreign trade monopoly, previously rigidly administered only by the ministries of foreign trade, has been relaxed in favour of other ministries, and many branch associations and enterprises have been granted the right of direct dealings in foreign markets. In several countries tariffs have been made an active instrument of trade policy, and the insulation of domestic from foreign markets has been relaxed in several respects. The system of material incentives, and the basis of settlements between foreign trade corporations and domestic enterprises, have been improved to promote the most efficient structure of exports and, to a lesser extent, of imports.

The common Western view is that the economic reforms in the European Socialist countries are simply a logical part and parcel of de-Stalinization in the economic sphere. This is only partly true. The political reaction against the Stalinist-type rule since the 20th Congress of the Communist Party of the Soviet Union (1956) has no doubt facilitated economic liberalization. However, history teaches us that one does not necessarily have to partner the other. In spite of political relaxations and moderating ideological fervour, most Socialist countries were not ripe for far-reaching departures from the old model as long as production was relatively simple and ample reserves for extensive growth were present. Viewed from the standpoint of economic development, the reforms have not been a fortuitous concession but a logical evolutionary step brought about by the increasing complexities of production processes and relations and an indispensable precondition for sustained growth.

The immediate effect of the reforms on growth rates was depressing and this could be observed not only in the case of CMEA countries but also of Yugoslavia. This is only natural considering the magnitude of the changes involved and the inevitable disruption before readjustments to the new system could be carried

---

are 10,000 private retail shops and the number of artisans working on their own account exceeds 100,000. In Romania the number of private workshops is over 40,000 and in Bulgaria the number of registered private tradesmen is about 30,000. In Czechoslovakia the number of privately owned enterprises exceeds 2,000 and the number of persons working on their own account is at least 17,000.

out. But even later no spectacular recovery of the rates followed
(see Table 2, p. 6). This can be partly explained by the fact that
the implementation of the reforms has taken longer than expected
(partly due to the opposition of, and even sabotage by, the Party
hardliners) and that the qualitative improvements in production
that have followed are not easily reflected in Socialist growth rates.

B. NATIONAL DIFFERENCES OF APPROACH

In the preceding section we have highlighted the salient elements
of the reforms typical of the region as a whole. But naturally the
content and process of reforms differed in each country, reflecting
its political set-up, the stage of economic development and geo-
graphical and historical circumstances. Before we consider the
differences, it should be realized that up to 1956, and in the case of
Yugoslavia up to 1950, the economic system in each European
Socialist country was virtually identical – a slavish imitation of the
Soviet prototype.

At the 20th Party Congress in 1956, the Soviet leadership conceded the possibility of 'different paths to Socialism'. One of the
most interesting consequences of the reforms has been the increasing diversity of the national economic systems. In effect, the
European Socialist countries can be considered a huge economic
laboratory where different principles are being tested and better
solutions evolved according to a variety of conditions. The
divergent national systems that are emerging demonstrate that
several economic models are compatible with the Socialist road to
development.

The immediate causes of reforms differed from country to
country. In Yugoslavia it was the expulsion from Cominform (in
1948), a reaction against outside interference and the need of the
leadership to cultivate popular support. In most other countries –
Czechoslovakia, the German Democratic Republic, Hungary,
Poland and the USSR – reforms of the system came more than a
decade later, when the political climate was less repressive and by
which time the ineptitude and waste of the old system became
unbearable.

But in Bulgaria and Romania, the situation was different again. Revisionist ferments were weak and the presence of extensive sources of growth did not yet make the inefficiency of the old system apparent. However, from the experience of the more developed Socialist countries the regimes knew what was in store for their own economies. Benefiting by the mistakes and successes of their neighbours, they embarked on forestalling reforms, in some respects more systematic and far-reaching.

In Bulgaria, the German Democratic Republic and Romania, and in Yugoslavia in 1950–52, the initiative and impetus for the reforms came largely from above, whilst in the remaining countries (including Yugoslavia after 1952) there was a good deal of pressure from theoretical and practising economists and popular opinion in general. In Bulgaria, Poland and the USSR considerable importance was attached to practical experiments extending over one to three years before actual reforms were embarked upon. Widespread theoretical discussions, conducted in a remarkably free atmosphere and advanced to a high degree of sophistication, prepared the ground for reforms especially in Czechoslovakia, Hungary, Poland, the USSR and Yugoslavia.

The process of the implementation of reforms also differed. In the German Democratic Republic the programme for the reforms had been most carefully prepared and carried out with military precision in three stages over the period 1964–68. On the other hand, in Bulgaria, Czechoslovakia, Hungary and Yugoslavia the reforms of the 1960s were put into practice in one major sweep (in 1968, 1967, 1966 and 1965 respectively). They were most effectively and smoothly implemented in Hungary and Yugoslavia with the perfect co-operation of the Party, whilst in Czechoslovakia and Poland Stalinist diehards were in a position to obstruct and even sabotage the implementation.

On the whole, the departures from the old centralized model have been most radical so far in Yugoslavia, and also in Hungary and Czechoslovakia, but least in Romania, the USSR and the German Democratic Republic. But there were differences in specific fields. The decentralization of price determination has advanced furthest in Yugoslavia, Hungary, Czechoslovakia, Bulgaria and to some extent in the German Democratic Republic.

There has been considerable decentralization of the banking system in Yugoslavia and some in Czechoslovakia, but not elsewhere. The wage fund has been largely decentralized in Yugoslavia, Bulgaria, Czechoslovakia and Hungary, but not in the German Democratic Republic, Poland, Romania and the USSR.

The organization and conduct of foreign trade has been decentralized most in Yugoslavia, to a considerable extent too in Bulgaria, the German Democratic Republic, Hungary and Romania, and least in Czechoslovakia, Poland and the USSR. Workers' self-management has been most firmly established in Yugoslavia and to lesser extents in Poland and Czechoslovakia, but it is least developed in Romania and the USSR. In Yugoslavia, Hungary and Czechoslovakia the emphasis in the reforms has been on incentives and disincentives, whilst the German Democratic Republic and Romania have been preoccupied with the organization and structure of the economy. Private enterprise is least restricted and most dynamic in Poland, and also in the German Democratic Republic and Yugoslavia, whereas in the USSR it is virtually non-existent.

C. THE COMPLEMENTARITY OF PLAN AND MARKET

Although, as a result of the reforms, there are now as many models of the Socialist economy as there are countries, there are no extreme cases of a centralized command economy and of a market economy. The systems that have emerged represent the peaceful co-existence of central planning and the market mechanism.

Traditionally in Socialist economic thought plan and market were commonly regarded as antagonistic and mutually exclusive – an example of Hegelian contradiction. The majority of Socialist thinkers and policy-makers now believe that in the advanced stages of economic development an organic coalescence of the two mechanisms is not only possible but in fact highly essential for intensive-based growth. Fascinated with the prospects of this happy synthesis, a Soviet Marxist economist described it as 'the dialectical unity of plan and market'.[1] At a conference on

[1] A. Bachurin, ('Reforms, Planning and the Science of Economics'), *Planovoe khoziastvo* (Planned Economy), Moscow, 2/1968, pp. 3–16.

the relation between the two mechanisms organized by the Czechoslovak State Planning Commission in Prague in 1967, the Deputy Chairman (M. Kohoutek) summed up the conclusions reached:

> ... we cannot operate with a plan which eliminates the market just the same as we cannot operate with the market in the absence of a plan, nor can the market be regarded only as an instrument for putting the plan into effect. The market represents an objective economic category which constitutes an object for the recognition and function of the plan.[1]

Major proportions in the economy of long-run macrosocial importance, i.e. conducive to high rates of growth, are still centrally planned (see Chapter 4 B, pp. 65, 68). They are set and adhered to more rigidly in some countries (the German Democratic Republic, Romania, the USSR) than in others (especially in Czechoslovakia, Hungary and Yugoslavia). However, the essence of this planning process is that it is not as arbitrary as in the past but largely based on signals revealed by the market, and in turn the construction and implementation of the plan provides for the utilization of the market mechanism.

A modicum of free markets existed even before the reforms, viz. in privately grown produce sold directly to consumers and in private services from tradesmen. But these markets did not determine the planning process and the planned allocation of resources. Under the new system, the market is used to enforce the adaptation of the structure of production to the preferences of the users (consumers as well as other enterprises). The regulation of the relations amongst enterprises is now entrusted – more in some countries (especially in Yugoslavia) than in others (Romania) – to the market mechanism.

In the past, under the central allocation of resources, errors were often made on a large (macroeconomic) scale and remained undetected and unrectified for long periods. Under the new system, it is hoped that the operation of the market mechanism will promote the optimum utilization of resources at the operational level,

---

[1] M. Kohoutek, ('The Problem of Plan and Market'), *Plánované Hospodářství* (Planned Economy), Prague, 9/1967, p. 17.

correct planners' decisions and in turn provide guidance to planners in their future allocations.[1] If these functions are to be performed effectively, buyers' markets must be developed (see Chapter 12 D, pp. 231–2).

The system in force in Yugoslavia since 1965 is what is sometimes described as 'market socialism'. Under this set-up the maximum extent of the social ownership of the means of production and the minimum degree of central planning are combined with a virtually freely operating market mechanism and workers' self-management. A similar system has been advocated in Bulgaria by G. Petrov, in Czechoslovakia by O. Šik, in the German Democratic Republic by F. Behrens, in Hungary by P. Erdös, in Poland by W. Brus and in the Soviet Union by G. S. Lisichkin. Some Socialist economists such as V. Bakarić of Yugoslavia and E. Löbl of Czechoslovakia, have urged the adoption of market socialism without planning.[2]

D. LIMITATIONS AND PROSPECTS

In countries so strongly dominated by ideology, the reforms are not merely a question of economics. In some ways, the most sacred truths of Marxian thought, for long accepted as axiomatic, have been undermined. In all these countries except Yugoslavia, the original proposals for reforms were much more radical than the watered-down versions actually put into practice. Some disappointed observers in Poland and in Romania described the changes as 'mini-reforms'.

Many ideologues regard the reforms as a retrograde step, only postponing the transition to Full Communism. As in the past, the hardliners are likely to be regrouping, especially in Czechoslovakia, Poland, Romania and the USSR, to resist 'the infiltration of alien

---

[1] I. Konnik, ('Plan and Market in the Socialist Economy'), *Voprosy ekonomiki* (Problems of Economics), Moscow, 5/1966, pp. 18–30.

[2] V. Bakarić, ('The Basic Economic Stimulus Must be the Working Man'), *Vjesnik* (Herald), Zagreb, 4/4/1965, pp. 2–3 (quoted from: M. Gamarnikow, *Economic Reforms in Eastern Europe*, Wayne State UP, 1968, p. 73); E. Löbl, ('Economic Democracy, but of What Sort?'), *Plánované Hospodářství*, 6/1968, pp. 67–72.

concepts and methodologies . . . peculiar to Capitalist monopolies'.[1]
Marginal utility, marginal cost, marginal revenue and the valuation
of land are yet to be explicitly recognized as rational and accepted
in practical economic accounting.

Contrary to many enthusiastic expectations in the West, there
is no evidence of these countries returning to Capitalism, not even
in Yugoslavia. The Marxian ideal of Full Communism is still the
declared ultimate goal of Socialist development, and outside
observers can easily mistake means for ends. Many new elements
incorporated into the Socialist economies, such as profit, economic
incentives to labour, interest, flexible prices, independence of
enterprises, are not identical with those operating under Capitalism
as they are conditioned in different ways. The limitations of the
market are recognized not only in Socialist countries but also in
the Capitalist world. The market is not the best mechanism to
shape structural developments, new production capacities and
progress in science and technology in accordance with long-run
social preferences.

There is a large body of economists which is convinced that in
actual practice the possibilities of linking plan and market into a
harmonious system are clearly limited. Even Ota Šik, whose
theoretical as well as practical work was directed towards an
integration of the two, conceded:

> It is not difficult to link the plan and the market in a theoretical
> abstraction and demonstrate the necessity of their unity under
> socialism. It is much more difficult to work out concrete forms
> of their interaction under specific social-economic conditions.[2]

This conflict often became apparent in the working of the Yugoslav
model between 1952 and 1965.[3] Thus in the future Socialist countries will be confronted with two alternatives – either further liberal
reforms and less planning, or more planning and restriction of the
role of the market.

---

[1] J. Mujżel, ('Politics, Economics, Economists'), *Życie gospodarcze* (Economic
Life), Warsaw, 28/7/1968, p. 6.
[2] Ota Šik, *Plan and Market under Socialism*, Prague, Czechoslovak Academy of
Sciences, 1967, p. 342.
[3] See, e.g., J. T. Bombelles, *Economic Development of Communist Yugoslavia
1947–1964*, Stanford, The Hoover Institute, 1968, pp. 75–181.

There is sufficient evidence to suggest that none of these countries will revert to the old system of directive centralized planning and management. The weakening of ideological fanaticism, the irritations of continued bureaucratic interference and the all-pervading yearning for more freedom and better living are, no doubt, conducive to further liberal reforms.

On the other hand, there will be forces opposing, and even restricting the scope of, the market mechanism. The remarkable progress made in the application of mathematical methods and the rapidly proceeding computerization are significant developments revolutionizing the process and implementation of planning. The system may be perfected to such an extent that centralized scientific management and 'shadow markets' may prove more acceptable to the Party and technocrats than the fragmentation of power inevitable under the invisible hand of the market mechanism. This question is taken up in the following chapter. It appears reasonable to assume that some Socialist countries will focus their attention on the former course whilst others will concentrate on the latter, but not to the exclusion of the other. But in whatever direction, further reforms are certain to follow because so far no spectacular improvements in growth rates are evident.

4 Planning and Management

A. THE OLD DIRECTIVE, CENTRALIZED SYSTEM

THE system of planning and management which prevailed in the European Socialist countries before reforms was noted for four distinctive characteristics.

(i) *The Centralization of Decision-making.* The State Planning Commission (SPC) was vested in each country with the power of determining not only the major proportions in the economy but also the detailed setting of production targets for each enterprise. The targets were laid down in perspective (15–20-year), medium (5–7-year), annual, quarterly and monthly plans. It was tacitly assumed that the SPC was the only competent entity to work out the ways and means of realizing the broad economic goals laid down by the Party and that the plan faithfully reflected the needs of society and the capacities of enterprises.

(ii) *The Hierarchical Nature of Economic Relations.* The SPC was also responsible for the methods of plan implementation. The disaggregated tasks were addressed to appropriate ministries, branch associations (if they existed) and enterprises. The links in the pyramid were vertical – from the highest to the lowest. Horizontal ties, i.e. direct transactions between (supplying and purchasing) enterprises, did not play an independent role because they were also vertically arranged.

(iii) *The Directive Nature of Planning and Management.* The instructions (called 'directives') were transmitted down the hierarchical ladder and were legally binding, overriding individual preferences. The shorter the plan period the more detailed and directive the targets were.

(iv) *Physical Balancing.* Economic accounting was done almost exclusively in physical units, both at the central and operational levels. Allocative decisions were based on the postulated output, and on the technical coefficients of production (indicating input–output relations). Prices (which did not reflect cost-preference relations anyway) did not perform the guidance function for the allocation of resources but were used merely for aggregation.

The system outlined above had a number of advantages in the early stages of economic development when extensive sources of growth were relied upon. Accelerated development and industrialization in backward countries require major shifts in the economy to harness existing under-utilized reserves of resources and to create new sources of raw materials, capital equipment and skilled labour. Centralized and directive planning and management in several ways provided the most effective framework for carrying out radical structural transformations swiftly and consistently. A Hungarian economist summed up the situation thus:

> The highly centralized system of economic planning and management . . . was the answer to the exigencies of the times and it enabled the implementation of the tasks confronting our society. A tendency towards centralization is typical of countries embarking on far-reaching social and economic transformation and determined to attain ambitious economic objectives.[1]

Oskar Lange, a well-known Polish scholar, planner and administrator, went even further when he pointed out that the centralized set-up was justified not only on the obvious economic grounds, but also by '. . . the very process of Socialist revolution whereby one social system is replaced by another demanding that the revolutionary regime exercise centralized control over the allocation and utilization of resources'.[2]

The advantages of this system were particularly obvious in the case of a large country such as the Soviet Union, but for a variety of reasons the Soviet model was adopted by other Socialist countries as well. In all these economies there was a shortage of trained

[1] G. Varga, ('The Reform of the Management of the National Economy'), in L. Lewandowicz and M. Misiak (eds), *Reformy gospodarcze w krajach socjalistycznych* (Economic Reforms in Socialist Countries), Warsaw, PWE, 1967, p. 330.
[2] O. Lange, *Pisma wybrane* (Selected Works), Warsaw, PWN, 1963, p. 138.

and experienced administrators and managers, and some of the most competent were concentrated in central planning offices. The most difficult decisions, such as those concerning the allocation of resources, the structure of production, the disposal of output, prices, wages and costs, and the settlement of accounts, were all worked out in detail by central planners and transmitted as directives to the managers of enterprises. The remaining tasks, consisting mostly of routine paper work and the hiring of labour, could be reasonably well handled by the local management, as they did not require great managerial skills. There was no need for enterprises to make an economic evaluation of their activities as these were carried out at the central level at the time of the plan construction.

Although the system was conducive to the maximization of targets in quantitative terms, at the same time it could not ensure the most suitable structure of output (with regard to use and quality) and the minimization of inputs. The method of planning by physical balancing merely ensured the internal consistency of the plan, but not the most efficient structure of output. Even the methods of production were prescribed for each enterprise in detail and imposed from above. Very little initiative could be exercised by managers to respond to changing conditions underlying costs and demand, and to introduce modern management methods and technology.

There was a prevalent atmosphere of unquestioned obedience or of apathy at the operational level, so that even where central directives were patently inconsistent and singularly unsuited to local conditions they were passively implemented all the same. The SPC, overburdened with a mass of detail, could not devote due attention to macroeconomic issues. At the same time its microeconomic decisions were often erroneous, owing to the lack of reliable and complete data and its inability to process the available information promptly.

Contrary to what might be expected, there was a good deal of instability. It was caused by tight planning – allowing for very small or no reserves – and providing for too optimistic targets. Owing to planners' errors, the incompetence of administrators and unforeseen contingencies at home as well as abroad, bottlenecks

frequently appeared, threatening a whole chain reaction of unful-
filled targets. Consequently, plans had often to be changed by
commands from above, thus undermining enterprises' morale.
For example, in the USSR in 1963, the plan had to be changed
twelve times in the Kiev *Sovnarkhoz* and sixteen times in the Lvov
Sovnarkhoz.[1]

From the above brief discussion it should be evident that
although the old system was effective in a restricted sense it was not
efficient in general. It was especially indifferent and even inimical
to the activation of intensive sources of growth. As a reaction
against the inadequacy of the old system to meet the new requirements for economic development, two seemingly opposite lines
of approach have been followed: decentralization on the one hand,
and the perfection of centralized planning and management on the
other. We shall examine these developments in the following parts
of this chapter.

B. DECENTRALIZATION

Under the new system planning has been streamlined in several
ways and adapted to the needs of intensive growth. In one respect,
the process of planning has been reversed – the old hierarchical
planning has given way to plans constructed 'from below'
('counter-planning') where branch associations and enterprises
participate in determining the structure of production according to
demand and their own capacities. A good deal of importance is
attached to industrial co-operation, where enterprises are allowed,
and indeed encouraged, to enter into contracts with other enterprises directly, and these now form the basis of economic plans
('horizontal planning').

In some countries – Czechoslovakia, Hungary and Yugoslavia –
annual plans have been virtually discontinued. In Yugoslavia compulsory targets have been dropped altogether, whilst in other
countries their number has been greatly reduced. Thus in the late
1960s such targets were decreased to less than 60 in Czechoslovakia,

[1] S. Góra, *Warunki produkcji a działanie bodźców* (Conditions of Production
and the Operation of Material Incentives), Warsaw, PWE, 1967, p. 118.

to about 60 in the German Democratic Republic and to 120 in
Bulgaria – compared with several thousands in the early 1960s.[1]
The number of directive indicators regulating enterprises' activities has also been pruned. For example, their number in the USSR
before 1965 ran to 30–40, but now it is only about 10.[2] In Bulgaria
the number of directive indicators has been reduced to five, plus
four 'orientational-analytical' indicators.[3] Their number is slightly
larger in the German Democratic Republic, Poland and Romania,
whilst in Yugoslavia they are no longer compulsory.

The accent is now on what has come to be known as 'flexible'
planning. This approach is particularly favoured in the consumer-
goods sector. Plans are constructed in broad categories and a good
deal of progress has been made in defining them in value terms.
Even in the USSR changes in production plans are allowed during
the year in response to demand. If plans are changed on the initiative of higher authorities, or if the original plan contained errors,
compensation is payable to affected enterprises for any losses
incurred.[4]

Another novel approach to planning is represented by 'structural
planning'. Most pioneering work in this field has been done in the
German Democratic Republic since 1967, but the practice has
been spreading to other planning-conscious Socialist countries as
well, especially Czechoslovakia, Poland, Romania and the USSR.
Under the traditional 'branch' approach, plans are worked out by
the relevant economic ministries with the participation of the
branch associations and enterprises concerned. Experience has
shown that this departmentalization produces sectional pressures

[1] J. Wilczynski, The Economics of Socialism, London, Allen & Unwin, 1970,
p. 35.
[2] The centrally allocated raw materials and components, the total value of
production, the quantity and quality of main products, the centrally determined investment, the wage fund, the total amount of profits and the profitability
rate, the payment of incentives, rental and fixed payments, the introduction of
new technology. Kommunist (The Communist), Moscow, 5/1968, pp. 94–5;
Życie gospodarcze (Economic Life), Warsaw, 29/3/1970, p. 11.
[3] Directive indicators – the total value of production, the volume of production
of specified basic products (in physical units), limits to investment, centrally
allocated raw materials and components and the foreign exchange spending;
'orientational-analytical' indicators – an increase in net production, an increase
in average wages, total wage fund, turnover taxes (Życie gosp., 1/10/1967, p. 11).
[4] See, e.g., Neues Deutschland (New Germany), East Berlin, 18/5/1968, p. 13.

for protecting narrow interests, in several ways impeding technological progress.

Under structural planning, the planners' preoccupation is not
with individual branches of the economy but with selected broad
goals or problems, especially with modernization, specialization,
concentration, industrial co-operation, applied research and innovations.[1] Structural plans do not merely consist in an extrapolation
of existing situations but in attempts to anticipate the desired
structure and direction of development in the future. It is widely
realized now that intensive growth critically depends on the
continuous assimilation of new technology. To facilitate this process, favourable conditions must be provided for in long-term plans
based on economic prognoses to promote the continuity of technical progress[2] (for further details, see Chapters 11 and 13).

The decentralization of planning would not be effective without
parallel developments in economic administration. These developments include the transfer of several responsibilities of the SPC
and economic ministries to intermediate organs, a greater independence of enterprises (including farms) and the growth of workers'
self-management. The intermediate organs include branch associations (also known as 'economic' or 'industrial' associations or
'centrals'), industrial trusts (in Czechoslovakia and Hungary) and
chambers of industry, commerce, transport, etc. (in Yugoslavia).

The intermediate level of economic administration is best
developed in the German Democratic Republic, Poland and
Romania and least in Czechoslovakia and Hungary. Its role
naturally varies from country to country. But in all countries the
intermediate organs have relieved central authorities of many
details of administration and management, they shield enterprises
against arbitrary central interference and they provide a valuable
basis for industrial co-operation.[3] They have proved more effective

[1] Diagrammatical models of structural planning in the GDR can be found in
Die Wirtschaft (The Economy), East Berlin, 8/5/1968, Supplement, pp. 4, 5, 9,
15.
[2] L. Rzhiga, ('Scientific and Technological Progress and Long-term Prognoses'), *Voprosy ekonomiki* (Problems of Economics), Moscow, 9/1969, pp. 39–
48.
[3] In the GDR there are over 80 industrial associations comprising at least
1,700 enterprises (12% of the total number, but responsible for 70% of industrial
output) plus about 100 scientific and technical centres. Poland has 40 large

than the regional decentralization experimented with in the USSR between 1957 and 1965 and in the German Democratic Republic between 1961 and 1965.

But of all the reforms of planning and management, the consequent increased independence and importance of enterprises is of greatest significance. In effect, enterprises now have a good deal of freedom in choosing their actual structure and methods of production. The market and the enterprises' own interests largely regulate the dealings amongst enterprises. There is evidence indicating that appointments to managerial positions are now more related to professional competence than to political reliability.

In a sense, the workers' self-management can also be considered as an aspect of the decentralization of management. Workers' councils were first created in Yugoslavia in 1949, then in Poland (1956), Hungary[1] and in Czechoslovakia (1968). They are elected by the members of each enterprise from amongst workers and the managerial staff and they share in the management of the enterprise. Where this system exists, it enhances the feeling of pride and responsibility of all the enterprise personnel and is conducive to the elimination of waste and to a constant search for improving enterprise performance. The system has been developed most successfully in Yugoslavia, where self-managed enterprises are now responsible for 60 per cent of the national income produced.[2]

The decentralization of planning and management is likely to cure Socialist economies, at least partly, of the two major weaknesses prevalent under the old system – the irrationality of decision-making at the microeconomic level and the faulty link between central authorities and the executors of the plan at the operational

---

branch associations covering most industries. In Czechoslovakia there are about 90 small industrial trusts; in Hungary 25 such trusts comprising 250 enterprises, whilst the remaining 600 enterprises are subject directly to their branch ministries. In the GDR and Poland membership is compulsory, but in Czechoslovakia, Hungary and Yugoslavia it is not. For details, see *Gospodarka planowa* (Planned Economy), Warsaw, 2/1968, p. 55; *Finanse* (Finance), Warsaw, 9/1968, p. 15.

[1] But in Hungary they had virtually disappeared by the end of the same year, after the collapse of the anti-Communist uprising.

[2] *Ekonomist* (The Economist), Zagreb, 4/1968, p. 732.

level. With the increasing possibilities of substitution amongst resources, amongst products and amongst technologies, enterprises
are in a better position to make rational decisions than are distant
central planners. At the same time, decentralization relieves the
SPC of a mass of routine work so that it can concentrate more
effectively on matters of long-run macroeconomic significance.
The new system also provides better bonds of harmony between
macro and micro levels in the form of economic incentives and
disincentives designed to reconcile the interest of enterprises and
their personnel with the long-run interest of society.

It would be unwarranted to conclude from the preceding account
that the reforms have completely done away with centralization.
The 'major proportions' (as they are commonly described) in the
economy of long-run macrosocial importance are still centrally
determined with little reference to the market and current consumers' preferences. These proportions include consumption and
accumulation, investment in productive and 'non-productive'
sectors, distribution of investment among the major branches of
the economy, private and social consumption and the personal
wage fund and the level of retail prices.

In some countries centralized economic administration has been
strengthened at the ministerial level. By the reforms of 1965, in
Czechoslovakia a number of specialized industrial ministries was replaced by two large ministries (of Mining and of Heavy Industry),
and in the German Democratic Republic and the USSR new economic ministries took over from regional economic councils. In
several ways the banking system has been further centralized and
financial controls tightened. In some respects branch associations
restrict the independence of enterprises. This is particularly so in
the German Democratic Republic, Poland, Romania and the
USSR, where the associations are not voluntary organizations
operated by enterprises, but largely the administrative organs of
central authorities. In some countries (especially in Romania) the
responsibilities of enterprises have been greatly increased but not
their powers. In Bulgaria in 1969 greater powers were given to the
Ministry of Foreign Trade to exercise stricter controls over the
entities engaging in external trade.

Even in the countries where decentralization has been advanced furthest (in Hungary and Yugoslavia), the State still has the power – and it has exercised it in recent years – to apply drastic direct controls. It is also likely that progress in the application of mathematical methods and computers to planning and management and further economic integration under the Council for Mutual Economic Assistance will promote a greater centralization.

C. MATHEMATICAL METHODS AND COMPUTERS

For a long time there was little interest amongst Socialist economists in econometrics and computers. This was further re-inforced by opposition on ideological grounds. Mathematical methods involve marginal analysis and the valuation of non-labour factors of production, and as such they were considered a threat to Marxian thinking and consequently 'anti-social'. On more practi-cal grounds, many leaders foresaw that the value judgements made by the Communist Party, which in the past were accepted without question, could be demonstrated to be erroneous.

Yet there was a number of mathematical economists who carried on work on linear programming and optimization models in re-search institutes or privately, even in the USSR under Stalin. The official attitude began to change after 1956, and in a few years a number of original studies appeared in published forms. Some of these works have been accepted as important contributions to world economic thought and have been translated into Western languages.[1] In fact it is now claimed in the USSR that linear programming was first discovered at the University of Leningrad in 1939 (by Kantorovich) long before its (independent) formu-lation in the West by G. B. Dantzig in 1947.

Advanced mathematical methods and computers are now revolutionizing the whole system of planning and manage-

[1] e.g. those translated into English include: L. V. Kantorovich, *The Best Use of Economic Resources*, Harvard UP, 1965; J. Kornai, *Mathematical Planning of Structural Decisions*, Amsterdam, North-Holland, 1967; O. Lange, *Introduction to Econometrics*, Oxford, Pergamon, 1959 (2nd ed., 1962); V. S. Nemchinov (ed.), *The Use of Mathematics in Economics*, Edinburgh, Oliver & Boyd, 1964; V. V. Novozhilov, *Problems of Measuring Outlays and Results under Optimal Planning*, New York, IASP, 1969.

ment.[1] They make possible the application of sophisticated statistical inference in variant thinking, optimal calculations and equilibrium analysis beyond the old-fashioned empirically developed method of physical balances.

Computers and mathematical techniques are used to collect, transmit and process a variety of data. They are employed not only in planning but also in mechanization and automation, in economic administration, transport, banking and warehousing. The combination of computers and self-regulating devices, or cybernetics, enable the automatic steering and control of production processes in the most effective ways, according to the objectives postulated in the plan. 'What is important in this mathematization and computerization drive,' concluded a Polish cyberneticist, 'is not so much the saving of immediate costs, but the placing of the economy on a higher and solid basis of efficiency.'[2]

With regard to the availability of modern computers, Socialist countries are behind the leading Western nations but rapid progress is being made. Of the total number of about 80,000 computers in the world (50,000 in the USA) in 1970, the European Socialist countries had nearly one-tenth. The USSR had over 5,000 whilst the number in the remaining countries (disregarding Albania) ranged from less than 50 in Romania to over 400 in Czechoslovakia. Most of the computers in use are small and medium-size and of the second generation.

However, imports of medium and large computers from Britain, France, Japan and the USA are increasing remarkably. The USSR, Poland, Czechoslovakia and the German Democratic Republic have recently stepped up,[3] and Bulgaria and Hungary have begun,

---

[1] Using integrated semiconductor circuits, high-speed computers can now perform up to 100m. arithmetic operations per second and, in principle, with the aid of semiconductor diode lasers it is possible to increase the performance to 10,000m. operations per second. In the Soviet Republic of Kazakhstan it took from one and a half to two months to work out annual plans, but with the aid of computers it is hoped to reduce the period to two to four days. *Ekonomika i organizacja pracy* (The Economics and Organization of Labour), Warsaw, 2/1970, p. 94; *Pravda* (Moscow), 5/2/1970, p. 2.

[2] W. Szyndler-Głowacki, ('Computers' Road to Management'), *Życie gosp.*, 29/1/1967, p. 5.

[3] The USSR produced her first computer as early as 1950; Poland began building experimental models in 1951 and Czechoslovakia and the GDR began producing small computers in the late 1950s.

the production of computers, including third-generation (with integrated circuits) machines. The annual output to be reached in the USSR alone by 1975 is planned to be 30,000.[1]

In all these countries the State Planning Commissions have been equipped with computers, and computer centres have been established and are being developed to serve selected enterprises, industries and regions. Given sufficient time, an integrated computer network may embrace the entire economy (which is more feasible than in a Capitalist country) and perhaps even the member countries of the Council for Mutual Economic Assistance. In a vision of the shape of things to come, a Socialist economist pointed out: 'It may be reasonably expected that the changeover from mechanized to automated production will be realized in its completeness only under Socialist conditions.'[2] Work is in progress, under the auspices of the CMEA Permanent Commissions for Economic Questions, Statistics, and Standardization, on a complete reorganization of statistical information in member countries to answer the needs of the new economic system. At the CMEA session held in Moscow in February 1969, a programme was prepared for co-operation in the installation and operation of computers in member countries.

D. OPTIMAL PLANNING

Until the late 1950s the question of optimization received little attention from planners. There was little guidance available from theoretical work, and planning techniques were still rudimentary. Moreover, as the growth strategy was dominated by extensive considerations, the waste and missed opportunities associated with the irrational use of resources were not apparent enough. Planners were preoccupied with the construction of balanced, i.e. internally consistent, plans. However, the practicability of a plan does not necessarily ensure its optimality.

[1] Based on the following sources: *Ekonomika i organizacja pracy*, 2/1970, p. 92; *Figyelö* (Economic Observer), Budapest, 2/10/1968, p. 5; *Viata economica* (Economic Life), Bucharest, 26/10/1969, p. 3.

[2] B. Miszewski, *Postęp ekonomiczny w gospodarce przemysłowej* (Economic Progress in an Industrial Economy), Warsaw, PWE, 1968, p. 59.

A more rational allocation and utilization of resources could either enable the attainment of the postulated targets at lower overall outlays, or the employed resources could yield greater effects. That is precisely what the leading planometricians argued in their contributions published in the late 1950s. Kantorovich stated the argument most convincingly:

> . . . the transition to a system of optimal planning with valuations of production corresponding to the full national economic costs, should lead to a fuller realization of the advantages of a Socialist system and to further increases in the rate of growth of its productive forces.[1]

By the early 1960s, the need for the optimization of planning was generally appreciated by the majority of economists and political leaders owing to, as Oskar Lange put it, 'the sufficient theoretical and technical basis, . . . the high degree of maturity of the Socialist economies and the need for the intensification of economic growth'.[2]

There is, of course, nothing absolute about the 'optimal plan'. Optimization is a relative concept depending on a postulated objective. This question has aroused most heated discussions because it strikes at the very rationale of the Socialist economy. For many years the quantitative maximization of national income (the 'fetishism of production') was usually regarded as the central goal. But more recently the maximization of consumption is being put forward by many theoreticians as a more reliable criterion of optimization.[3] Some economists believe that the maximization of production associated with a continuous growth of social welfare (increase in consumption, reduction in the hours of work, etc.) should be jointly adopted as the criterion.[4] Some writers go further

---

[1] L. V. Kantorovich, op. cit., p. 151.

[2] O. Lange, ('From Physical Balancing to the Selection of the Optimal Plan'), *Nowe drogi* (New Paths), 2/1965, pp. 40-1.

[3] See, e.g., A. Aganbegian and K. Barginovskii, ('Macroeconomic Optimum'), *Voprosy ekonomiki*, 10/1967, pp. 116-23; K. Kouba, 'The Plan and Economic Growth', *Czechoslovak Economic Papers*, no. 6, 1966, pp. 7-21; K. Porwit, *Zagadnienia rachunku ekonomicznego w planie centralnym* (Problems of Economic Accounting in the Central Plan), Warsaw, PWE, 1964, pp. 57-9.

[4] N. Kovalev, ('Some Methodological Problems of Macroeconomic Programming'), *Vop. ekon.*, 10/1966, pp. 68-80.

by postulating different criteria of optimization according to the four levels of planning – for enterprises, the branches of the economy, the national economy and the CMEA region.[1]

Optimal planning necessitates the valuation of all factors of production, i.e. not only labour but also capital and land, according to scarcity. As in most cases neither producers' nor retail prices in Socialist countries fully reflect scarcities, it appears that the planners' responsibility is to discover ideal programming prices instrumental to the attainment of the optimal plan. Historically, two methods have been suggested to provide a rational basis for such prices. The supporters of market socialism believe that basic information at least should be derived from the market for the determination of rational prices not only of products but also of the means of production.[2]

On the other hand, the exponents of the mathematical school oppose this approach in their conviction that modern mathematical methods and computers provide a more reliable and less wasteful solution.[3] Optimalists recognize the fact that some resources are scarcer (more productive) than others, and consequently they should be allocated in such a pattern – given the constraints and objectives inherent in the plan – as to maximize the overall production in the economy, not merely in each enterprise.

This process necessitates the calculation of opportunity costs, or as Novozhilov calls them 'the costs of the forgone alternative applications of resources' or 'feedback costs'.[4] The optimal plan is

---

[1] B. Miszewski, op. cit., pp. 217–25.

[2] The original proponent of this solution was the pre-war Oskar Lange, according to whom rational prices of the means of production could be established on the basis of market signals with corrections by central planners for social cost-benefit ('shadow prices'). On the other hand, some of the modern supporters of market socialism, such as K. Kouba of Czechoslovakia, are critical of Lange's shadow markets and instead advocate genuine traditional markets for the determination of rational prices of the means of production. See O. Lange, 'On the Economic Theory of Socialism', *Review of Economic Studies*, vol. I, no. 1, 1936/37, pp. 53–71; K. Kouba, ('The Plan and Market in a Socialist Economy'), *Politicka ekonomie* (Political Economy), Prague, 9/1967, pp. 773–83.

[3] See, e.g., L. V. Kantorovich, op. cit., p. 151.

[4] V. V. Novozhilov ('The Law of Value and Price Formation'), in *Problemy primeneniya matematiki v sotsialisticheskoi ekonomike* (Problems of the Application of Mathematics to Socialist Economics), Sbornik II, Leningrad, 1965, esp. p. 19.

arrived at by the process of successive approximations consisting in making adjustments to the combinations of different resources and methods of production according to the laid-down maximand(s) (national income, consumption, etc.) or minimand(s) (inputs, time, etc.). To pursue this process, it is essential to solve very large numbers of simultaneous equations when passing from one plan variant to another.

Thus optimal planning involves two fundamental departures from the traditional Marxian economics. Firstly, it necessitates the evaluation of the non-labour factors of production. Secondly, it resorts to marginal analysis, i.e. the determination of the marginal rate of substitution of inputs and of outputs. The optimal plan provides the ultimate basis for the derivation of the optimal prices of the factors of production. These prices in fact are coefficients representing the relative significance of the different resources to the attainment of the optimal plan. Kantorovich calls them 'objectively determined valuations'[1] (also see Chapter 5 A, pp. 78, 82).

The first practical optimization attempts were made in the USSR in the early 1960s, but other advanced Socialist countries (the German Democratic Republic, Hungary, Poland and Czechoslovakia) soon followed suit. So far most progress has been made in partial optimization. It has been applied to determine the optimum composition and distribution of production in selected branches of the economy, mostly on a regional basis and in those industries where possibilities for the substitution of inputs are limited and where fairly constant technical coefficients of production prevail.[2] The industries affected so far include coal-mining, fishing, iron and steel, food processing and transport. Optimization procedures have also been applied to specific problems, such as investment efficiency, the utilization of fixed assets and the effectiveness of exports. A good deal of work has been done on the optimization of the 1971–75 five-year plans, but little reliable information was available at the time of writing.

---

[1] L. V. Kantorovich, op. cit., pp. 5–12, 25, 123, 137–51.
[2] The technical coefficient of production indicates the relation between input and output in a particular industry or in the case of a particular product. It is derived by dividing the input outlay by the output obtained in physical terms and is usually expressed as a decimal fraction of six or more places.

There is still a good deal of scepticism amongst theoretical writers as well as practising planners on the feasibility of optimization covering the whole economy. There are many economists who believe that computers can be applied to best effect in large enterprises, and doubts have been cast on the practicability and advisability of a super-system on a macroeconomic scale.[1] Compared with the West, Socialist countries have a small number of computers even for ordinary needs,[2] and those they have are mostly of too small capacity and too obsolete to meet the needs of optimal planning. There are shortages of personnel qualified to undertake programming for economic planning and the standard of training in the 1960s was apparently low.

[1] See, e.g., A. Birman, ('One Hundred Million Nuts'), *Ekonomicheskaya gazeta* (Economic Gazette), Moscow, no. 13, 1963, p. 7; M. Draganescu, ('Production and Uses of Computers'), *Viata Economica*, 20/6/1969, p. 8; A. Yeremin and L. Nikiforov, ('On the Theory of the Constructive Political Economy of Socialism'), *Vop. ekon.*, 6/1969, pp. 112–24.

[2] According to Socialist sources, the number of computers per one million of population at the end of 1967 was as follows: USA, 200; UK, 50; EEC, 50; Japan, 30; Austria, 30; USSR, 12; Eastern European countries, 5–7. It was conceded that Poland was at least thirteen years behind the UK in the computerization of her economy and that she would not reach the 1967 British level till 1980. *Ekonomika i organizacja pracy*, 2/1970, p. 92; *Foreign Trade*, Moscow, 8/1968, p. 42; *Życie gosp.*, 26/10/1969, p. 3.

5 Prices

A. ECONOMIC RATIONALITY AND PRICING

THE philosophy underlying Socialist prices and the institutional set-up for price fixing that prevailed before the reforms were not conducive to intensive growth. On strictly ideological grounds, it was believed that prices should be based on the Marxian concept of value, i.e. the cost of live and materialized labour plus a macro-social mark-up proportional to prime costs. Thus rent, interest (to some extent), utility and scarcity, as well as fluctuations in supply and demand, were not considered as contributions to value. Similarly, marginalism (marginal utility, marginal cost pricing, marginal revenue) was rejected as being subjective and consequently anti-Marxian.

The actual price fixing was highly centralized in each country in the hands of the State Price Planning Commission, with the most crucial matters of pricing reserved for the Council of Ministers. The price determination process was guided by a hybrid mixture of objectives to serve particular purposes, in which the desired distribution of national income was the most important consideration.

In each country there was a two-tier price system, viz. producers' (or wholesale) prices and retail (consumers') prices. Producers' prices were, as a rule, based on the 'average cost of production' of the branch of industry. But these costs did not include rent and capital charges. Moreover, these prices were fixed in advance before the desired combination of resources and the structure of production were worked out in the plan, and they remained fixed for long periods. The prices for agricultural products payable by the State differed according to 'compulsory' and 'above-compulsory' deliveries, and were further differentiated according to regions (for details, see section B of this chapter). In the construction of the central plan, the allocation of resources was not guided by prices but by material balances expressed in physical terms.

Retail prices usually bore little relation to producers' prices, as the overriding objective in fixing the former was to ensure an equilibrium in the market for consumer goods by adjusting demand to the planned supply. Even the same product was often assigned different prices according to the type of article, its purpose and the class of user. In effect, the prices of retail consumer goods were insulated from producers' prices by substantial and highly differentiated turnover taxes or subsidies.[1] Consequently, consumers' preferences had hardly any influence on the size and structure of production until they were acknowledged by central planners prepared to make appropriate adjustments to producers' prices and the allocation of resources.

A description of the procedures associated with price determination and the consequent red tape and waste would read stranger than fiction. As an illustration, it may be mentioned that in the USSR in the mid-1960s there were 100,000 prices for articles of clothing – all centrally fixed. Even such insignificant items as fishing hooks had 107 different prices – all centrally determined in Moscow – according to the details of diameter, length, shape, purpose, etc. Yet the Soviet economy produced well over 10m. different types of goods.[2]

To conclude that the old price structures were irrational would be an over-simplification. They were certainly not arbitrary (barring planners' unintentional errors), but they performed functions which were logical in the context of the objectives adopted, and as such they had a rationality of their own. However, they were not rational from the standpoint of the efficiency of the allocation of resources and the requirements of intensive economic growth.

[1] For example, as was revealed by the Chairman of Hungary's Materials and Price Commission, before the price reform of 1968 only 10% of consumer goods in Hungary was retailed at prices reflecting costs (as understood in Socialist countries), 30% was sold above production costs (carrying heavy turnover taxes) and 60% below costs (i.e. produced under subsidization). Béla Csikós-Nagy, *Pricing in Hungary*, London, Inst. of Econ. Affairs, 1968, p. 11.

[2] N. Fedorenko, ('Prices and Optimal Planning'), *Kommunist* (The Communist), Moscow, 8/1966, p. 93.

It is now widely agreed amongst Socialist economists that for prices to be rational in the above sense (which coincides with the Capitalist concept of price rationality), the following conditions must be satisfied:

(a) Prices must be *either* determined in free competitive markets where consumer's sovereignty prevails,[1] *or* derived computationally from the optimal plan.

(b) The contribution of all resources (i.e. in addition to labour) to production must be accepted as cost and reflected accordingly in prices.

(c) Prices must be based on the costs of marginal enterprises in the industry producing a particular article.

(d) There ought to be a closer correspondence between retail and producers' prices. If they must differ (over and above wholesale and retail margins), the rates of turnover taxes should be reasonably uniform, at least for broad classes of products.

(e) Prices must be fairly flexible to indicate the conditions of supply and demand as reflected in conventional markets or in computationally simulated 'shadow markets'.

(f) Domestic prices of internationally traded products (including their close substitutes) must be linked to those prevailing in world markets.

It follows that if the efficiency function of prices is to be ensured, prices must not be manipulated for redistributive and non-economic considerations. Thus non-labour incomes should be absorbed by taxation, low-income and other groups in need could be assisted by the raising of minimum wages and social services, the State revenue could be raised mostly by deductions from enterprise profits or a general taxation of incomes (and perhaps fairly uni-

---

[1] Before the feasibility of computationally derived prices was known in the West, Mrs Joan Robinson, in an article written for a Polish journal, pointed out that 'The arguments for the determination of prices in accordance with market demand are stronger in the case of a Socialist economy than a Capitalist economy. Under Capitalism the distribution of purchasing power amongst families depends largely on the distribution of wealth – the basis of distribution which is justified neither on economic nor on ethical grounds. Thus under the latter system the manipulation of prices may be a desirable instrument of correcting the maldistribution of national income.' Joan Robinson, ('Philosophy of Prices'), *Ekonomista* (The Economist), Warsaw, no. 3, 1960, p. 541.

form turnover taxes as well), and market equilibrium could be maintained by enabling and inducing producers to respond to demand.

The reforms of the economic system in the Socialist countries under consideration[1] have also included major price reforms, particularly of those most relevant to efficiency, viz. producers' prices – in the German Democratic Republic in 1964–66, 1969–70; Yugoslavia, 1965; the USSR, 1967; Poland, 1967, 1971; Czechoslovakia, 1967–68; Hungary, 1968; and Bulgaria in 1968–69. More price reforms are envisaged to meet the needs of the 1971–75 five-year plans. Although the price reforms since 1964 have been more radical than the occasional price revisions carried out before, the Socialist price systems are still far from rational as understood in market economies. We shall now briefly bring out the main features of the price reforms relevant to the intensification of economic growth.

First, as the basic principle governing price formation, the Marxian concept of 'production price', as distinct from 'value', has been adopted.[2] This 'full-cost price', which includes the capital charge but not ground rent, reflects scarcity more closely than was the case previously and should encourage a more economical use of capital goods. Some steps have also been made towards taking account of differential rent in prices (see section B of this chapter).

Second, there has been a tendency to raise the level of producers' prices to increase the profitability of many branches of the economy and to eliminate the need for planned deficits. Thus by the Soviet reform of 1967, the prices of chemical products were increased by 5 per cent, the price of cement was raised by 13 per cent, timber products by 26–33 per cent, metal products by 43 per cent, rolled zinc by 64 per cent, coal by 78 per cent (coking coal by 93 per cent)

---

[1] With the exception of Romania up to the time of writing (end of 1970). The price reform of 1963 was in fact only a major revision of wholesale prices of the traditional type, not related to the economic reforms initiated in 1967. The decree of 1970 further tightened the central control of price fixing.

[2] 'Value' in Marxian terminology is expressed as $c + v + m$ (constant capital + variable outlays (wages) + surplus product mark-up proportional to variable outlays only). 'Production price', on the other hand, includes the surplus product mark-up proportional to constant capital and variable outlays combined $(c + v)$. Thus 'production price' is higher than 'value'.

D

and oil by 2·3 times.[1] As a result the planned profitability of most branches of the industry has been improved, as is illustrated by the figures below:

	According to Old Prices	According to New Prices
Coal	−17·0	8·0
Electricity	4·6	10·0
Woodworking	6·9	12·6
Industrial raw materials	5·4	13·6
Oil extracting and processing	10·4	14·6
Iron and steel	8·6	15·0–16·0

Source. Y. M. Zinoviev, *Pribil i povyshenie effektivnosti sotsialisticheskogo proizvodstva* (Profit and the Promotion of the Effectiveness of Socialist Production), Moscow, Mysl, 1968, p. 103.

In the German Democratic Republic, before the price reforms, the degree of State subsidization in selected branches of industry was: paper, 40 per cent; fuels mining, 45 per cent; timber, 50 per cent; and rolled metal products, 55 per cent. According to the reform of 1964–67 (carried out in three stages), the prices of selected producer goods were raised on the average by 70 per cent, then by 40 per cent and in the third stage by 4 per cent (the overall level of producers' prices having increased by 12 per cent over the period).[2] As a result of the Hungarian reform of 1968, producers' prices were increased on the average by 7·8 per cent; in light industry by 16·6 per cent, in the food industry by 10·9 per cent, in the machine-building industry by 10·0 per cent, but in the chemical industry they were reduced by 2·0 per cent.[3]

Since the price reforms, the average gross profitability (in relation to fixed and variable assets) in industry has been as follows: in Yugoslavia, 10 per cent; in Bulgaria, 13 per cent; in the German Democratic Republic, 15 per cent; and in the USSR also 15 per cent. In Hungary, net profitability (allowing for capital charges as a cost) has been about 8 per cent and the gross profitability rate fixed in Czechoslovakia has been 6 per cent of total cost plus 22 per cent of the wage fund.[4]

[1] *Planovoe khoziaistvo* (Planned Economy), Moscow, 7/1967, pp. 15–16.
[2] *Gospodarka planowa* (Planned Economy), Warsaw, 8–9/1967, p. 103.
[3] *Társadalmi szemle* (Social Review), Budapest, 6/1969, p. 6.
[4] W. Sztyber, ('Theoretical Foundations of the Reform of Producers' Prices in Socialist Countries'), *Ekonomista*, no. 6, 1969, pp. 1290–4.

Third, the opposition to marginalism, at least on the production side, has weakened, and such concepts as the marginal rate of substitution, marginal cost, marginal land, marginal enterprise have been generally accepted as economic realities. The increases in producers' prices, outlined above, were partly guided by production costs in marginal enterprises in some industries and an extension of this basis is advocated by many theoretical writers.

Fourth, there is an increasing inclination on the part of authorities to revise producers' prices, where they are still centrally fixed, more frequently according to major changes in costs and demand. Thus, the German Democratic Republic, which up to 1969 was noted for an extremely rigid price structure, has embarked on what is known as a 'dynamic price policy' to promote technical progress and desired structural changes in the economy. 'Flexible price policies', adopted in Bulgaria, Czechoslovakia, Hungary and Yugoslavia, can also be regarded as concessions to changing economic conditions (see section C of this chapter).

Fifth, the degree of insulation between retail and producers' prices has been considerably reduced. The operation of the market necessitates a closer link between production and distribution and the authorities are more inclined to accept guidance from consumers' preferences. Turnover taxes, as well as subsidies, have been substantially reduced,[1] and instead enterprise profits are becoming the main source of State revenue (see Chapter 12 C, pp. 221–6). Of all Socialist countries, Yugoslavia and Czechoslovakia have departed most from the insulatory two-tier price system.

Sixth, there has been considerable decentralization of price determination – most in Yugoslavia, Hungary, Czechoslovakia and Bulgaria and least in the German Democratic Republic and Romania. The prices of key products are still centrally fixed, but otherwise branch associations, regional or local authorities and even enterprises also participate. Under the so-called 'flexible price systems', producers' as well as retail prices of defined categories of products are freely determined by market conditions (see

---

[1] The general increases in producers' prices have not been passed on in higher retail prices, but mostly absorbed by the State in the form of lower turnover taxes.

section C). Finally, in most of these countries (Yugoslavia, Bulgaria, Hungary, Czechoslovakia, the German Democratic Republic and Poland) attempts have been made to link domestic prices with those prevailing in world markets (see section D).

There is also evidence indicating that the allocation of resources in central plans is increasingly guided by efficiency prices instead of merely consisting in endeavours to achieve a balancing in physical units. In most of these countries central planners now determine the broad allocation of resources on the basis of 'programming' or 'shadow' prices. Although these prices are not yet optimal as understood by econometricians, they are closer to scarcity prices. In the more advanced countries several variants of the 1971–75 plan for some branches of the economy were worked out in which these prices were used to gauge the opportunity costs associated with different patterns of resource allocation.[1]

B. THE PRICES OF PRIMARY PRODUCTS

The irrationality of the pricing of primary products (foodstuffs, raw materials of agricultural origin, timber, minerals) which prevailed in the past consisted in their unduly depressed level in relation to industrial prices and in widespread price differentiation. The traditionally low level of these prices was largely due to ideological and social considerations. In Marxian economics, based on the labour theory of value, land has no value because it is not a product of labour. Consequently land's contribution to production

---

[1] Although some theoreticians place great hopes in computationally established optimal prices for the whole economy (derived from the optimal plan), the feasibility of working out such prices appears to be no better than a decade ago. In fact, after the initial fascination with optimalists' concepts and promises, many Socialist theoretical economists, as well as planners, believe that 'all ideas of rational prices being worked out by computers solving simultaneous equations, instead of being determined by the market, must be treated as utopian'. B. Miszewski, *Postęp ekonomiczny w gospodarce przemysłowej* (Economic Progress in an Industrial Society), Warsaw, PWE, 1968, p. 195. Also see A. Boyarskii, ('Critique of a Model of Optimal Planning'), *Voprosy ekonomiki* (Problems of Economics), Moscow, 8/1969, pp. 107–16; K. Kouba, ('Plan and Market in a Socialist Economy'), *Politicka ekonomie* (Political Economy), Prague, 9/1967, pp. 773–83; H. Mann, ('Economic Effectiveness and Price'), *Wirtschaftswissenschaft* (Economic Science), East Berlin, 1/1969, pp. 49–61.

was not considered as a cost and thus ground rent was not taken
into account in price fixing.

Yet the range of natural conditions in primary production is
very wide and increases in output sometimes have to be achieved
by the extension of the margins of exploitation. In market economies, the prices of primary products are usually determined by the
cost of production on marginal (not on average, as is typical in
Socialist countries) land (so that differential rent increases in effect);
moreover, in many Western countries there are various support
schemes to agricultural prices. However, Socialist leaders regarded
the low cost of living for urban workers and low-priced raw materials as essential to the consolidation of working-class power and
to industrialization. But at the same time, the level of incomes in
agriculture was about one-quarter lower than in industry.[1]

The highly differentiated prices paid to the primary producing
enterprises were governed by the State's endeavour to intercept
differential rent. As far as agricultural products were concerned,
the differentiation was based on regions, quantities delivered to the
State and in some countries (such as the USSR up to 1966) on the
type of farms (State or collective). This is illustrated in Table 12,
where the ranges of price differentiation are demonstrated on the
example of Poland.

These pricing practices militated against efficiency in several
ways. There was widespread demoralization and neglect of
Socialist agriculture which, as is well known, led to disastrous failures in the early 1960s and which in turn impeded the development of other branches of the economy (see Chapter 2 B, p. 37).
The condition of the optimum utilization of resources from
the standpoint of efficiency is price uniformity, i.e. non-discrimi-
nation amongst users of resources and products, and furthermore
that the marginal productivity of resources is equalized in different
forms of production and that the prices of products are equal to
their marginal costs (the 'principle of equimarginality').

However, the irrational price relations between primary products and manufactures made the substitution calculation largely
meaningless. The relative cheapness of raw materials and food
encouraged their extravagant and misguided use. Thus in the

[1] For statistical evidence, see Chapter 7 D, note 2, p. 119.

TABLE 12 DIFFERENTIATION OF AGRICULTURAL PRICES IN
POLAND IN 1966
(In Złotys per Quintal)

PRODUCT	Regional Range of Procurement Prices Payable by the State		Regional Range of Prices Prevailing in Free Markets (Officially Tolerated)
	On compulsory deliveries	On above-compulsory deliveries	
Barley	156–249	268–328	319–407
Oats	148–158	265–283	297–417
Potatoes	53*	100*	84–143
Rye	175–186	284–297	298–386
Wheat	221–239	358–376	398–485

* National average. Data on regional differentiation not available.

Source. Based on: Central Statistical Office of Poland, *Rocznik statystyczny 1967* (Statistical Yearbook for 1967), Warsaw, 1967, pp. 361, 363.

early 1960s, in spite of critical shortages of grains, bread was often fed to pigs and cattle because it was cheaper than feeding stuffs.

The depressed price level of primary products, in spite of steeply rising costs, discouraged exports of raw materials to other Socialist countries (including the dishonouring of signed contracts). Consequently, acute shortages of such items developed on the CMEA[1] scale, whilst manufactures became 'soft' items. This question was first thoroughly analysed by a well-known Soviet economist, O. Bogomolov, in 1965.[2] He demonstrated that the

[1] The countries belonging to the Council for Mutual Economic Assistance (also known in the West as 'Comecon') – Bulgaria, Czechoslovakia, the German Democratic Republic, Hungary, Poland, Romania and the USSR; Mongolia is also a member, whilst Yugoslavia has only associate membership status.

[2] O. Bogomolov, *Ekonomicheskaya effektivnost mezhdunarodnogo sotsialistiche-skogo razdeleniya truda* (The Economic Effectiveness of the International Socialist Division of Labour), Moscow, Ekonomika, 1965. See also his articles: ('Current Problems of the Economic Co-operation amongst Socialist Countries'), *Mirovaya ekonomika i mezhdunarodnye otnosheniya* (World Economy and International Relations), Moscow, 5/1966, pp. 15–27; and ('An Important Stage in the Co-operation amongst CMEA Countries'), *Kommunist*, 18/1966, pp. 13–24.

rapidly proceeding industrialization in Socialist countries was producing a restructuring of costs, viz. costs in primary industries rising in relation to those in manufacturing. Bogomolov predicted that the shortages of raw materials would become even more acute, particularly in the more industrialized CMEA countries, unless the past price relation between primary and manufactured products in intra-CMEA foreign trade is reversed in the future (see section D of this chapter).

Now to illustrate how Socialist pricing policies sinned against the equimarginal principle. In the USSR in 1959, according to the existing price structure, to achieve production to the value of one rouble, the necessary investment outlays were: in the textile industry, 0·14 rouble, but in the fuels and energy industry, 2·23 roubles, i.e. 16 times higher.[1] In Poland in the early 1960s, to earn one foreign-exchange rouble it was essential to incur the following investment outlays: in machine-construction, 56 złotys; in coal mining, 187 złotys; and in copper mining, 522 złotys.[2]

The changes in economic thought and pricing policies since the late 1950s have been creating favourable conditions for removing some irrationalities of the past. First, the price levels of primary products in the Socialist countries have been increased in relation to manufactures. In the recent reforms of producers' prices, those of primary products have been increased more than those of manufactured articles. Thus in Hungary over the period 1966–68, the procurement prices of agricultural products were lifted by 17 per cent whilst industrial prices as a whole rose by only 7·8 per cent; the prices of chemicals were actually reduced by 2 per cent.[3] In the USSR by the 1967 reform of producers' prices, oil was increased by 2·3 times but chemical products by only 5 per cent.[4] In Yugoslavia according to the price reform of 1965, agricultural wholesale prices were increased by 33 per cent whilst the prices of industrial producer goods rose by only 13 per cent;[5] the relative

[1] A. Notkin, *Tempo i proporcje reprodukcji socjalistycynej* (The Rate and Proportions of Socialist Economic Growth), Warsaw, PWE, 1962, p. 224.

[2] O. Bogomolov, *Mir. ekon. i mezhd. otnosh.*, op. cit., p. 19.

[3] *Acta oeconomica* (Economic Papers), Budapest, vol. 4, no. 1, 1969, p. 13; *Társadalmi szemle*, 6/1969, p. 6.

[4] See section A of this chapter, pp. 80–1.

[5] *Statistički godišnjak Jugoslavije 1969*, p. 121.

change is even more striking if we consider the period since the economic reforms of 1952 – between 1952 and 1969 agricultural prices increased by 360 per cent but the prices of manufactures (wholesale in each case) by only 50 per cent.[1]

In contrast to previous practice in Socialist countries, the cost of geological surveys is now wholly or partly included in the prices of the minerals concerned, and similarly expenditure on research and experiments is now regarded as a cost of production (Chapter 13 B). It also appears that attempts have been made to introduce a uniformity of prices of some primary products, and instead to apply differentiated taxes to absorb differential rent.[2] Where this is done, any special advantages which are not due to the enterprises' own efforts are neutralized, which provides an equality of opportunity for the improvement of the methods of production. Many economists now believe that to promote intensive farming, which is the only practical basis for increasing agricultural output nowadays, at least a portion of differential rent II should be allowed to be retained by farms.[3]

The advocates of optimal planning, of course, accept differential rent as an essential component of the optimal prices of natural resources and implicitly of costs, at least at the central plan level. Kantorovich summed up their stand in the following words:

> In solving problems of the use of natural resources which are more efficient but in short supply, their use must be determined by allowing for differential rent. The magnitude of the latter is determined by the saving of labour obtained from the use of these resources in the optimal plan. If rent is included in expenditure then the principle of least cost is observed in the

---

[1] *Ekonomista*, no. 6, 1969, pp. 1380–1.

[2] e.g. in the USSR before the reform of 1967 the prices of gas and oil payable to producing enterprises were differentiated according to conditions of production in different basins, but in the new price system this differentiation has been removed. Differential rent was calculated by the Central Institute for Economics and Mathematics of the Soviet Academy of Sciences on the basis of a specially prepared algorithm.

[3] In Marxian terminology, differential rent II is that deriving from differences in the productivity of land brought about by man-made improvements (whilst differential rent I is due to natural differences in the quality of land, such as fertility and location).

optimal plan. Consequently the calculation of the rent should play an important role in questions of price formation.[1]

However, the reforms have produced certain developments whereby some prices (especially those of primary products) are held stable whilst those of luxuries and other industrial goods are allowed to fluctuate and rise. Moreover, the extension of financial incentives to encourage above-compulsory deliveries to the State (where they still exist, as in the German Democratic Republic, Poland, Romania and the USSR) has tended to accentuate price differentiation. We shall examine these questions next.

C. PRICE FLEXIBILITY

Up to about the mid-1960s, Socialist price systems were noted for their rigidity. The prices of producer goods remained unchanged for long periods, usually five to ten years, and even the retail prices of the most important items entering the cost of living were not changed frequently. Under directive central planning, dominated by the extensive approach to economic growth, the stability of prices had several advantages. But this is no longer so, as a Soviet economist observed:

> Some economists, justifiably, believe that price stability is one of the greatest advantages of the Socialist system. But the maintenance of stability for its own sake in the face of changing conditions underlying production and demand becomes the very opposite of an advantage.[2]

In a progressive economy, in the interest of efficiency, prices must provide guidance to the continuous process of substitution, both in the input and output markets, in accordance with changing cost-preference relations. The new economic system very largely depends for its success on this process, and the ability and inclination of sellers as well as buyers to respond to changing prices have been considerably enhanced by the economic reforms.

[1] L. V. Kantorovich, *The Best Use of Economic Resources*, Harvard UP, 1965, p. 99.

[2] I. Lukimov, ('Agricultural Production and Prices'), *Kommunist*, Moscow, 4/1968, p. 70.

To meet the challenge of intensive growth, all eight Socialist countries under consideration have introduced at least some elements of price flexibility. Yugoslavia has freed a large proportion of her prices from central control, especially since 1965, so that by 1970 about one-half of all prices was determined in free markets. Bulgaria, Czechoslovakia, the German Democratic Republic and Hungary have introduced highly elaborate price systems under which the degree of flexibility depends on the type of goods. Typically, there are four categories of prices in descending order of permitted fluctuations.

(a) *Fixed Prices*. These are fixed by the State and held constant for longer periods. The items usually covered include those which have a substantial effect on the level and structure of production costs and on the cost of living, such as fuels, metals, consumer necessities and basic services.

(b) *Ceiling Prices*. These prices are allowed to fluctuate below the maximum levels fixed by the State. They apply to many raw materials and less essential items of household use where competition amongst sellers is possible and desirable.

(c) *Free-range Prices*. In this case the State sets maximum and minimum levels applicable to selected articles (or groups of articles), so that prices can move freely within the range so laid down. The items covered are mostly less important raw materials, components and semi-luxury consumer goods (processed foods, clothing, mass-produced household effects).

(d) *Free Prices*. These are allowed to fluctuate freely according to market supply and demand. Included in this category are mostly luxuries and non-standardized items, such as jewellery, handicrafts, paintings, goods in seasonal supply and many imported articles.

The flexible price system as understood in the above sense is best developed in Hungary. In the late 1960s the following proportions of consumer goods (measured by the value of the retail trade turnover) fell into the above categories: fixed, 20 per cent; ceiling, 30 per cent; free-range, 27 per cent; and free prices, 23 per cent. Of all articles of clothing (also by retail value), 21 per cent was retailed under fixed prices, 54 per cent at free-range prices, and free-market prices applied to the remaining 25 per cent. In the case of basic materials, 25 per cent (by value) was subject to fixed, 50 per cent to ceiling, 5 per cent to free-range, and 20 per cent to free-market prices.[1] In the German Democratic Republic, enterprises in the most progressive industries are required to pass on the benefits of increasing productivity in price reductions (rather than in higher taxes on profits), which can also be considered as a form of price flexibility.[2]

But even in Poland and the USSR (and to a lesser extent in Romania) there is considerable price flexibility owing to the fact that some prices are now negotiated between enterprises in accordance with State-prescribed regulations. Furthermore, increasing proportions of consumer goods, especially foodstuffs sold directly to private consumers, are determined in (relatively) free markets. The practice of 'drastic price cuts' and 'sales' is no longer the preserve of Capitalist merchandising. A Soviet financial journal recently quoted the case of a trading enterprise in Leningrad which, to dispose of its large stocks, marked down the articles of haberdashery by 70–80 per cent, and of a co-operative shop in the Soviet Far East which 'slashed down' the prices of women's shoes from 28·50 to 5·00 roubles.[3]

The degree of price flexibility is further increased by the fact that the State is now inclined to initiate price changes more frequently to stimulate the operation of the market. Instead of relying on directives, the authorities are using price incentives to promote the attainment of objectives of macroeconomic importance. This is known as 'target (or goal) pricing'. This is done by applying price mark-ups and mark-downs to promote improvements in quality, a greater differentiation of products, the introduction of new articles and the discontinuation of obsolete lines (see Chapter 13 C, pp. 251–2). The acceptance of profit as an indicator of enterprise performance on the one hand, and the gradual development of

[1] *Figyelö* (Economic Observer), Budapest, 31/7/1968, p. 5; *Gospodarka planowa*, 8/1969, p. 36; *Planovo stopanstvo* (Planned Economy), Sofia, 4/1969, p. 53.
[2] For details, see *Gesetzblatt der DDR* (Law Gazette of the GDR), East Berlin, no. 9, Oct 1968, pp. 29–52.
[3] V. Mitrofanov, ('The Use and Misuse of Price Reductions'), *Finansy SSSR* (Soviet Finance), Moscow, 12/1968, pp. 30–1.

buyer's markets on the other, are making sellers and buyers more sensitive to price changes. Consequently target pricing is now a more effective weapon of economic policy than it could be before.

D. PRICES IN FOREIGN TRADE

Traditionally, domestic prices in each Socialist country were almost completely insulated not only from world market prices but also from those in other Socialist countries. Foreign trade corporations[1] paid the enterprises producing for export domestic wholesale prices, not equivalent prices obtained in foreign markets. Similarly, imported articles were sold domestically not at foreign-exchange equivalents but at the prices of the closest domestically produced substitutes, or (in the case of consumer goods) at prices designed to adjust domestic demand to the available supply.

These insulatory price differentials usually yielded the foreign trade corporations substantial 'profits' on imports and 'losses' on exports. This was largely a reflection of the over-valuation of Socialist currencies, especially in relation to Western currencies. These surpluses and deficits were not, of course, indicative of the corporation's efficiency or inefficiency, and were absorbed fully by the State budget.

In their trade with the Capitalist nations, Socialist countries normally use the prices prevailing in world Capitalist markets, and the transactions are carried out in Western currencies. However, in individual deals, prices are often negotiated and they may depart considerably from current world market prices. Thus it was not uncommon for Socialist exports to be sold at lower than world prices in the case of re-exports of unwanted goods acquired in the first instance in barter deals, owing to an urgent need for Western hard currencies, the desire to establish a foothold in markets dominated by well-entrenched Western suppliers, political considerations and sometimes as a result of poor marketing techniques and ignorance of the prevailing prices.

It also happened on occasions that Socialist importers paid

---

[1] Specialized entities responsible for carrying on the export and import of defined groups of products.

higher than world market prices. This could occur in the case of the very large purchases typical of Socialist import deals (and collusion amongst Capitalist suppliers), in the case of the items subject to Western strategic embargo, when Socialist imports were conditional upon the Capitalist partner accepting Socialist 'countersales', and when prospective non-commercial advantages were thought to justify the higher prices paid.[1]

In intra-Socialist foreign trade up to 1958 there was no systematic basis for determining prices. They were negotiated between trading partners, but apparently world Capitalist prices over the period 1949–50 were sometimes used for reference. In 1958 the member countries of the Council for Mutual Economic Assistance adopted what has come to be known as the 'Bucharest Agreement'. It was formally agreed that in intra-CMEA foreign trade average prices in the principal Capitalist markets over a selected period were to be used as a starting base. The periods chosen in the past under the Bucharest Agreement were 1957, 1957–58, 1960–64 (the latter base period applicable to the 1966–70 five-year plan period), and the late 1960s have apparently been chosen for the 1971–75 five-year plan period.

However, the Capitalist world market prices are not only 'cleansed of Capitalist fluctuations and speculative elements' but also carry 'correction mark-ups', so that their level is higher than Capitalist prices. Furthermore, the mark-ups are not uniform but differentiated, usually in proportion to the labour content. Thus in 1964, the CMEA mark-up on grinding machines ranged (according to size and complexity) from 28 to 78 per cent, on boring machines from 16 to 107 per cent and on turning machines from 54 to 128 per cent above the prices of identical (or near-identical) machines in world Capitalist markets. At the same time, raw materials normally carry 5–10 per cent mark-ups, and some agricultural products only 2 per cent or less.[2]

The traditional irrationalities of Socialist foreign trade prices

---

[1] For further details, see J. Wilczynski, *The Economics and Politics of East–West Trade*, London, Macmillan (and New York, Praeger), 1969, pp. 93–6.

[2] F. Bartha, ('Tendencies in the Development of Foreign Trade Prices under Socialism'), *Külkereskedelem* (Foreign Trade), Budapest, 9/1967, pp. 271–2, 274; Z. Knyziak, ('Socialist Integration – The Role of the Price System in Foreign Trade'), *Życie gospodarcze* (Economic Life), Warsaw, 2/6/1968, p. 11.

can be traced to three basic causes: the insulation of domestic from foreign prices, bilateralism, and the differentiated correction mark-ups above world market prices in intra-CMEA trade. The waste and missed gains from the international division of labour consequent upon the faulty system of pricing in foreign trade was recognized by many theoretical writers long ago, but little was done about it in practice up to about the mid-1960s. However, since that time several important changes have been initiated, specifically designed to promote a greater efficiency of foreign trade as a source of intensive economic growth.

Steps have been taken in most Socialist countries to establish links with world market prices – in Yugoslavia since 1965, in Czechoslovakia since 1967, in Hungary and Bulgaria since 1968, in the German Democratic Republic since 1969 and in Poland since 1971.[1] (In the Soviet price reform of 1967 world market prices were not taken into account and in Romania no price reform has been carried out so far.) Domestic enterprises producing for export are now generally paid according to the foreign prices obtained, so that it is in their interest to respond to the conditions in foreign markets. Many imports, especially of basic raw materials, are also priced domestically at foreign-exchange equivalents.

At the same time, attempts have been made to evolve 'realistic' exchange rates, more closely relating domestic to foreign prices. There is also a growing inclination to change over to single exchange rates, as distinct from the commonly administered multiple rates in the past. The USSR adopted a single rate in 1961, Yugoslavia in 1962 and in Romania by 1968 a single non-commercial rate replaced rates administered before (for further details, see Chapter 14 C, pp. 276–9). The aim is to eliminate the demoralizing automatic budgetary equalization payments in foreign trade, to enhance competition and to promote efficiency in general.

The problem of the rationalization of prices in intra-CMEA foreign trade is complex. This question has been subjected to widespread polemics in economic literature and several conferences were held on the subject in recent years. However, no generally acceptable scheme has been worked out yet, largely due to the

[1] e.g. in Bulgaria about 60% of all producers' prices have been linked to world market prices. W. Sztyber, op. cit., p. 1381.

divergent national interests of the member countries. Three distinct views have emerged so far – adopt Capitalist world market prices without qualifications, evolve a distinct CMEA price structure divorced from Capitalist prices or devise a compromise solution.

A full acceptance of Capitalist prices is mostly advocated in those countries which are most interested in trade with the Capitalist world and which would lose by the adoption of a CMEA own-price basis, especially in Czechoslovakia, Hungary and Poland (and, of course, Yugoslavia). It is pointed out that Capitalist prices can provide a rational basis for Socialist domestic prices, and thus guard against the misallocation of resources and inefficiency. The CMEA region is not a closed economic grouping and the use of these prices would facilitate economic relations with Capitalist countries. Such prices and closer trading links with these countries would provide healthy competition to Socialist industries and would promote the assimilation of Western technology. The countries of the CMEA region are not yet capable of working out a common price basis of their own owing to a lack of uniformity in the principles and procedures determining their national price formation – the differing treatment of the costs of materials, depreciation, capital charges, profit mark-ups, taxes and the absence of equilibrium exchange rates. Moreover, a separate price basis would further increase the already prevailing suspicion of exploitation in intra-CMEA trade. A Soviet economist concluded that a departure from world market prices would mean a setback to economic progress. He stated:

> In my opinion, a changeover to a separate Socialist price basis would only apply brakes on our continued progress in the co-operation amongst Socialist countries and their capacity to compete economically with the most advanced Capitalist nations.[1]

The supporters of a CMEA own-price basis are most vocal in Bulgaria, Romania and the USSR, which are important exporters of raw materials to other member countries. The adoption of a separate price system would mean high prices of such items in

[1] K. Popov, ('Objective Principles for the Construction of a Price System for Trade amongst Socialist Countries'), *Vop. ekon.*, 8/1968, p. 72.

relation to manufactures. These protagonists advance the following arguments. Capitalist prices are not equilibrium prices for the CMEA region as they do not reflect the conditions of supply and demand peculiar to the grouping.[1] These prices are misleading indicators of comparative advantage to Socialist countries and they do not provide the necessary incentive for overcoming shortages of 'hard' items and surpluses of 'soft' ones. On the contrary, they only promote the processes of adjustment to Capitalist markets. Moreover, the concept of 'world market' prices is in itself debatable. But even if an agreement is reached on their definition and method of determination, Socialist countries just cannot allow current fluctuations originating in Capitalist markets to govern intra-CMEA economic relations. If, on the other hand, average prices over some past period are accepted, they are currently out of date, and thus provide little guidance to Socialist economic development in the future.[2]

On the other hand, many moderates believe that whilst CMEA prices should be linked to world market prices, they should reflect regional cost-preference conditions. Such a price system would in fact be similar to those prevailing in the economic groupings of the Capitalist world, except that it would be adjusted on a planned basis and it would be noted for a greater stability.[3]

No final decision was made up to the time of writing. But whichever basis is adopted it will have considerable effects on individual CMEA countries because on the average two-thirds of their

[1] Thus it was reported in a Soviet source in 1968 that one vertical milling machine at world Capitalist prices was equivalent to 520 tons of iron ore, but the cost structure in the CMEA region was such that an identical machine was equal to only 140 tons of iron ore. Similarly, one railway passenger car was worth 3,400 tons of oil at world Capitalist prices but only 1,300 tons in terms of CMEA costs. N. Bautina, ('Production Relations amongst Socialist Countries'), *Mirov. ekon i mezhd. otnosh.*, 4/1968, p. 70.

[2] See especially V. Diachenko, ('Guidelines for the Improvement of Prices in Trade among the CMEA Member Countries'), *Vop. ekon.*, 12/1967, pp. 64–74; Z. Knyziak, ('The Role of the System of Foreign Trade Prices and of Domestic Prices in the Economic Integration of the CMEA Countries'), *Gosp. plan.*, 5/1968, pp. 1–6; T. Kutiev, ('Domestic Wholesale Prices and the Development of a Price base for Intra-CMEA Foreign Trade'), *Planovo stopanstvo*, 4/1969, pp. 47–58.

[3] B. Csikós-Nagy, ('Foreign-Exchange and Pricing Problems of Socialist Integration'), *Gosp. plan.*, 8/1969, pp. 26–30; O. Tarnovskii, ('Regional Value and the CMEA Market'), *Vop. ekon.*, 10/1967, pp. 81–92.

foreign trade is claimed by other member countries. In spite of the differences of opinion on the basis to be accepted, there is general agreement on the need for a uniformity of principles and procedures to govern the determination of prices and exchange rates and it is certain that efforts will continue to be directed towards these goals.

If a CMEA own-price basis is adopted, the process will be gradual, extending over several years. In such a case it is most likely that the distortion of prices in intra-CMEA trade would be the opposite of that in the past, i.e. the prices of raw materials would be relatively higher than those of manufactures in comparison with world market prices – in other words the Prebisch effect in reverse.[1] It is also likely that the prices of standardized raw materials would be fixed for long periods whilst those of manufactures would be more flexible. Such a price basis would work to the disadvantage of most Eastern European countries and would certainly benefit the USSR, which in the CMEA region is the main supplier of primary products and absorbs most of the manufactures exported by the member countries.[2]

[1] In world markets between 1953 and 1970 the prices of manufactured exports increased by 21% but those of primary products exported by only 2%. Based on United Nations *Monthly Bulletin of Statistics* (different numbers).

[2] In the late 1960s, the USSR supplied about 55% of other CMEA countries' needs of raw materials; in respect of the following key raw materials the USSR normally supplies 80–100% of these countries' import needs: crude oil, iron ore, coking coal, aluminum. At the same time the USSR absorbs about two-thirds of these countries' export of manufactures. *Izvestiya*, Moscow, 14/9/1968, p. 3; *Mirovaya ekon. i mezhd. otnosh.*, 4/1968, p. 65; *Vop. ekon.*, 4/1966, pp. 88–90; *Życie gosp.*, 3/11/1968, p. 11.

6 Enterprise Performance

A. THE CRITICAL IMPORTANCE OF THE ENTERPRISE

As is generally well known, orthodox Marxian economics is pre-occupied with macrosocial issues to the neglect of microeconomics. Many microeconomic concepts are in conflict with the labour theory of value, social justice and planned economic development. After the formation of Socialist States, the first reaction was to restrict the independence of enterprises and this was conditioned by two considerations. On the one hand, it was aimed at preventing the recurrence of some of the abuses typical of *laissez-faire* capitalism, such as the absolute power of the management over workers, the exploitation of the public, disruptive competition and anti-social production. On the other, owing to the shortages of competent managerial personnel, it was found desirable, and indeed necessary, that central authorities make all the crucial decisions for individual enterprises. This role of enterprises, as passive and obedient executors of commands from above, fitted quite well into the centralized directive planning and management under which efficiency was of little concern.

The 'great debate' on the economic model after the mid-1950s and the stagnation of the Socialist economies in the early 1960s have led to a thorough reappraisal of microeconomics, and in particular of the place of the enterprise. It became apparent to theoretical economists and political leaders that even if resources were allocated in optimum patterns at the central planning level, there could still be a wasteful utilization of such resources in individual enterprises. Consequently, enterprises must be freed from too much interference by central authorities in the details of operation, and moreover the system of incentives must be based on a criterion which combines micro- and macroeconomic interest, so that there is no contradiction between the interest of enterprises and that of society.

The success of the reforms depends largely on the extent to which the efficiency of the Socialist economy is improved. In this campaign the enterprise obviously represents the main battle-ground. Economy in the use of labour, capital equipment, raw materials and natural resources, the introduction and diffusion of new technology, an improvement in the quality and variety of products, the adaptation of production to demand and the development of buyers' markets – in other words the changeover to intensive-based growth – all depend in the ultimate analysis on enterprises.

B. CRITERIA OF ENTERPRISE PERFORMANCE

Experience had clearly demonstrated both in the USSR and in other European Socialist countries that, contrary to the hopes entertained by idealist Communist theoreticians, appeals, exhort-ations and other 'moral' inducements could not be relied upon to yield desired production results. To place enterprise performance on a solid basis, there must be some system of material motivation to the personnel. The question then arises as to the criterion for incentive payments. This problem has proved to be a formidable one under the social set-up in force, as attested by the different methods used in the past.

For many years in most industries the volume of output was adopted as the basis for incentive payments. The success of the enterprise was judged by the physical size of the output produced in a given period defined in weight, length, area, pieces, etc.This basis led to what became known as the 'fetishism of output', when production became an end in itself.[1] Producing enterprises strove to reach and exceed targets with little concern for costs, suitability or quality of the products turned out.

When incentives were based on the value of output, enterprises were mostly interested in producing articles using the most expen-sive raw materials and components. This anomaly was pushed to extremes when enterprises' output was valued at 'industry disposal

[1] M. Pohorille (ed.), *Ekonomia polityczna socjalizmu* (The Political Economy of Socialism), Warsaw, PWE, 1968, p. 72.

prices', i.e. factory price plus turnover tax. This practice, which prevailed for example in Poland before 1967, often defeated the State policy of discouraging the use of certain products by means of high turnover taxes.[1] In effect, the expensive and socially least desirable articles tended to be in plentiful supply.

In some cases, the so-called point system was experimented with, under which bonuses were payable not for reaching or exceeding targets but for undertaking additional tasks, such as extra types of goods produced or services rendered or for the improvement of quality. The main purpose was to discover enterprises' 'hidden reserves'. But this approach also proved wasteful. Enterprises tended to neglect their primary targets and also to hoard resources for as long as possible to be able to perform 'additional tasks' each year. Then it was thought that the value of production, i.e. the 'value added' in the enterprise, would provide a better criterion. But soon it was found that enterprises looked for labour-intensive articles to produce and were extravagant in the use of labour.

In trading enterprises the criterion commonly used was the value of the trade turnover. Their reaction was twofold. Firstly they looked for the most expensive sources of supply. Secondly, they tended to favour goods which carried high turnover taxes and thus promoted the use of those products which the authorities endeavoured to restrict. When the value of sales was calculated on net of turnover taxes, enterprises still preferred to handle expensive lines to the neglect and even exclusion of low-priced items, however essential they might have been to users.[2] The cost of distribution and the quality of service to customers were remote considerations. The number of transactions, or of customers attended, or of man-hours worked proved equally unsatisfactory and even more cumbersome.

It should be evident that the criteria of enterprise performance outlined above were typical of the extensive approach to economic growth, with waste becoming more and more obvious in higher stages of development. All these criteria favoured an extravagant

[1] J. Albrecht, ('The New Financial System – the First Results and Conclusions'), *Życie gospodarcze* (Economic Life), Warsaw, 25/6/1967, p. 1.

[2] W. Wilczyński, *Rachunek ekonomiczny a mechanizm rynkowy* (Economic Accounting and the Market Mechanism), Warsaw, PWE, 1965, pp. 162–4.

demand for resources, and moreover whichever method was adopted it tended to irrationalize the process of substitution. It was often in the enterprises' interest to substitute the more expensive (i.e. scarcer) factors for the more abundant ones, which further tended to aggravate the shortages of 'hard' items.

The administration of directive coefficients of material utilization, of technical coefficients of costs and of the limitations on wage funds helped prevent some abuses, but they were not positive inducements to efficiency because enterprises – in a true Parkinson spirit – usually rose to the limits admissible. At the same time, high proportions of output often proved unsaleable because incentive payments were based on what was produced and not necessarily sold. Thus it was not uncommon for the piling-up of stocks of useless goods to exist side by side with prevalent shortages of both consumer goods.

These wasteful practices became obvious enough to many economists but, with the exception of Yugoslavia after 1948, their views could not be easily articulated publicly before the mid-1950s, and even after they could, they did not arouse widespread interest until the early 1960s. The critics came to the conclusion that the best criterion of enterprise success was profit. This criterion was first adopted on a limited basis in Yugoslavia in 1952 and in Hungary in 1957, when profit sharing by the enterprise personnel was introduced. In the USSR, as is well known in the West, the most persistent and forceful arguments in favour of profit were advanced by Evsei G. Liberman. He first put forward his idea at a meeting of economists in 1948 but was told by his timid colleagues to keep quiet. Then, taking advantage of the first wave of de-Stalinization, he published a few articles on the subject in the latter 1950s, but they passed almost unnoticed. It is only his articles in 1962, followed by later writings, that have produced widespread interest.[1]

After several years of experimentation, profit was officially accepted in the USSR in 1965 as the main criterion of enterprise

---

[1] See his articles, especially: ('Planning Industrial Production and Material Incentives for Its Economic Development'), *Kommunist*, Moscow, 10/1956, pp. 75–92; ('On Economic Levers for Fulfilling the Plan in Soviet Industry'), *Kommunist*, 1/1959, pp. 88–97; ('The Planning of Production and Regulators of Lasting Effectiveness'), *Voprosy ekonomiki* (Problems of Economics), Moscow, 8/1962, pp. 102–12; ('Plan, Profit, Bonus'), *Pravda*, Moscow, 9/9/1962, p. 3.

performance, and the remaining European Socialist countries (except Albania) did likewise, including Romania in 1968. Romania has never been in the forefront of economic reforms but after several years of discussion and experiments it was concluded at the Congress of the Romanian Communist Party in December 1967 that 'profit is not merely a question of interest to individual enterprises but also a fact of critical importance to the national economy, because the growth of accumulation, of material production and of the standard of living depends on it'.[1]

The superiority of profit over other criteria consists in the fact that it is a 'synthetic' indicator. Profit maximization involves not only the minimization of costs but also the maximization of that production for which there is demand, i.e. which is actually sold. It is in the interest of the enterprise personnel to maximize profits because a portion of them is distributed to the management and workers in the form of bonuses and sociocultural and housing grants. After payments are made in the form of taxes and other deductions to central and local authorities, the remainder of the enterprise profit is retained for the financing of further development and the modernization of production, and to accumulate or replenish reserves for emergencies.[2] Thus, as a well-known Soviet economist stated, 'the earning and application of profits provide a unique link combining the interests of the State, the enterprise and the individual worker'.[3]

C. PROFIT VARIANTS AS INDICATORS OF PERFORMANCE

Profit can be used in different forms as a criterion of enterprise

[1] Quoted from I. Blaga, ('Profitability as a Goal and Criterion'), *Scinteia* (The Spark), Bucharest, 20/7/1969, p. 3.

[2] Taking the European CMEA countries, on the average about 60% of gross enterprise profits in industry is absorbed by central and local authorities, 20% is channelled into the enterprise production development fund, 10% is distributed to the personnel as individual and collective incentives and the balance is devoted to other purposes. Deductions from enterprise profits now represent the most important source of State revenue, having outranked turnover taxes. For further details, see Chapters 7 C, pp. 115–17, and 12 C, pp. 225–6.

[3] A. Birman, ('Profit Today'), *Kommunist*, 10/1967, p. 102.

performance. There are two lines of approach – the absolute amount and the rate. The absolute amount of profit is, of course, arrived at by deducting the enterprise's total cost from its total receipts. A distinction is also made between gross and net profit, the difference being represented by State deductions consisting of capital charges, differential payments for the advantages not created by the enterprise and, in some countries, payroll tax (as in Hungary), and where repayable loans are obtained from the State budget (as in the USSR), interest on such loans.

An alternative approach to the determination of enterprise performance is to express an enterprise's profit as a percentage of either its costs or its assets. The percentage ratio of profits to the prime cost is known as 'rentability', whilst the percentage ratio of profits to fixed and variable assets is generally described as 'profitability' or (more precisely) the 'profit rate'.

All three indicators – profit, rentability and profitability – have been used in the European Socialist countries (except, of course, Albania). But their exact calculation has differed from country to country, according to the accepted definition of the different components of costs, and even within each country depending on the branch of the economy or industry. In recent years there have been efforts made, under the auspices of the Council for Mutual Economic Assistance, to introduce some uniformity of procedures for the calculation of costs and profit mark-ups as a step towards the evolution of realistic exchange rates and perhaps to the CMEA region's own price basis.

Each variant of the profit criterion has its advantages and disadvantages. Gross profit is easy to calculate and simple to understand, and thus its inducement effect on ordinary workers may be greater. However, its size overstates the contribution of the enterprise because some social costs are not deducted. Moreover, a portion of this profit may be due to differential advantages, such as better natural resources, location, equipment, etc., through no extra effort on the part of the enterprise. These particular defects are removed if the amount of profit is shown on a net basis.

However, there is evidence suggesting that even a net basis tends to produce some adverse effects peculiar to extensive-based growth. Enterprises find that the size of net profits can be increased by concentrating on products which contain a large proportion of material inputs embodying high turnover taxes (where the latter are applied to producer goods). Enterprises also tend to be interested in large outputs of a limited range of standardized articles and not necessarily in a wide variety and better quality to suit different tastes.[1]

Some of the disadvantages of using the absolute figures of profits can be overcome by applying the rates of return, i.e. rentability or profitability. But experience has demonstrated that under this system enterprises tend to neglect the production of the articles showing lower rates of return, even though the production of such items is socially desirable and large-scale output could bring large profits in absolute terms.[2] Furthermore, incentives to the personnel have sometimes been based on *increased* rentability or profitability above the preceding year or some other period. In such cases, enterprises find it expedient to hoard resources and only gradually to utilize their surplus capacities in each succeeding year.[3]

The most common practice is to judge enterprise performance on the actual rentability or profitability attained in relation to planned directive rates which are highly differentiated according to industries, enterprises and products. The purpose is to neutralize the effect of the distorted prices and of differential advantages so that each enterprise has an equal start and the incentive fund is then directly related to the effort of the enterprise personnel. Thus in Poland in 1967 the planned rentability rates for different enterprises in industry ranged from 2·68 to 22·53 per cent, and those actually achieved from 2·99 to 22·77 per cent.[4] If planned rates are to serve their purpose, they have to be modified periodically to

---

[1] See, e.g., Krystyna Cholewicka-Goździk, ('Rentability and Quality of Production'), *Finanse* (Finance), Warsaw, 12/1968, p. 18; V. Garbuzov, ('Economic Reforms and Financial Matters'), *Kommunist*, 3/1968, p. 51.

[2] J. Pajestka, ('Directions of Perfecting the System of Management and Planning in Industry'), *Życie gosp.*, 22/9/1968, p. 4.

[3] B. Miszewski, *Postęp ekonomiczny w gospodarce przemysłowej* (Economic Progress in an Industrialized Society), Warsaw, PWE, 1968, p. 120.

[4] *Wiadomości Narodowego Banku Polskiego* (Communications of the National Bank of Poland), Warsaw, 1/1969, p. 18.

reflect changing cost and demand conditions. However, such changes, if too frequent, produce demoralizing and disruptive effects on enterprises.[1] Consequently, there is a tendency now for these rates to be announced well in advance and held constant for reasonably long periods – for example for up to five years in Czechoslovakia, the German Democratic Republic and Hungary.[2]

D. PERFORMANCE AND EFFICIENCY

It is generally agreed that the acceptance of profit as the main or only criterion of enterprise performance, and consequently as the basis for material incentives to labour, has produced beneficial effects. In their endeavour to maximize profits, or reach and exceed planned rates of return, enterprises have been searching for ways of rationalizing their production by reducing cost and adapting their products to buyers' preferences. The remarkable growth of profits in recent years suggests that not only has there been wide scope for improvement but also that the profit 'motive' can be quite strong even under Socialism.[3]

However, it must be realized that, with the exception of Yugoslavia, enterprises are not completely free to pursue their profit-maximizing activities. To a varying extent in different countries and branches of industry, enterprises are still bound by other criteria as well, such as the total value of production, the minimum volume

[1] e.g. in Poland in 1967 the directive rentability rates were changed for 95% of all enterprises, for some of them as many as four times during the year. *Finanse*, 2/1969, p. 35.

[2] R. Evstigneiev and V. Kaie, ('Economic Reforms in the CMEA Countries'), *Voprosy ekonomiki* (Problems of Economics), Moscow, 10/1968, p. 110.

[3] To quote a few examples. In Hungary, the planned net profitability for 1968 (the first year under the new system) was 7·6%, but the actual rate achieved was 9·4%. In Romania gross profits earned per unit of fixed assets increased between 1963 and 1969 by 60%, whilst national income during the period rose by only 53%. In the USSR gross profits in industry increased by 10% in 1966 (the first year under the new system), by 22% in 1967, by 9% in 1968, by 7% in 1969 and the expected rate in 1970 was 9%; the rate of growth of profits over the period was about one-quarter faster than that of national income and the average return per rouble of assets used increased from 0·18 to 0·25 rouble. In Yugoslavia net product per 100 dinars' assets used rose from 34·3 in 1962 to 41·6 dinars in 1966 (the first full year after the reforms of 1965). Based on: *Pénzügyi szemle* (Financial Review), Budapest, 2/1970, p. 90; *Scinteia* (The Spark), Bucharest, 20/7/1969, p. 3; *Kommunist*, Moscow, 3/1968, p. 47; *Pravda*, Moscow, 17/12/1969, p. 4; *Jugoslavenski pregled* (Yugoslav Survey), Belgrade, 5/1969, p. 203; *Życie gospodarcze*, 29/3/1970, p. 11.

of output of specified basic products, the size of allocated raw materials and components, and sales in foreign markets. There are also directions regulating the distribution of net profits into different enterprise funds and there are limitations on bonuses to the personnel. But of greater consequence is the fact that under Socialist economic conditions the maximization of enterprise profits is not necessarily coextensive with maximum efficiency.

Enterprise performance is a microeconomic concept. An enterprise may perform in the best possible way, by maximizing the applicable profit variant, within the framework imposed on it. Yet this alone does not ensure the optimum allocation and utilization of resources in a macroeconomic sense. In a competitive free-enterprise economy profits usually indicate not only enterprise performance but also efficiency. The prices of inputs (costs) and of products (revenue) are determined in free markets, and thus they reflect cost-preference; furthermore both producers and users are in a position to respond to changing market conditions, and the prevalence of competition ensures that they do so. The discrepancy between the microeconomic performance and efficiency in a broader sense can be traced to three basic causes: the irrationality of prices, widely differing profit rates and the absence of competition. We shall now examine the extent to which these conditions still exist in the Socialist countries under consideration.

Since the mid-1960s all the European Socialist countries except Romania (and disregarding Albania) have carried out major price reforms in the interest of a greater efficiency in the use of resources (see Chapter 5 A, pp. 78–82). However, in most cases such factor costs as rent and even capital charges have not been explicitly included as cost components (but are usually deducted *ex post* from enterprise profits). The reforms have largely by-passed retail prices, and even where they have been revised they still depart from costs.[1] The existence of the two-tier price system distorts

---

[1] e.g. in Hungary, if we disregard tobacco and alcoholic beverages (which carry heavy turnover taxes), retail prices of consumer goods and services as a whole in 1969 were still 2–3% below production costs (as defined in Hungary). The degree of subsidization by the State amounted to, in the case of basic foods, 20–40%; fuels and passenger transport, 45–50%; and housing rent, 165% (*Pénzügyi szemle*, 2/1970, p. 102). Since that time State subsidies on house rents have been substantially reduced.

enterprise profit as an indicator of efficiency, as producers' and retail prices are still largely insulated by differentiated turnover taxes and subsidies. This means that even if an enterprise is micro-economically profitable (according to producers' prices), it may be macroeconomically inefficient, and vice versa. Thus, profit is not such a synthetic indicator of efficiency under Socialism as is generally assumed.

The planned rates of return in different branches of the economy and even of industry in each country still differ remarkably (with the possible exception of Czechoslovakia, and of Yugoslavia where planned profit indicators are no longer set by the State). Thus in the German Democratic Republic, in the 88 industrial associations examined, the profitability rate ranged from −0·5 to 98·0 per cent.[1] In the USSR the average profitability in industry was reported in 1968 as 15 per cent, but the rate for peat mining was set at 7 per cent, for the agricultural machinery industry 10 per cent, and for the timber exploitation industry 20 per cent.[2] In Yugoslavia in 1966, the average profit in different branches of industry per 100 dinars of assets employed ranged from 15·50 dinars (in electric power) to 63·20 dinars (in the rubber industry).[3]

The profitability of individual enterprises within each branch of industry, of course, varies considerably. As producers' prices are, generally, based on the average costs for the branch, there are many enterprises permanently incurring losses and having to be subsidized. This produces a demoralizing effect on the enterprise personnel and its performance, not to say on efficiency.

In the late 1960s there were at least a dozen different profit variants used in the Socialist countries to indicate enterprise per-formance – the absolute size of profit, rentability, profitability, and furthermore each of these could be calculated on gross and net, planned and achieved, and on quarterly, annual and long-term bases. Where differentiated planned profitability or rentability indicators are set for different enterprises by higher authorities, errors are inevitable, and in practice some inefficient enterprises

---

[1] *Gospodarka planowa* (Planned Economy), Warsaw, 10/1969, p. 33.

[2] A. Komin, *Ekonomicheskaya reforma i optovyie tseny promyshlennosti* (Economic Reform and Industrial Producers' Prices), Moscow, Finansy, 1968, p. 10.

[3] *Jugoslavenski pregled*, 5/1969, p. 203.

are sheltered whilst in the case of the more efficient ones the point of incentive is blunted. Moreover, where such indicators are altered frequently, 'enterprises become adept at making only such changes as will induce the superior authority to readjust these indicators to their own advantage'.[1] Yet as a Soviet economist pointed out:

> The condition that can be deduced from the theory of optimal planning is that all producing units embraced by the optimal plan must be of equal profitability, because those enterprises which employ scarcer resources have to pay more for their use, while the price of a given product should be uniform.[2]

In other words, Fedorenko postulates adherence to the principle of equimarginality, long accepted in Western economic thought since V. Pareto as a condition of maximum efficiency (optimality), i.e. the marginal productivity of resources should be equal in all enterprises.

A reasonable degree of uniformity of the rates of return could be evolved only if all prices were rationalized, and tax scales so devised as to absorb differential rent. Moreover, there would have to be a substantial degree of mobility of resources and competition amongst producing as well as trading enterprises, so that buyers' markets are established. As long as sellers are in a privileged position (as, on the whole, they have been so far), enterprises find that profits can be increased by limiting output to a few standardized products, rather than by increasing the variety of articles and improving their quality.

Competition for a long time was rejected by political leaders and most economists as being synonymous with the 'anarchy of the market' and instability. The competitive mechanism is still rejected in most Socialist countries (Yugoslavia excepted) for the broad allocation of resources, but intra-industry ('microeconomic') competition is now generally accepted as an essential condition for intensive-based growth, because as F. Hornik, a Czechoslovak economist, put it, 'Economic competition promotes innovations, the technical level of manufacturing and a larger variety of goods

---

[1] R. Napiórkowski, ('Synthetic Indicators of the Economic Effectiveness of Enterprise Activity'), *Finanse*, 2/1969, p. 35.

[2] N. Fedorenko, ('Prices and Optimal Planning'), *Kommunist*, 8/1966, p. 89.

which, given buyers' markets, is conducive to cost reduction, stability and the meeting of buyers' preferences in general.'[1]

The decentralization of planning and management, the profit incentive, an increasing availability of substitutes in the factor as well as in product markets, a closer correspondence between production and distribution, the acceptance of advertising as a legitimate economic instrument and the liberalization of foreign trade are all creating favourable conditions for competition and a general evolution of buyers' markets (see Chapter 12 D, pp. 231–2). So far these developments have been advanced most in Yugoslavia and to a lesser extent in Hungary and Czechoslovakia. However, as long as central planning exists and the primacy of macrosocial considerations is adhered to, there will be definite limits to genuine competition and Western-style buyers' markets, so that the possibilities of the macroeconomic allocation and the microeconomic utilization of resources in accordance with the equimarginal principle are pretty remote.

[1] F. Hornik, ('Imports and Economic Competition'), *Hospodářské noviny* (Economic News), Prague, 30/5/1969, p. 10.

7 Economic Incentives to Labour

A. THE PROBLEM OF MOTIVATION IN A SOCIALIST ECONOMY

As is well known, Marx in his writings had a vision of an egalitarian society in which there would be no distinction between the remuneration of skilled and unskilled, of mental and physical, of urban and rural labour, but in which work and income would be governed by the principle 'from each according to his ability, to each according to his needs'.[1] After the Bolshevik Revolution, attempts were made to turn Marx's dream into reality. But the experiments proved unworkable, with disastrous effects on work discipline and production.

Consequently, as a concession under the New Economic Policy (beginning in 1921), a modified, Leninist, principle – 'from each according to his ability, to each according to his work' – was adopted to apply under socialism (called the 'lower phase of communism') as a transitional stage to 'full communism'. Later, other Socialist countries also adopted the Soviet practice, but the Marxian ideal has nowhere been abandoned as the ultimate goal. However, in the context of the new system of planning and management and the need for a greater efficiency, incentives have acquired new significance.

The problem of the motivation of labour in a Socialist society is, of course, much more complex than under Capitalism. There is virtually no private ownership of enterprises, and where private enterprise is tolerated, it is relegated to insignificant spheres and subjected to discriminatory treatment. The possibilities of private enrichment and of social distinction based on wealth are thus practically non-existent, and in fact largely pointless. The right to work is guaranteed, the fear of unemployment is virtually absent[2]

[1] K. Marx, *Critique of the Gotha Program*, Moscow, FLPH, 1947, p. 27.
[2] Except in Yugoslavia; see Chapter 1, note 4, p. 18.

and dismissal from work is usually strictly regulated. Moreover social security, in the form of generous benefits in cash and kind open to all in need, is very well developed and taken for granted.[1] At the same time, Socialism provides a wider scope than Capitalism for the manipulation of non-material inducements.

In Socialist thinking and practice, distinctions are made between material and moral incentives and between specialized and synthetic incentives. Material incentives are those which appeal directly to the workers' wants and are received in money or kind. On the other hand, moral incentives, which are remarkably well developed in Socialist countries, are of an ideological, political and ethical nature and are addressed to the worker's pride, sense of achievement, responsibility, craving for social esteem and professional recognition. They assume the form of patriotic appeals, mass slogans, boards and books of honour in factories, awards of pennants, certificates and medals, presentation to top political leaders, an offer of membership of the Communist Party, and the like.

Specialized inducements are those which are directed at some partial and clearly specified effect, such as economy in the use of materials or power, time saving, quality, invention, the completion of a task on time, export promotion, etc., whereas synthetic incentives are based on an overall result, such as the volume or value of output, the value added, turnover or profit. Incentives, material as well as moral, may be addressed either to individuals or to groups of workers. The awards are made accordingly – in the form of either personal bonuses, or collective sharing in special amenities, and of either individual distinctions (certificate, medal) or group awards (team commendation, factory banner).

A notable feature of Socialism is that economic motivation can be placed on a planned basis, where individual and collective and

---

[1] The proportion of total personal income on the national scale derived from social services ('social consumption') in the Socialist countries under consideration ranges from 20 to 30%, compared with 5 to 15% in the Capitalist world. For example, old-age pensions in the USSR are available at the age of 55 (for women) or 60 (men); the amount of the pension depends on the person's earnings on retirement, and ranges from 50% (in the case of the highest-paid employees) to 100% (unskilled labourers), the average pension being 60% of the average national wage. See J. Wilczynski, *The Economics of Socialism*, London, Allen & Unwin, 1970, pp. 92, 158–9.

material as well as moral incentives can be integrated into what a Bulgarian writer described as 'dialectical unity'.[1] Furthermore, the needs and tastes of the population can be influenced by the State (through 'consumption steering') to induce the operation of incentives in desired directions. The major proportions in the economy (see Chapter 4 B, p. 68) are centrally determined in advance. It follows that economic incentives can operate only within this planned framework.

B. INCENTIVES AND THE STAGE OF ECONOMIC DEVELOPMENT

Before the reforms, the prevailing official attitude was that material incentives had to be tolerated as unavoidable and temporary in a Socialist society still 'economically, morally and intellectually stamped with the birthmarks of the old [Capitalist] society from whose womb it emerges', as it was put by Marx and later reiterated by Lenin.[2] As a rule, economic incentives were narrowly conceived on an *ad hoc* basis from the point of view of special tasks, persons or enterprises. The system reflected the prevailing extensive approach to economic growth. It did little to promote efficiency, and in fact in some ways it hindered it.

Synthetic material incentives were based on the size of output (or production), more specifically on the fulfilment and over-fulfilment of the plan. But, as a Polish economist pointed out, 'basing the system of incentives on the reached and exceeded planned targets only creates contradictions in the process of economic planning, prodding the management of enterprises to minimize targets and maximize allocations of resources'.[3] The contradiction in fact went further, because the fulfilment or over-fulfilment of targets could usually be achieved more easily if costs and quality were disregarded.

[1] S. G. Tsonev, ('Material Motivation, Plan and Mo ral Inducements') *Planovo stopanstvo* (Planned Economy), Sofia, 4/1970, p. 71.

[2] K. Marx, op. cit., p. 24; V. I. Lenin, 'The State and Revolution', *Selected Works*, London, Lawrence & Wishart, vol. VII, pp. 83–6.

[3] S. Góra, *Warunki produkcji a dzialanie bodźców* (Conditions of Production and the Operation of Incentives), Warsaw, PWE, 1967, p. 105.

It must be mentioned that cost reduction and quality improvement were not altogether forgotten by central planners, but they were supposed to be taken care of by specialized material incentives and moral pleadings. However, neither of these proved effective in producing the desired results. Specialized incentives became most developed in those countries where centralized control was tightest and at the same time its inefficacy became most apparent. Thus in Poland by 1962 there were 81 specialized incentives in operation[1] (by the mid-1960s the number was reduced to about 30).[2]

Specialized incentives may be instrumental in achieving some narrow objective, but they often produce conflicting effects, impair the effectiveness of synthetic incentives and, of course, involve a large amount of paperwork. Specialized incentives are likely to apply more to some enterprises and workers than to others,[3] with consequent frictions and adverse effects on work morale. The features of production not rewarded become, of course, neglected so that there is a constant pressure for more 'supplementary' incentives.

Before the reforms there was also a tendency on the part of the authorities to attach excessive importance to moral incentives. Many thinkers believed, especially in the USSR, that Socialist society had advanced far ahead in evolving the 'new communist man', devoid of the crude acquisitive instinct but imbued with a natural altruistic desire to give society as much as he could and claim no more than he was legitimately entitled to. But Socialist reality proved quite different. Experience showed that, even in the USSR after half a century of transitioning towards the 'higher phase' of communism, most workers were not unlike those in Capitalist countries. There was a growing dissatisfaction with the continued low living standards and an irresistible trend towards

---

[1] M. Misiak (ed.), *Bodźce ekonomiczne w przedsiębiorstwie przemysłowym* (Economic Incentives in the Industrial Enterprise), Warsaw, PWE, 1963, p. 276.

[2] S. Borkowska, ('Specialized Incentives'), *Finanse* (Finance), Warsaw, 8/1967, p. 43.

[3] e.g. in Poland over the period 1961–63, the average annual value of specialized incentives in export promotion ranged from 110 to 23,897 złotys per enterprise concerned. M. Misiak, op. cit., p. 44.

E

what became known as 'consumerism'. The constant appeals and promises of a future Communist cornucopia had lost their previous fascination and effect.

These attitudes amongst workers must have been a great disappointment to the Communist leadership but, clearly, they could not be ignored. The reforms in all Socialist countries, even in Romania, have embodied a far-reaching reformulation of incentives. It is now widely agreed amongst theoretical writers as well as policy-makers that 'the elimination of extensive methods of development and the changeover to intensive sources of growth is unthinkable without strong material incentives'.[1]

Under the new system, special efforts have been made to place incentives on a broader and a more systematic basis so as to combine the individual interest of the worker with that of the enterprise and society. Material incentives are accepted as an indispensable element of 'Socialist competition' and they now represent higher proportions of total personal earnings, mostly 20–33 per cent but in some cases even more (see section C of this chapter).

There is a trend towards the phasing out of specialized incentives in favour of synthetic incentives.[2] The fact that enterprises have been freed from detailed central control provides a greater meaning to moral incentives. It gives the management and workers a greater sense of responsibility and reduces the danger of alienation (workers' indifference and even hostility to Socialist property and authority). In some countries, especially in Yugoslavia and to a lesser extent in Czechoslovakia, Hungary and Poland, workers' participation in the management and control of the enterprises has been enlarged.

The beneficial effect of the strengthened material incentives is already apparent. In spite of the relaxation of State controls, work discipline has improved and workers are prepared to work harder because they can see tangible rewards. Considering the relatively

---

[1] B. Fick, ('Differentiation of Wages'), *Nowe drogi* (New Paths), Warsaw, 11/1969, p. 45.

[2] But it is unlikely that specialized incentives will be discontinued altogether. Some economists believe that 'as a rule synthetic incentives should be applied to the management personnel whilst specialized incentives should be used to reward other personnel for carrying out desirable individual and group tasks of a specific nature'. Krystyna Cholewicka-Goździk, ('Incentives for the Promotion of Quality'), *Finanse*, 6/1969, p. 42.

low levels of income and unsatisfied demand in the past, there is a strong inducement to earn higher incomes for the purchase of consumer durables in particular. The authorities, to reinforce the operation of material incentives, are devoting more resources to consumer-goods industries to provide more and a wider range of consumer goods, especially luxuries. Previous experience had demonstrated that not even material incentives can produce the desired results if the availability, range and quality of consumer goods are narrowly limited.

The former wide disparity between the growth rates of the output of producer and consumer goods has been reduced and in recent years in some countries the production of consumer goods increased faster than that of producer goods (see Chapter 12 B, pp. 218–20). The improvement is most noticeable in the availability of consumer durables which, as Socialist market research has shown, have the strongest and most lasting incentive effect on work and saving. At the same time the investment outlays involved in expanding the production of most types of these goods are two to three times lower than in increasing the output of food.[1] Table 13 illustrates the improvement in the availability of selected electrical household appliances.

Steps have also been taken to establish or expand the motor-car industry. All the Socialist countries under consideration, except Hungary, now produce or assemble passenger cars. In the last five years, Bulgaria, Poland, Romania, the USSR and Yugoslavia signed contracts with such Western concerns as Daimler-Benz, Fiat, Renault, Volkswagen and Volvo to construct plants for the mass production of cars. In recent years the authorities have also yielded to the public demand for better housing and have allocated more investment for this purpose. The restrictions on consumer credit, which previously were rigidly enforced, have been relaxed (see Chapter 9 C, p. 154), and the progress being made towards the development of buyers' markets should further strengthen the effectiveness of material incentives.

---

[1] e.g. in Poland in 1968, output per 100 złotys' worth of productive assets in different industries was: in iron-ore smelting, 26 złotys; agriculture, 27 z.; electrical engineering, 82 z.; the textile industry, 96 z. *Życie gospodarcze* (Economic Life), Warsaw, 22/2/1970, p. 7.

TABLE 13 CONSUMER DURABLES SOLD PER 1,000 OF POPULATION
IN 1963 AND 1967

COUNTRY	YEAR	Radio Sets	TV Sets	Refrigerators	Washing machines	Vacuum Cleaners
Bulgaria	1963	19	6	3	13	n.a.
	1966*	18	15	7	14	n.a.
Czechoslovakia	1963	22	24	14	11	10
	1967	18	19	21	19	13
GDR	1963	31	32	15	18	21
	1967	43	26	24	21	19
Hungary	1963	15	15	3	14	5
	1966*	21	17	11	19	9
Poland	1963	18	12	4	17	8
	1967	21	15	9	13	10
Romania	1963	14	6	4	4	2
	1967	18	12	7	5	3
USSR	1963	19	10	4	9	2
	1967	21	18	10	17	4

n.a. = not available.
* Data for 1967 are not available.

Source. Central Statistical Office of Poland, *Rozwój gospodarczy krajów RWPG 1950–1968* (Economic Development of the CMEA Countries 1950–1968), Warsaw, 1969, p. 127.

C. ENTERPRISE PROFITS AND MATERIAL INCENTIVES

Under the old system, material incentives to the personnel were in almost all cases financed out of enterprise wage funds fixed by central planners in advance. The size of these funds was determined by reference to a variety of considerations, of which efficiency was only one and a remote one at that. But in any case enterprises had little direct influence on them.

The significance of profit as the criterion of enterprise performance stems mainly from the fact that material incentives to labour are based on the size of enterprise profit or a rate of return indicating overall performance. Of all bases for material incentives profit is most 'synthetic' in effect. It takes care of both the supply (cost) side and the demand (buyers' preferences) side, and it best combines micro- and macroeconomic interest. A portion of enterprise profits is channelled into the 'material incentives fund' and the 'sociocultural and housing fund'. Out of the former, bonuses are paid to the personnel of the enterprise concerned, whilst the latter is used to provide collective benefits in the form of reading rooms, entertainment, excursions, assistance for housing, etc. The portion allowed for individual and collective incentives is determined by State regulations.[1]

The proportion of enterprise profits allowed for material incentives varies from country to country, from one branch of the economy to another, and there are variations within most branches as well (especially in industry).[2] But to generalize, about one-tenth of enterprise gross profits (before taxes) is reserved for individual and collective incentives. The proportion of earnings of labour derived from incentives in most industrial enterprises is about one-quarter (about one-fifth in the German Democratic Republic and Romania). The distribution of profits is carried out at quarterly, six-monthly or annual intervals. At one stage, it was not uncommon to distribute the material incentives fund in some industries equally amongst the members of the enterprise, irrespective of their position, with consequent regressive effects on higher-paid occupations. But this practice appears to have given way to a less democratic basis of distribution, roughly in proportion to the capacity of different employees to influence the profitability of the enterprise.

Thus in Poland, incentives per person employed on State farms constituted only 0·2 per cent of their total earnings in 1962–63, but in 1968–69 the proportion rose to 23·3 per cent (from 400 to

[1] Some exceptions may be noted. In Poland and Romania the material incentives fund and the sociocultural and housing fund are combined into one fund. In Bulgaria, Czechoslovakia, Hungary and Yugoslavia the material incentives fund is combined with the standard wage fund. In Yugoslavia, once taxes are paid, enterprises are free to distribute their profits as they wish.

[2] e.g. in Hungary in 1968, the proportions of enterprise profits channelled into the Material Incentives Fund, the State Budget and other Funds were as follows: in agriculture, 21, 46, 33; in transport, 15, 64, 21; in construction, 12, 61, 27; in industry, 9, 59, 32; in trade, 8, 64, 28; and in services, 4, 60, 36. *Figyelö* (Economic Observer), Budapest, 29/10/1969, p. 3. For the differentiation according to the type of personnel, see this text further on.

5,000 złotys annually).[1] The percentage represented by incentives in a general manager's total salary averaged 28 per cent in 1960, but by 1968 the percentage rose to 50.[2]

In Hungary, the top managerial personnel may earn an incentive payment of up to 80 per cent of their standard salary, the middle-ranking personnel up to 50 per cent and ordinary workers about 25 (before 1970, 15) per cent or less of their wage. At the same time, if the enterprise suffers losses the State guarantees only 75 per cent of the standard salary of the top-grade personnel and 85 per cent of the middle group, whereas the standard wage of the workers is guaranteed 100 per cent. In 1968 (the first year under the new system), the average amount of incentives distributed per person in the top category was 13,000 forints, in the middle-ranking group 5,500 forints and to ordinary workers 1,300 forints.[3]

In all the Socialist countries under consideration, the personnel of the enterprise now has some freedom to determine the conditions on which the material incentives fund is to be shared. This freedom is unlimited in Yugoslavia and quite considerable in Czechoslovakia and Poland. In all these countries, even if an enterprise makes high profits, individual inefficient employees may be deprived of a portion or all the bonus to which they may otherwise be entitled. The adoption of profit as a basis for incentives, in a sense, transforms the employees of the enterprise into shareholders, and where workers' self-government exists, the workers' council acts as does a board of directors in a Capitalist company.

There is little doubt that material incentives based on enterprise profit are more conducive to efficiency and intensive growth than any of the previously used bases. These incentives promote the reduction of costs, improvements in quality in accordance with market demand and a fuller utilization of production capacities. However, the experience of the last few years has revealed several shortcomings and some adverse effects of the new system under Socialist economic conditions.

It is pointed out that in some countries, such as the USSR,

[1] Życie gospodarcze, 29/3/1970, p. 9.
[2] Gospodarka planowa (Planned Economy), 12/1969, p. 43.
[3] Figyelő, 29/10/1969, p. 3; Ekonomika i organizacja pracy (The Economics and Organization of Labour), Warsaw, 1/1970, p. 43.

where the material incentives fund is based on enterprise realized profits *and* on rentability, the system is too complicated to be easily understood by ordinary workers. This, combined with the multiplicity of the methods followed in the distribution of the fund to the personnel, weakens the spur of incentives.[1] Owing to great initial differences in the surplus capacity of different enterprises, the scope for the improvement of performance has varied, with consequent differences in the bonus payments received in different enterprises.[2]

As a result of a greater role assigned to the market, enterprise profits vary during the year and, of course, even more from year to year. This means that the incentive element of personal earnings is subject to fluctuations. Moreover, in some countries (Bulgaria, Czechoslovakia, Hungary and Yugoslavia) standard pay also partly depends on enterprise profits, i.e. the State guarantees apply only to a portion of standard wages or salaries.[3] In effect, Socialist workers now share in enterprise losses, and on this score they are exposed to greater instability than workers in Capitalist countries. Under Capitalism, workers do not normally share in business risk, whilst shareholders usually belong to higher income groups and are in a position to spread their risk so that they can absorb fluctuations in dividends more easily. This fact of modern Socialist economic life must have risen to the size of a problem because it has been found necessary to establish 'risk reserve funds' in enterprises (financed out of enterprise profits).

In a broader context, it may be observed that although material incentives are instrumental in promoting an enterprise's maximum performance (indicated by maximum profits), they do not necessarily ensure maximum efficiency on the macroeconomic scale. As

[1] J. Artemov, ('The Distribution and Utilization of the Material Incentives Fund'), *Voprosy ekonomiki* (Problems of Economics), Moscow, 5/1969, pp. 29–39.

[2] B. Sukharevskii, ('Material Motivation and Economic Reforms'), *Ekonomicheskaya gazeta* (Economic Gazette), Moscow, no. 29, 1968, p. 9.

[3] In Czechoslovakia, the State guarantees 92% of the average wage planned for the preceding year. In Bulgaria the guarantee covers 90%, 85% and 80% of the standard wage or salary of the lowest, middle and the highest occupational classification respectively; in Hungary the respective guaranteed proportions are 100%, 85% and 75%. R. Volodavskaya *et al.*, ('Material Incentives in the European CMEA Countries'), *Ekonomicheskie nauki* (Economic Studies), Moscow, 8/1969, p. 64.

is well known, price structures in Socialist countries, in spite of recent reforms of producers' prices, do not yet fully reflect all factor costs (especially rent and interest) and they are still largely insulated (in the form of highly differentiated turnover taxes) against changes in consumers' preferences. As long as price irrationalities remain, enterprise profit does not reliably reflect macroeconomic gain. Consequently, labour may be induced to engage in sub-optimal production because it may, paradoxically, lead to maximum enterprise profits.

D. THE DIFFERENTIATION OF INCOMES

For practical purposes it may be assumed that under Socialism income, if we exclude social service benefits, is derived from one's own labour.[1] On this score alone, one can expect a smaller differentiation of income in Socialist countries. Under Capitalism, rents, interests and dividends usually constitute more than one-tenth of personal income, and very large incomes are almost wholly derived from these sources. It may be observed that in Socialist countries, incentives received from distributed enterprise profits are treated as a part of wages (or salaries) because they are rewards only to those who actually work in the enterprise in question.

The earnings of labour are made up of standard pay plus incentive payments. The latter may consist of overtime pay and a bonus derived from enterprise profits. As was shown in the preceding section of this chapter, explicit incentive payments are now considerably differentiated. But in a sense, the incentive element may also be embodied in standard pay rates (i.e. before overtime

[1] Exceptions to this rule are of minor consequence. Personal income may also be derived from interest earned on savings deposits (at 3 % p.a.) and on government bonds (normally carrying 3–5 % p.a.) and, where private enterprise is still tolerated, from profits. However, these sources are of little significance in practice. With low income levels still prevailing, personal savings are low, the issue of government bonds to persons has been virtually discontinued in the last fifteen years or so, and profits from private undertakings are subject to highly progressive taxes (rising up to 90 %). In the isolated cases where income is received from abroad (emigrant remittances, royalties, etc.), its value is greatly reduced by the application of the official exchange rate (whereby foreign, especially Western, currencies are grossly undervalued) and even by special taxes. All these sources do not normally represent more than 1 % of personal income.

and bonuses are added). If this is done, the total range of personal earnings is increased further.

Even before the reforms, Socialist countries had found that a substantial differentiation of standard pay rates was essential. Of all resources, labour is least subject to central direction. To promote the desired distribution of manpower, consistent with the freedom of choice of occupation and the place of employment, differentials in standard pay rates became an important instrument.

These differentials were based on occupation, industry, region and working conditions. They tended to increase in the USSR up to the early 1950s and in other CMEA countries up to the late 1950s, when they were similar to those in Capitalist countries except that top managerial and professional salaries did not reach the higher extremes typical of the latter countries. Oddly enough, up to that time Socialist countries had no explicit minimum wage legislations. Then there was a tendency for the differences in standard pay rates to be narrowed, mainly by raising the level of wages in the lowest-paid occupations and in such depressed branches of the economy as agriculture,[1] trade and 'non-productive' services.[2]

However, since the reforms it has been widely agreed that the changeover to the predominantly intensive sources of economic growth necessitates a greater differentiation of earnings in order not only to encourage more effort from the most productive workers but also to promote a greater mobility of labour. Intensive growth

---

[1] As reported in 1969, all the Socialist countries under consideration except Czechoslovakia had legally defined minimum wages (per month): Bulgaria, 55 leva; the GDR, 300 marks; Hungary, 800 forints; Poland, 850 złotys; the USSR, 60 roubles; and Yugoslavia, about 300 dinars. The minimum wage ranges from 43 to 55 % of the average wage level. Based on: T. Krajkovic, ('The Control of Wages in Socialist Countries'), *Prace a Mzda* (Labour and Wages), Prague, 3/1969, pp. 148–52.

[2] Average wages in agriculture as a percentage of those in industry in 1955 were as follows (in brackets the percentage for 1965 is shown, to indicate the trend for improvement in most countries since that time): Bulgaria, 76 (87); Czechoslovakia, 70 (84); the GDR, 78 (82); Hungary, 75 (87); Poland, 70 (77); the USSR, 68 (72); Yugoslavia, 82% in 1959 (98% in 1966). Based on V. P. Gruzinov, *Materialnoe stimulirovaniye truda v stranakh Sotsializma* (Material Incentives to Labour in Socialist Countries), Moscow, Mysl, 1968, p. 239; Federal Institute of Statistics, *Statistički godišnjak FNRJ 1960*, (Statistical Yearbook of Yugoslavia for 1960), Belgrade, 1960, p. 257; *Statistički godišnjak Jugoslavije, 1969*, Belgrade, 1969, p. 275.

largely depends on the acquisition of skills and the structural transformation of the economy, with some industries declining and others expanding or being established.[1] Before the Socialist economy can afford a distribution according to needs, there must be a substantial rise in the general level of incomes comparable with those in Western countries.[2] Yet no dramatic increase can be expected without activating the workers' material motivation on a broad front.

To meet this challenge, since the late 1960s the regimes in most European Socialist countries have departed from the previous egalitarian dream in favour of a greater differentiation of earnings in respect of both standard pay rates and incentives. The increasing acceptance of marginal analysis on the production side makes the differentiation more meaningful and desirable.

Complete data on the size of personal earnings are not published in any Socialist country. But there is sufficient evidence, provided in recent studies carried out by Socialist private researchers, suggesting that these countries are far from becoming egalitarian societies. Poland is usually regarded as one of the countries where the disparity of incomes is smaller than in most other Socialist countries. Yet the differences are quite considerable even by Western standards. In 1967 earnings per person employed averaged 2,200 złotys per month. The minimum wage was 850 złotys, but there were 220,000 persons (representing 2·5 per cent of total employment) with incomes of over 5,000 złotys per month. Compared with 1961, the number of persons in this income group more than doubled and the upper range was increased. Within this group in 1967 there were 20,000 persons earning more than 8,000

---

[1] The highest earnings per person employed is usually found in the construction industry and in transport, and the lowest in trade and agriculture. To illustrate, the percentages above (+) and below (−) the national average in the respective industries (in that order) in the late 1960s were: in Bulgaria, +20, +10, −11, −11; in Czechoslovakia, +9, +4, −19, −16; in Poland, +10, −4, −21, −23; in the USSR, +15, +10, −18, −20. In Hungary in 1968, the average pay per month in health, culture and public amenities averaged 1,030 forints but in finance and management it exceeded 2,270 forints. V. P. Gruzinov, op. cit., p. 239; *Figyelö*, 29/10/1969, p. 3.

[2] In 1970 the estimated national income per head (taking the Western concept) in the eight Socialist countries averaged US $1,530, compared with $3,910 in the USA and about $770 in Capitalist countries taken as a whole. For further details, including prospective growth up to the year 2000, see Table 44, p. 336.

złotys, and 5,000 persons over 10,000 złotys per month. In the last category were included top managers in industry, construction and foreign trade, top administrators in government service and leading actors, scientists and writers.[1] Thus the incomes of 2·5 per cent of the persons employed were six or more times the minimum wage, and those of 0·1 per cent were twelve times or more the minimum wage.

In Bulgaria in 1968, the minimum monthly wage was 55 leva and the average monthly earnings in the economy amounted to 110 leva. Yet in the construction industry monthly earnings reached 500 leva. In the same year, actors earned up to 1,250, composers and musicians up to 2,100 and painters, sculptors and architects up to 2,500 leva per month.[2] Thus the earnings of some architects were forty-five times the minimum wage. When the Soviet poet, E. Evtushenko, was interviewed on Australian television in 1968, he was asked what his annual income was; his answer was, 'about 100,000 roubles', which works out at 138 times the minimum wage in the USSR.

It may be reasonably assumed that similar differences in earnings now exist in other Socialist countries as well. A well-known Hungarian economist and administrator advocates further differentiation of incomes. He is also in favour of limiting the growth of social consumption (social services provided free, or below cost, by the State) because private spending on consumption has a much greater motivating effect on persons to work harder.[3]

Investigations carried out in several Socialist countries show that popular attitudes to the differentiation of earnings from labour differ and they largely depend on the social group. The first-generation working class, recruited mostly from poor peasant and servant families and consisting mostly of unskilled workers, is in favour of the egalitarian principle. The old working class of several generations' standing supports considerable differentiation based on payments by results (i.e. piece-work wages). The intelligentsia

---

[1] B. Fick, op. cit., p. 42.

[2] I. D. Vuchev, ('Conditions of the Consumption of Luxury Goods under Socialism'), *Finansi i kredit* (Finance and Credit), Sofia, 4/1970, p. 33.

[3] Béla Csikós-Nagy, ('Problems of Improving the Economic Mechanism'), *Közgazdasági szemle* (Economic Review), Budapest, 4/1970, pp. 448–58, esp. p. 456.

favours substantial differentiation to be embodied in standard time rates.[1]

Although in the near future the authorities are certain to rely more on the differentiation of earnings than on moral incentives, in the long run their role is likely to be reversed. There has already been a trend away from piece-work wages in favour of time wages, which tends to produce smaller differences in earnings.[2] Similarly, overtime work is not as welcome as it was in the past and holding more than one job will certainly be less common than it used to be.

Incentive payments as separate elements of earnings, especially if they represent substantial proportions, are unpredictable and they often produce inflationary effects, particularly in the countries where price controls have been relaxed, as in Yugoslavia.[3] The levels of income will, no doubt, be increasing in the future. This is likely to make workers less responsive to extra incentive payments, considering that in Socialist countries the scope for the acquisition of private property is clearly limited.

The regimes in Socialist countries are committed to two long-run goals – a reduction of differences in the earnings from labour and a continued expansion of social consumption. The long-run pursuit of the first goal was clearly reaffirmed at the 22nd Congress of the Communist Party of the Soviet Union in 1961 by 'removing the class distinctions between workers and peasants, the essential distinction between town and country, and creating conditions for an organic fusion of physical and mental work'.[4] Social consump-

[1] J. Kleer, ('Observations on the Principle of Distribution'), *Nowe drogi*, 9/1968, pp. 95–6.

[2] Up to the mid-1950s, Socialist countries were noted for their preference for piece-work wages – about three-quarters of workers were paid on this basis (compared with about one-third in most Western countries). In addition to the high cost of administration, this practice contributed to poor quality and disregard for costs. Moreover, unskilled labourers on piece-work wages often earned more than skilled workers on time rates, which adversely affected the acquisition of higher qualifications. Since the mid-1950s the proportion of workers paid on a piece-work basis has declined to about one-third and the trend is likely to continue further.

[3] In Yugoslavia in the 1950s (after the reforms of 1952) retail prices were rising on the average by 3% and in the 1960s by 11% annually. *Statistički godišnjak Jugoslavije 1961*, p. 249, and *1969*, p. 267.

[4] Documents of the 22nd Congress of the CPSU, *The Road to Communism*, Moscow, FLPH, 1961, p. 247. According to the Programme presented at the Congress, the USSR was scheduled to enter the 'higher phase of Communism' after 1980.

tion, which is a form of distribution according to needs, in contrast to private consumption reduces the inclination to earn higher incomes. Yet in the next decade or two, social consumption is planned to increase from its present share of about 25 per cent to about 50 per cent of total consumption.[1]

On the other hand, the conditions for enhancing the effectiveness of moral incentives are likely to improve. Increasing levels of income and the shortening of hours of work[2] will promote better attitudes to work and to the social system in general. The role of unskilled routine manual tasks will continue to decline in favour of work requiring higher qualifications and providing greater interest and personal satisfaction. Progress in workers' self-management will further strengthen their responsibility.

[1] See, e.g., ibid., pp. 512, 538–9, 545; S. Góra, op. cit., p. 72.
[2] On the reduction in the hours of work, see Chapter 8 B, p. 128.

8 Labour Productivity

A. THE QUESTION OF OPTIMUM EMPLOYMENT

UNDER the extensive approach to economic development optimum employment was identified with maximum employment. This attitude was further reinforced by political and ethical considerations. As the Socialist State was responsible for providing sustenance to the population anyway, any addition by labour to total production was regarded as socially gainful, so that there was a tendency to push employment up to the point where the marginal product of the labour force approached zero. The system of incentives was such that it favoured additional employment irrespective of its efficiency (see Chapter 6 B, pp. 97–8). The policy of maximum employment, as a Polish economist described:

> undoubtedly yielded several important benefits, such as a rapid growth of production enabling a mighty investment leap forward and the incorporation of hundreds of thousands of persons into production processes at higher occupational levels. But at the same time, the policy of maximum employment produced a number of adverse effects. Above all, it was not conducive to the growth of labour productivity because it led to over-full employment and a high labour turnover, and it weakened labour discipline and conscientious application to work.[1]

With the emphasis switched over to intensive sources of growth – the growth of labour productivity in particular – it is now widely believed that optimum employment is below maximum employment. In Yugoslavia, the determination of the optimum level of employment is largely left to the market forces and in recent years

[1] M. Syrek, *Wpływ substytucyjnego i niezależnego postępu technicznego na wydajność pracy* (The Influence of Capital-Using and Independent Technical Progress on Labour Productivity), Katowice, Wyd. Śląsk, 1967, p. 259.

this proportion represented 92 per cent of total employment.[1] However, in the remaining European Socialist countries the official view, supported by a large majority of economists, is that optimum employment is much higher – at least 99 per cent of the labour force, i.e. allowing less than 1 per cent for frictional unemployment, and all able-bodied persons willing to work can find employment within a reasonably short period of time.[2] This means that the number of vacancies should be about equal to frictional unemployment, but no more than that. The proportion allowed for frictional unemployment appears to be low by Capitalist standards (where 2 per cent or more is regarded as normal). But this is not unreasonable, considering that under Socialism much more effective anticipatory and current adjustments are possible owing to central planning and the social ownership of the means of production.

To avoid excessive demand for labour, greater attention is now given in economic plans to setting more realistic targets. At the enterprise level, the application of the profit criterion tends to limit employment to the point where the marginal product of labour is equal to its marginal cost. In Bulgaria, Czechoslovakia and Hungary, to counteract over-full employment, a payroll tax has been recently introduced.[3] A similar approach is advocated by some economists in other Socialist countries, and furthermore it is proposed that credits at concessional rates be made available to industries where the replacement of labour by capital is feasible.[4]

It is also reported that some economists and technocrats are in favour of creating a small pool of unemployment as a means of improving the discipline and efficiency of labour. This question

---

[1] In the late 1960s persons seeking employment averaged 300,000, representing about 8% of total employment. In addition, there were 350,000 Yugoslavs working in Western Europe. Based on: Federal Institute of Statistics, *Statistički godišnjak Jugoslavije 1969* (Statistical Yearbook of Yugoslavia for 1969), Belgrade, 1969, pp. 94, 104; *Problemi spoljne trgovine i konjunkture* (Problems of Foreign Trade and Cyclical Fluctuations), Belgrade, 2/1969, p. 165.

[2] Z. Łaski, ('Economic Accounting and the Optimization of Employment'), *Życie gospodarcze* (Economic Life), 11/9/1966, p. 3.

[3] e.g. in Hungary the tax amounts to 25% of the wage (including salary) bill, and wage increases are taxed on a progressive basis rising to 70% above the payroll tax.

[4] See, e.g., *Figyelö* (Economic Observer), Budapest, 28/5/1969, p. 2; *Trud* (Labour), Moscow, 12/5/1968, p. 2.

was widely debated at the Conference on the Use of Resources arranged by the Council for Mutual Economic Assistance and held in Budapest in September 1968. But the majority of the country delegates strongly repudiated such a step.[1] On another occasion, a Hungarian economist summed up the prevalent Socialist view on the subject:

> . . . under Socialist conditions the free flow of labour necessary for economic growth, structural changes and the equilibrium of employment must not rely upon a reserve army of unemployed. *Planned economy offers us other means and methods for this purpose.* [Emphasis in the original.][2]

An important aspect of the optimization of employment is the distribution of the labour force amongst the different branches of the economy, and some remarkable changes have taken place in this respect in all the Socialist countries under discussion. The most dramatic redistribution of manpower has occurred between agriculture and industry. Taking the eight Socialist countries as a whole (including Yugoslavia), over the relatively short period between 1950 and 1968 the proportion of the working population engaged in agriculture declined from over 50 to less than 33 per cent, whilst in industry it rose from 20 to 30 per cent (in absolute numbers, the decline in agriculture was from 58m. to 52m., and the rise in industry from 26m. to 38m.).[3] There has also been a relative and absolute decline of employment in domestic service and some relative and absolute increases in construction and transport (see Table 24, p. 190).

This process must be regarded as one of the important elements of the intensification of economic growth, because the redistribution has consisted in transfers (absolute and relative) of labour from the less efficient to the more efficient branches. Productivity in industry in these countries is some three times higher than in agriculture (see section C of this chapter, p. 139). Socialist economies are undergoing similar structural transformations to those

---

[1] Y. Yakovleva, ('Labour Resources in the CMEA Countries'), *Voprosy ekonomiki* (Problems of Economics), Moscow, 1/1969, p. 152.

[2] J. Timar, 'The Level of Employment and Its Equilibrium in Socialism', *Acta oeconomica* (Economic Papers), Budapest, vol. 4, no. 2, 1969, p. 173.

[3] Based on Table 24, p. 190, and its sources.

experienced by developed Capitalist countries in the past,[1] except that under Socialism these processes are taking place on a planned basis and are being squeezed into shorter periods.

To promote the optimal redistribution of manpower, employment offices have been established, even in the USSR.[2] Whilst transfers of manpower from agriculture to industry are still continuing, the accent is now shifting to redistribution within the non-agricultural sector. Owing to the rapid technological changes, the declining industries and those lending themselves to a greater mechanization and automation tend to release manpower, most of which are skilled workers. In the past, newly established and the most dynamic industries had often been allocated unskilled rural labour, whilst the available skilled workers did not necessarily find themselves in the forms of employment to which they were most suited.

Some attempts have been made in recent years to increase the mobility of labour amongst Socialist countries. For example, a group of Bulgarian workers has been engaged in the USSR in the timber-cutting, building and iron industries in order to assist in the production of the raw materials needed by Bulgaria and to acquire new skills. For similar reasons, Hungarian workers have been employed in East German industrial enterprises, and Polish workers in constructing power stations in Czechoslovakia and the German Democratic Republic. It appears that this form of cooperation in the utilization of manpower will be further expanded in the future.[3] In addition, *ad hoc* movements of labour have been intensified in recent years under the auspices of CMEA in respect

[1] According to estimates made by S. Kuznets, inter-branch shifts of labour accounted for four-tenths of the total growth of the net national product per worker in the USA over the period 1869–1948 (quoted from: J. T. Dunlop, 'Evaluation of Factors Affecting Productivity', in *Problems in Economic Development*, ed. E. A. G. Robinson, London, Macmillan, 1965, p. 351). In Socialist countries the proportion has probably been higher owing to a greater productivity gap between agriculture and industry.

[2] In the USSR employment offices were abolished in 1936 because 'unemployment does not and cannot occur under Socialism'. In 1969 plans were announced to establish employment bureaux in cities of over 100,000 people (at least 30 such bureaux were in existence in that year). See K. Novikov, ('Problems Associated with the Effective Utilization of Labour Resources'), *Kommunist*, Moscow, 13/1969, p. 107.

[3] K. Mikulskii, ('Urgent Problems Facing the CMEA Countries in the Distribution of Labour'), *Voprosy ekonomiki*, 7/1969, pp. 139–40.

of training programmes, the lending of experts, study tours, etc. (see Chapter 13 D, pp. 253-6).

B. LABOUR PRODUCTIVITY AND INTENSIVE GROWTH

The Socialist victory over imperialist powers in the economic arena ultimately depends on the growth of labour productivity, together with rapid improvements in science, technology and the quality of production. At the present stage, when the Leninist thesis of 'who–whom' is being put to the test on a world-wide scale, increasing labour productivity is the most lethal weapon in the Socialist arsenal to ensure the victory of the new social order.[1]

This was the resolution that emerged from the 23rd Special Session of CMEA in Moscow in April 1969, attended by the Secretaries of Communist Parties and Heads of Governments of the member countries. The resolution reflects the degree of importance now attached to the growth of labour productivity, not only from the standpoint of the intensification of economic growth but also on political and ideological grounds.

The need for a faster growth of labour productivity, especially per man-hour, has been further accentuated by the reduction in the standard hours of work, the workers' decreasing inclination to work overtime (owing to the recent substantial increases in the wage rates of the lowest-paid workers) and the prospects for slow-downs in the growth of employment in the future. The standard working week in the Socialist countries was reduced from about 48 hours in the late 1950s to about 44 hours in the following decade, and it is planned to be further reduced to about 35 hours or less by 1980. Birth rates have been declining in recent years and the natural increase is expected to be quite low in the next decade at least (1·0 per cent p.a., or less, for the region),[2] so that the pro-

---

[1] *Pravda*, Moscow, 2/7/1969, p. 4.

[2] According to recent population prognoses, the rates for the individual countries are: the GDR, 0·2%; Hungary, 0·3%; Czechoslovakia, 0·4%; Bulgaria, 0·7%; Poland, 0·9%; Romania, 1·0%; Yugoslavia, 1·0%; and the USSR, 1·0%. The expected rate for non-Socialist Europe is 0·7%, for the USA 1·4%, and for the world as a whole 2·0%. For further details, including projected populations for 1985 and 2000, see Table 43, p. 332.

portion of the working-age group is likely to be declining in favour of the old-age bracket.[1]

In analysing the problem of labour productivity, Socialist economists draw a distinction between macrosocial and microeconomic productivity.[2] Macrosocial labour productivity is indicated by national income per head and it is determined by such factors as institutional arrangements, conditions of life, social attitudes to work, the proportion of national income invested and structural developments in the economy. On the other hand, microeconomic labour productivity (which is the conventional concept as usually understood in Capitalist countries) is measured by output per worker (or output per man-hour). It is influenced by factors operative in individual enterprises, viz. the organization of work, management–workers relations, incentives, the personnel's skills and application to work. Whilst macrosocial productivity normally increases with the expansion of employment, microeconomic productivity increases rather with a reduction of employment.

Historically speaking, Socialist countries for a long time were preoccupied with the creation of favourable macrosocial conditions for the growth of labour productivity. According to J. Pajestka, now the vice-chairman of the Polish State Planning Commission, this is a prerequisite for any country, Socialist or Capitalist, embarking on accelerated development if solid found-

---

[1] The peak of growth of the working-age group was reached in Czechoslovakia during 1961–65, whilst in Poland, Romania and the USSR the peak was entered in the late 1960s and is likely to continue into the early 1970s. During the decade of 1971–80, the growth is expected to be lower than during the preceding decade in Bulgaria, Czechoslovakia and Romania, but in Poland the rate will be maintained. The growth of this group of the population will be slower over the period 1976–80 than over 1971–75 in all CMEA countries except the GDR, where the rate will be higher. In Yugoslavia, the proportion of 'active' population will start declining after 1971. By 1980, the proportion of the total population in the old-age group (65 and over) is expected to be as follows: Bulgaria, 12·1% (compared with 8·9% in 1967); Czechoslovakia, 13·2% (10·4%); the GDR, 16·5% (15·1%); Hungary, 14·3% (10·9%); Poland, 10·4% (7·4%); Romania, 11·2% (8·1%); the USSR, 9·6% (7·6%); and Yugoslavia, 9·7% (7·2%). Based on: Central Statistical Office of Poland, *Rozwój gospodarczy krajów RWPG 1950–1968* (Economic Development of the CMEA Countries 1950–1968), Warsaw, 1969, pp. 51–5; periodical publications of the countries concerned.

[2] See, e.g., J. Pajestka, 'Stages of Industrialization and Labour Productivity', in *Problems in Economic Development*, op. cit., pp. 257–61.

ations are to be laid down for the continued growth of productivity. However, as economic development reaches higher stages, factors influencing labour productivity at the operational level should increasingly assume the focus of attention.[1]

It is not difficult to see that the macrosocial emphasis was a logical feature of the extensive approach to economic growth, and under that system 'it was easier for workers to increase their incomes by overtime and from illegal sources than by becoming more efficient'.[2] On the other hand, intensive growth is critically dependent on microeconomic conditions directly inducing increases in labour productivity. The economic reforms have been primarily directed at creating such conditions, and all major facets of the Socialist economies have been affected. They are considered in detail in other chapters of this book, but the most relevant are: (i) a greater independence of enterprises, allowing them more initiative to exploit the opportunities for increases in efficiency (Chapters 4 B, 6 A and B); (ii) the acceptance of profit as the main or only criterion of enterprise performance (Chapter 6 C); (iii) making enterprise profits the criterion for bonuses, and in some cases even standard pay (Chapter 7 B and C); (iv) a greater differentiation of standard pay rates according to skills and productivity (Chapter 7 D); and (v) the introduction of special profit mark-ups to spur enterprises and their personnel to technological progress (Chapter 13 B and C). In effect, material incentives to labour have been recognized as being more reliable than moral appeals.

In some countries where central planning is still dominant (such as the German Democratic Republic and the USSR) experiments have been undertaken in recent years on the introduction of the index of labour productivity as one of the bases for the determination of the wage fund and the bonus fund, especially in labour-intensive industries. This task will be easier in the future because, in contrast to the past, more reliable methods for measuring labour productivity are being developed. It also appears that labour organizations – trade unions, workers' councils, factory committees

[1] Ibid., p. 257.
[2] S. Góra, *Warunki produkcji a działanie bodźców* (Conditions of Production and the Operation of Incentives), Warsaw, PWE, 1967, pp. 45–6.

– are now more concerned than in the past with raising productivity because it is now more directly related to workers' earnings (however, see section D of this chapter, pp. 142–3).

At the same time, macrosocial conditions are not being neglected. At the central planning level, special attention is given to the development of those industries which show a rapid growth of productivity and those with the greatest potential (see Chapter 11). Far-reaching reforms of producers' prices have been carried out in which cost-preference relations are more closely reflected than in the past. A variety of financial incentives and disincentives (differentiated interest rates, subsidies, depreciation rates, quality mark-ups) are now also commonly applied, designed to induce structural developments in favour of the most efficient industries.

Furthermore, the previous policy of high levels of accumulation is continued so that the capital–labour ratio is on the whole rising. This is demonstrated in Table 14, showing the relation between the growth of investment and employment. Even though the ratio has varied from year to year, largely caused by 'recessions' and the changeover to the new economic system, there are several indications that the rising trend will continue in the near future at least.

The effectiveness of this growth is in fact greater than the rising ratios would imply. As part of the anti-extensive campaign, the authorities have reversed their previous emphasis on capital-widening to capital-deepening. This has assumed two forms. Firstly, the plans laid down are more realistic and at the same time enterprises are discouraged from attempting too many investment schemes, and instead are induced to complete planned projects in the shortest possible time. Secondly, great efforts are being made to increase working equipment in enterprises (machinery and tools) and to reduce the emphasis on passive fixed assets, such as buildings (for further details, see Chapter 10 B, pp. 173–5).

Before we leave this section it may be of interest to examine the rates of growth of those facets of labour productivity for which complete statistics are available. Table 15 shows the average annual rates of increase in *per capita* national income, industrial production, agricultural production, labour productivity in industry

TABLE 14 INCREMENTAL INVESTMENT–EMPLOYMENT RATIOS,
1950–1968*

YEAR	BULGARIA	CZECHOSLOVAKIA	HUNGARY	POLAND	ROMANIA	USSR
1950–60 (annual av.†)	2·0	2·1	1·2	1·9	3·1	2·1
1961	1·0	2·0	—2·0	2·3	2·6	0·7
1962	3·5	—1·0§	3·0	2·8	1·9	1·3
1963	2·5	—5·5¶	5·0	1·0	1·6	1·7
1964	2·5	5·5	1·0	2·0	2·0	2·3
1965	1·3	2·3	ind.‖	2·5	1·8	1·6
1966	2·4	3·7	10·1	2·3	2·5	1·8
1967	5·0	3·0	9·5	2·8	4·3	2·7
1968	0·0‡	4·5	2·5	2·0	3·0	2·0

* The ratio is derived by dividing the percentage increase in investment (at constant prices) by the percentage increase in total employment. The ratio of 1·00 indicates that there is no change in the amount of capital (investment) per person employed. A negative ratio means that investment increased by a smaller (or declined by a greater) percentage than employment. The comparability of the figures between different years, and particularly between different countries, is limited. (No complete data are available for the GDR and Yugoslavia.)

† Based on indices of investment (at constant prices) and of employment, with 1950 = 100.

‡ Investment increased by 0%, whilst employment rose by 5%.

§ Investment declined by 3%, whilst employment increased by 3%.

¶ Investment declined by 11%, whilst employment increased by 2%.

‖ Indeterminate; investment increased by 1%, whilst there was no change in employment.

Source. Based on: Central Statistical Office of Poland, *Rozwój gospodarczy krajów RWPG 1950–1968* (Economic Development of the CMEA Countries 1950–1968), Warsaw, 1969, pp. 16–43.

and real wages. Unfortunately, no complete figures are available for changes in output per man-hour or output per person in the material sphere. The table must naturally be treated with caution, but the following trends are indicated by the figures. In general, the 1950s were noted for high rates of growth of productivity in the four ways defined in the table. The low rates of the 1960s can be explained on three grounds:

(i) the economic stagnation that prevailed in most of these countries;

(ii) the dislocations caused by the reforms in changing over to the new system;

(iii) the reduced standard hours of work by about 10 per cent between the late 1950s and the late 1960s (from about 48 to 44 hours per week);

(iv) the decline in the degree of over-valuation of industrial production (especially in relation to agricultural production; as industrial production represents such high and increasing proportions of total material production (see Table 25, p. 194), a relative decrease in its valuation (compared with the past) unduly depresses the rate of growth of national income (see also Chapter 1 C, pp. 14, 19).

Although some improvements can be seen in the late 1960s (except in Yugoslavia), there is little evidence yet to suggest that the recent economic reforms have produced spectacular results. Perhaps the period is too short for the new economic system to demonstrate its real viability. It will be noted that real wages in all these countries have lagged well behind the growth of national income per head. This is an outcome of the deliberate State policy of restricting current consumption in favour of high accumulation. However, Socialist views on this question appear to be changing now.

C. INCREASES IN LABOUR PRODUCTIVITY AND EMPLOYMENT AS SOURCES OF ECONOMIC GROWTH

In Socialist discussions on the intensification of economic growth, a good deal of importance is attached to the relative

TABLE 15 TRENDS IN PRODUCTIVITY AND REAL WAGES, 1950–1968

(Average Annual Rates at Constant Prices)*

COUNTRY	YEARS	National Income per Head of Population	Indus-trial Output per Head of Population	Agri-cultural Output per Head of Population	Indus-trial Produc-tivity†	Real Wages
Bulgaria	1950–60	11	13	6	5	7
	1961–64	6	10	3	6	2
	1965–68	8	12	2	7	6
	1968 (index‡)	438	853	196	322	270
Czechoslovakia	1950–60	5	10	2	7	5§
	1961–64	1	4	0	3	1
	1965–68	6	6	3	5	2
	1968 (index‡)	247	371	124	275	160
GDR	1950–60	n.a.	12	6	6§	6§
	1961–64	3	7	1	6	2
	1965–68	5	6	5	5	3
	1968 (index‡)	396	502	204	328	360
Hungary	1950–60	6	10	2§	4	5
	1961–64	5	8	2	5	2
	1965–68	6	6	2	4	2
	1968 (index‡)	249	424	135¶	211	182
Poland	1950–60	6	11	1	8	5§
	1961–64	5	7	1	5	2
	1965–68	6	7	6	5	1
	1968 (index‡)	265	494	126	326	149‖
Romania	1950–60	6§	12	5	9	n.a.
	1961–64	8	13	1	8	4
	1965–68	7	12	3	8	5
	1968 (index‡)	426	759	177	433	140**

TABLE 15—*Continued*

COUNTRY	YEARS	National Income per Head of Population	Industrial Output per Head of Population	Agricultural Output per Head of Population	Industrial Productivity†	Real Wages
USSR	1950–60	8	10	3	8	2††
	1961–64	5	7	3	4	2
	1965–68	7	8	4	5	4
	1968 (index‡)	348	448	158	302	140‡‡
Yugoslavia	1952–60	9	12	n.a.	8	5
	1961–64	7	10	n.a.	7	6
	1965–68	3	3	n.a.	4	6
	1968 (index§§)	290	480	213	210	242

n.a. = not available.
* The rates and indices are based on official statistics likely to embody an upward bias. The comparability of the figures between different years and particularly between different countries is limited.
† Industrial output per person employed in industry.
‡ 1950 = 100.   ** 1960 = 100.
§ For 1955–60.   †† For 1958–60.
¶ 1954 = 100.   ‡‡ 1958 = 100.
‖ 1955 = 100.   §§ 1952 = 100.

Sources. Based on: *Rozwój gospodarczy* . . ., op. cit., pp. 16–43; Federal Institute of Statistics, *Statistički godišnjak Jugoslavije 1969* (Statistical Yearbook of Yugoslavia for 1969), Belgrade, 1969, pp. 121, 165, 172.

shares contributed by the increases in labour productivity and employment to the growth of national income or industrial production. Socialist economists use a number of different methods for calculating these shares, and although none is perfectly satisfactory the results produced are interesting, even though only approximate.

A commonly used formula for the calculation of the proportion contributed by the increase in labour productivity to the increase in national income is as follows:[1]

$$Pl = 100 - \frac{\Delta E}{\Delta Y} 100;$$

Pl = percentage contribution of the increase in the productivity of labour to the increase in national income;

E = employment in the whole economy;[2]

Y = national income (at constant prices).

Table 16 shows the role played by the growth of labour productivity in the eight Socialist countries over the period 1950–68 as calculated by the above formula. Taking the group of countries as a whole, roughly a little less than two-thirds of the growth of national income in the late 1960s was due to increases in the productivity of labour. The highest proportions were reached in the most developed countries (Czechoslovakia, and the German Democratic Republic[3]) or where there was substantial unemployment (Yugoslavia[4]). The role of employment increases in the growth of national income was highest in the less developed countries and where increases in employment also happened to be unusually high (Bulgaria, Poland and the USSR[5]).

[1] Adapted from B. Minc, *Postęp ekonomiczny* (Economic Progress), Warsaw, PWN, 1967, p. 249.

[2] Rather than in material production. Although national income is calculated on a material basis, it would be unreasonable to assume that only labour employed in the material sphere creates national income and that this production would be possible without the contribution of the non-productive sphere. This fact is recognized even by Socialist economists. If changes in employment in only the productive sphere are taken into account, the tendency for the share of labour productivity in the rate of growth of national income to increase would be accentuated, because in the last decade the proportion of the working population engaged in the material sphere has tended to decrease (see Chapter 11 D, pp. 210–11). On the other hand, in considering the role of labour productivity in industrial output we shall restrict changes in employment only to those in industry.

[3] Besides, employment rose very slowly – only 1% annually over the four-year period 1965–68, compared with a 5% annual rise in national income.

[4] Over the 1965–68 period, unemployment was about 8% (averaging 290,000 persons). Over this period employment actually fell by 2% (80,000 persons) whilst national income increased by 18%.

[5] Over the four-year period 1965–68, the average annual increase in employment in these countries was 6%, 4% and 4% respectively (compared with the natural increase in population of 0·7%, 0·9% and 1·1%), whilst that in national income was 8%, 7% and 7% respectively.

TABLE 16 PERCENTAGE SHARE OF THE INCREASE IN LABOUR
PRODUCTIVITY IN THE GROWTH OF NATIONAL INCOME,
1950–1968*

YEAR	BULGARIA	CZECHOSLOVAKIA	GDR	HUNGARY	POLAND	ROMANIA	USSR	YUGOSLAVIA
1950–60 (annual av.†)	22	32	53	11	31	43	40	20‡
1961	−33	43	150	67	62	36	14	−50
1962	67	−200	100	40	−100	−75	33	50
1963	14	−200	100	50	57	50	25	83
1964	60	−100	80	20	71	58	56	54
1965	−17	0	80	100	43	50	29	0
1966	20	70	83	87	43	50	50	122
1967	56	86	60	78	33	50	57	150
1968	50	67	80	20	56	71	50	80

* The rate of increase in national income is treated as 100%, so that the
residual percentage represents the contribution of the increase in employment
to the increase in national income. Negative percentage figures mean that in
each case employment increased by a higher proportion than did national
income. In Czechoslovakia in 1962 employment rose by 3%, whilst national
income increased by 1%, and in 1963 an increase in employment of 2% was
accompanied by a decline of 2% in national income. Figures greater than 100 (in
the GDR in 1961 and in Yugoslavia in 1966 and 1967) mean that there was a
decline in employment accompanied by an increase in national income. The
figures should be treated as crude approximations.
† Based on the index of employment and the index of national income for
1960, with 1950 = 100.
‡ For 1952–60.

Sources. As for Table 15, p. 135.

It can be concluded that, on the whole, the growth of national
income is increasingly due to the growth of labour productivity
rather than to that in employment, especially since the mid-1960s.
This trend is due to three main causes. Firstly, it is typical of the
growth of labour productivity that it assumes increasing importance in the higher stages of economic development. If we examine

the statistical evidence pertaining to the leading developed Capitalist countries, more than three-quarters of the growth of national income is normally due to increases in labour productivity and only one-quarter or less is contributed by increases in employment. By comparison, in the less developed countries these proportions are reversed (which also applied to Western countries earlier in this century).[1]

Secondly, there is little doubt that in recent years the economic reforms, with their emphasis on intensive growth, have also enhanced the role of labour productivity. Their precise effect is impossible to estimate because the period which has elapsed since is too short and there are no sufficient and reliable data. It seems that their main contribution so far has been to remove some of the obstacles to the growth of efficiency, so that Socialist economies can naturally follow similar evolutionary paths to those traversed by developed Capitalist countries in the past.

It can be reasonably assumed that the role of productivity in the growth of national income will continue to increase in the future and the 1971–75 five-year plans explicitly provide for such increases. This trend will be accentuated by the declining increases in employment (see note 1, p. 129).

The role of the increases in labour productivity in the growth of industrial output is demonstrated in Table 17.[2] If comparison is made with Table 16, it is evident that the share of labour productivity increases (compared with employment increases) is much higher in industrial output than in national income. Its share in industrial output in the late 1960s ranged from nearly six-tenths in Bulgaria and Poland to nine-tenths in the German Democratic Republic. In spite of annual fluctuations, the rising trend in the role of labour productivity is unmistakable.

This strikingly higher share in industrial output than in national income is attributable to a number of reasons. Industry has benefited from priority allocation of resources, including a better quality of labour (in respect of training, age, sex), in contrast to

---

[1] Estimates based on United Nations sources: *Yearbook of Labour Statistics* and *Yearbook of National Accounts Statistics*.

[2] The figures were arrived at in the same manner as for Table 16, p. 137, i.e. by the application of the formula found on p. 136 and where both employment and output are limited to industry only.

TABLE 17 PERCENTAGE SHARE OF THE INCREASE IN LABOUR PRODUCTIVITY IN THE GROWTH OF INDUSTRIAL OUTPUT, 1950–1968*

YEAR	BULGARIA	CZECHOSLOVAKIA	GDR	HUNGARY	POLAND	ROMANIA	USSR	YUGOSLAVIA
1950–60 (annual av.†)	44	49	52	37	56	55	53	31‡
1961	82	56	117	70	70	47	56	29
1962	70	50	117	62	50	50	70	57
1963	40	—100	100	57	60	58	62	69
1964	60	75	83	67	78	71	43	50
1965	53	75	83	80	44	54	67	50
1966	33	57	100	71	57	73	67	120
1967	62	86	86	70	50	71	70	0
1968	75	80	83	40	56	67	62	100

* The rate of increase in industrial output is treated as 100%, so that the residual percentage represents the contribution of the increase in employment to the increase in industrial output. Percentage figures higher than 100 in three cases (GDR in 1961 and 1962, Yugoslavia in 1966) mean that employment declined whilst industrial output increased. The negative figure (for Czechoslovakia in 1963) denotes unchanged employment combined with a decline in industrial output. The percentages should be treated as crude approximations.

† Based on the index of employment and the index of industrial output for 1960, with 1950 = 100.

‡ For 1952–60.

Sources. As for Table 15, p. 135.

such branches of the economy as agriculture and trade. At the same time, there is a greater scope in industry than elsewhere in the material sphere for the introduction of technological innovations, including labour-saving devices. The higher share is also due to the over-valuation of industrial output, especially in relation to agricultural output. As a result of these three conditions, labour productivity in industry in most Socialist countries appears to be two to four times higher than in agriculture.

To make calculations of the role played by the increases in labour productivity in agriculture is a much more ungrateful task than in national income and industrial output. Although it is commonly known in Socialist countries that both the level and the growth of productivity increases in agriculture are lower than in other major branches of the economy, it is virtually impossible to make even crude statistical calculations. Some agricultural output is valued at compulsory-delivery prices, some at above-compulsory prices and some at free-market prices (see, e.g., Table 12, p. 84), and moreover the proportions of the output realized in these categories have been changing widely even in the same country. The situation is further complicated by the existence of State, collective and private farms, in each of which the definition of employment is usually different.

The growth of the productivity of labour is dependent not only directly on labour but also on capital and technology. We shall examine their role in Chapters 10 and 13.

D. PROBLEMS AND LIMITATIONS

Economic reforms have not removed all the obstacles to the continuous growth of labour productivity, and in fact they have created new problems. An excessive demand for labour still prevails in most Socialist countries, especially in Czechoslovakia, the German Democratic Republic, Hungary and the USSR.[1] The consequent labour shortages have been accentuated by the introduction of capital charges (see Chapter 10 C, pp. 176–80), because the latter tend to enhance the demand for labour rather than for capital. It also appears that the substantial increases in minimum wages in recent years have led in many cases to absenteeism, with consequent adverse effects on production and productivity.[2]

---

[1] e.g. in Czechoslovakia in 1969 excess demand for labour outside agriculture and forestry alone was estimated to have been at least 107,000 persons. In the USSR in the Russian Republic (representing about one-half of the USSR's total work force), the number of unfilled vacancies was 600,000 in 1967 and 900,000 in 1968. *Życie gospodarcze*, 16/8/1970, p. 11; *Kommunist*, 13/1969, p. 106.

[2] S. Góra, op. cit., pp. 57–8.

In effect, slack labour discipline is still common, and in fact in some respects it appears to be a greater problem now because many strict administrative controls have been lifted. In a study of this topical question, a Soviet economist reflected with obvious disillusion: 'Liberalization and a lenient attitude are just as harmful to the cause of efficiency as administrative controls.'[1] In another study carried out recently in Poland, it was revealed that the utilization of the working time in Polish enterprises ranges from 70 to 80 per cent, i.e. the daily working time, instead of being eight hours, in practice amounts to only 5·5–6·0 hours owing to 'conversations with workmates, loafing, late commencement and early finishing of the work day, reading in work time, excessively long breaks for morning tea, etc.'[2] Another problem appears to be the increasing labour turnover.[3]

Although large sums are paid out in incentives and increased standard wages, in many cases they are not matched by corresponding productivity increases. For a variety of reasons, enterprise profits can change due to no merit or fault of the personnel and yet it may benefit from undeserved windfalls or suffer from unexpected losses beyond its control. In some countries (such as the USSR) incentive funds are still tied to the standard wage funds of the enterprises and the method of determining the wage funds is still largely independent of labour productivity and in fact is such that it favours the hoarding of labour.[4]

[1] V. Khvorin, ('Lenin and Labour Discipline'), *Pravda*, Moscow, 10/1/1970, p. 3.

[2] M. Syrek, op. cit., p. 242.

[3] In the USSR the turnover increased after 1956 when the law prohibiting the unauthorized leaving of employment was repealed. No comprehensive statistics are published, but from official statements it appears that it is a problem, particularly in the construction industry and the northern and eastern regions. In Poland over the ten-year period 1958–67, 8m. persons changed employment (when average employment was 13m.); in 1964 the turnover in socialized industry was 26 %. In Hungary, the annual turnover before the reforms was 15–20 %, but by 1970 it rose to 40 %. See Emily C. Brown, *Soviet Trade Unions and Labor Relations*, Harvard UP, 1966, pp. 33–9; Central Statistical Office of Poland, *Rocznik statystyczny 1965* (Statistical Year-book for 1965), Warsaw, 1965, p. 154; B. Miszewski, *Postęp ekonomiczny w gospodarce przemysłowej* (Economic Progress in an Industrialized Country), Warsaw, PWE, 1968, pp. 187–8; *Acta oeconomica* (Economic Papers), Budapest, vol. 4, no. 2, 1969, p. 170; *Figyelö*, 20/5/1970, p. 5.

[4] V. Rzheshevskii, ('Reforms and Labour Productivity'), *Kommunist*, 12/1969, pp. 65–76, esp. p. 66.

Thus in Hungary, where of all Socialist countries labour short-ages appear to be most acute, a recent survey carried out by the Hungarian Academy of Sciences showed that in industrial enter-prises on the average 12 per cent of workers were surplus to legitimate requirements; on the national scale, this amounted to 200,000 hoarded workers.[1] Another illustration of the continued extravagance in the use of labour is provided by the Shchekino Chemical Complex in the USSR. In 1968 the management re-duced the number of workers in the fertilizer plants by about 1,000 (and yet the output increased by 80 per cent) and was allowed to distribute one-half of the saved wages to the remaining personnel. This case is often quoted by Soviet leaders with pride as evidence of efficiency under the new system. The fact which is not generally known is that most of the 'dismissed' workers were transferred to the newly constructed synthetic fibre plants belonging to the same complex. These plants had been designed by Dutch (Verkspoor) and Italian (Snam Progetti) firms providing for the employment of 278 persons, but in reality the management employed 806 persons. In another case, a Western contractor designed six chemical plants which could normally be operated by 90 persons, but in fact the management manned the plants with 720 workers.[2]

The low level and slow growth of labour productivity in Socialist agriculture, trade and 'non-productive' services are well known. This is a consequence of the long period of planned neglect in respect of investment and the quality of manpower. It was conceded in a Soviet source that in 1960–61 the productivity of labour in agriculture in the USSR was 20–25 per cent of that in the USA.[3] Over the period 1964–68 labour productivity in Soviet collective farms rose by less than one-third, and yet the personal earnings of collective farmers nearly doubled (from 2·26 to 4·38 roubles per man-day) during the same period.[4]

Finally, there are some indications in several Socialist countries

[1] *Figyelő*, 20/5/1970, p. 5.
[2] E. Manevich, ('Problems of the Growth of Manpower and the Methods of Improving the Utilization of Labour in the USSR'), *Voprosy ekonomiki*, 10/1969, pp. 33–4, 37.
[3] *Kommunist*, 1/1968, p. 41.
[4] F. Senko, ('The New Statute for Collective Farms'), *Kommunist*, 8/1969, p. 86.

(Czechoslovakia, Hungary and Yugoslavia) suggesting that trade unions may not necessarily continue to act as blind 'transmission belts' for the State industrial policies. Instead, they may assume a quasi-protective function (similar to that in Capitalist countries) against bureaucracy and technocrats. The technological revolution, the trend towards greater industrial integration and the acceptance of the profit criterion have strengthened the position of the managers versus the workers. These developments have also increased the threat of dismissal from work or forced transfers of labour to other enterprises, industries or regions. The possibility of trade unions evolving into champions of workers' rights has been discussed by a number of Socialist writers in recent years, and, contrary to what might be expected, the Communist Parties have not condemned such discussions.[1] If the unions do evolve into such organizations actively protecting workers' interests, their ability to promote increases in productivity may be smaller than in the past.

But even if it is assumed that productivity per man-hour will rise in the future, this will be partly offset by the expected continued reduction of the standard working week (to about 35 hours by 1980).

[1] For details, see M. Gamarnikow, 'New Tasks for Trade Unions', *East Europe*, 4/1967, pp. 18–26; W. Solyom-Fekete, 'Hungary's New Labour Code', *East Europe*, 3/1968, pp. 17–20; A. Rozehnal, 'Revival of the Czechoslovak Trade Unions', *East Europe* 4/1969, pp. 2–7.

F

9 Banking and Finance

SOCIALIST economic thought and policy were for a long time dominated by a restricted view of the role of money. On ideological as well as practical grounds it was widely believed that under Socialism all functions of money should be strictly planned by the State. It was accepted that the role of money should be reduced to that of a passive recording and accounting device, to facilitate the administration and control of planned production and distribution, and that it should wither away under 'full communism'.

In practice, before the reforms money was allowed to play an active role – within a strictly planned framework – in three spheres: the labour market, the distribution of a predetermined mass of consumer goods and in the private sector where it was permitted to operate. Otherwise, production processes and the circulation of the means of production amongst enterprises were determined in detail by planning, and accounted for by bookkeeping entries and cashless transfers administered by the State Bank. Money was no measure of value – even if defined as the socially necessary labour embodied in a product – because of the different criteria applied in the pricing of different items, and in addition money in private hands could not be used to purchase producer goods (outside the private sector). Financial results of enterprises were in no way indicative of their efficiency, or even performance.

The main function of the banking system was to administer the distribution of finance for the purposes predetermined in detail in the economic plan. Typically, in each country the financing of investment was in the hands of a specialized investment bank which simply administered non-repayable budgetary grants, whilst short-term credits for current production were provided by the State Bank or some other bank. This system facilitated the establish-

ment of new projects and the creation of extra job opportunities for
the manpower released from agriculture and domestic service and
further accentuated by the rapidly increasing proportion of the
population in the working-age group (see Chapter 2 A, pp. 26-9).
The expansion of production capacities and the quantitative
growth of output received such high priorities that quality and
efficiency were neglected. Thus it can be seen that the monetary
and banking system of the type in existence was logical in the context of the highly centralized and directive planning and management, and at the same time it was quite effective in promoting
economic development based on extensive sources.

However, in the 1960s, the more developed Socialist economies
reached a stage where a full utilization of the existing production
capacities, and the careful selection and most efficient execution of
investment projects, could equally or better contribute to economic growth than the mere proliferation of new schemes. In this
drive towards intensive growth, a flexible use of finance has assumed
a strategic role. The more decentralized an economy is, naturally,
the more important becomes monetary and banking policy.

Financial instruments have proved in many ways to be more
effective than detailed directives imposed from above in promoting
efficiency. Enterprises are now more sensitive to financial terms
(interest, depreciation allowances, the period of credit, etc.) because their profits are directly affected, which in turn determines
material incentives to the personnel. Financial incentives and
penalties, unlike directives, are still consistent with enterprises'
independence. Enterprises are in a better position to judge local
supply and demand conditions, and financial incentives not only
allow them a greater freedom of initiative but also spur them to
adopt such methods of production and to pursue such processes
of substitution as lead to maximum performance.

B. INSTITUTIONAL CHANGES

To meet the challenge of the new economic system, the banking
systems in the Socialist countries have had to be adapted accordingly. So far banking reforms have been carried out in Yugoslavia
(1954, 1961, 1964-65), Bulgaria (1967, 1969), Romania (1968), the

German Democratic Republic (1968), Czechoslovakia (1969) and Poland (1969–70). The reforms in Soviet banking in 1959 and 1963, although effected before the main economic reforms of 1965–67, can be considered as partly relevant to the new economic system. To generalize, the banking system has been changed in three respects: the structure, the principles governing the functioning of banks and the relation between banks and enterprises.

The structural changes have assumed two forms – diversification and centralization. The number of separate banks catering for different needs has increased most in Yugoslavia, Czechoslovakia, the German Democratic Republic and Bulgaria. In Yugoslavia before 1954 there was virtually one bank, but by the early 1960s the number had increased to over 200. Since the 1964–65 reform, the number has been reduced to about 100, of which 10 are investment banks, 40 are investment-commercial banks and 50 are commercial banks. A peculiarity of the Yugoslav banking system is that it also has about 380 independent 'social accounting offices', with which enterprises keep accounts and records of transactions to facilitate public control. According to the 1964–65 reform, socio-political communities and enterprises are permitted under certain conditions to establish new banks, and founders and customers are allowed to participate in the distribution of profits.[1] Since 1967 banks, in addition to the National Bank of Yugoslavia, are allowed (under certain conditions) to engage in foreign exchange operations.[2]

In Czechoslovakia up to 1969, central banking functions, as well as the financing of investment and of current production, were concentrated in one bank (the State Bank).[3] In 1969 seven new

[1] The conditions laid down are: the minimum number of founders is 25, the minimum amount of initial capital is 1,500m. dinars for an investment bank, and 500m. dinars for a commercial bank. *Ekonomist*, Zagreb, 2/1969, pp. 507–9; *Finansije* (Finance), Belgrade, 7–8/1969, pp. 359–60.

[2] In the late 1960s, there were 17 banks which held a 'great charter' permitting them to perform payment transactions with foreign countries and to obtain credits from abroad, whilst 36 banks were in possession of a 'small charter' authorizing them to operate residents' foreign exchange accounts only.

[3] In 1965 (before the economic reforms) the Czechoslovak Bank of Commerce was established to assist the State Bank in carrying on foreign exchange operations to promote foreign trade. There was also a bank for handling non-commercial foreign transactions (Zivnostenská Banka) and a number of credit and loan companies – both still in existence.

banks were set up – two banks (the Czech National Bank and the Slovak National Bank) to share in some central banking responsibilities (with the Czechoslovak State Bank), two general-purpose banks (the Czech Economic Bank and the Slovak General Bank), a bank for financing non-productive and new centralized investments (the Investment Bank) and two savings banks (the Czech State Savings Bank and the Slovak Savings Bank, replacing the former Czechoslovak Savings Bank). The banking reform was partly conditioned by the new federal system of government.

New banks have also been established in Bulgaria – the Maritime Commercial Bank (1968), the Bank for Agriculture and Commerce (1969) and the Bank for Industry, Construction and Transport (1969); in the German Democratic Republic – the Bank for Industry and Commerce (1968); and in Romania – the Agricultural Bank (1968) and the Romanian Bank of Foreign Trade (1968).

The other development, i.e. a greater centralization, may appear paradoxical in view of the institutional diversification and the economic decentralization in general. As a consequence of the reforms of planning and management, enterprises have acquired a greater independence and they are left with larger financial resources at their disposal (see section D of this chapter). Thus, to compensate for the dispersion of finance at the enterprise level and to prevent intentional and unintentional misuse of cash and credit, there is a need for a concentration of banking resources for whatever purposes, for a stricter financial control and for a strengthened overall co-ordination.

The centralization effect can be detected in four developments. First, in the last decade or so there has been a tendency for a decline and disappearance of small co-operative banks which up to about the early 1960s played a very important role in catering for the financial needs of retail shops, peasant farms, private and co-operative workshops, and for private and co-operative construction and the maintenance of houses. Instead, these functions have been largely taken over by 'business' and savings banks. In fact, in Bulgaria, Hungary and Romania (and, of course, long ago in the USSR) co-operative banks have completely disappeared.

Second, in some countries the extension of long-term finance (for investment) and short-term credit (for production, trade, etc.)

is now handled by the same bank. Under this set-up one specialized bank provides all types of finance to a whole branch of the
economy (e.g. the Agricultural Bank in Poland) or even more
branches (e.g. the Bank for Industry and Commerce in the German
Democratic Republic and the Bank for Industry, Construction and
Transport in Bulgaria).

Third, in some countries the financing of investment, of current
production and of trade has been transferred to the State Bank (the
central bank). Thus the National Bank of Poland, which previously (in addition to its central bank responsibilities) extended
only short-term credits, in 1970 took over the functions of the
liquidated Investment Bank and now provides all finance to the
economy, with the exception of agriculture and foreign trade
(whose needs are catered for by specialized banks).

A similar effect was produced in the USSR when in 1956 the
Bank of Trade, and in 1959 the Agricultural Bank, the Central
Municipal Bank and the Industry Bank, were wound up and their
functions were taken over partly by the State Bank (*Gosbank*) and
partly by the newly created (in 1959) Investment Bank (*Stroibank*).
In 1963 the State Bank also took over all savings banks. The two
Soviet banks are the largest in all Socialist countries. The State
Bank operates 80,000 branches, including 76,000 savings bank
branches and agencies. Its functions include currency issue,
foreign payments (also partly handled by the Bank of Foreign
Trade, or *Vneshtorgbank*), the provision of short-term credits, the
financing of investment in agriculture and in all the co-operative
sector, the servicing of the State budget, the administration of the
accounts of over 1,000,000 enterprises and the settlement of cashless payments amongst them. The Investment Bank has over
1,000 branches and administers investment grants and credits to
all branches of the economy except agriculture and the co-
operative sector.

The structure of the banking system in each of the eight Socialist
countries is represented in Table 18, pp. 150–1.

Another notable development is the increasing attention being
given to central bank policy along Western lines. In Bulgaria,
Czechoslovakia, the German Democratic Republic, Romania
and Yugoslavia all or most of the general banking functions have

been transferred to other, specialized, banks. Instead, central banks are concentrating on overall co-ordination and supervision. Such functions as the 'bankers' bank' and the 'lender of last resort', rather meaningless in the past, are beginning to be treated as inevitable modern facts of financial life.

The relaxation of price controls, the increasing role of material incentives and the closer links being established with foreign markets are creating new sources of inflationary pressure and instability, so that the challenge to central banks to maintain monetary stability and the balance of payments equilibrium is greater than before. In all the eight countries, not only the responsibilities but also the status of central banks have been substantially enhanced. Thus the State Bank of the German Democratic Republic, which was reorganized in 1968, has assumed several functions previously performed by the Ministry of Finance and is now directly responsible to the Council of Ministers. In all the remaining countries except Poland, central banks also enjoy a good deal of independence and they are not responsible to their respective ministries of finance but to the councils of ministers.

The status and responsibilities of other banks have also been increased in several ways. They are no longer administrative offices of the ministries of finance merely enforcing financial plans, but have become active promoters of efficient investment, production and trade. They are usually run now like business enterprises, and competition is encouraged not only between different banks (especially in Czechoslovakia and Yugoslavia) but also between different branches of the same bank. Banks act as financial advisers to enterprises and are usually charged with the responsibility of ensuring that finance is used economically and for the most efficient projects.

Another recent development of growing consequence is that the role and business of savings banks have been considerably extended. In addition to their traditional function as passive collectors of private savings and subscribers to State loans, they have become important sources of credits for peasant farming, private plots, small workshops, private and co-operative housing and for the hire-purchase of consumer durables.

TABLE 18   THE BANKING SYSTEMS IN THE

COUNTRY	Central Bank (CoM or MoF*)	Investment or Branch-of-Economy Bank
BULGARIA	Bulgarian People's Bank (CoM)	Bank for Industry, Construction and Transport; Bank for Agriculture and Commerce
CZECHOSLOVAKIA	Czechoslovak State Bank† (CoM)	Investment Bank
GDR	State Bank of the GDR (CoM)	Bank for Industry and Commerce; Bank for Agriculture and Food
HUNGARY	Hungarian National Bank (CoM)	Hungarian Investment Bank
POLAND	National Bank of Poland (MoF)	Agricultural Bank
ROMANIA	National Bank of Romania (CoM)	Investment Bank; Agricultural Bank
USSR	State Bank of the USSR (CoM)	All-Union Bank for Investment
YUGOSLAVIA	National Bank of Yugoslavia (CoM)	About 10 investment banks; about 40 investment–commerce banks;

* CoM = responsible directly to the Council of Ministers. MoF = responsible to the Ministry of Finance.
† Plus Czech National Bank and Slovak National Bank.
‡ It handles non-commercial transfers of foreign exchange and other assets.

EUROPEAN SOCIALIST COUNTRIES

Savings Bank	Bank of Foreign Trade	Other Banks
Popular Savings Bank	Bulgarian Bank for Foreign Trade	Maritime Commercial Bank
Czech State Savings Bank; Slovak Savings Bank	Czechoslovak Bank of Commerce	Czech Economic Bank; Slovak General Bank; Živnostenská Bank;‡ credit and loan co-operatives
State Savings Bank	German Bank for Foreign Trade	Berlin People's Bank;§ Berlin Municipal Bank;§ co-operative banks for farmers and tradesmen
National Savings Bank	Hungarian Foreign Trade Bank	General Banking and Trust Company‡
Popular Savings Bank	Commercial Bank	Polish Guardian Bank;‡ savings and credit co-operatives
State Savings Bank	Romanian Bank of Foreign Trade	
Savings branches of the State Bank of the USSR	Foreign Trade Bank	
Post Office Savings Bank	Yugoslav Bank for Foreign Trade¶	About 50 commercial banks; about 380 social accounting offices

§ Also handles transactions between the GDR and the FRG.
¶ There are 16 other banks with a right to conduct foreign exchange transactions.

Sources. Based on: *Wiadomości Narodowego Banku Polskiego* (Communications of the National Bank of Poland), Warsaw, 3/1969, pp. 109–16, 120–1; and 11/1969, p. 442.

C. THE ROLE OF CREDIT AND INTEREST

Before the reforms, practically all investment was financed by free budgetary allocations even though they were administered by (special 'investment') banks, and although credit for current production and trade was subject to interest charges the rates were very low. Neither type of finance was used by the authorities as a flexible instrument of economic policy. The provision of all types of finance was more or less automatic if the purpose was embodied explicitly or implicitly in the general economic plan, because the latter had a counterpart in a financial plan approved by the legislature at the same time.

Under the new system, bank credits have come to play an active role. The general level of interest rates has been increased and the rates have become highly differentiated according to the purposes of credits, and finance is usually extended on the basis of the equality of the bank and the borrower, i.e. by voluntary contracts. The bank's responsibility is threefold: to refuse credits for purposes of doubtful soundness and contrary to social interest, to encourage enterprises to choose the most effective projects and to ensure – within their capacity – that the selected projects financed are carried out in the most efficient manner. In other words, not so much need but profitability is the main criterion for credit extension. Material incentives to a bank's personnel are partly based on the effectiveness of the bank's lending. Banks now have well-developed research offices and teams of field experts. They offer financial and broader economic advice and participate in the preparation of plans.

In addition to ordinary financing, special credits have been introduced for the modernization of plant, for innovations and for the promotion of technological progress in general. Not only enterprises but also research institutes, design bureaux and experimental stations are entitled to these credits. Banks are expected to pursue, as was stated in the East German ordinance in 1968, 'an active credit policy to strengthen Socialist economic relations and to shape the desired structural developments in the economy'.[1]

---

[1] *Gesetzblatt der DDR* (Law Reports of the GDR), East Berlin, I/9, 1968, p. 223.

The State policy is to use bank credits and the conditions under which they are extended selectively and flexibly, to facilitate and induce structural changes in the economy in favour of the technologically most dynamic industries. Banks also engage in policing deliveries according to the agreed specifications, quality and date, and apply financial penalties when necessary.

Traditionally, the financing of investment on the one hand, and of current production and trade on the other, was separated. Typically, long-term financing was administered in each country by a specialized investment bank, whilst short-term credits were extended mostly by the central bank. The main purpose of this dichotomy was to enable the State strictly to control the size and direction of investment and to prevent transfers of finance within enterprises that might interfere with the planned distribution of resources. Up to the mid-1960s, most investment allocations were free, whilst working capital was subject to very low interest rates. This separation of the two forms of financing still prevails in Hungary, Romania and the USSR, but in the remaining five countries the extension of these two types of credit has been institutionally combined.[1]

The provision of investment and working capital by the same bank has several advantages under the new economic system.

(i) There is a greater concentration of financial resources in one bank, which is highly desirable to counteract the scattering effect of decentralization.

(ii) The extension of credits is based on broader information available to the bank about the competing uses for finance. This facilitates a balanced evaluation of the projects to be financed and is conducive to the optimum overall distribution of resources.

(iii) It is easier for the bank and central authorities to control the application of financial resources. There is evidence

[1] Although in Czechoslovakia there is now an Investment Bank (not to be confused with the former 'Investments Bank', which was concerned with the liquidation of banks) established in 1969. Its function is to finance: (a) investment in the non-productive sphere and (b) centralized new investment in the productive sphere. Most credits are now extended by the general-purpose banks – the Czech Economic Bank, the Slovak General Bank and the Czechoslovak Bank of Commerce (the latter extending short- and long-term credits to promote foreign trade).

indicating that in the case of the institutional separation of the two types of credits, enterprises endeavoured to extract the maximum amount of finance from each bank, taking advantage of bureaucratic inertia and the difficulty of communication inherent in a highly centralized planned economy.[1]

(iv) In a rapidly changing planned economy bottlenecks are likely to appear, with a threat of disruption. The concentration of finance in one bank servicing all the needs of a particular branch (or several branches) of the economy makes the tackling of bottlenecks easier and more effective.

(v) From the point of view of a bank, the system enables a better utilization of the expert personnel and modern equipment which can be equally used to service both investment and circulating credits.

(vi) From the standpoint of the users of credit, it is less time-consuming to deal with one bank which is in a position to cater for all the financial needs of an enterprise or institution.[2]

In addition to the increased role being played by credits for investment, current production and trade purposes, there has been a remarkable growth of consumer credit. Formerly, the authorities did not favour the expansion of this type of credit because they feared that it would excessively increase consumption and furthermore interfere with the planned allocation and utilization of resources. But under the new system economic plans are no longer as tight as before, and at the same time the availability of consumer credit provides powerful support for material incentives to labour. This credit is extended by savings banks and consumer co-operative shops for the repair and construction of dwellings, owned privately and on a co-operative basis, and more importantly in recent years for the purchase of consumer durables. The steady expansion of

[1] This practice was accentuated under the old system when investment allocations were usually interest-free and circulating credits were subject to very low interest rates (see section D of this chapter for further details).

[2] Based on: *Die Einheit* (Unity), East Berlin, 8/1968, pp. 955–65; *Finansi i kredit* (Finance and Credit), Sofia, 5/1969, pp. 3–13; *Finansije* (Finance), Belgrade, 7–8/1969, pp. 357–67; *Pénzügyi szemle* (Financial Review), Budapest, 8–9/1969, pp. 632–8; *Wiadomości Narodowego Banku Polskiego* (Communications of the National Bank of Poland), Warsaw, 11/1969, pp. 439–45.

these credits indicates that the authorities are willing to divert more resources to the production of semi-luxuries and luxuries, which was deliberately neglected in the past. The proportion of consumer goods sold on hire-purchase is about one-tenth; in the less liberal countries (such as Poland and the USSR) the percentage is about 5 per cent, whilst in others (such as Czechoslovakia, Hungary and Yugoslavia) it is about 15 per cent or more.[1]

Consumer credit is also becoming a valuable instrument for regulating demand. The freer operation of the market mechanism under the new system has made consumer demand more changeable and unpredictable, and certainly more fluctuating than supply. As under Socialism much greater significance is attached to market stability, alterations in the terms of hire-purchase offer a useful weapon for ensuring market equilibrium without having to resort to frequent changes in retail prices. A flexible use of consumer credit is compatible with both the market system and central planning. It can be effectively employed as an instrument of 'consumption steering' to overcome shortages and surpluses and also to promote the consumption and production of those goods and services where the economies of scale are the greatest.

Although interest existed under the old system, it was hardly used as an economic lever. Investment finance was normally granted free of any charges. Circulating credits carried only nominal rates of interest, less than 3 per cent a year, the main purpose of which was simply to cover administrative costs. In addition, interest was payable on savings banks deposits (3 per cent or less annually) and on State bonds (5 per cent or less p.a.). Otherwise, interest was ideologically despised as one of the hallmarks of Capitalism and a source of private accumulation. One of the most remarkable developments stemming from the changeover to intensive sources of economic growth has been the fact that interest has been seized upon by the authorities as a powerful weapon for regulating the most effective application of finance. Since the mid-1960s (and in Yugoslavia partly after 1952) the general level of interest rates has been substantially increased to an

[1] Based on: *Acta oeconomica* (Economic Papers), Budapest, vol. 2, no. 1–2, 1967, p. 96; *Durzhaven vestnik* (Official Gazette), Sofia, 30/7/1968, pp. 1–4; *Nova trgovina* (New Trade), Belgrade, 5/1968, pp. 221–5; *Życie gospodarcze* (Economic Life), Warsaw, 23/3/1969, p. 9.

average of about 7 per cent, and the differentiation of the rates has reached the upper limit of 20 per cent p.a. – which is in fact higher than in the bourgeois countries! The interest rates charged on bank credits and payable on deposits in the Socialist countries are set out in Table 19.

The differentiation of interest rates is governed by several criteria. As a rule, the longer the term the higher the rate. But this consideration is very often more than outweighed by the purpose of the credit. The rate on investment loans is in many cases lower than on short-term circulating credits. Furthermore, projects of high social priority may be charged concessional rates, and schemes specifically approved by the council of ministers may be financed interest-free. Credits classified as directly promoting technological progress are extended at preferential rates. For example, in Poland ordinary investment credit carries 3 per cent a year, but modernization credit costs only 1·5 per cent p.a.[1]

Credits for purposes not covered by the economic plan are not necessarily refused now, but may be extended at twice the ordinary rates. In some countries, such as the German Democratic Republic, mark-ups are allowed to be charged above basic rates according to the degree of risk borne by the bank.[2] Particular importance is now attached to the repayment of credits on time. Penalty rates on over-due loans range from 8 per cent in Bulgaria to 20 per cent in Yugoslavia (see Table 19, p. 157); the ceiling rate of 8 per cent in Bulgaria and the USSR is likely to be lifted in the future. Some writers have advocated that the penalty rate under Soviet conditions should be 18 per cent p.a.[3]

So much for the role assigned to credit and interest under the new economic system. However, the effectiveness of these instruments under present Socialist conditions can be easily exaggerated. First of all, credits and interest rates cannot have such a decisive influence on the distribution of resources as is the case in a Capitalist economy. As long as central planning exists, the broad pattern of the allocation of the factors of production is centrally determined in the light of the existing capacities and future needs

[1] *Finanse* (Finance), Warsaw, 7/1969, p. 48.
[2] *Finanse*, 5/1969, p. 66.
[3] I. Levchuk and A. Cheblokov, ('Credit and the Economic Reform'), *Diengi i kredit* (Money and Credit), Moscow, 2/1968, p. 15.

TABLE 19 INTEREST RATES CHARGED AND PAYABLE IN THE
EUROPEAN SOCIALIST COUNTRIES IN 1969
(*Per cent per annum*)

TYPE OF CREDIT OR DEPOSIT	BULGARIA	CZECHOSLOVAKIA	GDR	HUNGARY	POLAND	ROMANIA	USSR	YUGOSLAVIA
Delivery (trade) credit	2	8–12	1·8	8	4	2	1	10*
Credit for seasonal stocks	2	6	3·6	8	4	4	2	10*
Credit for continuous stocks	2	6	3·6	8	4	4	6	10*
Credit for odd purposes	4–8	12	5–12	4–10	4–10	12	7	10*
Penalty rate on circulating credit	8	12	10–12	14–16	12	12	8	20*
Investment credit	2	6	1·8	5–8	3	1	2*	10*
Demand deposits	n.a.	0·5	1	0	0	0	0·5	3*
Time deposits	n.a.	3*	5*	3–7	2–6	0	0·5	8*

n.a. = not available.
* Maximum rate.

Sources. Bank i kredyt (Bank and Credit), Warsaw, 5/1970, pp. 199–200;
Finanse (Finance), Warsaw, 1/1969, p. 52; *Pénzügyi közlöny* (Financial Gazette),
Budapest, 30/12/1968, p. 785; *Socialisticke zemědělství* (Socialist Agriculture),
Prague, 1/11/1968, p. 4;*Vesnik Jugoslavenske Investicione Banke* (Bulletin of the
Yugoslav Investment Bank), Belgrade, no. 146, Feb 1969, p. 9; *Wiadomości
Narodowego Banku Polskiego*, 9/1969, p. 382, and 11/1969, p. 470.

of society, irrespective of current interest rates. It is also accepted as axiomatic that economic development must not be handicapped merely by a lack of finance. If resources are available, credits are provided as a matter of course. As the total amount of credit is planned, the role of interest is in fact largely limited to the shaping of the most effective application of resources at the microeconomic level.

But even the above function is not necessarily efficiently performed, because of substantial differences in the profitability of enterprises. For example, in Czechoslovakia and Hungary in 1968 and 1969 the profits of many enterprises were so high that penalty rates did not deter them from over-borrowing and lagging behind in repayment of due loans. Concessional rates allowed to some branches (e.g. agriculture) or regions (less developed) or specified projects only, produce distorting effects on the distribution of resources, conflicting with the optimization principle.[1] Some financial experts advocate a uniform basic rate of interest for investment and circulating credits and that it should be equal to the capital charge[2] (see Chapter 10 C, pp. 178-9).

In a sense, the highly differentiated interest rates can be looked upon not as an active and ingenious device but rather as a cumbersome method of compensating for the widely differing profitability of different enterprises (including farms) as a consequence of the continued distortions in the Socialist price structures. Finally it must be realized that, owing to the long neglect of banking and finance in the past, Socialist countries lack a sufficiently large pool of suitably qualified and experienced personnel to answer the complex needs of modern business under rapidly changing conditions.

D. SOURCES OF INVESTMENT FINANCE

Finance for investment purposes in Socialist countries is normally derived from three main sources: budgetary grants, enterprises' own accumulated funds and bank credits. Under the old

[1] See, e.g., S. Shteinshleigher, ('Some Problems of the Role of the State Bank of the USSR in the Economy'), *Diengi i kredit*, 8/1968, p. 23.

[2] e.g. P. Yakovlev, ('Some Problems of the Organization of Financing State Capital Investments'), *Finansy SSSR* (Soviet Finance), Moscow, 8/1968, p. 33.

system, interest-free budgetary allocations were the predominant form of financing investment, contributing about two-thirds of the total.[1] Since the mid-1960s (and in Yugoslavia since 1952) this proportion has declined to about one-third, and in some countries to much less.

In Czechoslovakia and Yugoslavia this basis of financing is now exceptional and where it exists it requires the sanction of a top-level authority (usually the council of ministers). Free budgetary grants have in principle been abandoned in Yugoslavia since 1967, but subsidies are still continued (mostly to agriculture, the power industry and transport). In the remaining countries, only State-initiated projects specified in advance in the central plan can be financed in this way. But even in the latter countries, the number of such projects tends to decrease, which is in line with the general trend towards the decentralization and self-financing of enterprises.[2] These grants play the largest role in Romania, Hungary and Bulgaria. To generalize, budgetary grants are resorted to in the following cases:

   (i) the establishment of new enterprises;

  (ii) projects which are too large for the financial resources of ordinary enterprises and branch associations;[3]

 (iii) undertakings which have long periods of recoupment (e.g. in the USSR of over five years);

 (iv) schemes which are of decisive significance in changing the structure of the economy in desired directions;

  (v) industries incurring planned losses or earning very low profits (as in Bulgaria);

 (vi) entities which are not on commercial accounting.

Budgetary grants are normally non-repayable and interest-free.

---

[1] The proportions in the individual countries in 1963 were as follows: Hungary, 75%; Bulgaria, 70%; Czechoslovakia, 68%; Romania, 61%; the USSR, 60%; Poland, 48%; and the GDR, 46%. Based on: *Finanse*, 12/1967, p. 35.

[2] e.g. in Hungary the number of such projects centrally named was 1,200 in 1967, but only 85 in 1968. *Finanse*, 8/1969, p. 65.

[3] e.g. in Hungary, according to the regulations introduced in 1968, investment projects exceeding the following costs in different industries (in forints): in mining, 300m.; in chemical and machine-building industries, 200m.; in light and food-processing industries and in trade, 100m. *Życie gospodarcze*, 25/8/1968, p. 7. At the official basic exchange rate, 100 forints = £3·55 = US $8·51.

But in some countries (e.g. Bulgaria, Czechoslovakia and Hungary) central authorities may use their discretion and specify repayment in part and an appropriate interest rate. This practice is likely to spread in the future.

The most important source of investment finance today lies in enterprises' own funds. As a result of the reforms of producers' prices and a change in the State taxation policies, enterprises are now in a position to accumulate substantial funds of their own. Moreover, they can now retain larger portions of depreciation allowances, they are encouraged to sell surplus fixed assets and they can earn interest (up to 8 per cent p.a.) on their bank deposits.[1] Enterprises' own accumulated funds play the largest role in Yugoslavia, and also in Czechoslovakia, the German Democratic Republic and Poland.

This source of investment finance is used first of all for undertakings on the enterprise's own initiative directed towards increasing enterprise profitability in the manner best known to the local management. Centrally planned investments are also partly or wholly financed from these funds. There is little doubt that this form of financing effectively enhances the enterprises' independence, their financial responsibility and pride, and consequently is more conducive to efficiency than the allocated budgetary grants.

Bank credits, although playing an incomparably greater role now than ever before, represent a supplementary source of finance. The proportion of total investment financed in this way ranges from about 5 per cent in Romania to about 25 per cent in the German Democratic Republic. In Czechoslovakia and Yugoslavia, where enterprises are able to accumulate considerable financial resources in short periods, banking control over investment is less than in Bulgaria, Poland and the USSR. In Romania, only minor centrally laid-down projects and smaller investments undertaken on the enterprises' own initiative are financed by bank credits. In all the eight Socialist countries, bank credits are repayable out of the enterprises' own funds, and the repayment takes precedence over the financing of new ventures.

---

[1] A portion of enterprises' funds may be held by branch associations and in some cases by regional authorities for joint investment undertakings and the most desirable new projects.

TABLE 20 SOURCES OF INVESTMENT FINANCE IN THE EUROPEAN
SOCIALIST COUNTRIES

COUNTRY	Budgetary Grants	Enterprises' Own Accumulated Funds	Bank Credits
Bulgaria	Centrally specified investments and those in deficit-incurring industries	Centrally planned investments and those on the enterprise's own initiative	All types of investments in profitable industries
Czechoslovakia	Exceptional	All types of investments	All types of economically sound investments
GDR	Exceptional	All types of investments	All types of economically sound investments
Hungary	Only centrally named projects	Centrally planned investments and those on the enterprise's own initiative	All types of economically sound investments
Poland	Centrally specified investments	All types of investments	All types of investments
Romania	All new investments centrally determined	Centrally planned and decentralized investments	Minor centrally planned and decentralized investments
USSR	Centralized investments whose period of recoupment exceeds five years	All types of investments	All types of investments
Yugoslavia	Practically non-existent	All types of investments	All types of economically sound investments

Sources. Mostly based on: *Finanse*, 8/1969, p. 71.

The sources of investment finance in each Socialist country under consideration are summarized in Table 20. How the actual proportions compare under the old and the new systems is illustrated by the percentage figures applying to Bulgaria, Hungary and Poland in 1963 and 1968:

	Bulgaria		Hungary		Poland	
	1963	*1968*	*1963*	*1968*	*1963*	*1968*
Budgetary grants	70	43	75	49	48	28
Enterprises' own funds	29	31	24	39	44	52
Bank credits	1	26	1	12	8	20
Total	100	100	100	100	100	100

Sources. *Finanse*, 12/1967, p. 35; *Planovoe khoziaistvo* (Planned Economy), Moscow, 3/1970, p. 74.

In addition to the three usual sources of investment finance, other occasional sources may be briefly mentioned:

(a) *Share Capital.* In most Socialist countries, especially in Czechoslovakia, the German Democratic Republic, Hungary, Poland and Yugoslavia, there are joint-stock companies in which the initial capital was provided by other enterprises, or institutions or even (in Yugoslavia) by private persons. The shareholding entities are usually major suppliers of components, finance or some service and they participate in the management and profits of their 'subsidiary'. Such companies with limited liability are mostly found in foreign trade and manufacturing. In Yugoslavia, private persons can own share capital but they normally have to work in the enterprise concerned, and their dividends cannot exceed current bank interest.[1]

---

[1] Examples of joint-stock companies with limited liability are: Czechoslovakia – Centrotex Ltd (the export and import of textiles and leather goods), Tuzex Ltd (domestic retailing of goods for foreign currencies); the GDR – Isocommerz Ltd (the export and import of radioactive materials and nuclear equipment), Limex Ltd (the training of foreign personnel and students); Hungary – Inter-Co-operation Co. Ltd (agency company for foreign transactions); Poland – Dal Ltd (foreign trade in miscellaneous goods and services).

(b) *Debentures*. This form of raising capital exists in Yugoslavia.
For example, in 1969 Yugoslav Railways floated debentures of 500
and 1,000 dinars, repayable in six years and bearing 6 per cent
p.a. interest, plus free and concession rail tickets and other
prizes.[1] A similar issue was made by the Red Banner Auto-
motive Works and the Slovenijales Furniture Manufacturing
Enterprise.

(c) *Intra-CMEA Investment Credits*. A good deal of credit has
been extended by the more developed or richer CMEA[2] countries
(Czechoslovakia, the German Democratic Republic and the
USSR) to other member nations. To place the extension of multilateral investment credits on a systematic basis, the CMEA
countries (with the exception of Romania) established the International Investment Bank in 1970. The initial capital of the Bank
is 1,000m. transferable roubles, of which 30 per cent is in convertible currencies. Its function is to finance projects, including
joint ventures, which promote specialization and industrial co-
operation amongst member countries. The credits extended are
for medium terms (up to five years) and for long periods (up to
fifteen years).[3]

(d) *Western Capital*. A small flow of investment from the advanced Capitalist countries has begun since the early 1960s with
the growth of joint East–West business undertakings. There is no
legal barrier to Capitalist investors owning assets in Socialist
countries, but the latter insist on owning more than 50 per cent of
the share capital. Western capital has come to play a significant role
in some industries in Yugoslavia, where special legislation was
passed in 1967 and in 1969 to protect Yugoslav interests as well as
foreign investors. At the end of 1969 there were at least 14 joint
Yugoslav–Western undertakings, with total investment capital
amounting to 2,037m. dinars, of which 27 per cent ($43m.) was

---

[1] *Vesnik Jugoslavenske Investicione Banke* (Communications of the Yugoslav
Investment Bank), Belgrade, 4/1969, pp. 5–6.

[2] The Council for Mutual Economic Assistance, also known as 'Comecon'
to which Bulgaria, Czechoslovakia, the GDR, Hungary, Poland, Romania and
the USSR (and Mongolia) belong.

[3] *Ekonomicheskaya gazeta* (Economic Gazette), Moscow, no. 30, July 1970,
p. 20.

foreign capital[1] (for further details of joint East–West business ventures, see Chapter 15 C, pp. 317–22). To facilitate this flow of Western capital to Yugoslavia, the International Investment Corporation was set up in 1969 with the initial capital of $12m. contributed by the International Bank for Reconstruction and Development, the International Finance Corporation, private banks in eight Western countries (Britain, France, the Federal Republic of Germany, Italy, Japan, the Netherlands, Switzerland and the USA) and twelve Yugoslav banks.[2]

[1] V. Dragojević, ('The Growth of Foreign Investments in the Yugoslav Economy'), *Nova trgovina* (New Trade), Belgrade, 1/1970, pp. 12–14.
[2] *The American Review of East–West Trade*, 10/1969, p. 9.

10 Capital Formation and its Efficiency

A. CAPITAL ACCUMULATION AND ECONOMIC GROWTH

SOCIALIST thinking and policy have traditionally been dominated by the postulate of a high level of accumulation.[1] This attitude was particularly strong under centralized planning and management when high proportions of savings were considered to be both necessary and possible. It was generally assumed that high rates of economic growth were feasible only if supported by high and rising investment rates. There was a prevalent conviction that the output of producer goods should grow at a faster rate than that of consumer goods. In other words, it was assumed that economic progress could be achieved only by a growing capital–output ratio. Yet, owing to the Cold War and ideological considerations and pride, Socialist countries (except to a minor extent Yugoslavia) could not obtain economic aid from the developed Capitalist nations.

The need for large accumulation was further accentuated by two developments peculiar to Socialist economies. Firstly, in their accelerated industrialization drive each of these countries chose to develop heavy industries and the sources of raw materials first – the branches of production which are highly capital-absorptive (see Chapter 5 B, pp. 85–7). Secondly, the developmental strategy was based predominantly on extensive sources of growth. Large amounts of capital were essential for the construction of new

---

[1] In Socialist terminology that part of national income (i.e. net material product) not consumed during the year in which it was produced. Disregarding minor exceptions, it assumes the form of fixed assets in the productive and non-productive spheres, net additions to stocks and reserves and the foreign trade balance. It can be calculated by the following formula: $A = Y(1 - cm) - Yn - Sc$ (Y = net material product, cm = consumption rate of the labour force in the material sphere of production, Yn = income of the labour force in the non-productive sphere, Sc = social consumption). The formula is adapted from: B. Minc, *Postęp ekonomiczny* (Economic Progress), Warsaw, PWN, 1967, p. 202.

projects, not only to give employment to the rapidly expanding labour force but also to absorb under-utilized labour released from agriculture and domestic service (see Chapter 2 A, pp. 26–9).

This demand was magnified by the tremendous waste associated with the extravagant use of capital. Projects were often built more for the sake of what may be termed 'conspicuous development' than for their suitability and efficiency (Chapter 2 B, pp. 34–6). Investment decision-making was centralized more than any other segment of the Socialist economy. Investments were usually financed by non-repayable budgetary grants on which no capital charges were made, and interest rates on circulating capital were very low (see section D of this chapter).

The accumulation rate was fixed at the top political level, usually between 20–30 per cent of national income (by the Socialist definition). The official percentages for the eight countries under consideration in selected years are given in Table 21. It must be

TABLE 21 PERCENTAGE OF NATIONAL INCOME DEVOTED TO ACCUMULATION IN SELECTED YEARS*

COUNTRY	1950	1955	1960	1965	1967
Bulgaria	20	21	27	21	33
Czechoslovakia	17	20	18	20	22
GDR†	10	12	18	12	24
Hungary	23	22	25	23	26
Poland	21	23	24	23	27
Romania	18	18	20	25	29
USSR	27	25	27	26	27
Yugoslavia	36‡	35	34	28	21

* At current prices. The Socialist concept of national income is used (net material product at realized prices). The comparability of the figures between the years and especially between the countries is limited.

† Productive investment only.

‡ In 1952.

Sources. Central Statistical Office of Poland, *Rozwój gospodarczy krajów RWPG 1950–1968* (Economic Development of the CMEA Countries 1950–1968), Warsaw, 1969, p. 62; *Ekonomista* (The Economist), Warsaw, no. 6, 1968, p. 1453; *Probleme economice* (Problems of Economics), Bucharest, 3/1970, pp. 83–4; statistical yearbooks of the countries concerned.

pointed out that, owing to the heavy undervaluation of producer goods in relation to consumer goods, real proportions were much higher – particularly before the mid-1960s, when the degree of undervaluation was higher. If Socialist national income figures were brought to the Western basis, the proportion of saving in national income would be closer to 20–40 per cent. The high share of planned saving, considering the low levels of *per capita* income, meant great sacrifices to the public in current consumption. In Capitalist countries, at comparable stages of economic development, the proportion usually falls within the range of 10–25 per cent.

To enforce the planned levels of accumulation, it was essential to limit current consumption through the control of wage funds, heavy turnover taxes, low procurement prices paid by the State to farms for food and agricultural raw materials, more or less compulsory subscriptions to State loans, a strict control of imports of consumer goods and tight restrictions on foreign travel. Not only was the level of accumulation maintained, but it also tended to grow faster than national income. This is demonstrated in Table 22. It will be noted that this disparity was particularly large in the 1950s. This tendency continued in the late 1960s, although it was less pronounced. In fact, in the countries where the foundations for basic industrialization involving capital-intensive industries had been laid down earlier (as in Czechoslovakia and the USSR), the trend appears to be towards an equalization of the two rates.[1]

As with other aspects of Socialistic economics, the traditional thinking and practice relating to accumulation have been subjected to thorough reappraisals in the context of the economic reforms and the requirements of intensive-based growth. Experience showed that depressing current consumption beyond certain levels tended to produce demoralization and alienation amongst workers in the form of absenteeism, a large labour turnover, pilfering in factories and on farms, damaging socialized property and even open riots (as in Berlin in 1953, in Poznan in 1956 and in Gdansk in 1970).

[1] Nevertheless, in each Socialist country over the 1950–69 period there were at least two years when the growth of investment was slower than of national income, usually during economic crises, e.g. in Bulgaria 1956–57; Czechoslovakia 1953–55, 1962–63; Hungary 1950–56, 1964–65; Poland 1954–57, 1963–64; the USSR 1952–53, 1960–62.

The waste associated with excessive accumulation may actually depress rates of economic growth below the levels possible with higher consumption standards. A Czechoslovak economist showed that if over the period 1955–61 Czechoslovakia had relied on predominantly intensive growth stragegy, she would have achieved the same rate of economic growth as she did (5·9 per cent p.a.) with a volume of accumulation 15 per cent lower.[1] The principle rigidly adhered to in the past, that the growth of output of producer goods should be faster than that of the articles of consumption, has been questioned in recent years by both theoreticians and policy-makers (for details, see Chapter 12 B, pp. 219–20).

In the changeover towards predominantly intensive sources of growth, accumulation, particularly investment in the productive sphere, has assumed strategic significance. Both planning and the implementation of investment has been considerably

TABLE 22 AVERAGE ANNUAL RATES OF GROWTH OF INVESTMENT AND NATIONAL INCOME, 1951–1968*

COUNTRY	1951–60		1961–65		1966–68	
	I	NY	I	NY	I	NY
Bulgaria	16	11	9	7	19	9
Czechoslovakia	11	8	2	2	7	9
GDR†	16	10	5	3	9	5
Hungary	7	6	5	4	11	9
Poland	10	8	7	6	9	7
Romania	16	10	11	9	12	7
USSR	13	10	6	7	8	7
Yugoslavia	16	8	15	8	7	5

I = Investment, NY = National Income.
* At constant prices.
† At current prices.

Sources. Based on: *Rozwój gospodarczy krajów RWPG 1950–1968*, op. cit., pp. 44, 46; *Gospodarka planowa* (Planned Economy), Warsaw, 4/1969, pp. 5–6; Federal Institute of Statistics, *Statistički godišnjak Jugoslavije 1969* (Statistical Yearbook of Yugoslavia for 1969), Belgrade, 1969, p. 253.

[1] V. Nachtigal, 'Extensity and Efficiency in Economic Growth in Czechoslovakia', *Czech. Econ. Papers*, no. 9, 1967, p. 45. Also see Chapter 1 D, p. 23, and Chapter 2 B, pp. 34–8.

decentralized,[1] so that enterprises and branch associations now actively participate in planning new developments, are encouraged to use their initiative and pursue the most economical methods of carrying out the projects.

There is a trend away from capital-widening in favour of capital-deepening, i.e. the old preoccupation with sheer size and large numbers of new projects has given way to a greater attention being paid to selective investment in the most efficient industries and those crucial to technological progress. The development is most pronounced in the German Democratic Republic, where about one-half of capital formation in industry has assumed the form of what is now officially called 'intensification investment'.[2]

During the basic industrialization drive 'at any cost', many mistakes were inevitably made and much of the equipment installed was of poor quality, with little concern being displayed for the latest technology and efficiency.[3] As this equipment becomes due for replacement, special attention is now being given to the construction of the most modern plants. It is known that since the late 1950s several Socialist countries have carried out comprehensive surveys of their capital,[4] to determine the extent of obsolescence and replacement needs with a view to rationalization. In this modernization drive, Western technology and even complete imported plants are playing a significant part (for further details see Chapter 15 C, pp. 317–21).

[1] With the exception of Romania, where in the late 1960s over 95% of investment was still financed out of centralized funds. See *Annuarul Statistical Republicii Socialiste România 1969* (Statistical Yearbook of the Romanian Socialist Republic for 1969), Bucharest, 1969, p. 452.

[2] See *Statistisches Jahrbuch der Deutschen Demokratischen Republik 1968* (Statistical Yearbook of the German Democratic Republic for 1968), East Berlin, 1968, p. 18.

[3] Typical of the extensive strategy of economic development was the Socialist approach to reconstruction after the Second World War. In the Western European and Japanese reconstruction programmes, the opportunity was seized to update the layout of factories, equipment and the processes of production. But in the USSR and in other Socialist countries effort was concentrated on recreating pre-war installations so that, as an American economist concluded, 'After the reconstruction (1950), Soviet technology was about at the same level as it was in 1940'. M. Boretsky, 'Comparative Progress in Technology, Productivity and Economic Efficiency: USSR versus USA', in US Congress, Joint Economic Committee, *New Directions in the Soviet Economy*, Washington, GPO, 1966, Part II-A, p. 149.

[4] e.g. in Poland (1959–61), the GDR (1963), Romania (1965), Hungary (1968).

In the foreseeable future, the proportion of national income planned for accumulation is likely to be maintained at the recent high levels of 15–30 per cent of (Socialist) national income. Selective development, associated with intensive growth, implies concentration on the most modern industries, neglected in the past, which require high capital outlays. At the same time, with rising *per capita* incomes, the maintenance of the same proportion of accumulation is a decreasing burden on the population. The proportion will tend to be closer to the higher limit of the range in the less developed countries (such as Bulgaria and Romania) where there are still many gaps in basic industries and in infrastructure, but lower in the more developed economies (especially in Czechoslovakia and Hungary).[1]

B. THE STRUCTURE OF CAPITAL

In this part of the chapter, we shall examine the distribution of accumulation between productive and non-productive investment and between fixed and circulating assets. We shall also consider the problem of the technical structure of capital, and in general the relevance of extensive and intensive approaches to economic development.

(a) Productive and Non-productive Investment

Under the Socialist growth strategy, productive investment is given preferential treatment by authorities because it directly contributes to the growth of material production.[2] The share of this

---

[1] e.g. in the Romanian 1971–75 five-year plan, the proportion of accumulation is scheduled to be 28–30% to support the planned annual rate of increase in national income of 8%. In the Czechoslovak perspective plan for 1971–80, 17–18% of national income is to be reserved for accumulation to support the average annual rate of economic growth of 6·5%. Reported in: *România libera* (Free Romania), Bucharest, 21/6/1969, pp. 1, 3; *Gospodarka planowa* (Planned Economy), Warsaw, 12/1968, p. 50.

[2] Non-productive investment is that directed to the 'non-productive' sphere (roughly corresponding to service industries in Western national income accounting), viz. commerce (except buildings) and sales promotion, banking and insurance, education, science, culture and church, health, sport, entertainment, public administration (including local government) and defence.

type of investment in the European Socialist countries in the past averaged three-quarters, ranging from 55 to 85 per cent of total investment, compared with the 30–60 per cent typical of Capitalist countries.

If we examine the Socialist investment patterns, two significant conclusions emerge. First, in the five to ten years immediately following the Communist takeover, the proportion of productive investment tended to be lower. In each country, these periods coincided with post-war reconstruction, and also with large defence programmes owing to tense relations with the leading Capitalist powers. The regimes found it morally binding and politically expedient to provide all the most basic amenities and opportunities (health, education, housing, etc.) to protect the welfare of the poorest masses. But then the proportion tended to rise slowly. The second worth-while observation is that the highest shares of productive investment have been exhibited in the less developed countries, viz. in Bulgaria and Romania, whilst the lowest proportions have been recorded in such countries as Czechoslovakia, the German Democratic Republic and the USSR.

Economic reforms have produced two conflicting effects. On the one hand, to promote intensive growth it is advisable to channel investment into the most productive industries away from the non-productive sphere. On the other hand, intensive growth also presupposes rapidly rising labour productivity. On this score, it is highly desirable to divert more investment resources to the non-productive sphere in order to make increasingly better provisions for education, research, housing, shopping, passenger transport, entertainment, etc. (for further details, see Chapter 11 D, pp. 210–11). On balance, some Socialist economists believe that it is possible that in the higher stages of economic development a rising rate of growth of non-productive investment may be just as effective in the future as the rising rate of productive investment was in the past.[1]

[1] W. Iskra, ('Investment and the Economic Development of the East European Countries'), *Ekonomista* (The Economist), Warsaw, no. 6, 1967, p. 1462.

(b) Fixed and Circulating Assets

Under Socialist economic planning in the past, the authorities endeavoured to channel as much capital into fixed assets as possible and to reduce reserves and the stocks of circulating capital to the minimum.[1] In the 1950s, the authorities aimed to keep down the level of circulating assets in the economy to about one-quarter of total productive assets, but since the early 1960s the proportion has tended to increase.[2]

The size of circulating assets is related to economic development in several ways. Socialist economists essentially view such assets as tied resources reducing effective supply, and if excessive they tend to reduce the rate of economic growth. It can be expected that, under tight centralized planning, reserves and stocks can be kept to a bare minimum, although in reality planners' ambitions may be partly defeated by enterprises resorting to hoarding. With a greater role assigned to the market, the need for reserves and stocks is naturally greater. The unusually large (absolute and relative) increase in circulating assets since the early 1960s in all the Socialist countries under consideration can be partly explained on these grounds. To this extent they are not necessarily wasteful, as they may forestall the bottlenecks with which Socialist economies had been frequently plagued before.

However, it appears that a considerable portion of the increases in stocks is wasteful and causing serious concern to the authorities.[3] This unhealthy trend bears evidence of two ills still inherent in

---

[1] In Socialist practice a distinction between these two concepts is considered significant. Reserves are passive, and include only those goods which are held as an insurance against unexpected contingencies, whilst stocks consist of raw materials, semi-finished and final products held in the normal course of production and distribution.

[2] The increase was fastest, at least up to the late 1960s, in Yugoslavia, where by 1968 circulating assest reached 65% of total assets, or 14% of national income. See *Ekonomist*, Zagreb, 2/1969, p. 50.

[3] To illustrate, in Hungary between 1962 and 1969 the size of stocks increased from 8,000m. to 15,000m. forints, or from 4·9 to 6·5% of national income. In Poland the actual (and planned in brackets) stocks as percentages of national income for the years between 1961 and 1968 were as follows: in 1962 – actual, 5·1 (planned, 5·6); in 1963 – 7·4 (4·2); in 1964 – 7·6 (5·2); in 1965 – 8·3 (5·9); in 1966 – 8·4 (6·1); and in 1967 – 6·2 (5·3). *Pénzügyi szemle* (Financial Review), Budapest, 7/1969, p. 569; *Wiadomości Narodowego Banku Polskiego* (Communications of the National Bank of Poland), Warsaw, 7/1969, p. 273.

Socialist economies. Enterprises are caught between what may be described as the 'scissors of transition'. On the one hand, as buyers of raw materials and components, enterprises are still largely confronted with seller's markets, and consequently are taking recourse to hoarding and much more so now than before because they have greater freedom. On the other, the enterprises are facing developing buyers' markets for their finished products (see Chapter 12 D, pp. 230–2, for details), with the consequent growth of unsaleable stocks.

(c) The Technical Structure of Capital

The most important portion of capital from the standpoint of technological progress, the quality of production and the potential for rapidly rising productivity is that consisting of machinery, machine tools and other implements directly used in productive processes. This portion of capital is regarded as 'active' capital or 'working equipment', in contrast to buildings (in the productive sphere, of course), usually described as 'passive capital'. The relation between the two types of assets is referred to in Socialist literature as the 'technical structure of capital'.

Compared with Western countries, the Socialist economies were noted in the past, and still are, for the high proportions of building and construction in their total productive investment. According to a comparative study of the pig-iron industry carried out in Poland, this proportion in some of the leading Socialist and Capitalist countries was as follows (averages over the period 1953–65):[1]

USSR	65%
Poland	50%
Yugoslavia	35%
USA	35%
UK	15%

[1] M. Syrek, *Wpływ substytucyjnego i niezależnego postępu technicznego na wydajność pracy* (The Influence of Capital-Using and Neutral Technical Progress on the Productivity of Labour), Katowice, Śląsk, 1967, p. 152.

Taking the eight Socialist countries as a whole, it appears that before the reforms the proportion was about one-half.

Three explanations can be given for this fact. First, for a variety of reasons, a high proportion of buildings in total productive capital is typical of economies in the early stages of industrialization, and before the economic reforms Socialist countries were in that stage in comparison with advanced Capitalist nations.[1] Second, the two largest Socialist countries under consideration (Poland and the USSR), owing to severe climatic conditions, have to make extra provisions for more solid and a larger number of buildings (including extra storage facilities) and have to bear higher maintenance outlays than is necessary in most Western countries.

However, the most important explanation lies elsewhere, viz. in the extensive approach to economic development which prevailed in the past.[2] The investment process was highly centralized and largely divorced from the conduct of current production. Enterprises had little influence on, and interest in choosing, the most economical and effective internal composition of the project. Moreover, most investment allocations to enterprises were free anyway.

Planners made extravagant provisions for space per worker, large halls for meetings, impressive frontages, excessive external additions and embellishments and extensive storages, depots and courtyards. Political leaders, who were usually better communists than economists, and to whom popularity with the masses mattered more than economic common sense, favoured imposing projects for propaganda purposes. This attitude was further nourished by the widely accepted philosophy according to which the archi-

---

[1] e.g. in the USA the ratio of outlays on buildings to outlays on working equipment decreased from 3·0 over the period 1869–98 to 1·8 during 1899–1928 and to 0·8 by 1950. R. A. Gordon, 'Investment Opportunities in the United States before and after World War II', in *The Business Cycle in the Post-War World*, Proceedings of the International Economic Association, ed. E. Lundberg, London, Macmillan, 1955, p. 291.

[2] For Socialist support of this interpretation of the unfavourable technical structure of capital under the old system, see, e.g., Gy. Cukor, 'Long term Planning and Technical Progress', *Acta oeconomica* (Economic Papers), Budapest, vol. 4, no. 3, 1969, pp. 239–58, esp. p. 251; E. Rychlewski, ('The Technical Structure of the Capital–Output Ratio'), *Ekonomista*, no. 3, 1968, pp. 639–76, esp. pp. 663, 671–4.

tectural expression of the Socialist society – which had no palaces for capitalists – inevitably had to find its outlet in 'palaces of work'.

The adverse effects of this practice on efficiency became obvious to some economists long ago, but its full significance has been appreciated only in the context of intensive growth. The drive towards increasing the share and effectiveness of working equipment has become one of the essential elements of the new system. The former enthusiasm for building 'work palaces' has been abandoned in favour of investment efficiency, where the size of the site, the planning of buildings and the location of working equipment within plants are subject to objective evaluation.

The accent is on modernization, continued rationalization and working efficiency. Greater attention is given to the improvement of the quality of materials and designs used in building and in the construction of machinery, which should lead to a reduction of outlays on buildings and foundations.[1] A slow improvement is already evident and this trend, no doubt, will continue in the future as Socialist countries advance to higher and higher stages of economic development.[2]

[1] According to Soviet estimates made in the early 1960s, mechanization and the use of prefabricated building materials to the extent practised in the West could reduce construction costs in the USSR by 30–40%. A Czechoslovak economist estimated in 1969 that the weight of buildings in tons per square metre in Czechoslovakia would decline from 0·43–0·66 in 1969 to 0·30–0·57 'in the next few years'. N. A. Cagalow (ed.), *Wykład ekonomii politycznej* (Textbook of Political Economy), Warsaw, KiW, 1965, vol. II, p. 390; M. Bláha, ('Construction and the Materials Base'), *Plánované hospodářství* (Planned Economy), Prague, 12/1969, p. 5.

[2] The percentage of productive investment channelled to working equipment and other working assets increased between 1959 and 1968 as follows: in Bulgaria, from 30 to 42%; in Poland, from 35 to 40%; in Romania (working equipment only), from 32 to 36%; in the USSR, from 27 to 32%. However, in the GDR the proportion remained constant, at 52%, and in three countries it declined: in Czechoslovakia, from 34 to 31%; in Hungary, from 40 to 38%; and in Yugoslavia, from 38 to 28%. In Czechoslovakia the ratio of working equipment to output is planned to rise (from 0·98 in 1955) to 1·33 in 1975 and to 1·79 by 1985. Based on: Central Statistical Office of Poland, *Rozwój gospodarczy krajów PWPG 1950–1968* (Economic Development of the CMEA Countries 1950–1968), Warsaw, 1969, p. 65; Federal Institute of Statistics, *Statistički godišnjak Jugoslavije 1969* (Statistical Yearbook of Yugoslavia for 1969), Belgrade, 1969, p. 117; *Czechoslovak Economic Papers*, Prague, no. 10, 1968, p. 78.

G

C. CAPITAL CHARGES

Up to the mid-1960s (up to the early 1950s in Yugoslavia), capital allocated to enterprises for investment was not only free (non-repayable) but also there was no annual charge for its use. Although such capital was subject to depreciation charges, the rates were low and they did not apply until the project or the piece of equipment was actually in use.

The opposition to capital charges was essentially ideological in nature and was based on the following thinking. First, they were looked upon as a form of surplus value accruing to a non-labour factor of production. Second, it was feared that they would induce enterprises to substitute labour for capital, and thus impede mechanization, automation and economic progress in general. However, the disadvantages of this largesse became too obvious to be ignored. As capital costs to enterprises were negligible and material incentives to the personnel were not affected, enterprises incessantly pressed for the largest possible allocations. This practice resulted in hoarding and idle capacity in some enterprises and in shortages in others, with the consequent waste.

To prevent that waste, after periods of experiment, all European Socialist countries except Romania (and Albania) have introduced capital charges – Yugoslavia as early as 1953, whilst the remaining countries did so between 1963 and 1967. The charge levied represents a percentage of the value of the enterprise's assets and the amount is calculated for each quarter, the payment being made to the State budget. The most common rate ranges from 3 per cent (in Bulgaria) to 6 per cent p.a. (in the German Democratic Republic and the USSR). In most countries both fixed and circulating capital are now subject to the charge, but in Poland only fixed assets are liable to it. In most countries the initial (undepreciated) value of the assets is taken as the basis of valuation. The details of the charges in the individual countries are presented in Table 23.

Although the common rate in each country appears uniform, in reality there is considerable differentiation in the form of total exemption from the charge, concessional rates, and in some countries (in the German Democratic Republic and the USSR) excess rates applicable to some industries. As a rule, agriculture, fishing, transport as well as the non-productive sphere are exempt from the charge. In addition, in Czechoslovakia no charge applies to the equipment installed to counteract pollution and in the German Democratic Republic to rescue facilities even if provided by enterprises. Concessional rates often apply to mining, construction, local

TABLE 23 CAPITAL CHARGES IN THE EUROPEAN SOCIALIST COUNTRIES

COUNTRY	Year of Introduction	Usual Annual Rate*	Type of Capital Subject to Charges†
Bulgaria	1964	3‡	Gross value of fixed§ and circulating assets in industry
Czechoslovakia	1966	5¶	Net value of fixed and circulating assets in industry
GDR	1964	6	Gross value of fixed and circulating assets in industry and trade
Hungary	1964	5	Gross value of fixed§ and circulating assets in the non-agricultural branches of the productive sphere
Poland	1966	5	Gross value of fixed assets in industry
USSR	1966	6	Gross value of fixed and circulating assets in industry
Yugoslavia‖	1953	4	Net value of fixed and circulating assets in non-agricultural branches

* For other rates of capital charges, see the text, pp. 176–8.
† Gross value = initial (replacement) value; net value = current (depreciated) value.
‡ Up to 1/1/1969 the rate varied from 1 to 6.
§ Including land.
¶ Up to 1/1/1970 the rate on fixed assets was 6 and on circulating assets 2.
‖ It is planned to discontinue capital charges from the early 1970s.

Source. Based on daily and periodical publications of the countries concerned.

handicraft industries and trade.[1] The concessions may also take the form of a postponement of the date from which the charge is applicable to the acquired assets. As a rule, no charge is levied on fixed (and in Bulgaria also on circulating) capital if financed by bank credits until they are repaid.[2] Productive assets purchased out of enterprises' own liquid resources are also exempt in some countries (for two years in the USSR and for five years in Czechoslovakia). On the other hand, in some countries (as in Bulgaria and Hungary) private plots of land are also subject to capital charges.[3]

There is little doubt that capital charges have become an important instrument for promoting intensive growth. Once profit is accepted as the criterion of enterprise performance and material incentives to the personnel are linked to it, enterprises are interested in reducing costs and selecting those projects promising maximum returns. Capital charges discourage enterprises from making extravagant demands for capital for ill-conceived schemes and at the same time induce them to choose only such undertakings as will yield annual returns in excess of capital charges. Enterprises are also encouraged to dispose of the assets they do not need. The effectiveness of capital charges is further reinforced by the fairly high interest rates offered by banks on deposits. This policy is most actively pursued in Czechoslovakia and Hungary. Thus in Hungary, where the capital charge is 5 per cent and the deposit

[1] Thus in Bulgaria, the common capital charge of 3% applies to industry, but in construction the rate is 2% and in the small local handicraft industry it is only 1%, with no charges applying to the rest of the economy (as yet). In the GDR since 1968 trade is also subject to capital charges ranging from 1% (in catering) to 8% (for some establishments in food distribution).

[2] An interesting loophole appears to have been discovered by enterprises for evading capital charges, particularly in those countries where bank interest is lower than the capital charge (cf. Tables 19 and 23, pp. 157 and 177). As capital charges are based on the net value of the assets (minus bank credits) at the end of each quarter or month, enterprises have found it expedient to borrow funds from the bank just before the end of the period in question and to repay the loan a few days later at the beginning of the next period. To close this loophole, Hungary passed a law in 1969 whereby 'mortaged' assets are also subject to capital charges (i.e. in addition to the interest on the bank loan), and apparently other countries have also tightened the regulations.

[3] Based on: *Bank i kredyt* (Bank and Credit), Warsaw, 2/1970, p. 68; *Ekonomista*, no. 6, 1969, pp. 1385–8; *Pénzügyi szemle*, 2/1970, p. 89; *Planovoe khoziaistvo* (Planned Economy), Moscow, 3/1970, p. 73; *Voprosy ekonomiki* (Problems of Economics), Moscow, 8/1968, p. 110; *Wiadomości Narodowego Banku Polskiego*, 10/1969, pp. 426–7.

rate 7 per cent, it is in the enterprises' interest to select investment ventures promising more than 7 per cent annual return (i.e. gross profitability of at least 12 per cent annually).

It would be far from the truth to assume that the operation of capital charges is ideal under the conditions prevalent in Socialist countries at present. The differentiation of the rates of charges – a crude attempt to compensate for the distorted price structures – can be criticized on similar grounds to the excessively differentiated interest rates (see Chapter 9 C, pp. 156–8), i.e. it hinders the optimum distribution and utilization of capital resources. The uniformity of capital charges is regarded by the Council for Mutual Economic Assistance as a necessary element for evolving comparable and rational price structures in member countries and in turn a necessary condition for the complete economic integration of the grouping. However, there is little chance of this objective being attained in the foreseeable future.

Some Socialist economists, whilst rejecting the present basis of differentiation (i.e. as between different industries), advocate differentiation between 'passive' and 'working' capital – a lower rate for the latter to improve the technical structure of capital[1] (see section B of this chapter, pp. 173–5). Some economists believe that the present rates of charges are too low to produce the desired results.[2] Others maintain that the charges can be effective only if they are deducted not from the enterprise's general receipts or profits but directly from the material incentives fund, especially from that portion which is earmarked for the management personnel.[3]

It seems that in the long run capital charges will disappear. As accumulation is likely to continue at high levels, capital will become more and more abundant – not unlike the Keynesian 'euthanasia of capitalists'. Furthermore, under the new system –

---

[1] e.g. Romana Stala, ('Capital Charges on Fixed Assets'), *Wiad. Nar. Banku Pol.*, 1/1969, p. 20.

[2] This argument is put forward even in the USSR, where present capital charges are higher (up to 9% p.a.) than in other Socialist countries. See, e.g., V. Gribov, ('Important Reserves for the Increase in the Effectiveness of the Distribution of Working Assets'), *Diengi i kredit* (Money and Credit), Moscow, 6/1968, p. 22.

[3] S. Shvarts, ('The Economic Reform and the Problem of Credit Relations'), *Diengi i kredit*, 9/1968, p. 10.

with the extension of the self-financing of enterprises, better management training and accumulated experience – management and financial responsibility are likely to improve. Under such conditions, if there is still a need for capital charges, they could be embodied in suitably designed scales of depreciation charges. Capital charges are scheduled to be discontinued in Yugoslavia in the early 1970s, and a similar possibility is envisaged in other Socialist countries in the future.[1]

D. THE EFFICIENCY OF INVESTMENT

In the earlier stages of industrialization in Socialist countries, the problem of the efficiency of investment was largely neglected. The main directions of investment were decided at the political level, and the centralized planned development by stages left little choice in the selection of main projects. The missed gains from priority and extensively conceived investment schemes were not apparent to Socialist leaders because according to orthodox Marxist thinking, which is opposed to the concept of scarcity and marginalism, the principle of diminishing returns did not apply in a Socialist economy.

The investment field is still subject to State intervention more than any other sphere of the Socialist economy. But the central authorities now concentrate on the long-run macroeconomic effectiveness of investment, i.e. on the major proportions between different branches and regions of the economy, and particularly on those developmental needs which are strategic to technological progress. Otherwise the microeconomic details of planning and construction of investment projects are left to enterprises, branch associations and banks.

Investment efficiency studies had been carried out in all the eight Socialist countries for many years before the economic reforms,[2] but the demands of intensive growth under the new

[1] See, e.g., M. Breiev, ('Theoretical Problems of Perspective Planning'), *Planovoe khoziaistvo* (Planned Economy), Moscow, 3/1969, pp. 61–9.

[2] See, e.g., the following studies available in English: G. R. Feiwel, *Soviet Quest for Economic Efficiency*, New York, Praeger, 1967, esp. pp. 163–73, 382; H. Fiszel, *Investment Efficiency in a Socialist Economy*, Oxford, Pergamon,

system place special responsibilities on the selection and implementation of investment undertakings. Socialist economies have reached those stages of economic development where on the one hand the number of alternatives for investment has been multiplying rapidly, and on the other – seemingly paradoxically – optimization requirements in fact narrow down the choice to the most efficient pattern.

To assist in the selection of the most effective investment undertakings at the planning level, Socialist economists have developed a number of formulae in which, to generalize, investment costs are related to investment effects. These formulae, or indexes of investment efficiency, were at first quite crude, but in the last decade or so the complexity of the indexes and the degree of sophistication in the measurement of costs and effects have greatly increased. As one would expect, there are considerable national differences of approach, and methodological studies are still in the process of evolution. In the following discussion, we shall outline the main indexes embodying the common principles involved in the evaluation of investment projects under Socialist conditions.

In planning the modernization of production, an index is used to determine whether the proposed more capital-intensive project is more economical than the existing one with high operating costs, assuming the same flow of production. This is done by calculating the period of recoupment, i.e. the time during which the additional investment outlay is recovered from the annual savings brought about by lower operating costs:

$$T = \frac{I_2 - I_1}{C_1 - C_2};$$

T = time of recoupment;
I_1 = investment outlay incurred on the existing plant;
I_2 = investment outlay on the proposed project;
C_1 = annual operating cost of the existing plant;
C_2 = annual operating cost of the proposed project.

1966; D. Granick, *Soviet Metal-Fabricating and Economic Development*, Univ. of Wisconsin P., 1967, esp. pp. 127–38, 171–206; M. Rakowski (ed.), *Efficiency of Investment in a Socialist Economy*, Oxford, Pergamon, 1966.

The shorter the period of recoupment, *ceteris paribus*, the more preferable is the proposed project. If the period of useful life of the proposed project exceeds the time of recoupment T, the contemplated modernization is economical. The degree of efficiency is indicated by annual savings in operating costs $(C_1 - C_2)$ multiplied by the period of the excess life of the project.

If modernization necessitates the dismantling of the old plant, the costs involved must be reflected in the formula. Thus the index assumes the following form:

$$T = \frac{iP_1}{W} \cdot \frac{P_2}{P_2 - P_1};$$

i = average coefficient of capital intensity in the branch of the economy;

P_1 = average productivity of labour in the old plant;

P_2 = average productivity of labour in the proposed project;

W = average annual wage in the branch of the economy.[1]

The authorities, of course, can alter the normative periods of recoupment. This weapon of investment policy is in a way equivalent to the rate of interest in Capitalist countries, and it has a bearing on the composition of growth. If the period is increased from five to ten years (equivalent to a reduction of the interest rate from 20 to 10 per cent p.a.), more investment projects will qualify for acceptance, and mechanization will be promoted rather than labour-intensive projects. On the other hand, if the period is reduced from five to four years (amounting to a rise in the interest rate from 20 to 25 per cent), more labour-intensive undertakings will become eligible for implementation, and consequently the growth of production will be attained more via increases in employment.[2]

---

[1] Using this formula, the normative periods of recoupment T in years, as calculated by the Institute for Economic Research attached to the Polish State Planning Commission, for selected industries in Poland are (valid up to 1975); fuel mining, 30·8; electric power, 14·9; the smelting of non-ferrous metals, 9·0; ferrous metallurgy, 5·8; food processing, 3·6; the textile industry, 2·3; the chemical industry, 1·8; machine-building, 0·8. The average for the economy is 6·0 years. Based on: R. Chwieduk *et al.*, *Ekonomia polityczna* (Political Economy), Warsaw, PWN, 1966, vol. II, pp. 259–64.

[2] B. Miszewski, *Postęp ekonomiczny w gospodarce przemysłowej* (Economic Progress in an Industrial Country), Warsaw, PWE, 1968, pp. 214–16.

To ensure the overall optimum allocation of investment, it is necessary to carry out the evaluation of the contemplated projects, so as to select those which are most effective. This is done by applying the formula for investment efficiency:

$$Ie = \frac{\frac{1}{T}I + C}{V}$$

Ie = index of investment efficiency;

T = time (in years) for the recoupment of the investment outlay; it is either fixed as a uniform number of years for the whole economy (e.g. six years in Poland) or differentiated according to industries (e.g. three to ten years in the USSR);

I = investment outlay;

C = annual production cost of operating the project during its useful life; either prime cost (as in Poland) or total cost (as in the USSR) may be taken into account;

V = annual value, or volume, of production during the lifetime of the project.

The implementation of an investment project involves not only direct outlays on materials, equipment and wages but also an indirect cost to society during the period of construction when resources are idle from the production standpoint. This 'freeze' period differs, of course, according to the size of the project and the type of industry. Moreover, operating costs as well as the capacity for production may vary during the lifetime of the completed project. To take account of these qualifications, a synthetic index of investment efficiency has been developed:

$$sIe = \frac{\frac{1}{T}I(1 + d \cdot f) + Cn \cdot vc}{Vn \cdot vp}$$

sIe = synthetic index of investment efficiency;

d = coefficient of discount indicating annual losses caused to the economy during the period of construction of the investment undertaking; it is usually fixed for the whole economy (e.g. in Hungary it is 0·20 and in Poland 0·16);

f = the freeze period, i.e. the number of years necessary to complete the investment project;

$Cn =$ total cost of exploitation of the project including maintenance and repairs during the whole period n;

$vc =$ coefficient of cost variation during the period of exploitation;

$Vn =$ total value of production in the entire period n;

$vp =$ coefficient of production variation during the period of exploitation.

The coefficients are either constants for the whole economy, or otherwise can be established from special tables prepared by the State Planning Commission.[1]

For a long time land was regarded in Socialist countries as having no value, as it was not a product of labour, and thus land's contribution to production was not treated as a cost. Consequently, the size and quality of land were disregarded in the evaluation of investment efficiency. This practice led not only to the extravagant occupation of land for investment projects, but also distorted the efficiency calculation. The omission of land made the initial effectiveness of the investment outlay appear unduly high, because the increase in production seemed to be due only to this outlay, as if there were no contribution from land. Then, additional investment outlays on labour and capital appeared to lead to disproportionately low increments to production in the project in question.

This only exaggerated the extensive approach to investment, because new projects on other land promised higher returns on paper. Furthermore, if land is not assigned value (according to location, fertility, physiography, etc.), the substitution of the factors of production is devoid of economic rationality. To overcome this weakness, the price of land (L) is included, and the formula so obtained is known as the index of the total synthetic investment efficiency:

$$tsIe = \frac{\frac{1}{T}(I + L)(1 + d \cdot f) + Cn \cdot vc}{Vn \cdot vp}.$$

[1] The State Planning Commission of Poland, *Instrukcja ogólna w sprawie metodyki badań ekonomicznej efektywności inwestycji* (General Instruction Concerning the Methodology of the Evaluation of the Economic Efficiency of Investment), Warsaw, PWE, 1962, pp. 30–5, 60–107; B. Miszewski, op. cit., pp. 214–27.

Although methods of the valuation of land differ widely, all the eight Socialist countries now at least partly take land into account in their evaluation of investment efficiency.[1]

The efficiency of investment depends not only on the selection of the comparatively most effective projects at the planning stage but also on their most economical implementation, i.e. the shortest possible period of construction and the lowest possible material and labour outlays. One of the features associated with the extensive approach to economic development was a strong tendency to exceed planned construction periods. This was largely due to the poor preparation and documentation of the designs,[2] the scattering of investment resources on too many new undertakings, and at the same time to the weakness of material incentives to the personnel. Excessive periods of construction prolong the freezing of resources, enhance obsolescence in the days of rapid technological change, lead to bottlenecks with magnifying effects, and consequently depress the rate of economic growth. Similarly, capital equipment was bulkier and heavier than necessary and little care was

[1] Thus in Hungary, when a census of the capital stock was carried out (in 1968), urban land was also included and valued at 100–500 forints per sq. metre (100m.–500m. forints per hectare). In the case of new investment projects, urban land has to be purchased, and in addition a capital charge of 5% (as in the case of man-made capital) of the purchase price is levied annually. If agricultural land is taken over for non-agricultural purposes, compensation has to be paid to titleholders on the basis of cadastral records (preserved from pre-Communist times) ranging from 80,000 to 100,000 forints per hectare. In Poland, where most land (85%) is still privately owned, if the State takes over urban sites for building purposes it pays compensation of up to 40 złotys per sq. m. (400,000 złotys per hectare). Market prices of land have been regularly quoted for years now in official statistics; for example, in 1966 regional variations of agricultural land ranged from 16,000 to 42,000 złotys per hectare. See M. Loiter, ('Problems of Raising the Effectiveness of Capital Investment in the CMEA Countries'), *Vop. ekon.*, 1/1970, p. 139; Central Statistical Office of Poland, *Rocznik statystyczny 1966* (Statistical Yearbook 1966), Warsaw, 1967, p. 252.

[2] e.g. a study of the Polish iron and steel industry over the period 1961–65 revealed that one-third of the investment projects was based on 'intuition' and 'guesswork', one-third was partly documented and no more than one-third was properly worked out and supported by documentation. In the case of the Warszawa Iron and Steel Works, the planned construction period was three years, but the actual period was seven years, and it took an additional four years of testing to bring the project to its full production capacity. Taking the Polish economy as a whole, the proportion of investment projects completed on time in different years was: in 1964, 80%; in 1965, 77%; in 1966, 77%; in 1967, 87%. M. Syrek, op. cit., pp. 153–5; *Finanse* (Finance), Warsaw, 1/1969, p. 56. See also Chapter 2 B, note 1, p. 35.

exercised in the use of materials, so that material costs were excessively high compared with those in Western countries.[1]

In recent years several steps have been taken to eliminate, or at least to reduce, these forms of inefficiency. The emphasis is on the concentration of investment outlays on a smaller number of new projects, and the modernization of existing capacities is regarded as equally important. Efforts are made to ensure a better territorial co-ordination of investment to avoid a duplication of facilities where enterprises are under different ministries, in which branch associations and regional authorities now play a prominent part. Thorough preparation of designs and documentation is promoted by special material incentives and penalties to the personnel in design offices. The enterprises undertaking investment projects have a direct stake in keeping construction costs and periods to a minimum because their profitability is increased thereby. Their interest is further strengthened by concessional and penalty interest rates applied by banks.[2]

There are also bonuses payable to construction enterprises for the efficient execution of projects.[3] Similarly, bonuses are payable to the enterprises which produce equipment for economizing on materials and components, and particularly for reducing the size and weight where practicable. To prod the enterprises into putting

[1] To illustrate, as recently reported, Polish machine tools and equipment were 10–20% heavier than the corresponding items in the West. The weight per unit of power of near-identical automated turning machines were (in kilogrammes per kW): Polish, 480; Swedish, 417; West German, 350. In the machine-building industry 25% of crude metal was wasted in the process of production, compared with 10–20% in Western countries and 10% in Japan. *Ekonomista*, no. 3, 1968, p. 663; *Nowe drogi* (New Paths), Warsaw, 8/1969, p. 140.

[2] Thus in Poland, where the basic interest rate on investment credit is 3%, if the project is completed on time the interest rate on the investment credit is reduced by 0·3%, if planned costs are not exceeded the interest rate is also reduced by 0·3%, and if both are not exceeded, by an additional 0·4%, i.e. by 1·0% in all. On the other hand, if the period of credit is exceeded, the penalty rate rises to 6%, and if extra credits are applied for in order to finance the cost above the planned level the rate charged rises up to 9%. *Finanse*, 7/1969, pp. 48–9, and 4/1970, p. 34.

[3] e.g. in the USSR bonuses are payable for the work carried out according to the plan. Moreover, if the period of construction is reduced below the norm specified by 10%, the bonus fund is increased by 10%; if the construction period is reduced by 30%, the bonus fund rises by 50%. In the case of design offices, if blueprints are completed ahead of schedule the incentive fund is now raised by 5% (previously by 2·5%). *Ekonomicheskaya gazeta* (Economic Gazette), Moscow, no. 3, Jan 1970, p. 9.

the project into full operation immediately, capital charges now generally apply as soon as construction is completed. Some economists would like to go further, and advocate the application of capital charges from the planned date of completion (not the actual date, if the latter is later than the former).[1]

In addition to the drive to increase the efficiency of investment in each Socialist country, there have been renewed efforts in recent years to promote the rationalization of investment policies on a wider, international, scale, especially under the guidance of the Council for Mutual Economic Assistance. Up to 1956, when autarkic national policies prevailed, CMEA's role was almost wholly limited to the co-ordination of trade. However, since that time increasing attention has been given to the economic integration of the grouping along five lines relevant to the efficiency of investment. First, agreements have been initiated on specialization with a view to eliminating the duplication of capital equipment and the consequent surplus capacities in member countries. To place this form of co-operation on a systematic basis, over a dozen specialized Permanent (or 'Standing') Commissions have been established for the most important branches of the economy.[2] Specialization is now pursued along agreed lines in more than twenty branches of manufacturing industries alone.

Second, since 1958 this form of co-operation has been further strengthened by the co-ordination of national economic plans. Third, since 1962 steps have been taken specifically to co-ordinate long-term investment plans. Fourth, this co-ordination has been facilitated by a consistent policy of standardization of equipment and parts since the early 1960s. In 1962 the member countries established the Permanent Commission for Standardization (with

---

[1] J. Trendota, ('Directions for the Further Perfection of the Financial System in Industry'), *Finanse*, 7/1969, pp. 27–8.

[2] Agriculture (in 1956, with its headquarters in Sofia), Coal (1956, Warsaw), Electric Power (1956, Moscow), Oil and Gas (1956, Bucharest), Ferrous Metals (1956, Moscow), Non-ferrous Metallurgy (1956, Budapest), Engineering (1956, Prague), Chemicals (1956, East Berlin), Light Industries (1958, Prague), Food Industries (1958, Prague), Building and Construction (1958, East Berlin), Transport (1958, Warsaw), the Peaceful Utilization of Nuclear Energy (1960, Moscow), Radio and Electronics (1963, Budapest). In addition, there are seven other Permanent Commissions concerned with other, more general aspects of co-operation.

its headquarters in East Berlin) and the Institute for Standardization (head office in Moscow) in the following year.

But the most obvious example of the economizing of investment resources is represented by the jointly established and operated schemes. The most important joint undertakings of this type are:

   (i) the Arkhangelsk Paper and Cellulose Corporation (Bulgaria–USSR);

  (ii) the Common Freight Railcar Pool (Bulgaria–Czechoslovakia–GDR–Hungary–Poland–Romania–USSR);

 (iii) the Friendship Oil Pipeline (Czechoslovakia–GDR–Hungary–Poland–USSR);

 (iv) the Haldex Coal Extraction Corporation (Hungary–Poland);

  (v) the Intermetal Iron and Steel Community (Bulgaria–Czechoslovakia–GDR–Hungary–Poland–USSR);

 (vi) the Kingisep Potash Works in the USSR (Bulgaria–Czechoslovakia–GDR–Hungary–Poland–USSR);

(vii) the Komi Timber Exploitation Corporation in the USSR (Bulgaria–USSR);

(viii) the Peace Electric Grid (Czechoslovakia–GDR–Hungary–Poland–USSR).

11 Structural Developments

A. INTER-BRANCH AND INTRA-BRANCH STRUCTURAL CHANGES

As is well known, the Socialist economies have undergone far-reaching structural changes in the last two decades. The statistical evidence of these changes can be found in the distribution of the working population amongst the different branches of the economy, the contribution of different branches of the economy to national income in different years and the comparative rates of growth of different industries.

If we take the eight Socialist countries as a whole, the proportions of the working population engaged in the different branches of the economy in 1950, 1960 and 1967 were as follows:

	1950	1960	1967
Industry	20	25	29
Construction	4	6	7
Agriculture and forestry	50	40	31
Transport and communications	6	6	7
Trade and other productive services	7	8	9
Non-productive services	13	15	17
	100	100	100

The rapid transformation of these countries from predominantly agricultural to semi-industrialized economies is evident. The details for individual countries are presented in Table 24. It will be noted that there are still considerable differences in the degree of industrialization attained by each country, largely reflecting the stage of economic development inherited from pre-Communist regimes.

It must be realized that the employment figures for industry

TABLE 24 PERCENTAGE DISTRIBUTION OF WORKING POPU-
LATION ACCORDING TO THE MAIN BRANCHES OF THE ECONOMY,
1950, 1960 AND 1967

COUNTRY	YEAR	Industry*	Construction	Agriculture†	Transport‡	Other§
Bulgaria	1950	11	4	73	2	10
	1960	22	5	55	4	14
	1967	28	7	43	2	20
Czechoslovakia	1950	30	6	39	5	20
	1960	37	8	20	6	29
	1967	39	8	18	7	28
GDR	1950	39	6	23	7	25
	1960	42	6	16	7	29
	1967	42	6	15	7	30
Hungary	1950	20	3	51	4	22
	1960	28	6	38	6	22
	1967	33	7	29	6	25
Poland	1950	19	4	57	4	16
	1960	22	6	47	5	20
	1967	24	6	42	5	23
Romania	1950	12	2	74	1	11
	1960	15	5	65	3	12
	1967	20	7	54	4	15
USSR	1950	22	4	46	7	21
	1960	25	6	39	7	23
	1967	29	7	30	8	26
Yugoslavia¶	1953	8	3	67	2	20
	1961	14	4	57	3	22
	1967	19	5	48	4	24

* Includes manufacturing, mining, quarrying and crude processing of
primary products.
  † Including forestry.
  ‡ Including communications.
  § Includes trade, other productive branches and the non-productive sphere.
  ¶ Data for the whole economy (as distinct from the socialized sector) are
available only for census years (1953, 1961). Figures for 1967 are the author's
estimates.

Sources. Central Statistical Office of Poland, *Rozwój gospodarczy krajów RWPG 1950–1968* (Economic Development of the CMEA Countries 1950–1968), Warsaw, 1969, p. 56; Federal Institute of Statistics, *Statistički godišnjak Jugoslavije 1969* (Statistical Yearbook of Yugoslavia for 1969), Belgrade, 1969, p. 84.

understate its overall growth. The production capacity and output in this branch of the economy usually rise faster than the labour force employed in it, owing to the relatively more generous allocation of investment to industry than (particularly) to agriculture and trade. Thus the proportions of total investment directed to these three branches of the economy in the European member countries of the Council for Mutual Economic Assistance (CMEA) over the period 1960–67 were as follows (the proportions of the labour force employed are stated in brackets):[1]

	Industry	Agriculture	Trade
Bulgaria	48 (25)	23 (50)	3 (5)
Czechoslovakia	44 (38)	14 (19)	2 (9)
GDR	55 (42)	8 (15)	3 (11)
Hungary	39 (30)	16 (33)	3 (8)
Poland	41 (23)	15 (44)	3 (7)
Romania	47 (18)	20 (60)	2 (4)
USSR	35 (27)	17 (34)	3 (9)

Structural changes can normally be represented more reliably by the contribution of different branches of the economy to national income. In Socialist national accounts these changes are partly distorted and obscured. Firstly, the contribution of different branches is not valued at factor cost but at realized prices. In this valuation, the share of industry is exaggerated whilst that of agriculture is understated[2] (see also Chapter 1 C, p. 141).

[1] Based on: *Rozwój gospodarczy krajów RWPG 1950–1968*, op. cit., pp. 56, 63, and statistical yearbooks of the countries concerned.
[2] To take the example of the USSR, according to the official valuation the contribution of industry to the gross social product in 1964 was 64·1% and of agriculture 16·4%. If Soviet national income accounts are brought to the Western basis, viz. the gross national product at factor cost, then the contributions of the selected branches of the economy were in the same year as follows (comparative figures are also given for the United Kingdom and the United States):

Secondly, the distortion has not been uniform. In general, the undervaluation of agricultural production in relation to industrial production was lower in the late 1960s than it was in the 1950s, owing to substantial increases in the prices of agricultural products and the declining role of turnover taxes (see Chapter 12 C, pp. 224–5). Consequently, the growth of industry and the relative decline of agriculture are not fully reflected in the official production figures. Thirdly, Socialist national income figures omit the contribution of the non-productive sphere, yet the state of development of the services usually closely reflects the stage of economic development.

Nevertheless, if we bear these qualifications in mind, Socialist figures are still of value in revealing general trends at least. Table 25 represents the contribution of the main branches of the productive sphere to national income in the eight Socialist countries in selected years.

It is widely held by Socialist economists and political leaders that a relative decline of primary production in favour of a faster expansion of industrial production is indicative of economic progress, and according to Table 25 this applies to most of the Socialist countries. However, it will be noted that, by the official Socialist valuation, the share of industrial production in the USSR actually declined from 57 to 51 per cent between 1950 and 1969. Soviet leaders like to use this statistical evidence as proof that the USSR is prepared to sacrifice her industrial development for the sake of assisting the industrialization of the 'fraternal' CMEA

	Industry	Agriculture	Services	Other	TOTAL GNP
USSR	33·9	25·2	16·5	24·4	100·0
UK	40·1	3·7	29·7	26·5	100·0
USA	32·3	4·1	36·0	27·6	100·0

Based on: Central Statistical Office of the Council of Ministers of the USSR, *Narodnoe khoziaistvo SSSR 1964* (The National Economy of the USSR in 1964), Moscow, 1965, p. 67; S. H. Cohn, 'Soviet Growth Retardation . . .', in US Congress, Joint Economic Committee, *New Directions in the Soviet Economy*, Washington, GPO, 1966, Part II-A, p. 110. For the composition of the GNP of Bulgaria, Czechoslovakia, the GDR, Hungary and Poland in 1960, see M. Ernst, 'Postwar Economic Growth in Eastern Europe . . .', in *New Directions in the Soviet Economy*, Part VI, p. 878.

countries, i.e. she is increasingly engaged in producing cheap raw materials for them and at the same time is willing to provide an expanding market for their high-priced manufactures.[1]

However, Soviet protestations of beneficence cannot be accepted at face value without circumspection. The Soviet kindliness can also be interpreted as a desire to make the CMEA countries dependent on Soviet supplies and markets. Besides, as an independent study by S. H. Cohn indicated, if uniform valuation is applied on the Western basis, between 1950 and 1964 the share of industrial production in the Soviet GNP actually increased from 22·3 to 33·9 per cent and that of agricultural production declined from 35·1 to 25·2 per cent.[2]

Within industry the fastest expansion has been recorded in heavy industry and chemicals. This is brought out in Table 26. Thus production in the metals and the machine-building industry over the period 1950–67 was rising nearly twice as fast as in the food-processing industry.

The structural changes in the Socialist economies, even those before the reforms, can be interpreted as a process contributing to intensive economic growth. They produce intensive effects to the extent of increased productivity brought about by shifts of resources from the less to the more efficient branches of the economy. Structural changes caused by new resources, such as net investment and school leavers, directed to the branches of higher than average productivity in the economy, also contribute to intensive growth.

One of the consequences of the economic reforms is a new approach to structural developments. The structural changes which took place in the Socialist economies under the old system were mostly those between the major branches of the economy. These changes are likely to continue in the future. But the new attitude is much more sophisticated, the focus of attention being rather on intra-branch developments.

[1] e.g. I. Dudinskii, ('Some Problems of Fuel and Other Raw Materials in the CMEA Countries and the Ways of Overcoming Them'), *Voprosy ekonomiki* (Problems of Economics), Moscow, 4/1966, pp. 84–94; O. Bogomolov, ('An Important Stage in the Co-operation Amongst CMEA Countries'), *Kommunist*, Moscow, 18/1966, pp. 13–24.

[2] S. H. Cohn, loc. cit.

TABLE 25 CONTRIBUTION OF THE MAJOR BRANCHES OF THE
ECONOMY TO NATIONAL INCOME, 1950, 1960 AND 1969*
(In Value Percentages)†

COUNTRY	YEAR	INDUSTRY‡	CONSTRUCTION	AGRICULTURE§	TRANSPORT¶	TRADE	OTHER PRODUCTIVE BRANCHES
Bulgaria	1950	37	7	42	2	8	4
	1960	46	7	32	4	9	3
	1969	46	8	30	5	8	3
Czechoslovakia	1950	62	9	16	3	8	2
	1960	63	11	15	3	6	2
	1969	62	12	12	4	8	3
GDR	1950	56	5	12	6	19	1
	1960	65	6	10	5	13	1
	1969	59	8	14	5	12	2
Hungary	1950	49	7	25	4	n.a.	15‖
	1960	58	11	22	4	4	1
	1969	57	10	21	5	6	1
Poland	1950	37	8	40	n.a.	n.a.	15**
	1960	47	9	26	6	9	3
	1969	49	9	21	6	10	5
Romania	1950	43	6	28	6	12	5
	1960	42	9	35	5	6	3
	1969	51	9	28	6	5	2
USSR	1950	57	6	22	4	7	5
	1960	52	10	21	5	7	5
	1969	51	9	23	6	6	5
Yugoslavia	1950	38	8	35	6	9	5
	1960	43	6	27	6	11	6
	1967	49	7	20	6	12	5

n.a. = not available.
* National income produced in the material sphere.

† At current prices, except Poland where constant prices of 1961 were used. The percentages may not add up to 100 owing to rounding. The figures are based on official valuation at realized prices whereby, compared with Western valuation, industrial production is overstated and agricultural production understated. The comparability of the figures between years and especially between countries is limited.

‡ In addition to manufacturing it also includes mining, quarrying and the crude treatment of primary products.

§ Including forestry in the GDR, Romania and Yugoslavia. Elsewhere forestry is included under 'Other Productive Branches'.

¶ Including communications.

‖ Including trade.

** Including transport and trade.

Sources. Rozwój gospodarczy krajów RWPG 1950–1968, op. cit., p. 61; *Statistički godišnjak Jugoslavije 1963*, p. 109, and *1969*, p. 107; *Życie gospodarcze* (Economic Life), Warsaw, 31/5/1970, p. 10.

This new approach is now known as 'structural policy'. It is pursued in the most systematic manner in the German Democratic Republic, which of all Socialist countries has to rely most on intensive sources for growth. Its significance and content were clearly described by an East German economist:

In the context of the scientific and technical revolution, structural policy is acquiring increasing importance. A proper

TABLE 26 AVERAGE ANNUAL RATES OF GROWTH OF PRODUCTION ACCORDING TO THE MAIN BRANCHES OF INDUSTRY IN THE CMEA COUNTRIES, 1951–1967*

INDUSTRY	1951–55	1956–60	1961–65	1966–67	1951–1967
Metals and machine-building	17·3	14·4	11·8	11·8	14·2
Chemicals	17·0	11·8	13·0	11·8	13·7
Food processing	9·9	7·7	6·3	6·3	7·9
Industry as a whole	13·6	10·1	8·3	8·9	10·5
National income	10·7	8·3	6·1	7·5	8·2

* The countries included are: Bulgaria, Czechoslovakia, the GDR, Hungary, Mongolia, Poland, Romania and the USSR. The figures are based on official national statistics.

Source. Rozwój gospodarczy krajów RWPG 1950–1968, op. cit., p. 4.

appreciation and implementation of this policy has become a question of survival for Socialism . . .. It consists chiefly in the development of those products and technologies which exert a revolutionizing effect on the methods of production, and which decisively shape the structure of production up to world standards.[1]

The link between the structural transformation of the economy and the scientific and technical revolution was stressed by a Soviet economist:

> The introduction of new methods and technologies and of new types of products inevitably leads to changes in the structure of production, the emergence of new branches of industry and the acceleration of the rates of growth of some industries and a decline in others.[2]

The emphasis is on the development of research, specialization in production, industrial co-operation, standardization and, above all, on the improvement of quality and efficiency. Although planning and management are still essentially continued on the branch basis (economic ministries), they are now increasingly supplemented and even dominated by 'propulsive developmental drives' laid down by the Council of Ministers and the State Planning Commission. In the German Democratic Republic there are now sixteen key spheres enjoying priority treatment, viz. electronics, electronic data-processing equipment, scientific apparatus, automation, the technology of production, the higher stages of petrochemical processing, light metals, containerized transport, atomic power stations, and others.[3]

The implementation of structural policy is promoted mostly by a flexible use of financial instruments, such as quality price markups, interest rates, depreciation rates, taxes and subsidies. They

[1] L. Teuben, ('Planning of Structural Developments of the Economy'), *Die Wirtschaft* (The Economy), East Berlin, 8/5/1968, Supplement, p. 3.

[2] S. Kheinman, ('Scientific and Technical Revolution and Structural Changes in the Soviet Economy'), *Kommunist*, 14/1969, p. 64.

[3] K. Steinitz, ('The Development of the Structure of Production as a Decisive Factor in Economic Growth'), *Wirtschaftswissenschaft* (Economic Science), East Berlin, 8/1968, pp. 1233–47; H. Kriedemann, G. Langendorf and H. Nick, ('The Shaping of the Modern Economic Structure and the Role of the Socialist State'), *Wirtschaftswissenschaft*, 2/1969, pp. 181–90.

are all highly differentiated to induce the production of desirable items known as 'structural products' and to discourage obsolete lines. However, in some countries, especially in the German Democratic Republic, Poland and Romania, the authorities believe that direct intervention from above is still essential, in addition to financial incentives and disincentives, to ensure swift major structural changes.

B. THE PROBLEM OF INDUSTRIAL INTEGRATION

Although the processes of industrial integration were present under the old system, the economic reforms of the 1960s have widened the scope and pace of all three forms of integration – vertical, horizontal and territorial. There has been a marked trend towards the combination of several stages of production in one enterprise, illustrating backward integration in some cases and forward integration in others. Thus in Czechoslovakia, Hungary and Poland a number of concerns in the machine-building industry have taken over mining enterprises. In the German Democratic Republic and in Hungary, the enterprises engaged in the production of chemicals and of machine tools have been taking over smaller enterprises and workshops producing relevant components.

In all the countries under consideration, there is a growing number of enterprises which produce consumer goods opening factory shops to retail their products. Similarly, in all these countries, except the USSR, many enterprises producing for export have either taken over the foreign trade corporation concerned with the procurement of the necessary imports and the marketing of their products, or have developed specialized departments of their own for the purpose.

Of the three forms of industrial consolidation, vertical integration fitted best into the old system of hierarchical and directive planning and management based on the branch-of-industry organization. There was a temporary tendency towards disintegration in those countries which had changed over to the regional basis, as was the case in the USSR (1957–65) and in the German

Democratic Republic (1961–65). On the other hand, the new system has made horizontal and territorial integration much easier owing to decentralization and the official policy of encouraging enterprises to establish direct horizontal links with other enterprises in whatever industry they may be.

Consequently there has been a wave of amalgamations of the enterprises producing related articles or using similar processes. This trend has been most noticeable in the industries producing chemicals, processed foodstuffs, clothing and consumer durables. Many enterprises in the same area, although under different ministries, are similarly being consolidated into larger units. In this process, the intermediate level of economic administration is playing a vital role – branch associations and economic councils in the USSR, industrial associations in the German Democratic Republic and Poland, industrial trusts in Czechoslovakia, economic associations in Bulgaria, the German Democratic Republic and Yugoslavia, and industrial centrals in Romania.

The most far-reaching integration effect is produced by the Romanian centrals which have come into existence since 1967. Each central is almost an independent economic unit formed by the amalgamation or a loose association of several enterprises to form a larger operational or management unit. A central conducts research, co-ordinates investment, arranges for supplies, markets the output and holds the accumulated funds on behalf of the member enterprises. Industrial centrals are now regarded as the most dynamic element in the Romanian industrial structure.[1]

In the drive towards the improvement of the quality and efficiency of production through the structural transformation of the economy, integration yields many obvious benefits. In many industries, especially in those most instrumental to technological progress, large capital outlays and complex processes are involved. If the production of such goods is carried on in large enterprises, society can benefit from the economies of scale, deriving from a better utilization of expensive capital equipment, management talent and expert advice, and a greater specialization. Larger entities are in

[1] G. Popescu, ('The Industrial Central – A Lever for Increasing Economic Performance'), *Finanţe şi credit* (Finance and Credit), Bucharest, 5/1969, pp. 17–26.

a better position to undertake research and engage in innovation.[1]

Integration also facilitates a concentration of finance, which is of considerable advantage under the new system relying heavily on self-financing. It also promotes a better technical structure of capital (see Chapter 10 B, pp. 173–5), because in larger integrated enterprises economies can be achieved in passive capital (buildings) and more sophisticated working equipment can be provided instead. Integrated entities are less subject to disruptions which otherwise may be caused by the discontinuity of supplies from outside. They are also in a better position to utilize by-products as well as off-season labour, which is of considerable importance in agro-industrial *kombinats* (see section C of this chapter, p. 206).

However, experience has shown that industrial integration is not without defects. There are several indications that the degree of concentration in some European Socialist countries is higher than in the mature Capitalist economies. Thus in Bulgaria (valued at constant prices), the proportion of enterprises in possession of more than 3m. leva's worth of fixed assets in industry was only 5 per cent in the early 1950s, but in the late 1960s the proportion in this category rose to 19 per cent.[2] In Hungary the proportion of industrial labour working in enterprises employing 1,000 workers or more is 50 per cent, compared with 40 per cent in the Federal Republic of Germany, 35 per cent in Great Britain and only 32 per cent in the USA.[3] In the electrical engineering industry in the late 1960s, the proportion of enterprises employing less than 100 persons was 10 per cent in Poland, 28 per cent in the German Democratic Republic but as much as 38 per cent in France. On the other hand, the proportions of large enterprises with more than 1,000 workers in the same countries were 21 per cent, 15 per cent and 3 per cent respectively.[4] In Yugoslavia, in spite of rapid

---

[1] According to a Soviet economist, under the conditions prevailing in Socialist countries, the optimum annual size of output for an enterprise producing trucks was 15,000–20,000 units in the 1950s, 100,000 units in the early 1960s and the present optimum number is 200,000 trucks a year. Y. Medvedkov, ('The Scientific and Technical Revolution and Economic Co-operation Amongst the CMEA Countries'), *Mirovaya ekonomika i mezhdunarodnye otnosheniya* (World Economy and International Relations), Moscow, 12/1969, p. 33.

[2] *Ikonomicheski misul* (Economic Thought), Sofia, 3–4/1969, p. 6.

[3] *Acta oeconomica* (Economic Papers), Budapest, vol. 4, no. 1, 1969, p. 8.

[4] *Życie gospodarcze* (Economic Life), Warsaw, 7/1/1968, p. 9.

industrialization the number of enterprises over the period 1959–68 was reduced from over 25,000 to less than 14,000, so that the typical size of an enterprise more than doubled.[1] Curiously enough, in the USSR, the Socialist country most noted for gigantomania, industrial integration has not been advanced yet as far as is generally believed.[2]

The concentration of production in fewer and larger enterprises tends to eliminate competition and to strengthen monopolistic elements in Socialist economies. This danger is now very real because – in contrast to the centralized directive system before the reforms – enterprises enjoy considerable independence and are often in a position to restrict output and even fix their own prices. The abuses of monopoly power have become most apparent in Czechoslovakia, Hungary and Yugoslavia. Where prices are subject to strict controls, as is mostly the case in the remaining five Socialist countries, monopolistic enterprises turn out low-quality, mass-produced goods, taking advantage of their privileged position and the prevailing sellers' markets.[3] Moreover, the integrated concerns, in an endeavour to rationalize their production, often tend to produce a smaller range of articles than did the previously independent smaller enterprises considered as a whole. And yet, further economic progress necessitates a greater and steadily rising variety of both consumer and producer goods.[4]

It is widely believed in several Socialist countries that industrial

---

[1] *Privredni pregled* (Business Review), Belgrade, 8/12/1969, p. 13.

[2] This question was discussed in a recent article in *Pravda* (9/2/1970, p. 2) where it was pointed out that there were still too many small enterprises in Soviet industry. It was revealed that one-half of Soviet enterprises employed 200 workers or less, and three-quarters of the enterprises 500 workers or less. However, one-quarter of the enterprises employing more than 500 workers each produced 75% of the total industrial output.

[3] For examples of recent evidence, see: *Ekonomicheskaya gazeta* (Economic Gazette), Moscow, 27/1969, p. 9; *Figyelö* (Economic Observer), Budapest, 20/8/1969, p. 4; *Hospodářské noviny* (Economic News), Prague, 13/6/1969, p. 4; *Neues Deutschland* (New Germany), East Berlin, 1/7/1969, p. 3; *Nova trgovina* (*New Trade*), Belgrade, 4/1969, pp. 177–80; *Życie gospodarcze*, 4/2/1968, p. 2.

[4] e.g. the USSR, after the USA, has the largest heavy industry in the world, producing over 100m. tons of steel annually (and according to the current plan the USSR is to catch up with the USA in steel output by 1975). Yet in 1965 Soviet industry produced only 900 sections of rolled products compared with several thousands in the USA (and in Western Europe). S. Kheinman, ('Towards a Consistent Policy in the Field of Technological Progress'), *Kommunist*, 2/1967, p. 50.

integration has gone too far. Instead, some economists advocate greater specialization amongst independent enterprises, stronger and more varied links amongst different entities based on agreements enforceable by stricter penalties for the unsatisfactory fulfilment of contracts. Some go even further, arguing for moderate industrial disintegration, at least in some industries.[1]

It is likely that in the near future, whilst industrial integration continues in some spheres, industrial disintegration may set in in others. Such processes are typical of mature Capitalist economies in higher stages of development than the present Socialist countries.

C. CHANGES IN AGRICULTURE

As was shown in section A of this chapter (pp. 189–90), in 1950 agriculture in the eight Socialist countries as a group absorbed as much of the working population as all other branches of the economy combined, but by 1960 the proportion fell to 40 per cent and today it is less than 30 per cent. However, even the German Democratic Republic (with 15 per cent) and Czechoslovakia (18 per cent) are still behind the most advanced Capitalist countries.[2]

The economic reforms have produced two conflicting effects on employment in agriculture. On the one hand, the increased prices of agricultural products (see Chapter 5 B, pp. 85–6), the relaxation of restrictions on private farming, the extension of some social services to farmers and the lightened burden of taxation, have all substantially raised agricultural incomes. In the 1950s, average earnings in agriculture were only about two-thirds of those in industry, but by 1970 the level rose to about four-fifths.[3]

---

[1] e.g. M. Jagodziński, ('The Scientific and Technical Revolution and Central Planning'), *Gospodarka planowa* (Planned Economy), Warsaw, 8/1969, p. 32.

[2] The proportion in the late 1960s was: UK, 3%; Belgium, 5%; USA, 5%; Australia, 9%; Netherlands, 10%; Federal Republic of Germany, 10%; Sweden, 12%. However, the proportions in Socialist countries are quite respectable compared with such Western countries as: Portugal, 40%; Greece, 50%; and Turkey, 70%. Based on: International Labour Office, *Year Book of Labour Statistics 1969*, Geneva, 1969.

[3] For details, see V. P. Gruzinov, *Materialnoe stimulirovaniye truda v stranakh Sotsializma* (Material Incentives to Labour in Socialist Countries), Moscow, Mysl, 1968, p. 239; *Acta oeconomica*, vol. 2, no. 4, 1967, pp. 345–62; *Novo vreme* (New Times), Sofia, 8/1969, p. 16; *Rozwój gospodarczy krajów RWPG 1950–1968*, op. cit., p. 128.

This, together with improvements in amenities in rural areas (housing, electricity, entertainment) and the tendency to combine industrial production with agricultural pursuits (see below), has exerted some restraining influence on the 'drift to the cities'.

On the other hand, the authorities realize that, in the interest of intensive economic growth, it is highly desirable to continue transfers of rural labour to the more efficient branches of the economy. Even by present pricing, agriculture is still less efficient than most other productive branches (see Chapter 8 C, p. 139). On the whole, larger proportions of investment are now allowed to agriculture,[1] and the consequent improvements and mechanization tend to release more labour than in the past.[2] A greater freedom to leave rural employment and substantial improvements in urban housing are making the rural exodus less difficult than in the past.

On balance, it is pretty certain that the relative decline of agricultural employment will continue at high rates in most Socialist countries in the near future at least. This will mostly take place not so much by physical shifts of the labour force to other branches but rather through a higher rate of retirement than of replacement in agriculture.[3] According to a recent projection, the number of agricultural workers per 100 hectares of cultivated land in the CMEA

[1] Taking the region as a whole, the proportion of investment channelled to agriculture – as judged by official statistics – rose from an average of 15% in the 1950s to 17% in the late 1960s, even though the share of agricultural production in national income declined from about 25 to 20%.

[2] Between 1959 and 1968 in the European CMEA countries as a whole, the number of combines increased from 620,000 to 770,000, drills from 870,000 to 1,150,000 and calculational tractors (reduced to 15 h.p.) from 2,400,000 to 4,400,000. During the same period, the amount of arable land per calculational tractor fell from 120 to 60 hectares. Based on: *Rozwój gospodarczy krajów RWPG 1950–1968*, op. cit., pp. 102–3.

[3] e.g. in Poland between 1960 and 1969 the proportion of persons engaged in agriculture aged 60 years and over increased from 16 to 25%, and of those between 20 and 34 years dropped from 27 to 20%. The decline in agricultural employment is expected to be in the future as follows: 1970–75, by 0·6% annually; 1975–85, by 1·2% annually; and over the period 1985–2000, by 2·0% a year. M. Krukowski, ('The Most Important Tasks: Rational Proportions in the Economy and the Growth of Labour Productivity'), *Życie gosp.*, 21/9/1970, p. 9; W. Herer, ('The Choice between the Rate of Fall in Agricultural Employment and the Rate of Increase in the Industrial Work Force'), *Ekonomista* (The Economist), Warsaw, no. 2, 1970, p. 300.

region will decline from 14 in 1970 to 8 by 1980 (the number in 1960 was 20).[1]

The socialization of most farming, i.e. the transformation of private holdings into large State and collective farms, had been achieved in most European Socialist countries by 1960 (in the USSR by the mid-1930s). Yugoslavia and Poland represent interesting exceptions. In the former country, the peak of socialization was reached in 1951 (when 22 per cent of farming land was socialized) and in the latter in 1955 (with 23 per cent of farming land in the socialized sector).[2] However, since that time a part of that land has been de-socialized, so that today as much as 85 per cent of farming land in these countries is privately owned. Another interesting development in Socialist agriculture since the late 1950s has been the growth of personal plots cultivated by collective farmers and also by non-agricultural households. These plots now represent up to 10 per cent of the cultivated land. The distribution of agricultural land in each Socialist country in selected years is shown in Table 27.

In fact, the role of private and personal farming in agricultural production has become much greater under the new system than the area occupied would suggest. In the case of individual farming (private farms and personal plots), relatively little land is used in combination with a large amount of labour, animal manure and artificial fertilizers. As a rule only the most productive crops and livestock are selected – vegetables, fruit, potatoes, dairy cows, pigs and poultry. Even in the USSR, individual farming – occupying less than 2 per cent of agricultural land – has come to contribute about 20 per cent of total agricultural production, and as much as 70 per cent of eggs, 60 per cent of potatoes and 40 per cent of vegetables, milk and meat. These proportions are higher in other Socialist countries. Thus individual farms contribute 60 per cent of agricultural output in Hungary and over 90 per cent in Poland and in Yugoslavia.[3] The proportion of livestock raised privately

[1] W. Herer, op. cit., p. 301.

[2] B. Strużek, *Rolnictwo europejskich krajów socjalistycznych* (Agriculture in the European Socialist Countries), Warsaw, LSW, 1963, p. 125; *Rocznik statystyczny 1960* (Statistical Yearbook for 1960), Warsaw, 1960, p. 191.

[3] M. Pohorille (ed.), *Ekonomia polityczna socjalizmu* (Political Economy of Socialism), Warsaw, PWE, 1968, p. 737; *Acta oeconomica*, vol. 2, no. 4, 1967, p. 349.

TABLE 27 PERCENTAGE DISTRIBUTION OF AGRICULTURAL LAND
ACCORDING TO THE TYPE OF HOLDERS, 1950, 1960 AND 1967

COUNTRY	YEAR	State Farms	Collective Farms	Private Farms	Personal Plots
Bulgaria	1950	n.a.	42·7*	n.a.	3·9*
	1960	10·9	79·9	1·1	8·1
	1967	19·5	69·7	0·5	10·3
Czechoslovakia	1950	13·0	14·4	69·2	1·0
	1960	20·3	63·1	11·7	4·8
	1967	29·6	55·8	9·7	4·1
GDR	1950	5·7	—	94·3†	—
	1960	8·0	73·2	7·6†	11·2
	1967	7·9	76·3	6·0†	9·8
Hungary	1950	13·5	3·6	82·5	0·2
	1960	19·3	48·6	24·6	7·5
	1967	15·7	68·3	5·7	10·3
Poland	1950	9·6	0·8	89·6	—
	1960	11·8	1·1	86·9	0·2
	1967	13·5	1·1	84·7	0·1
Romania	1950	21·5	1·9	76·4	0·2
	1960	29·4	50·2	18·1	2·3
	1967	30·2	54·4	8·8	6·6
USSR	1950	16·9	80·7	0·5	1·7
	1960	42·2	56·4	—	1·4
	1967	58·1	40·4	—	1·5
Yugoslavia	1951	—— 22 ——		—— 78 ——	
	1960	—— 14 ——		—— 86 ——	
	1967	9·0	7·0	—— 84 ——	

n.a. = not available.
* In 1955.
† Including private plots cultivated by non-agricultural workers.

Sources. Based on: *Rozwój gospodarczy krajów RWPG 1950–1968*, op. cit., p. 84;
Gospodarka planowa, 6/1969, p. 27; *Statistički godišnjak Jugoslavije 1968*, p. 132.

has recently been in individual countries as follows: Poland, 85 per cent; Yugoslavia, 85 per cent; Hungary, 51 per cent; Romania, 50 per cent; Bulgaria, 45 per cent; the German Democratic Republic, 39 per cent; the USSR, 29 per cent; and Czechoslovakia, 20 per cent.[1]

On the other hand, State and collective farms mostly limit themselves to grains, industrial crops and pastoral activities – as is typical of extensive farming. This function has been accentuated to some extent by the continued consolidation of farms in the socialized sector into larger units.[2] Thus it can be seen that private farms and personal plots are playing an important part in the intensification of agriculture and in intensive economic growth in general.

The intensification of agriculture is further promoted now by financial incentives which have largely replaced directive administrative methods. Compulsory deliveries to the State at artificially low prices have been virtually abolished in all these countries except Poland.[3] Instead, the contract system has been adopted, whereby price incentives play a key role in stimulating production and deliveries. The level of agricultural prices in relation to industrial prices has been considerably raised, not only by large increases in the former but also by some reductions in the latter. There has been a remarkable liberalization of credits available to both socialized entities and private farms and personal plot holders.

Financial incentives are playing a strategic part in what has come to be known as the 'commercialization and industrialization of agriculture'. Large proportions of food products are now sold by farmers directly to private consumers at free-market prices, and

---

[1] *Gospodarka planowa*, 6/1969, p. 26.

[2] e.g. between the late 1950s and the late 1960s in Bulgaria the average size of collective farms rose from 850 to 3,850 hectares and of State farms from 1,100 to 4,150 hectares. During the same period in the USSR the average collective farm increased from 4,500 to 6,100 hectares and the average State farm from 5,000 to 7,000 hectares (1 hectare = 2·47 acres). *Życie gosp.*, 17/11/1968, p. 7; *Narodnoe khoziaistvo SSSR 1960*, pp. 492, 508, and *Nar. khoz. SSSR 1968*, pp. 423, 436.

[3] But even in Poland the quotas have been drastically reduced. Although peasants receive lower prices for compulsory than for contractual deliveries, the difference is not absorbed by the State but paid to the 'agricultural circles' (associations of private farms) for the common benefit of the member farms.

even State and collective farms can now sell their produce directly to restaurants and retail shops. Farms are motivated by price incentives to turn to industrial crops (flax for oil seeds and for fibre, rapeseed, sunflower, hemp, sugar beet, etc.) and animal feedingstuffs, apparently with considerable success.[1] The purpose is to facilitate industrialization and to provide more superior food products (meats, milk, milk products, eggs) to strengthen the appeal of material incentives to labour.

Furthermore, the former strict limitation on the farms' non-agricultural activities have been lifted, and both collective and State farms are now encouraged to develop industrial production based on their agricultural raw materials and even to run local workshops and restaurants. The growth of this vertical integration has been most remarkable in recent years in Hungary, Romania, the USSR and Yugoslavia. Enthusiasts describe it as 'agro-industrial symbiosis' or the 'highest form of agro-industrial integration', whereby the Marxist ideal of equalization between town and countryside will be realized. In the USSR 15,000 articles are now produced in this way.[2] This type of combination provides several advantages, such as the savings that can be achieved from the local processing of perishable products, the use of waste as fertilizers, the utilization of seasonally idle agricultural labour and the diffusion of technical skills in the countryside. At the same time, many industrial enterprises have taken to the production of agricultural commodities for their own use, and even for sale. For example, it was reported recently that the Soviet petroleum enterprises alone now grow enough food to feed a city of 100,000 people.[3]

One of the most determined drives directed towards the intensification of agriculture has consisted in the expansion of the production and application of artificial fertilizers. Between 1960 and 1967

---

[1] Thus in the CMEA region as a whole only about 20% of cultivated land was devoted to these raw materials in the 1950s, but in the late 1960s the proportion reached was 35%. Over the same period, the proportion of animal products in total agricultural output rose from 45 to 50%. Based on: *Rozwój gospodarczy krajów RWPG 1950–1968*, op. cit., pp. 83, 85.

[2] *Materialno-tekhnicheskoe snabzheniye* (Material and Technical Supplies), Moscow, 5/1969, p. 44.

[3] *Ekonomicheskaya gazeta*, no. 20, May 1969, p. 17.

the use of these fertilizers per hectare of arable land in the CMEA region nearly trebled. By 1967 all the European Socialist countries, except the USSR, used more artificial fertilizers per unit of cultivated area than the world average, but most of them were still behind the most advanced Western countries; see Table 28 for

TABLE 28 THE USE OF ARTIFICIAL FERTILIZERS, 1950–1967
(Kilogrammes per Hectare of Arable Land*)

COUNTRY	1950	1960	1965	1967
GDR	130	190	267	276
Czechoslovakia	49	94	166	173
Bulgaria	1	34	79	133
Poland	22	46	71	102
Hungary	6	29	63	91
Romania	1	8	29	47
USSR	6	11	27	33
European CMEA Countries	10	17	38	47
European Economic Community	n.a.	127	177	183
WORLD	11	21	31	34

n.a. = not available.
* Different types of fertilizers brought to a common calculational basis.

Source. Based on: *Rozwój gospodarczy krajów RWPG 1950–1968*, op. cit., pp. 7, 101.

details. The yields have been rising, but judging by the principal crops Socialist countries are still lagging not only behind the leading Western nations but also in comparison with world averages; see Table 29.

In recent years, there have been renewed efforts amongst the CMEA countries to extend their co-operation in the agricultural field. In May 1970 the CMEA Executive Council accepted a five-year plan for 1971–75, prepared by the Permanent Commission for Agriculture, designed to promote the systematic rationalization

H

TABLE 29 YIELDS OF GRAINS, POTATOES AND SUGAR BEET,
1960–1967
(In Quintals per Hectare)

PRODUCT	REGION	1961–65*	1966	1967
Grains†	CMEA	11	15	13
	EEC	26	27	32
	WORLD	13	15	14
Potatoes	CMEA	111	124	133
	EEC	200	215	252
	WORLD	119	127	137
Sugar beet	CMEA	184	222	252
	EEC	372	410	420
	WORLD	237	270	285

* Annual averages.
† Wheat, rye, barley and oats.

Source. Based on: *Rozwój gospodarczy krajów RWPG 1950–1968*, op. cit.,
pp. 6, 7.

and intensification of agriculture in the member countries. The
plan provides for joint planning and prognoses, the co-ordination
of scientific and technical research, further improvements in the
strains of crops and the breeds of animals and extended specialization and co-operation in the production of artificial fertilizers.

D. A NEW APPROACH TO NON-PRODUCTIVE SERVICES

Traditionally, Socialist countries were noted for the under-
development of the so-called 'non-productive' services.[1] Thus
before the reforms, less than 15 per cent of the working population

[1] The services which do not directly contribute to material production, and
as such are not regarded as part of national income. In official statistics they
are usually classified under eight headings: (i) public administration and justice;
(ii) education, science and culture; (iii) health, social welfare and sport; (iv)
finance and insurance; (v) local government and housing; (vi) defence;
(vii) political, social and religious activities; (viii) other services (including
postal services to non-productive users, domestic service, tourism, etc). Some
services, viz. transport, communications and trade, are regarded as productive to
the extent they constitute a continuation of the productive process.

in the region was engaged in the non-productive sphere, whilst the proportion in most Capitalist countries was twice, and in the most advanced ones three times, as high. The Socialist attitude could be explained on the following grounds.

First, the Socialist economies were relatively undeveloped, and it is typical of the lower stages of economic development that both the demand for and the supply of services are clearly limited. The second reason was more significant; it consisted in deliberate official restrictions placed on the non-productive sphere. The authorities, relying predominantly on extensive sources of growth, endeavoured to divert the largest possible amount of labour, capital and land to material production which alone – by the Socialist national income accounting – was indicative of economic development. At the same time, the need for quality, efficiency and a solid backing for the material motivation of labour was not fully appreciated. However, these attitudes and practices appear to be changing now.

Most services are instrumental in promoting increases in pro- ductivity, which is the main source of intensive economic growth. A further extension of education and, particularly, of vocational training improves workers' skills. Research leads to the improve- ment of existing methods of production or discoveries of new techniques. Regular and competent maintenance and repair services keep buildings and equipment in good working order and extend their useful life. Professional services supplied by technical bureaux, market research establishments, advertising agencies, management consultants and legal advisers may also help to minimize costs and maximize effects in desired directions. All these entities, although in the first instance classified as non-productive, play their part in productive processes. Even according to the Socialist national income accounting, if their services are sold to productive enterprises, the value of such services is reflected in material production.[1]

But even if services are rendered to the population for direct

[1] But such services appear statistically as having been produced by the purchasing enterprises, not by the sellers of the services. This is so because the value of material production is calculated by adding up enterprises' production, and the enterprises from their total output deduct only expenditure on material inputs (including depreciation).

consumption, their role in raising efficiency in the material production sphere is now widely recognized. A better provision of such
services as housing, child care, further education, personal services
(beauty salons, counselling, etc.), dry cleaning, passenger transport, repairs of private vehicles, various communal facilities,
entertainment and culture (sport, theatre, ballet, music, cinema,
exhibitions) not only may release (mostly female) labour for outside employment, but also cultivate better attitudes to work and
a greater respect for social property. With the rising levels of
income, consumer spending is increasingly directed (absolutely
and relatively) to luxuries, of which most services are very good
examples. Experience under the old system had demonstrated only
too well that unless luxuries are available in reasonable quantity
and variety, neither moral nor material incentives could be relied
upon to work effectively.

For these reasons, the official policy with regard to the growth of
non-productive services has been liberalized and some effects are
already apparent. In most Socialist countries (Czechoslovakia,
the German Democratic Republic, Hungary, Poland, the USSR,
Yugoslavia), the proportion of the working population engaged in
the non-productive sphere had risen to 20 per cent by 1970, compared with 15 per cent in 1960; in Bulgaria and Romania the proportion had increased from about 10 to 15 per cent during the
same period. In the USSR the volume of services rose over the
first four years under the new system (1966–69) by 90 per cent
(by 140 per cent in rural areas).[1] In these developments, private
enterprise is now playing an active part (see Chapter 3 A, p. 52).

For a long time, Socialist countries did not attach much importance to tourism, and they are still enforcing severe restrictions on
tourist travel to Capitalist countries. However, since the early
1960s they have lifted many restrictions on other tourist traffic, i.e.
including tourists coming from Capitalist countries. The dramatic
growth of tourism is indicated by the number of foreign tourists
who visited the eight Socialist countries in 1960 and in 1967 (the
percentage for 1967 in brackets represents foreign tourists from
CMEA countries):

[1] S. Kosyachenko et al., ('The Reform and Problems of the Economics of
the Service Industry') Vop. ekon., 3/1970, p. 149.

	1960	*1967*
Bulgaria	200,000	1,750,000 (37%)
Czechoslovakia	1,320,000	4,120,000 (81%)
GDR	90,000	350,000 (78%)
Hungary	240,000	2,420,000 (57%)
Poland	180,000	1,570,000 (83%)
Romania	100,000	1,200,000 (66%)
USSR	710,000	1,760,000 (49%)
Yugoslavia	870,000	3,680,000 (15%)
TOTAL	3,710,000	16,850,000 (55%)

Sources. Based on: *Rozwój gospodarczy krajów RWPG 1950–1968*, pp. 139–40; *Statistički godišnjak Jugoslavije 1969*, op. cit., p. 242.

This new policy is prompted above all by the desire to earn foreign exchange. It has been discovered that capital outlays and operating costs in the tourist industry yield much higher returns than those in visible exports.

The most immediate scope, or need, for the improvement in the quality and effectiveness of the provision of services appears to be mostly in the consolidation of small inefficient workshops and agencies into larger establishments. Such entities would be in a better position to install modern equipment and hire highly trained personnel to perform specialized tasks and to apply the system of material incentives based on profit. According to a Soviet administrator, these are the lines along which rapid progress is being made in the USSR.[1]

What are the prospects for further development of non-productive services? It appears that the conclusion reached by T. Riabushkin, a Soviet economist, points the direction:

> In the future, the scope of the non-productive sphere in Socialist countries will continue to increase, but it will never reach such a high degree of development as in Capitalist economies.[2]

The economic reforms have also produced an impact on productive services, i.e. trade and transport. We shall examine these developments in the following chapter.

[1] L. Ovsiannikov, ('Continued Expansion of Personal Services'), *Ekonomicheskaya gazeta*, no. 29, July 1969, p. 14.

[2] T. Riabushkin, *Pokazatieli ekonomicheskogo razvitiya sotsialisticheskikh stran* (Indicators of the Economic Development of Socialist Countries), Moscow, Mysl, 1966, p. 282.

12 The Relation between Production and Distribution

A. THE CHANGING ROLE OF TRADE

TRADE normally provides a link between production and consumption (including 'productive consumption', i.e. the use of intermediate goods in the process of production). However, its actual functions performed in a Socialist economy depend on the stage of economic development, the system of planning and management, the organization of production, the role of the consumer, the nature of markets and the accepted strategy of growth in general.

Under the old system, the role of trade was narrowly circumscribed.[1] The function of trade was limited to the distribution of the production predetermined by central planners, and the volume of sales handled was small. The ambitious drive to build up capital stock, in order to accelerate the pace of industrialization, meant severe limitation of the consumption fund. At the same time, dealings between producing enterprises were not, as a rule, handled by the trade network but were more or less automatic – determined by the centrally fixed allocations in which the enterprises concerned had no choice as to their partners and terms.

Thus trade had little effective power over the size of production and only a very limited influence on the structure of consumer goods. For many obvious reasons, the divorce between production and distribution facilitated centralized directive planning and management. Trade also suffered from a neglect by central

[1] Trade in Socialist terminology includes wholesale and retail trade, the procurement of agricultural products by the State and catering. In national accounts, trade ranks as the least important branch of material production (after industry, construction, agriculture, transport and communications). Only those trading activities are considered productive which involve an improvement of the goods handled (packaging, weighing, delivery to final consumers). In national income accounts, goods are valued at retail prices but most retail trade services (recording, settling payments, sales promotion, the administration of consumer credit) are regarded as non-productive.

planners in respect of the allocation of investment, the level and differentiation of wages and the quality of attracted personnel. There was little inclination to improve distribution because central planners, preoccupied with extensive development, considered that investment and labour (particularly the most productive labour) enhanced the rates of economic growth much more if directed to industry and construction than to trade. The ability to maintain the cost of distribution at very low levels was regarded as evidence of the superiority of Socialism over Capitalism.

As a result, Socialist trade was noted for its depressed state and poor performance. Even in the commercially most advanced Socialist country, Czechoslovakia, the number of shops was insufficient, and most of those in existence had a drab appearance with insufficient floor area. The personnel, who largely consisted of married women and persons in search of better opportunities, was poorly trained and remunerated, with a consequent high labour turnover, absenteeism and not infrequent closing of shops.[1] A small variety of goods, queues, overcrowded shops and poor service were familiar facts of daily life.

The authorities were, of course, aware of the shortcomings in trade, but the typical way of dealing with these problems was by resorting to administrative methods. These included State inspection, the intervention by trade unions or local consumer protection societies, complaints in the press – usually without much lasting improvement – rather than going to the basic causes of these deficiencies.

The new economic system places extra responsibilities on trade. One of the most important reasons for the decentralization of

---

[1] In Czechoslovakia in the mid-1960s the floor space per 1,000 residents was less than 200 sq. metres, compared with over 370 sq. m. in Western Europe. In Poland over the four-year period 1964–67, one-half of the personnel changed their place of employment and a retail shop had to be closed on the average for 28 working days a year; the occupational status of persons employed in trade ranked near the bottom of the scale – only above unskilled labourers and charwomen. In the CMEA region as a whole, the proportion of total investment channelled to trade was 2–4% (8–20% in the West). The proportion of working population employed in trade was only 6% (10–15% in Western countries). Average wages in trade were about 15% below the national average. Trade margins allowed to trading enterprises were less than 10%, whilst in Capitalist countries they normally represent 30%. See J. Wilczynski, *The Economics of Socialism*, London, Allen & Unwin, 1970, pp. 164–5.

planning and management was the relief of central planners from routine microeconomic decisions with regard to the structure of production, and furthermore the creation of conditions for the adaptation of production to consumption so that resources are utilized to yield maximum effects. In this process trade can become an effective transmitter of buyers' preferences to producing enterprises, and also a promoter of new products and socially desirable patterns of consumption through active salesmanship. A Polish economist described the new role of trade in the following words:

> The acquisition of goods by the trade network should be based on the assumption that the articles are produced not merely for the sake of plan fulfilment but for the satisfaction of ultimate users armed with the freedom of choice.[1]

This declaration may sound naïve to Western readers, but it is amazing how long it took Socialist leaders to grasp the significance of this simple truth.

The criteria formerly used for determining the success of trading enterprises and bonuses to the employees – the gross or net value of the sales turnover, the number of transactions, man-hours worked – all proved unsatisfactory from the point of view of efficiency and as an effective link between production and consumption (see Chapter 6 B, p. 98). The new responsibilities are likely to be discharged more effectively by the acceptance of profit as the indicator of trading enterprises' performance and the basis for material incentives to their personnel.[2] To reinforce the effectiveness of profit, new scales of trade margins (wholesale and retail) have been or are being drawn up to make even low-priced items and new and unknown articles profitable enough to handle.

The centralized system of the allocation of supplies has been

[1] T. Sztucki, *Plan i rynek w obrocie towarowym* (Plan and Market in the Flow of Trade), Warsaw, PWE, 1966, p. 195.

[2] e.g. in the USSR up to 30% of the planned profit and 60% of the above-plan profit of the trading enterprise can be placed in the material incentives fund. Up to 30% of the standard pay of the highly qualified personnel can be paid in bonuses. If the retail sales turnover does not reach the planned target, the material incentives fund is reduced – by 2% for each 1% of the retail sales target unfilled, and by 2% for each 1% of the planned profit underfulfilment. V. Dementsev, ('Economic Incentives in Trade'), *Finansy SSSR* (Soviet Finance), Moscow, 2/1970, pp. 13–14.

largely replaced by horizontal links where enterprises themselves have a good deal of freedom in negotiating contracts. In some industries, there are trading agencies specializing in handling intermediate products, and there are indications that this practice will spread further. Increasing importance is being attached to competition. Some steps have been taken by the authorities (especially in Czechoslovakia, the German Democratic Republic, Hungary and, of course, Yugoslavia) to create competing enterprises so that both selling and purchasing entities have a choice of several partners. Even in the remaining countries, producing enterprises sometimes open their own display rooms and retail sales divisions to publicize their new products and compete with trading enterprises.

It is now widely accepted that advertising, even in a Socialist economy, can enhance the effectiveness of economic processes. Under centralized and directive planning, advertising was regarded as not only wasteful but in fact positively harmful because it could interfere with the planned allocation. But the situation is different in the context of decentralization and developing buyers' markets. A high-ranking Soviet economic administrator pointed out recently:

> Advertising is one of those media which can assist in regulating production and consumption. . . . New products must be made widely known so that the economies of scale can be achieved. . . . Advertising can be employed to shape socially desirable tastes. . . . Producer goods also need advertising because even specialists find it difficult these days to keep abreast of modern developments and to know what is available in the way of new equipment and materials.[1]

The same Soviet writer observed that 'as a result of the economic reforms, the demand for advertising has increased two to three times'.[2] In the USSR there are now hundreds of different bodies concerned with advertising, and commercial advertisements commonly appear in newspapers, magazines, trade directories and on radio and television.

[1] A. Nastenko, ('Advertising – What Should Its Functions Be?'), *Ekonomicheskaya gazeta* (Economic Gazette), Moscow, no. 28, July 1969, p. 11.
[2] Ibid.

One of the common practices in dealings between the supplying and receiving enterprises in the past was the poor performance of contracts. Owing to prevailing shortages (sellers' markets), suppliers were often lax in fulfilling contracts, and receiving enterprises were hesitant to complain. But such deficiencies are now treated most seriously by the authorities. In all these countries legislation has been passed requiring the parties explicitly to indicate all the relevant conditions in contracts as to quality, specifications, packing, date, etc. Penalties for non-observance have been substantially increased, to which not only offending suppliers but also recipient entities are liable.[1]

The increased responsibility of trade is indicated by the remarkable growth of the volume of retail sales in most Socialist countries since the mid-1960s, as shown by the following annual averages:

	1961–65	1966–69
Bulgaria	6·8	8·8
Czechoslovakia	3·4	10·1
GDR	2·5	4·9
Hungary	5·2	8·0
Poland	6·0	6·4
Romania	9·9	8·4
USSR	6·0	8·5
Yugoslavia	9·6	7·0*

* 1966–68

Sources. *Gospodarka planowa* (Planned Economy), Warsaw, 4/1970, p. 12; *Statistički godišnjak Jugoslavije 1969* (Statistical Yearbook of Yugoslavia for 1969), Belgrade, 1969, p. 121.

[1] Thus in Poland, the increased penalty rates as of 1967 applicable to purchasing enterprises were as follows: accepting items not ordered, 5% of the value of the goods involved; accepting faulty articles, 10% in fine; agreeing to a breach of contract, 15% in fine. Suppliers were also subject to fines, which in the case of delays, if repeated in the same calendar year, were increased 100%. At the same time, bonuses are payable to State controllers of technical quality (attached to trading enterprises) according to the value of the penalties imposed. In the USSR, according to the new scale effective since 1/1/1968, suppliers of producer goods are fined 3% of the value of the goods involved if the delay is up to ten days and 5% if the delay exceeds ten days. If the goods supplied are not up to the standards laid down by the State, suppliers pay a fine amounting to 20% of the value of the rejected items. Similar penalties also apply to transport enterprises in the case of delays, damage, loss, etc. For further details, see *Finanse* (Finance), Warsaw, 12/1968, p. 24; *Ekonomicheskaya gazeta*, no. 47, Nov 1967, pp. 3–4.

Other evidence of the growing role of trade may be briefly mentioned. There is a trend towards slightly larger shares of investment being channelled to trade (in general, from less than 3 per cent in the 1950s to more than 3 per cent in the late 1960s) and more generous credits. Even in the countries which lagged behind in the past (Bulgaria, Poland, Romania, the USSR) provisions have been made in the 1971–75 plans for increases in the number of shops, the modernization of existing facilities, an improved system of training, a greater differentiation of pay and better working conditions. Pre-packaging, self-service, automated vending, home delivery, postal shopping, hire-purchase – for long neglected in comparison with Western practice – are being extended in all Socialist countries.

B. PRODUCER AND CONSUMER GOODS

In Socialist economic theory and practice, based on the Marxian analysis of the process of 'extended reproduction' (positive rate of economic growth),[1] a good deal of significance has always been attached to the composition of production. In particular, the division of output into producer goods (meant for further use in production) and consumer goods (meant for direct consumption) has been considered to be of crucial importance.[2] The relation between these two streams of production has been regarded as one of 'basic proportions' in the economy, and to ensure continuous economic progress the rate of growth of producer goods must be higher than that of consumer goods. This thinking was based on

[1] K. Marx, *Capital*, Moscow, FLPH, 1957, pp. 392–469.

[2] The goods falling into the first category are known as 'Department I' production and those into the second as 'Department II' production. This distinction is also made in industrial output, where 'Group A' represents industrial producer goods and 'Group B' industrial consumer goods. In practice, no complete statistics are compiled on Department I and II production, but in most Socialist countries data are published on Group A and B output. In Hungary, the classification into Group A and B output in official statistics began only in 1958 (before that date distinctions were made between the fuel-producing industry, the machine and metal industry, the chemical and rubber industry, the textile industry and the food-processing industry. In the GDR and in Yugoslavia the division into Group A and B output has not been adopted yet; instead, similar classifications are still used as in Hungary before 1958.

the implicit assumption that economic progress is capital-using, so that an increasing share of total production is necessary to maintain a given rate of economic growth.

Guided by this philosophy, the authorities were not only planning for higher growth rates of the output of the means of production, but also insisted on priority fulfilment of these rates – often at the expense of reduced growth rates of consumer goods. This essentially reflected an extensive approach to economic development. The differences in the rates of growth of industrial producer and industrial consumer goods over the period 1951–68 are demonstrated in Table 30.

TABLE 30 RATES OF GROWTH OF GROUPS A AND B INDUSTRIAL OUTPUT, 1951–1968

COUNTRY	1951–60*		1961–65*		1966		1967		1968	
	A	B	A	B	A	B	A	B	A	B
Bulgaria	18	12	14	10	13	12	14	12	n.a.	n.a.
Czecho-slovakia	12	9	5	5	7	6	12	5	5	6
GDR	14†	12‡	7	4	6	4	7	5	n.a.	n.a.
Hungary	15§	8‡	8	8	8	6	7	11	n.a.	n.a.
Poland	15	11	10	6	8	6	9	5	10	7
Romania	15	11	16	10	12	10	14	13	n.a.	n.a.
USSR	13	10	10	6	9	7	10	9	8	8

n.a. = not available.
* Annual averages.
† Machine-building industry.
‡ Food processing.
§ Machine and metal industry.

Sources. Based on: Rozwój gospodarczy krajów RWPG 1950–1968, op. cit., pp. 14–43, and daily and periodical publications of the countries concerned.

The practical effect of the pursued policy was that the share of producer goods in total production was steadily increasing. This is illustrated by 'Group A' in total industrial output ('Group B' in brackets) in different years:

	1950	1960	1967
Bulgaria	38 (62)	47 (53)	53 (47)
Czechoslovakia	47 (53)	58 (42)	60 (40)
Hungary	... (...)	66 (34)	65 (35)
Poland	53 (47)	59 (41)	64 (36)
Romania	53 (47)	63 (37)	68 (32)
USSR	69 (31)	72 (28)	74 (26)

Source. Central Statistical Office of Poland, *Rozwój gospodarczy krajów RWPG 1950–1968* (Economic Development of CMEA Countries), Warsaw, 1969, p. 66.

The postulate of the growth of producer goods outpacing that of consumer goods remained unquestioned for a long time, and indeed in the earlier stages of economic development a rising rate of accumulation was justifiable on several grounds (see Chapter 10 A, pp. 165–6). But the validity of this time-honoured view has been critically reappraised in recent years by both theoretical writers and policy-makers. The changing official attitude to this question is reflected in the Theses of the Central Committee of the Communist Party of the Soviet Union, put forward in 1967:

The reconciliation of the growth rate of the output of consumer goods with that of the means of production . . . is one of the important requirements of the modern structural changes in the economy.[1]

The vice-president of the Hungarian Central Statistical Office, I. Huszar, clearly stated in 1968:

There is no justification for the assumption in the theory of economic development that accumulation should grow faster than consumption. The growth of investment beyond a certain optimum level is likely to lead to lower efficiency. Therefore, the Hungarian economic policy in the future must not be designed to increase the proportion of accumulation in national income.[2]

M. Kalecki, the late Polish economist well known for his studies on economic growth, drawing on experience in Socialist and Capitalist countries, pointed out that 'the capital–output ratio

[1] Quoted from: A Strogova, ('The Production of Consumer Goods in CMEA Countries'), *Voprosy ekonomiki* (Problems of Economics), Moscow, 5/1968, p. 127.
[2] *Figyelö* (Economic Observer), Budapest, 6/11/1968, p. 4.

does not necessarily have to be rising to ensure a continuous growth of productivity'.[1] Similarly, a Soviet economist, M. Usiyevich, concluded that extended reproduction can be sustained even if production in the Department I sector does not rise faster than that in the Department II sector, if the capital–output ratio declines.[2] In fact K. Łaski, a Polish economist, went further by showing that the pursuit of accelerated economic growth by means of higher rates of accumulation may force the economy towards a higher capital–output ratio; by slowing down the rate of economic growth, the economy may be forced into a lower capital–output ratio, which in the long run may lead to higher rates of growth.[3]

There is already some evidence available that since the reforms the gap between the rates of growth of producer and consumer goods has been narrowing down, in some cases equalized and in some even reversed, especially since 1967. Thus to illustrate by reference to the USSR:[4]

	Group A	Group B
1928–67[5] (annual averages)	10·5	4·5
1968	8·0	8·3
1969	6·9	7·2
1970 (Plan)	6·1	6·8

In recent years, the rate of increase of the Group B output exceeded that of Group A also in Hungary (in 1967) and in Czechoslovakia (in 1968).

The willingness of the authorities to allow more resources for current consumption has been conditioned by three consider-

[1] M. Kalecki, *Zarys teorii wzrostu gospodarki socjalistycznej* (Outline of the Theory of Growth in a Socialist Economy), Warsaw, PWN, 2nd ed., 1968, p. 25.

[2] M. Usiyevich, ('Leninist Doctrine on the Two Departments of Social Production and the Experience of Socialist Development in the CMEA Countries'),*Voprosy ekonomiki*, 1/1969, pp. 111–22.

[3] K. Łaski, *Zarys teorii reprodukcji socjalistycznej* (Outline of the Theory of Growth under Socialism), Warsaw, KiW, 1965, pp. 306–14.

[4] Based on: *Kommunist*, Moscow, 11/1967, p. 90; *Pravda*, Moscow, 11/12/1968, p. 1; *Izvestiya*, Moscow, 17/12/1969, p. 2.

[5] During this period, the rate of increase of the Group B output exceeded that of Group A in 1937, 1945 and 1946, whilst in 1947, 1951, 1952, 1954 and 1956 the rates were very close.

ations. First, the pressure for better living – for long ignored or suppressed under the old authoritarian system – could no longer be disregarded in the context of the liberalization associated with the economic reforms. Second, the Socialist countries have reached higher stages of economic development, with solid foundations for continued industrialization firmly established. Consequently, these economies – especially the more mature ones (Czechoslovakia, the German Democratic Republic, Hungary, the USSR) – are in a better position to provide higher living standards than in the past. But the third consideration has probably carried the greatest weight. The new economic system relies heavily for its success on incentives. It had become painfully obvious before the reforms that neither moral appeals nor even financial rewards produced the desired results if not backed up by substantial improvements in the consumer-goods market. Experience had demonstrated that the only way to spur labour to more and better work was to provide more and a greater variety of consumer goods, especially luxuries.

C. TURNOVER TAXES

Turnover tax, a peculiarity of the Socialist economic system, is a type of indirect tax levied on goods and services passing from producers to consumers (although in some cases final producer goods may also be subject to it, even if they are not sold for consumption). It can be fixed in three different ways: (i) as the difference between the predetermined retail price (minus wholesale and retail margins) and the price receivable by the producer; (ii) as a specific tax (an absolute amount per unit of the commodity); or (iii) as an *ad valorem* tax (a percentage of the producer's price).

The first method has been the most common basis – in the past it covered about three-quarters of the items subject to the tax. In the case of the other two methods, the size and rates have also been highly differentiated and subject to such periodical readjustments as will ensure the desired stability of retail prices (determining the cost of living). To this extent, Socialist turnover taxes can be regarded as a residual element depending on the predetermined level of retail prices. This contrasts with indirect taxes in Capitalist countries, where it is the level of retail prices that is dependent on indirect taxes. Another significant feature is that Socialist turnover taxes constitute a very high proportion of retail prices – from one-third to two-thirds was common in the past (whilst indirect taxes in Capitalist countries normally represent less than half that proportion). The functions of turnover taxes were to raise revenue for the State, to control the profitability of enterprises in the socialized sector, to regulate the real incomes of different social groups and to ensure equilibrium in the market for consumer goods.

The manner in which turnover taxes were administered in the past fitted well into the centralized and directive economic system and the extensive strategy of growth. They were used above all as an instrument of insulating distribution from production. This insulation was achieved by maintaining a two-tier price system. Under this set-up, producers' and retail prices remained constant or moved independently of each other, because each was determined by reference to different criteria. Producers' prices, centrally fixed and rigidly enforced, were usually based on the average cost of production in the branch of industry concerned, at the time of the price reform, plus a planned profit margin. As a rule, these prices remained unchanged for long periods (five years or more). The stability of these prices was regarded as highly desirable, because it facilitated planning and social accounting. Retail prices were fixed at such levels as would adjust consumer demand to the planned or existing supply.

Of course, even under a highly centralized system, the conditions underlying supply and demand were bound to change. But if production costs increased or decreased, the effect on the enterprises' profitability was neutralized by reducing or increasing turnover taxes. Similarly, if consumers' preferences changed, or if planners decided to change production plans for consumer goods, or if targets were under-fulfilled or exceeded, retail prices were adjusted accordingly by varying turnover taxes. In each case, market equilibrium could be achieved via prices and not necessarily via supply responding to demand.

It should be clear from the preceding discussion that the manipulation of turnover taxes could absorb changes in cost-preference relations, and consequently they had adverse effects on the growth of productivity. In any economy, especially where rapid structural changes take place, the costs of producing some consumer (and producer) goods increase and of others decrease, and at the same time the demand for some goods falls and for others rises. But turnover taxes as they were administered in the past rendered enterprises insensitive to the requirements of economic progress. There was little to discourage them from producing articles at increasing costs and obsolete lines even though there was an increasing scarcity of 'modern' items.

To create conditions for the continuous growth of productivity, enterprises should find it to their advantage to be constantly adapting their productions in such ways as to use those inputs which are becoming relatively cheaper (and thus more abundant) and to expand their output of those goods for which demand is growing. At the same time, retail prices should reflect changes in production costs, so that the consumption of those goods produced from increasingly scarce resources is reduced whilst that of the more abundant articles (produced at lower costs) is encouraged.

For these reasons, turnover taxes should be transformed from a residual element into a price-forming component, so that prices provide a reliable guideline to both producers and consumers. Consequently, turnover taxes should be reformed in five respects. Firstly, the basis of assessment should be *ad valorem*, i.e. a fixed percentage of the producers' price. Secondly, the rates should be stable for reasonably long periods, so that changes in supply or demand are reflected in both producers' and retail prices. If the authorities want to regulate consumer demand to suit their short-run policy objectives, a change in the terms of consumer credit is a sounder instrument to rely upon (see Chapter 9 C, p. 155).

Thirdly, the rates should be fairly uniform, at least for broad classes of products, to avoid distortions between producers' and retail prices beyond those warranted by social cost–benefit considerations. This would provide additional opportunities for enhancing the growth of productivity, by not only reducing the cost of administration of these taxes but also strengthening the effectiveness of incentives to labour. In the past, many consumer durables and other luxuries were most heavily taxed, and yet it is the production of these goods that can be increased at the lowest extra cost (see Chapter 7 B, p. 113). A smaller differentiation of these taxes would mean reduced retail prices of those goods which have the greatest motivating effect towards a greater work effort. At the same time, the high-cost inferior foods and other 'necessities' – in the past exempt from turnover taxes, or even heavily subsidized – would be priced closer to their factor costs.

Fourthly, the size of turnover taxes should be reduced so that the disparity between the level of producers' and retail prices is not excessive, otherwise the guidance function of these prices can be impaired. Lastly, it is advisable that these taxes be collected by the trade network (preferably at the wholesale level), not by producing enterprises, so that the latter base their equilibrium production on factor cost. This would also prevent the cumulative tax effect in the case of goods passing through a large number of production stages in different enterprises. To be effective, the suggested reforms imply that producers' and retail prices are flexible and that both producers and consumers are in a position to respond to price changes.

So far, in contrast to many other important spheres of the Socialist economies, no drastic departures have been made from long-established policies and practices. But the disadvantages of the traditional approach are now widely realized in the context of the intensification of economic growth, and some reforms have already been initiated in several Socialist countries – in Yugoslavia (1958, 1965, 1968), the German Democratic Republic (1965, 1969), Poland (1966, 1969), Czechoslovakia (1967), Hungary (1968), Bulgaria (1969). The procedures for setting turnover taxes have been somewhat simplified and there is a definite trend towards the extension of the *ad valorem* basis to a larger proportion of consumer goods. In many cases, the differentiation of the explicit or implicit rates has been reduced. Thus in Hungary before 1968 there were 'tens of thousands' of turnover tax rates and specific levies, but by 1970 the number was reduced to 700. According to the president of Hungary's Price and Materials Commission, Béla Csikós-Nagy, this differentiation will be further decreased 'to ensure a close correspondence between producers' and retail prices. Only those differentiated rates should be tolerated which are in the interest of Socialist society on social, cultural and hygienic grounds.'[1] Even so, the extent and degree of differentiation is still considerable.[2]

By the price reforms carried out in all the eight Socialist countries since the mid-1960s, the levels of producers' prices have, on the whole, been increased, largely at the expense of turnover taxes because retail prices have been hardly affected. In fact, some consumer goods have been freed from these taxes and there has been a tendency to phase out subsidies (negative turnover taxes). In Poland, goods exported are now subject to a uniform rate, and in Bulgaria, Czechoslovakia, the USSR and Yugoslavia they are no longer subject to turnover taxes. Similarly, some imports, such as those used for humane purposes, have been freed from these taxes and in other cases there is a tendency to replace them with *ad valorem* import duties. On balance, the gap between producers' and retail prices, represented by turnover taxes, has been substantially reduced.[3] There has been a relative decline in turnover taxes as a percentage of the State budget-

---

[1] Béla Csikós-Nagy, ('Features and Tasks of the Price Policy'), *Pénzügyi szemle* (Financial Review), Budapest, 2/1970, p. 101.

[2] In Hungary the number of different tax rates and tax mark-ups for textile made-up articles is 360, for footwear and leather goods 200, and for knitted articles 100. The tax rates on women's shoes range from 0 to 47% and on brandy and liqueurs from 57 to 93%. Even the same article often carries different rates or mark-ups, depending on the type of raw materials used and the type of buyers; for example, in the case of underwear, the tax rates are as follows:

	Adults	Teenagers	Boys & Girls	Children	Infants
Cotton	20%	10%	0%	−15%*	−58%*
Synthetic	50%	40%	40%	40%	−58%*

* denotes a subsidy

In Poland (as reported towards the end of 1969), the range of tax rates works out from 1·0 to 50·2% on cotton goods; woollens are subject to tax rates ranging from 10·2 to 60·4%, but some are subject to subsidies ranging from 2·7 to 54·5%; in the case of the articles of confectionery (933 in all) most carry tax rates ranging from 0·3 to 61·4%, but 14 items are not subject to the tax and 193 items are subsidized. Based on: *Figyelő*, 23/8/1969, pp. 1–3; *Társadalmi szemle* (Social Review), Budapest, 6/1969, p. 8; *Życie gospodarcze* (Economic Life), Warsaw, 23/11/1969, p. 5.

[3] To illustrate, the average share of turnover taxes in retail prices in different years was as follows: in the GDR in 1956, 38%; over the period 1957–67, 14%; and in 1968, 4%; in Hungary in 1956, 53%; in 1959, 37%; and in 1968, 3–4%. *Ekonomista*, no. 6, 1969, pp. 1383–4; *Gospodarka planowa* (Planned Economy), Warsaw, 4/1970, p. 59; *Voprosy ekonomiki*, 3/1970, p. 72.

ary revenue (in favour of deductions from enterprise profits).[1]

Judging by the statements made on this subject by political leaders in recent years, further reforms are inevitable, but they are likely to be cautious and gradual. Some Socialist economists have gone further by advocating the abolition of a turnover in favour of a net production tax to be levied not only on consumer goods but also on producer goods,[2] in line with the practice recently adopted in a number of Western countries (such as France, the Netherlands and Sweden).

D. MARKETS AND ECONOMIC GROWTH

The most fundamental feature of the economic reforms has consisted in the fact that the market mechanism has been harnessed – to varying extents in the different Socialist countries – to participate in shaping economic processes in the interest of a greater efficiency. In *ex-ante* planning it is, of course, impossible to avoid errors, and as they are made at the central, macroeconomic, level the consequent losses to the economy assume large proportions. In an analysis of this subject, a Soviet economist made the following observation:

> It has been demonstrated beyond doubt that the market provides the mechanism for the verification of the extent to which social labour is distributed in optimum patterns, i.e. the extent to which labour outlays correspond to social needs . . . whether the structure of production is in accordance with consumers' preferences, whether production is of the required quality and whether costs are exceeded or not. Therefore, the study, understanding, and analysis of its operation is an essential pre-

---

[1] e.g. in the Soviet budgetary revenue the percentages represented by turnover taxes (and by deductions from enterprise profits in brackets) in selected years were: in 1950, 56 (10); in 1960, 41 (24); in 1965, 38 (30); in 1969, 32 (35); and in 1970 (planned), 32 (35). The percentages applicable to the GDR were: in 1956, 53 (19); and in 1968, 7 (33). The proportions of the State budget revenue derived from turnover taxes in the early and late 1960s in some other Socialist countries were: Bulgaria, 65 and 35%; Czechoslovakia, 45 and 30%; and Hungary, 30 and 15%. *Izvestiya*, 17/12/1969, pp. 4–5; *Gospodarka planowa*, 4/1970, p. 59; *Planovo stopanstvo* (Planned Economy), Sofia, 8/1968, p. 54.

[2] See, e.g., K. Ivanov, ('The Turnover Tax under the New System'), *Planovo stopanstvo*, 10/1968, pp. 54–6.

requisite for flexible and efficient planning. The signals supplied by the market indicate the extent to which production plans must be subjected to continuous corrections.[1]

Another Socialist economist described the market as 'the sword of Damocles hanging over the heads of those producers who are tempted to disregard buyers' requirements'.[2] The general role of the market in relation to planning has been examined in Chapters 3 and 4, whilst in the remaining part of this chapter we shall consider some specific aspects of the market, viz. the market for consumer goods and for the means of production, sellers' markets and buyers' markets.

Contrary to what has often been believed in Capitalist countries, markets have always existed in one form or another in Socialist economies, particularly in the sphere of distribution. Thus the sale of a part or whole of the privately grown produce directly to private consumers has always been carried on in free (in Socialist literature described as 'unorganized') markets. Since the discontinuation of rationing (in the early 1950s), the distribution of practically all consumer goods has been conducted on the basis of free choice. Even under the old system, although total consumption was strictly controlled, its structure was influenced to some extent by consumers' preferences registered in the market, as planners were anxious to avoid shortages and surpluses. The distribution of the planned production was, of course, carried on in 'organized markets', where the State could counteract changes in consumers' preferences by appropriately readjusting retail prices – not necessarily supply – and so an equilibrium in the market was still preserved.

But there were virtually no markets for the means of production. Producer goods in the socialized sector were simply allocated to producing enterprises by the central authorities in accordance with the plan – with the date, quantities, specification, prices and other terms laid down by the State. This practice was based on the long-established conviction that the socialized means of production, in contrast to consumer goods sold in retail markets, were not commodities, and consequently could not be subject to ordinary commercial exchanges.[1] There was a limited market in the private sector and foreign trade, particularly with Capitalist countries, was carried on on the basis of world market conditions. However, there are several indications that the markets for the means of production are already developing, and further progress in the near future appears to be certain.

The problem of the market for the factors of production in a Socialist economy is complex and the controversy on this subject has a long history.[2] Here we are concerned not so much with the rationality of the prices but rather with the institutional set-up for their distribution. Yugoslavia has, of course, been in the forefront in developing such markets after 1952, and especially since 1965. There is a large number of virtually independent trading enterprises which handle both producer and consumer goods in the socialized sector. In fact there is a possibility of a capital market being developed. The radical reduction of taxation has enabled many enterprises to accumulate considerable liquid balances, which are now often invested in debentures floated by other enterprises in immediate need of large financial resources (see Chapter 9 D, p. 163). Some Yugoslav economists have advocated the establishment of a debenture market to facilitate the mobilization of idle liquid resources and to enable debenture

---

[1] The crystallization of this view can be found in J. Stalin's last book (published in 1952), *Economic Problems of Socialism in the USSR*, Moscow, FLPH, 1952, pp. 13–22.

[2] The controversy goes back to 1920, when L. von Mises came to the conclusion that in the context of the socialization of the means of production there could be no market for them, and consequently no rational prices of the factors of production were possible under Socialism. In the 1930s, L. Robbins and F. von Hayek argued that rational prices of the means of production could be established mathematically but, as this would involve a huge number of calculations, it was not possible in practice (in the pre-computer age). At about the same time, O. Lange contended that rational prices could be arrived at not necessarily in conventional markets but by central planners in 'shadow markets', by the process of successive approximations ('trial and error') on the basis of the information supplied by enterprises and of consumer's free choice. The modern mathematical school (represented by L. V. Kantorovich and V. V. Novozhilov) maintains convincingly that rational prices can be established econometrically with the aid of high-memory computers. See Chapter 4 D, pp. 71–5, on optimal planning.

holders to sell their portfolios at short notice when needed.[1]

In Yugoslavia as well as Poland, since the substantial de-collecti-vization of farming land (see Chapter 11 C, p. 203), there has been a flourishing private trade in land, agricultural machinery and building materials. Even if the State takes over private land, it pays compensation to its owners roughly in accordance with the market value of the land, and land values are regularly quoted in official publications (see Chapter 10 D, pp. 184-5).

In Hungary since the reforms of 1968 many enterprises have been established which specialize in supplying raw materials and semi-finished products to industrial (including building) enter-prises. Special efforts are being made to promote competition by the creation of several trading entities handling the same type of producer goods so that both selling and purchasing enterprises have considerable choice. In 1969 there were trade monopolies for only 58 key products and they handled only 20 per cent of the trade amongst enterprises.[2]

Some progress along these lines was also made in Czechoslovakia in the late 1960s, but the military intervention by the Warsaw Pact countries and the reactionary regime of Dr G. Hušak have produced a setback. In the USSR, markets for the means of production have been advocated by a number of leading econo-mists, particularly since 1966 when it was announced at the 23rd Party Congress that wholesale trading enterprises would be gradu-ally established to take over the distribution of producer goods.[3]

Whilst trade in the means of production was probably not feasible under centralized and directive planning and management, its development is highly desirable under the new system to facili-tate intensive processes of economic growth. With the continu-ously expanding range of producer goods, it is beyond the capacity of central administrative organs to cater for increasingly specialized

[1] I. Dvornik, ('The Money Market and the Capital Market'), *Finansije* (Finance), Belgrade, 9-10/1968, pp. 542-51.

[2] B. Csikós-Nagy, 'First Experience Gained in the Implementation of the Economic Reform in Hungary', *Acta oeconomica* (Economic Papers), Budapest, vol. 4, no. 1, 1969, pp. 7-9.

[3] See especially: A. Birman, ('Trade in the Means of Production'), *Materialno-tekhnicheskoe snabzheniye* (Material and Technical Supply), Moscow, 11/1967, pp. 21-30; L. Leontyev, ('Processes of Distribution in a Socialist Economy'), *Kommunist*, 3/1967, pp. 70-1.

needs in production, particularly in these days of rapid technological changes. A viable trade network promotes a greater
mobility of producer goods, it reduces the need for hoarding and it
introduces an element of competition where in the past it was
conspicuously lacking. It also provides a larger choice of inputs
and thus enables enterprises to pursue the patterns of substitution
which are more conducive to efficiency.

Socialist economies have traditionally been noted for the prevalence of sellers' markets. Such markets exist whenever total demand
for producer and consumer goods exceeds total supply at the
official prices, which places producers and distributors in a
privileged and intolerant position. These markets were closely
associated in the past with the extensive road to economic
development. On the one hand, they were caused by tight balancing with no or insufficient reserves, the over-commitment of
resources, ill-designed incentives based on the quantitative fulfilment and over-fulfilment of targets irrespective of costs, excessive
incomes in relation to the productivity of labour and by too small
proportions of total output for current consumption. At the same
time there were austere restrictions on imports (especially of consumer goods) whilst price controls were rigidly enforced for all
types of articles.

On the other hand, sellers' markets contributed to waste and
inefficiency typical of extensive-based growth. The prevailing
shortages led to recurring bottlenecks and impelled enterprises to
adopt widespread precautionary hoarding. Producers and sellers,
being assured of excess demand, abused their strong position so
that the quality, variety and punctuality of deliveries were adversely
affected, and recipients and buyers were reluctant to complain.
Queues and low standards of service, with all the inevitable irritations and waste of time, were typical in retail distribution. In
effect, enterprises were largely deprived of independent decision-
making because the structure of output was often determined by
the availability of supplies. Similarly, the level of consumer satisfaction from spending given incomes was below optimum because
consumers often purchased goods which happened to be available
at the time.

It has often been maintained by some Socialist economists that –

as a consequence of the social and economic set-up – under normal conditions developed Capitalist countries are inevitably dominated by buyers' markets and at the same time attain low rates of economic growth, while Socialist economies achieve high rates of growth largely made possible by sellers' markets.[1] It is an interesting generalization which begs for a number of qualifications, and certainly it is at least doubtful whether Socialist experience in the past will be applicable in the future.

Although sellers' markets still exist in all Socialist countries, they are not as widespread and acute as in the past. The authorities realize that at this stage buyers' markets can play a strategic role in the intensification of economic growth, and several developments since the economic reforms suggest that at least 'shallow buyers' markets'[2] may be developed even under Socialism. First, as Socialist economies have now reached higher stages of development, they have a greater capacity to produce more goods and services of a larger variety and of better quality.

Second, excessive and detailed targets are no longer prescribed by central planners. Enterprises have a good deal of freedom in choosing their structure of production according to market conditions. Third, it appears that the authorities have reconciled themselves to the maintenance of larger reserves of resources for emergencies to avoid bottlenecks which were common in the past. The increasing stocks of industrial products reported in Socialist countries in recent years suggest that shortages are not as prevalent today as they used to be and that buyers' markets are developing for particular articles. Fourth, material incentives are now based on profit, so that it is in the interest of enterprises to minimize costs (the consumption of resources in the process of production) and to maximize output for which there is demand (and can thus be sold).

Fifth, there is growing competition facilitated by decentral-

---

[1] See, e.g., Z. Bosiakowski, ('The Quality of Production as an Economic Problem'), *Ekonomista* (The Economist), Warsaw, 3/1969, p. 756.

[2] Markets characterized by only a slight excess of aggregate supply over aggregate demand. This concept appears to have been used first by a Polish economist W. Brus in *Ogólne problemy funkcjonowania gospodarki socjalistycznej* (General Problems of the Functioning of the Socialist Economy), Warsaw, PWN, 1961, p. 263.

ization and the commercialization of economic processes. In several countries (especially in Czechoslovakia, the German Democratic Republic, Hungary and Yugoslavia) import restrictions have been liberalized with a view to exposing local enterprises to foreign competition. Sixth, the price reforms carried out since the mid-1960s whereby the prices of producer goods have been on the whole substantially increased, have brought supply and demand closer to equilibrium. A better appreciation and understanding of money and monetary policy (see Chapter 9 A, p. 145) should further contribute to the maintenance of balance. Finally, the progress made in the development of trade is likely to increase the mobility and availability of resources and products.

There is a well-rooted conviction amongst Socialist leaders that buyers' markets are a luxury because they promote more consumption than production. They involve social cost in the form of larger stocks and reserves, which as such represent idle resources not used in current production. They also necessitate some diversion of resources into non-productive services (retailing, sales promotion, finance).

However, buyers' markets and high rates of growth are not necessarily mutually exclusive. Such markets can eliminate many forms of waste associated with sellers' markets, and in addition can activate intensive sources of growth through a better adaptation of the structure of production to buyers' preferences and by strengthening the effectiveness of material incentives to labour. Buyers' markets are highly desirable to counteract the ever-present danger of monopolistic practices by producers and distributors. Indeed, it may be reasonably assumed that the success of the new decentralized system will largely depend on the extent to which these markets are developed. Only in buyers' markets can demand be taken as a reliable reflection of purchasers' preferences. In a study of this problem a Polish economist pointed out:

> Buyers' markets and competition prove to be an effective means of overcoming the inherent contradiction between the rate of growth of national income in quantitative terms and the rate of growth of the satisfaction of society's needs.[1]

[1] B. Miszewski, *Postęp ekonomiczny w gospodarce przemysłowej* (Economic Progress in an Industrialized Country), Warsaw, PWE, 1968, pp. 108–9.

13 Technological Progress

A. THE CHANGING BACKGROUND

TECHNOLOGICAL progress is usually understood in the Socialist countries as embodying the following elements:

(a) Improvements in the methods of production, consisting in a more effective management, more advanced specialization, a better utilization of labour, equipment and materials and in the rationalization of productive processes in general.

(b) Improvements in the quality of resources in the form of more highly skilled labour, a greater degree of power, durability, precision and the functional differentiation of capital, the drainage and irrigation of land, etc.

(c) Improvements in the quality of products in such respects as weight, durability, design, safety, aesthetic appearance, etc.

In a broader sense, technological progress also includes a fourth element:

(d) A rising capital–labour ratio, i.e. an increasing amount of productive fixed capital per worker, especially of power-driven tools and machines.[1]

In practice these elements of progress cannot be easily isolated, as one often involves one or more other elements and they naturally influence each other. In its final effect, technological progress is reflected in an increasing economy in the use of resources, or in a greater output from existing resources, or in the improved

[1] As in the West, in all the European Socialist countries the designations 'technological' and 'technical' progress are in use. In the most common usage, 'technological progress' includes elements (a), (b) and (c). However, some economists restrict its meaning to only (a), and apply the designation 'technical progress' to (b) and (c), but some regard the latter designation as including (a), (b) and (c), and still others as including all four. Some writers describe (a), (b) and (c) as constituting 'independent' (or 'pure') technological (or technical) progress and (d) as 'substitutional' or 'capital-intensive' technological progress.

quality of output, or simply in the rising national income per head.

The economic system which prevailed in the Socialist countries before the reforms was not conducive to technological progress. Under the detailed and directive centralized planning, emphasis was laid on the quantitative fulfilment and over-fulfilment of targets, and the system of incentives was such that cost reduction and improvement in quality were largely ignored. The planned allocations of producer goods restricted enterprises' freedom to pursue the most rational combination of resources, and the prevailing sellers' markets meant that whatever was produced could be easily disposed of anyway. Even if better technology was available, the inevitable disturbance of the established methods and patterns of production adversely affected the directive indicators of success, and consequently bonuses to the personnel. There was no certainty that enterprises and their employees would benefit from the introduced improvements in the long run either.[1]

It does not mean that the authorities were not anxious to promote technological progress. Indeed, a good deal of applied research was undertaken and innovations were made by central direction. Yet, as a Socialist economist observed, 'technical progress must be willingly absorbed, not imposed from above'.[2] What happens when technological changes are forced upon enterprises by administrative methods is illustrated by Polish experience. The authorities decided that technological progress could be achieved *inter alia* by decreasing the weight of equipment. The aim was to encourage enterprises to economize on materials, and material incentives to the personnel based on such economies were devised accordingly. As a result, enterprises producing equipment used deliberately to construct a very heavy first model by incorporating heavy and useless metal bars which could be easily removed one by one in subsequent 'new models' without much effort. In this way handsome bonuses were assured for long periods, and both the enterprise personnel and central planners were very pleased with

[1] D. Butakov and V. Bochkova, *Finansirovaniye tekhnicheskogo progressa v stranakh SEV* (Financing Technical Progress in the CMEA Countries), Moscow, Scientific Research Institute for Finance, 1966, pp. 45–6.

[2] B. Miszewski, *Postęp ekonomiczny w gospodarce przemysłowej* (Economic Progress in an Industrialized Country), Warsaw, PWE, 1968, p. 69.

themselves.[1] Many similar examples could be quoted indicating the ways in which the ingenuity of the management, designers and inventors was consummated.

The inducements provided to labour to improve skills were in most cases too weak to produce the desired effects. The differentiation of the standard rates of pay was small and the prevalence of piece-work wages meant that unskilled labourers could often earn more than skilled workers (see Chapter 7 D, p. 122). As was typical of the extensive approach to development, the quantity of labour was often regarded as being more important than its quality.

The preoccupation with the extensive sources of growth was also reflected in the official emphasis on increases in the amount of capital per worker. It was widely accepted amongst Marxist economists, including such Soviet authorities on the subject as S. G. Strumilin and T. S. Khachaturov, that the capital–labour ratio was 'the most reliable measure of the level of technology and its progress'.[2] As fixed capital was allocated free and there were no capital charges for its use, enterprises pressed for the highest possible allocations and hung on to the equipment in their possession even if they did not use it. The contrast between the Western and the Socialist approaches to technological progress was brought out in an interesting way by a Polish economist reflecting on post-Second World War experience: 'That is why from the defeated Germany the United States was anxious to extract technical documentation, patents, scientists – and not factory plants.'[3] The reader will, no doubt, note the merciful, but conspicuous, omission of explicit reference to the USSR.

It was revealed in Socialist sources that the percentage of the net material product (i.e. national income calculated by the Socialist method) spent on research and the development of

[1] Ibid., p. 71.
[2] S. G. Strumilin, ('On the Economic Effectiveness of the New Technology'), in *Ekonomicheskaya effektivnost kapitalnykh vlozhenii i novoi tekhniki* (The Economic Effectiveness of Capital Investments and the New Technology), Moscow, 1959, p. 50; also T. S. Khachaturov, ('The Economic Effectiveness of Capital Investments in the National Economy'), in ibid., p. 23 (quoted from: A. Rybarski, *Kryteria wyboru techniki w krajach słabo rozwiniętych* (Criteria for the Choice of Technology in Underdeveloped Countries), Warsaw, PWE, 1968, p. 40).
[3] Z. Lewandowicz, ('The Art of Management'), *Życie gospodarcze* (Economic Life), Warsaw, 9/11/1969, p. 11.

technology in the leading Capitalist and Socialist countries was in the early 1960s as follows:[1]

USA (1962)	5·1%
Great Britain (1961)	4·0%
FR of Germany (1961)	2·0%
France (1961)	2·0%
USSR (1962)	2·6%
Czechoslovakia (1962)	2·4%
GDR (1962)	1·6%
Hungary (1964)	1·5%

According to an American economist, M. Boretsky, although in 1962 the USSR had practically all the know-how that the USA had, the Soviets were on the whole twenty-five years behind the USA in the industrial application and diffusion of technology – in terms of twenty-five specific indicators selected, the lag ranged from five to forty years.[2] Productivity in the Soviet economy was only 40 per cent of the American level, in spite of the fact that the rate of accumulation in the USSR was three times as high as in the USA.[3] Boretsky's conclusion was that the Soviet lag in civilian technology behind the USA was greater in 1962 than in 1940.[4] The lag of Poland in 1960 was estimated to have been forty-three years behind Great Britain, or nine years behind France.[5]

The German Democratic Republic is technologically one of the most progressive Socialist countries, particularly in electrical engineering. Yet in the mid-1960s, per 1,000 employees in this industry, she had only one-fifth the number of research workers as the USA, and one-third the number in other advanced Capitalist countries.[6] Compared with 1950, the amount of rolled steel per

[1] *Czechoslovak Economic Papers*, Prague, no. 8, 1967, p. 48; *Figyelö* (Economic Observer), Budapest, 4/6/1969, p. 3; *Gospodarka planowa* (Planned Economy), Warsaw, 6/1968, p. 46.

[2] M. Boretsky, 'Comparative Progress in Technology, Productivity and Economic Efficiency: USSR versus USA', in US Congress, Joint Economic Committee, *New Directions in the Soviet Economy*, Washington, GPO, 1966, Part II-A, pp. 149–50, 156–9.

[3] Ibid., pp. 150, 152.   [4] Ibid., p. 150.

[5] *Życie gospodarcze*, 10/8/1969, p. 3.

[6] *Gospodarka planowa*, 6/1968, p. 44.

unit of industrial output by 1970 fell 38 per cent in the USA and
by 45 per cent in the Federal Republic of Germany, but in the
German Democratic Republic it actually increased by 4 per cent.[1]
In Czechoslovakia in the late 1960s, the production of building
materials in respect of quality, range and *per capita* figures was
five to fifteen years behind the levels in advanced Capitalist
countries.[2] As late as 1968, the Socialist countries were well behind Western nations in the output of synthetics, as indicated by
the following figures (kilogrammes per head of population):[3]

FR of Germany	49·8
Japan	36·3
USA	33·3
Italy	26·5
France	19·8
Czechoslovakia	13·7
Romania	6·6
Poland	6·2
USSR	4·9

However, in view of the critical importance of intensive sources
of growth under the new system, it is widely realized now that a
more radical approach is necessary to the speeding up of technological progress, particularly of its 'pure' component. Socialist
leaders, even in the more advanced countries, have now become
more conscious than ever of the 'technological gap' separating
their economies from the West. The Socialist upsurge of interest
in technology is reflected in the huge output of literature on technical achievements and management methods in the leading
Capitalist countries, even though on ideological grounds Socialist
leaders have nothing but contempt for Capitalism as a social system.

It is realized that in the advanced Capitalist economies about
one-half of growth is derived from 'pure' technological improvements, whilst in the Socialist countries, even in the 1960s, the

---

[1] J. Sołdaczuk (ed.), *Handel zagraniczny a wzrost krajów RWPG* (Foreign
Trade and the Economic Growth of the CMEA Countries), Warsaw, PWE,
1969, p. 197.

[2] *Hospodářské noviny* (Economic News), Prague, 19/5/1970, p. 8.

[3] T. B. Kozłowski, ('Novelty in the Chemical Industry'), *Gospodarka
planowa*, 4/1970, p. 35.

proportion was only about one-quarter – and in the countries where extensive tendencies kept reasserting themselves, much less, as in Poland – see Table 31. According to Soviet economists,

TABLE 31 SOURCES OF ECONOMIC GROWTH IN POLAND, 1961–1967

YEAR	Percentage Contribution to Economic Growth by			TOTAL
	Increase in Employment	Increase in Capital	Pure Technological Progress	
1961	22·7	36·1	41·2	100·0
1962	46·1	23·2	30·7	100·0
1963	46·5	81·0	−27·5	100·0
1964	17·6	52·6	29·8	100·0
1965	49·5	20·2	30·3	100·0
1966	46·5	69·7	−16·2	100·0
1967	55·0	51·9	−6·9	100·0
1961–67 (simple av.)	40·6	47·8	11·6	100·0

Source. S. Szwedowski, ('The Role of Technological Progress'), *Życie gospodarcze*, 26/10/1969, p. 4.

who discussed this question widely at the time of the implementation of the economic reforms, the amount of production in the USSR could be increased by 50 per cent merely by perfecting the technology of production (i.e. without having to increase the volume of resources).[1] A Polish economist summed up Socialist thinking on the subject thus:

> The utilization of the scientific and technical revolution is now viewed in Socialist countries as a means of rapidly increasing labour productivity, the rate of economic growth and the standard of living, in addition to such immediate goals as the improvement in the quality of industrial products and

[1] I. Kotkovskii, ('Present Conditions of Economic Rivalry between the USSR and the USA'), *Voprosy ekonomiki* (Problems of Economics), Moscow, 4/1967, pp. 74–5.

the expansion of exports. Another important consideration is the rivalry of the social systems.[1]

We shall next examine the measures recently adopted in Socialist countries to accelerate technological progress.

B. ACCELERATING TECHNOLOGICAL PROGRESS

One has to study Socialist literature and to travel in Eastern Europe and the USSR to appreciate the tremendous determination in these countries to modernize their production rapidly, and indeed to surpass the leading Capitalist countries in the technological field. It seems that the whole national life, from the top macro-level to the minute microeconomic units, is now permeated more than ever with these objectives.

Planning and management at the central level have become more flexible and are focused on long-term structural changes, and these are promoted more by incentives than by directives. Technical progress itself, especially the application of mathematical methods, cybernetics and computers, provides better and better techniques for working out and implementing optimal plans. The current five-year plans (1971-75) in all these countries also include 'scientific-technical plans'.

According to the methodology adopted in Socialist countries, the carriers of technological progress are the following eight propulsive developments:

1. Electrification.
2. Chemicalization.
3. The production of new kinds of materials, tools, machines and other types of equipment.
4. Mechanization.
5. Automation.
6. The perfection of the processes of production.
7. The concentration of production.
8. Discoveries.[2]

[1] M. Jagodziński, ('The Scientific and Technical Revolution and the Planned Economy'), *Gospodarka planowa*, 8/1969, p. 30.

[2] *Yugoslav Survey*, Belgrade, 5/1969, p. 101.

I

The previous developmental planning based on the branches of the economy is now being supplemented or partly replaced by 'structural planning' guided by 'complex technological goals', involving a number of branches. Examples of specific developments receiving priority treatment include synthetic fibres, plastics, precision engineering, section assembly lines and electronic equipment.

There is nothing new in the Socialist countries' determination to develop the industries producing power. These efforts are naturally still continuing, but in the last decade or so special emphasis has been placed on the development of superior sources of fuels (oil, natural gas, hydroelectricity).[1] There has been a remarkable growth of the electric power industry, in which preference has been given in the supply of electricity for production purposes rather than for household uses (see Table 32). The rapid increase in the consumption of power has exceeded the growth of its production in most Socialist countries, so that they now obtain about one-fifth of their requirements from the USSR, which is very well endowed with most sources of fuels (Poland has ample deposits of coal and also some oil, whilst Romania has good supplies of oil and coal). It is realized in the smaller Socialist countries that nuclear power is the only feasible answer to their growing fuel deficit and great strides are being made to develop nuclear power stations.[2]

[1] Taking the region as a whole, the percentage composition of the different types of fuels consumed changed between 1957 and 1965 as follows: solid fuels (black coal, brown coal, wood), from 72 to 50%; oil, from 20 to 30%; natural gas, from 5 to 15%; hydroelectricity, from 3 to 5%. In the USSR, the share of oil and gas rose from 19·7% in 1950 to 59·5% in 1968. These trends are similar to those in the West. Although the Socialist countries compare fairly favourably in this respect with most Capitalist countries, they are well behind the United States, where the proportion represented by oil and gas was nearly 80% in the late 1960s. See S. Wasowski, *Implications of the Development of Nuclear Industry in Eastern Europe*, Arlington (Virginia), Institute of Defense Analyses, 1969, p. 83; *Sotsialisticheskaya industriya* (Socialist Industry), Moscow, 8/4/1970, p. 3.

[2] The locations of nuclear power stations are: Bulgaria – Kozlodui; Czechoslovakia – Jaslovce and Pilsen; the GDR – Greiswald, Rheinburg, and Tierbach; Hungary – Paks; Yugoslavia – Videm Krasko. The officially announced figures for the output of electricity produced, or to be produced, in this way in different years are as follows (in megawatts): Bulgaria – 1972–73, 800; 1974, 1,200; Czechoslovakia – 1968–69, 150; 1974, 500; 1985, 5,900; the GDR – 1966, 100; 1974–75, 750; after 1980, 4,600; Hungary – 1975, 800; Romania – 1975, 1,200; Yugoslavia – 1970–75, 600; 1980, 1,400. All these countries including Poland

In each Socialist country under consideration there is now a high-level body responsible for the promotion of technical and scientific progress.[1] In each country the chairman of this body has the status of a minister and in all of them except Hungary he is also a member of the Council of Ministers.[2] The principles and the programme laid down by the top policy-making body is put into effect by various organizations. For example, in Bulgaria the main entity charged with the implementation of the policy of the State Committee for Scientific and Technical Progress is the Institute for Inventions and Rationalization, which in turn is assisted by Inventions and Rationalization Offices recently created by government departments and other major organizations for 'a swift and most effective implementation of the law'.[3] Research and technical bureaux, trade unions, the Communist Party organs and local councils now also actively participate in this work. The responsibilities of the Institute for Inventions and Rationalization (according to the new law passed in June 1969) are typical of similar entities in other Socialist countries, and they include:

(i) to study, evaluate and disseminate inventions;

(ii) to review and make decisions on the registration of inventions and to issue patents;

(iii) to publish a bulletin on current developments;

(iv) to exercise overall supervision of innovations;

(v) to declare topics for research and arrange for contests for the solution of major scientific and technical problems;

(vi) to patent Bulgarian inventions abroad;

---

and the USSR (but excluding Yugoslavia) also operate a joint research institute for the peaceful utilization of nuclear energy at Dubna, near Moscow. The above details have been obtained from S. Wasowski, op. cit., pp. 105, 109.

[1] In Bulgaria, the State Committee for Scientific and Technical Progress; Czechoslovakia, the Committee for Technology and Investment Development; the GDR, the Ministry of Science and Technology; Hungary, the Technical Development Committee; Poland, the Committee for Technical and Scientific Affairs; Romania, the National Council for Scientific Research; the USSR, the State Commission for Science and Technology; Yugoslavia, the Federal Council for the Co-ordination of Scientific Work.

[2] In the USSR, also the vice-chairman of the State Commission for Science and Technology is a member of the Council of Ministers.

[3] *Durzhaven vestnik* (Official Gazette), Sofia, 20/6/1969, pp. 1-7.

TABLE 32 ANNUAL CONSUMPTION OF ELECTRICITY IN
EUROPEAN COUNTRIES

COUNTRY	kWh per Head of Population		1967/1950 —100	10^3 kWh per Person Employed
	1950	1967		1966
1. Norway	5,356	13,552	253	n.a.
2. Sweden	2,595	6,763	261	22·1
3. Switzerland	2,126	4,025	189	n.a.
4. Gt. Britain	1,319	3,566	270	7·5
5. GDR	853	3,491	409	6·9
6. Finland	1,000	3,489	349	n.a.
7. FR of Germany	908	2,711	299	12·0
8. Austria	799	2,697	337	9·6
9. CZECHOSLOVAKIA	748	2,602	348	5·8
10. USSR	440	2,488	565	13·3
11. Belgium	996	2,358	237	11·1
12. France	795	2,290	288	11·9
13. Netherlands	698	2,232	320	n.a.
14. Denmark	514	2,226	433	9·0
15. Italy	535	1,827	341	11·2
16. BULGARIA	111	1,655	1,491	n.a.
17. POLAND	356	1,496	420	9·1
18. Ireland	324	1,446	446	n.a.
19. HUNGARY	294	1,285	437	5·1
20. Spain	249	1,216	488	n.a.
21. ROMANIA	133	1,172	881	7·3
22. YUGOSLAVIA	151	900	596	n.a.
23. Greece	80	776	970	n.a.
24. Portugal	111	617	556	n.a.
25. Turkey	33	179	542	n.a.

n.a. = not available.

Source. *Życie gospodarcze*, 17/8/1969, p. 4.

(vii) to establish and maintain the Central Patent Library;
(viii) to formulate lines of research and experimentation in Bulgaria in fulfilment of international agreements;
(ix) to organize the training of required cadres on the national scale.[1]

For a number of years now there have been intensified campaigns to attract more personnel with tertiary qualifications into research and experimentation. According to Socialist sources, the eight Socialist countries now have one million persons (including supporting staff) employed in scientific and technical research, i.e. one-third of the world's total; the USSR claims 500,000 research workers, the same number as the USA.[2]

But the most important feature of the new economic system relevant to technological progress is that, owing to decentralization and a greater independence of enterprises, it has released initiative and resourcefulness at the operational level. When profit was first adopted as a criterion of enterprise performance, it was soon found that the enterprise personnel was sometimes opposed to major modernization because it often involved an immediate diminution of the material incentives fund.[3] But this disadvantage has been removed by the introduction of special concessions applicable to experimenting and innovating enterprises.

Under the old system, which was first introduced in the USSR in the 1930s and later adopted by other Socialist countries, the financing of technological progress was mostly done by centrally allocated budgetary grants. Only minor outlays, not involving investment, were financed out of enterprises' own working capital so that, as a Polish economist observed, 'until recently technological progress in Socialist countries was in fact introduced almost exclusively only via the construction of new projects'.[4]

---

[1] Ibid.
[2] J. Metera, *Współpraca naukowo-techniczna krajów RWPG* (Scientific and Technical Co-operation Amongst the CMEA Countries), Warsaw, PWE, 1969, pp. 13, 99; *Soviet News*, Soviet Embassy in London, 3/2/1970, p. 60.
[3] M. Smirnov, ('Credit and Technical Progress'), *Planovoe khoziaistvo* (Planned Economy), Moscow, 4/1968, p. 12.
[4] M. Marlewicz, *Finansowanie postępu naukowo-technicznego w krajach socjalistycznych* (Financing Scientific and Technical Progress in Socialist Countries), Warsaw, PWE, 1968, p. 32.

The new system of financing technological progress is noted for a greater versatility and adaptability to changing conditions and opportunities. There are now four sources of finance:

(*a*) *Budgetary financing* is concentrated on research and innovations of macrosocial significance involving the highest degree of risk. Most fundamental research carried on in the leading institutes and the work arising out of scientific and technical co-operation under the auspices of the Council for Mutual Economic Assistance (CMEA) are also financed in this way. This source of finance is, with minor exceptions in some countries, interest-free and non-repayable. The distribution of these funds is administered in each country by the committee for science and technology, branch ministries and in some cases by other central organs.

(*b*) *Centralized and decentralized non-budgetary financing* is administered at the intermediate administrative level (branch associations in co-operation with enterprises). It is concerned with research and innovations involving several enterprises and extending over long periods. The risk is spread on a branch basis and the funds are derived mainly from the member enterprises' profits.

(*c*) *Earmarked enterprise funds in the form of 'technological progress funds'*[1] are used for financing experiments and innovations of local importance on the enterprise's own initiative. The main function of these funds is to protect the enterprises against short-term risk. They are replenished by explicit mark-ups on enterprise costs.[2]

(*d*) *Bank credits* are available to enterprises, branch associations and research establishments for projects involving irregular ex-

---

[1] In the USSR it is called the 'production development fund'. This fund had also existed before the reforms but had then represented less than 1% of the value of enterprise fixed assets. The size of the fund increased to 4% of fixed assets by 1969 and it is anticipated that it will reach 20%. In the GDR, the technological progress fund on the average represented about 10% of the enterprises' total revenue in 1969, but its share is to rise to 15–16%. *Voprosy ekonomiki*, 12/1968, pp. 35–44; *Die Wirtschaft* (The Economy), East Berlin, 23/10/1969, p. 14.

[2] e.g. in Bulgaria enterprises are required to add a mark-up on their prime cost according to the laid-down norms; the percentage ranges from 0·1 to 3·5 according to the type of industry or the branch of the economy. In the USSR the mark-up ranges from 0·3 to 3·0% of the enterprise's prime cost.

penditure. These credits are naturally repayable and low interest is charged on them.

Thus it can be seen that the risk involved to enterprises and research entities, which previously acted as a deterrent, has been largely removed.

Closer links have also been established between research and production. Research institutes have been granted a greater administrative and financial independence from central authorities, and many of them have been linked by direct ties with the relevant branches of the economy or industry. These ties have been substantially strengthened by what can be described as the 'commercialization of research'. By 1970 all these countries had placed most research entities on commercial accounting, i.e. such entities now have to rely mostly or exclusively for their income on the work done for enterprises and other bodies. Thus the work carried on by these entities – in such forms as the provision of information and expert advice, testing and experimenting, furnishing designs and documentation and the development of new processes, materials and products – is now bought and sold like commodities. One wonders how many times Stalin, who once decreed in his writings that not even tangible producer goods were commodities, has turned in his already disturbed grave.

The authorities have devised generous scales of charges that can be made by research establishments, including substantial profit mark-ups,[1] so that they can become financially self-supporting. Profits made by these entities are used for material incentives to the personnel, for the acquisition of better research facilities and for conducting pure research. Some research institutes, especially in Hungary, engage directly in industrial production closely related to their research. In view of the quickening pace of technological change, the authorities endeavour to shorten the periods of experimentation and accelerate the application of new

---

[1] e.g. in the GDR the profit mark-up on research work initiated by the commissioning enterprises is 5–10% above cost. The work classified by the authorities as leading to desirable planned structural changes in the economy carries a 10–40% mark-up and, in the case of structural changes of major significance, up to 80%. J. Schulze, ('Efficiency Mark-ups According to Scientific and Technical Results'), *Die Wirtschaft*, 23/10/1969, p. 14.

methods by various incentives and penalties.[1] Experience in the
CMEA countries over the past two decades shows that under
Socialist conditions the approximate number of years that elapses
between the initiation of the research project and its full application in production is as follows: in basic research, fifteen years;
in applied research, ten years; in *ad hoc* development work, five
years; and in the case of acquired licences, two years.[2] These
periods appear on the whole to be longer than in the most advanced Capitalist countries. According to the well-known Soviet
authority on technology, V. A. Trapeznikov, the period of arriving
at and applying technological solutions in the Soviet economy
could be reduced from the recent average of eight to twelve years
to four years.[3]

A new deal has been spelled out in some respects for individual
inventors. For a long time, inventions were essentially viewed as a
form of social property. Consequently, payments to private inventors either did not exist or were very small, because such extra
sources of income were regarded as ideologically objectionable.
But this view has changed in the last decade or so. Patent legislations have been modified to give greater protection and provide
for more generous payments. Thus according to the new patent
law in Bulgaria, effective since 1969, inventors are paid an initial
fee ranging from 30 to 200 leva and receive the title of 'rational-
izer'. Subsequently, royalties are paid according to the economic
effect of the innovation and may total up to 10,000 leva for
rationalization and up to 20,000 leva for an invention (the minimum monthly wage, effective since April 1970, is 60 leva).
Inventors are also entitled to extra paid leave of up to twelve days
annually for five years.[4] In the USSR, payments for rationalization
may amount to up to 5,000 roubles and for an invention up to

---

[1] Thus in Bulgaria, maximum mandatory periods have been laid down recently
for different industries, during which the newly constructed investment projects
are to reach full capacity and the required scientific and technical norms: in
the textile industry, 9 months; the chemical, electric power and food-processing
industries, 12 months; the iron and steel and machine-building industries,
24 months; and in the coal industry, 36 months. *Voprosy ekonomiki*, 1/1970, p. 134.
[2] J. Metera, op. cit., pp. 38, 45.
[3] See his article in a Polish journal, ('Problems of Steering Economic
Systems'), *Gospodarka planowa*, 12/1969, p. 58.
[4] *Durzhaven vestnik*, 20/6/1969, pp. 1–7.

20,000 roubles (compared with the minimum monthly wage of 60 roubles).[1] Similar scales of awards have been introduced in the other Socialist countries under consideration.

The attempts to reorganize scientific and industrial research were made in all these countries in the late 1950s and early 1960s. But the elaborate changes in the methods of financing outlined above took place mostly in the late 1960s, and they are still in the process of evolution. These changes clearly indicate that the general economic reforms of planning and management were not sufficient to induce rapid technological progress. This development appears to indicate that research and innovations are becoming increasingly costly, the element of risk is very high,[2] but at the same time there is little doubt as to the social benefit deriving from technological progress.[3]

According to V. A. Trapeznikov, a rouble spent on research and development in the USSR yields 1·45 roubles' increase in national income, i.e. four times more than the expenditure on material investment does.[4] Calculations made for the German Democratic Republic[5] and for Poland[6] support this conclusion. The growing appreciation of the role of technological progress in economic development is reflected in the rising proportions of national income being spent in Socialist countries on science and technology. Between 1960 and 1970, these proportions (of net material product) increased in Czechoslovakia from 2·0 to 3·5 per cent,

[1] For a scale of payments, see J. H. Giffen, *The Legal and Practical Aspects of Trade with the Soviet Union*, New York, Praeger, 1969, p. 222.

[2] A Polish economist who carried out a thorough study on technological progress in the CMEA countries formulated a 'law of outlays on research and development': the outlays increase as the square of the number of additional research workers, and the number of research workers increases as the square or cube of the improvement in technology. In other words, to double the stock of technological knowledge, outlays on research and innovations have to increase up to 16 times. J. Metera, op. cit., pp. 13–14.

[3] This is so even in the most advanced market economies, such as France, the Federal Republic of Germany, Japan, the UK and the USA, where governments disburse increasingly large funds for this purpose.

[4] Quoted from J. Metera, op. cit., p. 13.

[5] M. Steinbeck, ('Social Benefit as the Objective of Scientific Research'), *Die Wirtschaft*, 2/10/1969, p. 14.

[6] J. Moszczyński, ('The Prospects for the Perfection of the Principles Governing Commercial Accounting in Industrial Research Entities'), *Finanse* (Finance), Warsaw, 2/1969, p. 2.

in the German Democratic Republic from 1·5 to 3·0 per cent, in Hungary from 1·5 to 2·0 per cent, in Poland from 1·0 to 2·0 per cent and in the USSR from 2·0 to 3·5 per cent.[1]

C. THE PROBLEM OF QUALITY

In the past, Socialist countries were often noted for the poor quality of their production, especially when comparisons were made with developed Capitalist countries. Even in Czechoslovakia in the mid-1960s, the country usually regarded as the most mature Socialist economy at that time, only 40 per cent of the products of the machine-building industry measured up to world standards, 40 per cent were partly obsolete and 20 per cent were completely out of date. The respective proportions which applied to the Hungarian machine-building industry were 14, 39 and 47 per cent.[2] But even in 1968 the proportion of new (including improved) products in the Czechoslovak industrial production was only 10 per cent, one-third of which was not up to world standards (and as far as engineering and metallurgical products were concerned, 51 per cent was below world standards).[3] The share of new products in the East German industrial production in the early 1960s was less than 5 per cent, compared with 15 per cent in the Federal Republic of Germany.[4]

In 1959, losses to the Polish economy caused by faulty products were estimated to have been between 4,000m. and 6,000m. złotys, or 1 per cent of national income (as calculated by the Socialist method).[5] But even as late as 1968 these losses were valued at more than 3,000m. złotys, or 0·5 per cent of total material production.[6]

[1] *Hospodářské noviny*, 19/5/1970, p. 8; *Pravda*, Moscow, 17/12/1969. p. 4; *Życie gospodarcze*, 16/11/1969, p. 5.
[2] These figures were established by the State testing centres in the respective countries. Quoted from: I. Oleinik, ('The Material and Technical Base of the Socialist Camp'), *Voprosy ekonomiki*, 9/1967, p. 128.
[3] *Rudé právo* (Red Jurisprudence), Prague, 20/5/1969, p. 5; *Hospodářské noviny*, 19/5/1970, p. 8.
[4] *Gospodarka planowa*, 10/1969, p. 38.
[5] W. Wilczyński, *Rachunek ekonomiczny a mechanizm rynkowy* (Economic Accounting and the Market Mechanism), Warsaw, PWE, 1965, p. 154.
[6] *Finanse*, 12/1968, p. 25.

The proportion of industrial production in the socialized sector of the Polish industry in 1969 measuring up to world standards was only 53 per cent.[1] In 1963 per one ton of machinery and equipment exported, Poland received $793 compared with $1,610 earned by Japan and $1,830 by Italy. In 1964 per one ton of metal embodied in machine tools exported, Romania received £420 and Bulgaria £500, whilst France scored £946 and Switzerland £1,724.[2]

The poor quality standards prevailing in the past can be explained on two principal grounds. On the one hand, the authorities endeavoured to maximize the rate of economic growth through quantitative increases in production, and the system of incentives was designed primarily to promote this goal. Central planners realized that both quantity and quality competed for the limited resources, but the insistence on high qualitative standards would have simply reduced the possibilities of high quantitative growth. In the lower stages of economic development this approach is not necessarily devoid of rationality because, all in all, the social cost of high quality is likely to be higher than the social benefit. It may be generalized that at any stage of development there is an optimum degree of sacrifice of one for the other.

On the other hand, there is enough evidence to suggest that the quality of production turned out by many enterprises reached alarmingly low levels, leading to widespread waste, well beyond the proportions the central planners were prepared to tolerate. In their attempts to counteract these tendencies, the authorities resorted to administrative measures and specialized incentives. But neither produced results up to official expectations. It was physically impossible for the State inspection centres to test all products. Moreover, the penalties for poor quality were too small, at least in relation to the bonuses payable for the quantitative fulfilment and over-fulfilment of the plan. 'Consequently it was an economic proposition for enterprises to pay fines for faulty deliveries, rather than attend to quality and avoid penalties, but fail to reach the targets and forfeit bonuses.'[3]

[1] *Nowe drogi* (New Paths), Warsaw, 1/1970, p. 94.
[2] Y. F. Kormnov, *Mezhdunarodnaya spetsializatsiya proizvodstva* (International Production Specialization), Moscow, *Ekonomika*, 1968, p. 67.
[3] Krystyna Cholewicka-Goździk, ('Rentability and Quality in the Past'), *Finanse*, 12/1968, p. 23.

There were incentives for the production of new articles. But the enterprises' response in many cases was to use the most expensive materials (at least to start with) and introduce only minor changes, not necessarily leading to better quality. Owing to strong sellers' markets, even inferior products could be sold without difficulty, and it was easy to reduce costs in the future – and thus qualify for 'fulfilling the cost-reduction plan'.[1]

The incidence of sub-standard production, of course, varied in different industries and from one enterprise to another. Some products could escape quality control more easily than others, and in addition the degree of competence and honesty of the personnel naturally varied in different enterprises. In effect, the actual product-mix turned out by enterprises was often distorted not only qualitatively but also quantitatively compared with the planned structure. This, under the tight planning conditions prevalent in the past, frequently led to bottlenecks occurring side by side with idle stocks. Thus it can be seen that a slack quality discipline may adversely affect even the quantitative growth of production.

But the problem of quality has grown to different proportions altogether in recent years. In the higher stages of economic development the range and the degree of the sophistication of needs – both among consumers and producers – expand rapidly. In particular, the changeover to the predominantly intensive sources of growth demands a continuous expansion of the technologically most progressive industries and products, where exact specifications, the reliability of supplies and more effective ways of serving specialized needs are of strategic importance.

To meet the challenge of these requirements, several measures have been taken in the Socialist countries designed to:

(i) prevent enterprises from turning out sub-standard products, i.e. below the level of quality that is possible at the existing state of technology;

(ii) induce enterprises to constantly strive to introduce new products with superior qualities unknown before.

First, the inspection systems have been widened and tightened up. Penalties have been increased and they are also payable by the

[1] S. Góra, *Warunki produkcji a działanie bodźców* (Conditions of Production and the Operation of Incentives), Warsaw, PWE, 1967, p. 133.

enterprises and other entities which agree to accept sub-standard deliveries (see Chapter 12 A, p. 216). This system has also been extended to foreign trade. For this purpose specialized corporations have been established to exercise quality control over exports and imports.[1] Second, differentiated profit mark-ups are now commonly allowed to producing enterprises according to the quality classification of the goods they manufacture. In most of these countries selected groups of industrial products are now classified into three categories – high, medium and obsolete quality.

In Bulgaria, high-quality goods are awarded a 10 per cent price mark-up, while obsolete goods are marked down by as much as 20 per cent.[2] In the German Democratic Republic high-quality, mark-ups range from 2 to 5 per cent, and poor-quality mark-downs from 5 to 10 per cent.[3] In Poland, top-quality articles carry a 12–15 per cent mark-up and medium quality 7–10 per cent, and in the case of poor-quality goods the personnel may forfeit bonuses even if its enterprise makes profits on the sale of such goods.[4] As a result, between 1964 (when the system was introduced) and 1969 the proportion of top-quality products in the heavy and machine-building industry increased from 32 to 55 per cent, whilst the share of obsolete articles was reduced from 14 to 4 per cent.[5] In the USSR, price mark-ups are allowed for novelty for nine to fifteen months in the case of new products. In addition 'certificates of quality' are now awarded to deserving enterprises which, in addition to publicity and prestige, in effect usually benefit from larger sales and profits. By 1970, 1,400 such certificates had been awarded to enterprises producing TV sets, bicycles, watches, textiles, machine tools, excavators, granary cranes, etc.[6] In Czechoslovakia, Hungary and Yugoslavia, the flexible price systems – under which many prices are free to rise according to

---

[1] In Bulgaria, Bulgarkontrola; Czechoslovakia, Inspekta; the GDR, Inter-kontrol; Hungary, Mert; Poland, Polcargo; Romania, OCM (Goods Control Office); the USSR, the Commodity Export Examination Department of the All-Union Chamber of Commerce; and in Yugoslavia, Jugoinspekt.

[2] *Voprosy ekonomiki*, 8/1969, p. 60.

[3] *Życie gospodarcze*, 23/11/1969, p. 11.

[4] *Życie gospodarcze*, 11/5/1969, p. 7.

[5] *Gospodarka planowa*, 12/1969, p. 37.

[6] *Pravda*, 11/2/1970, p. 6.

market supply and demand – provide the inducement (see Chapter 5 C, pp. 88–90). In Romania, the introduction of production quality courses is advocated in vocational as well as general and higher education.[1]

The third line of approach to promote technological improvements consists in the greater degree of discretion now allowed to the trade network. In some countries, trading enterprises have been given the right to offer margins above the official prices to producing enterprises for fashionable goods. For a long time, the official view in Socialist countries was highly critical of changes in fashions, identifying them with the excesses typical of Capitalist societies. But this view has been almost wholly abandoned and it is conceded that fashions can usefully serve psychological and social needs. Trading enterprises now also have a special 'trade risk fund' to provide for novelty margins as well as for enabling them to dispose of obsolete items quickly at reduced prices.

Before the reforms, the authorities in Socialist countries generally regarded trade marks as Capitalist tricks employed by monopolies to squeeze out small businesses. However, judging by the recently introduced or revised legislations in several Socialist countries (such as Bulgaria, Romania and the USSR) on the registration and protection of trade marks, the latter are now considered as useful and legitimate instruments of promoting high standards of production and safeguarding deserving enterprises.

D. INTRA-CMEA TECHNOLOGICAL CO-OPERATION

In these days of peaceful co-existence, economic co-operation amongst Socialist countries will facilitate the victory of Socialism over Capitalism, in particular in the decisive arena of this rivalry – in the sphere of scientific and technical progress.[2]

This recent declaration by the Secretary of the Council for Mutual Economic Assistance sums up the prevalent determination in the

[1] See, e.g., M. Florescu, ('The High Quality of Production as a Requirement for Economic Progress'), *Scinteia*, Bucharest, 22/4/1970, p. 3.

[2] N. Faddeyev, ('The Source of Great Power'), *Izvestiya*, Moscow, 27/3/1970, p. 3.

CMEA[1] countries today towards ever closer co-operation in the field of technology.

There are four practical considerations prodding the CMEA countries to co-operation in this sphere:

(i) the need for the concentration of research resources on the most important common problems and the avoidance of the unnecessary duplication of effort and equipment;

(ii) the need to shorten the period of research and application, which is of increasing importance in an era of rapid technological change;

(iii) the determination to reach the best possible solutions measuring up to the highest world standards;

(iv) the desirability of reducing the risk of failure or spreading its cost.

The beginnings of technological co-operation go back to the late 1940s, but it has been placed on a more systematic basis only since the early 1960s, and by 1970 the following channels had been well established:

(a) *Multilateral co-operation* under the auspices of CMEA, usually involving national 'commissions for science and technology' (see section B of this chapter, p. 241).

(b) *Bilateral co-operation* between national scientific and technical institutes and similar bodies under the auspices of a bilateral inter-governmental agency. It is based on bilateral long-term agreements, usually covering twenty years. The importance attached to this form of co-operation is indicated by the fact that the national committee of the bilateral agency is headed by a vice-premier or minister.

(c) *Multilateral and bilateral* co-operation directly involving ministries. It is based on inter-governmental agreements.

(d) *Multilateral and bilateral* co-operation involving national academies of sciences.

---

[1] CMEA, or CEMA, or CEA, or Comecon, was established in 1949. Its membership includes Bulgaria, Czechoslovakia, the German Democratic Republic, Hungary, Poland, Romania, the USSR and Mongolia. In 1964 Yugoslavia was also admitted as an associate member to some CMEA bodies, *inter alia* the 'Permanent Commission for the Co-ordination of Scientific and Technical Research'.

(e) *Multilateral and bilateral* co-operation involving intermediate levels of economic administration, such as branch
associations, industrial trusts, chambers of commerce.

(f) *Direct co-operation* between enterprises.

The focal position in multilateral co-operation is occupied by
the Permanent Commission for the Co-ordination of Scientific
and Technical Research, established in 1962 with its headquarters
in Moscow.[1] Its main responsibility is to prepare a 'Research Co-
ordination Plan' and then promote its implementation. The first of
these plans was prepared for 1964–65, but since then they have
covered five-year periods corresponding with the national economic
plans. The 1966–70 Research Co-ordination Plan covered eight
directions of research, involving 50 major problems broken down
into 200 topics with about 500 specific research tasks.[2] In 1967 it
was agreed that the member countries could submit research
problems to the Commission to be handled jointly in anticipation
of future developments up to 1985.[3]

The actual implementation of the Research Co-ordination Plan
is in the hands of the CMEA Permanent Commissions in co-
operation with the relevant national economic ministries. Most of
the work arising out of the technological co-operation is carried out
in the national scientific and technical entities, as agreed by the
member countries.[4] But there is a growing body of opinion in
favour of specialized joint research institutes, considered to be a
'higher form of co-operation'. Such jointly owned and operated
establishments can be staffed with the top experts in their field,

---

[1] Other Permanent Commissions directly relevant to technological co-
operation established at about the same time are those for Standardization
(1962, with headquarters in East Berlin), Radio and Electronics (1963, Budapest)
and Geological Surveys (1963, Ulan Bator).

[2] The eight directions of research were: I. The perfection of the generation
and transmission of electricity. II. The improvement of geological exploration
and surveys. III. The application of synthetics. IV. The perfection of certain
processes in industry, construction and transport. V. Further development of
techniques in electronics, computing and automation. VI. The intensification of
agriculture and forestry. VII. Scientific bases of the organization of work and
management. VIII. New methods of protecting and improving health. J.
Metera, op. cit., pp. 67–71.

[3] Ibid., p. 43.

[4] e.g. in 1968, 700 institutes and designing bureaux in the member countries
participated in co-ordinated research projects. *Voprosy ekonomiki*, 2/1970, p. 117.

whose talents can be more fully utilized, they warrant more and superior equipment, and moreover they represent a forward step towards the higher phase of Communism. There are already several establishments of this nature in existence:

(i) The Nuclear Research Institute (owned and operated by all CMEA countries) at Dubna, the USSR (established in 1956).

(ii) The Organization for Co-operation in the Ball-Bearings Industry (Bulgaria, Czechoslovakia, the German Democratic Republic, Hungary, Poland and the USSR) (about 1960).

(iii) The Institute for Standardization (all CMEA countries), Moscow (1962).

(iv) Intransmash (a Bulgarian–Hungarian centre for the design and perfection of machines for the mechanization of transport between factory plants), Sofia (1965).

(v) Agromash (a Bulgarian–Hungarian–Soviet centre for the design and perfection of machines for the mechanization of processing vegetables and fruits), Budapest (1965; the USSR joined in 1968).

(vi) The Bureau for Tractor Research and Development (Czechoslovak–Polish), Brno, Czechoslovakia (about 1965).

(vii) Interchim (a centre for chemical research and manufacturing operated by Bulgaria, Czechoslovakia, the GDR, Hungary, Poland and the USSR), Halle, GDR (1970).

There are also research entities attached to the joint business undertakings (see Chapter 10 D, p. 188).

The most important practical forms of co-operation conducive to technological progress are as follows.

(a) *Standardization.* The adoption of common standards in production is regarded not only as facilitating mutual trade and economic integration but also as a means of promoting specialization, the economies of scale and high quality. In addition to the CMEA Permanent Commission for Standardization (a policy-formulating body) there is also the Institute for Standardization (a technical research body), both established in 1962. By 1968 the member countries had adopted at least 1,474 recommendations.[1]

[1] *Foreign Trade*, Moscow, 7/1969, p. 19.

In 1968 the CMEA Executive Council laid down three principles for raising the technological level through standardization: (i) concentration on products involving technology which affects the CMEA countries as a whole; (ii) the shortening of the period of recommendation for common norms to not more than eighteen months; and (iii) the speeding up of the standardization of products involving the latest technology.[1] In the same year the CMEA agencies adopted 1,600 recommendations for standardization.[2]

(b) *Technical Personnel.* Member countries co-operate in training personnel, providing experience for specialists, lending experts and organizing conferences on common technological problems.

(c) *The Provision of Know-How.* Scientific and technical information, results of experiments, complete documentation and designs are freely provided to the interested member countries.

The transfer of technological know-how from one country to another naturally poses the question of payment. According to orthodox Marxist thinking, technology – like the material means of production – should belong to society, and no individuals or groups of persons are morally entitled to remuneration for selling inventions or discoveries. Consequently, when CMEA was established (in 1949), the so-called 'Sofia Rules' were adopted, whereby the exchange or unilateral transmission of technology in any form amongst the member countries is free of any charge.[3]

However, under the new economic system, noted for the commercialization of production processes and research, as well as for self-financing, the incongruity of the Sofia Rules has become increasingly apparent to many theoretical and practising economists. There are three main arguments advanced in favour of placing the transmission of know-how on a commercial basis.

---

[1] *Standardisierung* (Standardization), East Berlin, 6/1969, p. 210.

[2] For instruments, machines and installations, 346 recommendations; for metals and metal goods, 285; for chemical products, 125; for power and electrical engineering installations, 119; for electronic equipment and communications, 109; other products, over 700 recommendations. *Ratsionalizatsiya i standardizatsiya* (Rationalization and Standardization), Moscow, 5/1969, pp. 1–2.

[3] Charges may be made only to cover the cost of reproduction and postage. But if these charges are likely to exceed 250 roubles, the country receiving the know-how in this form must be consulted beforehand.

First, there is an inevitable trend towards intra-CMEA specialization in research, which necessitates transfers of research findings
from one country to another on a larger scale than in the past. Yet
the incidence of research cost is not evenly spread because some
countries are engaged in research more than others and moreover
some types of research are more costly than others.

Second, in the higher stages of economic development the
costs of research rise steeply,[1] so that there is a greater need for
placing its financing on a broader and more systematic basis.
Third, charges for inventions would help remove certain iniquities
that have arisen in the interested countries' foreign trade. The
nation receiving free know-how for the production of exports un-
fairly competes with the donor country's exports, whether in
CMEA or in Capitalist markets. Alternatively, in the case of the
specialization of production, it is not fair that the country donating
technology should pay for it itself when importing goods embodying such technology from the recipient nation (it may be observed
that the CMEA countries use world market prices in their mutual
trade).

Consequently, the Sofia Rules are not conducive to the undertaking of costly research and the dissemination of technology. And
yet intensive growth critically depends on technological progress.
Of all the CMEA countries, the USSR – not surprisingly – is the
most enthusiastic supporter of payments for know-how.[2] But it
appears that there is a large and growing body of opinion in the
German Democratic Republic – also understandably – sympathetic
to this view.[3] Two bases have been proposed for the calculation of
such (lump-sum) charges:

(i) A percentage (ranging from 2 to 7 per cent) of the value of
production where the acquired know-how is used. This

[1] See this chapter, note 2, p. 247.
[2] Some Soviet economists have endeavoured to estimate the value of technology exchanged between the USSR and other CMEA countries, using world
market prices. According to one estimate, up to 1965 the USSR supplied over
12,000m. foreign exchange roubles' worth (about US $13,000m.) of technological
data, but received only 2,000m. roubles' worth (about $ 2,200m.). S. Yovchuk,
'Socialist Countries Co-operate in Science and Technology,' *International
Affairs*, Moscow, 11/1966, p. 111.
[3] See, e.g., M. Humml, ('The Need for Lump-Sum Payments for Scientific
Findings'), *Sozialistische Wirtschaft* (The Socialist Economy), East Berlin,
10/1968, pp. 12–15.

implies that the larger the country the more it would have to pay in absolute terms.

(ii) A contribution by each country using the know-how to cover the cost of research. This contribution could either be based on the expected value of the relevant production in each using country, or represent a uniform amount payable by each using country.[1]

In fact, there are already several developments suggesting a trend towards the commercialization of the exchange of technology in the CMEA region. Since the early 1960s all CMEA countries have established special foreign trade corporations responsible for the purchase and sale of patents and licences in relation to Capitalist countries, and by 1966 all these countries (including Yugoslavia) had acceded to the International Union for the Protection of Industrial Property. This means that the Socialist countries now agree in principle to pay for Western know-how and in turn insist on being paid for their own inventions exported to Capitalist countries.

In 1967 the CMEA Executive Council extensively discussed the exchange of technology among the member nations. Although it was not in favour of repealing the Sofia Rules, it conceded the possibility of charges being made in the case of costly research and in the case of substantial commercial benefits being reaped by the recipient country. This escape clause was further reaffirmed and extended in 1969. Furthermore it is an accepted fact now that if an invention is made in a joint research establishment owned and financed only by a few CMEA countries, the non-participating countries – whether CMEA members or not – wishing to use the invention have to make a payment to the establishment (or individuals concerned) according to their own national scale (see section B of this chapter, pp. 245–7).

An interesting solution has been evolved in Czechoslovakia, a country endeavouring to work out a compromise between the inexorable political facts of life and economic common sense. Domestically, all the exchange of technology between the Czechoslovak research institutes and enterprises is now based on a com-

---

[1] Y. Kormnov, ('Scientific and Technical Co-operation among CMEA Countries'), *Voprosy ekonomiki*, 5/1969, pp. 57–68.

mercial footing. But to conform to the Sofia Rules, the State established a centralized Compensation Fund. When a Czechoslovak invention is transmitted to other CMEA countries, the Czechoslovak research entity (or an inventor) receives payment from this Fund, according to the domestic scale of royalties. If a Czechoslovak enterprise receives technology from a CMEA country, it has to make a payment into the Fund. If the Fund happens to be exhausted (which is likely in the case of Czechoslovakia), grants are made from the State budget.

14 International Specialization and Trade

A. ECONOMIC GROWTH AND FOREIGN TRADE

THE reliance on the extensive sources of growth in the Socialist countries in the past also found its reflection in foreign trade. This was most evident up to the early 1950s, when each country strove towards the ideal of self-sufficiency, particularly in industrial production and raw materials. Imports were strictly controlled and limited almost exclusively to industrial equipment and other producer goods, primarily to widen the manufacturing base by establishing new enterprises and industries.

Imports of consumer goods were restricted to the bare minimum, mostly to overcome bottlenecks which could not be tackled otherwise. This practice contrasted with that under the pre-Communist regimes when imports largely consisted of luxury consumer goods. For example, as a Polish economist noted, 'in the pre-war Poland more foreign exchange was devoted to the imports of cosmetics than of machinery'.[1] Exports were essentially treated as a sacrifice to pay for a predetermined level of imports. Exports were dominated by bulky raw materials, the exploitation and handling of which required large capital outlays.

This vertical nature of the Socialist countries' foreign trade further accentuated extensive tendencies in exports. As they were mostly exporters of primary products and importers of manufactures, they suffered – and they still do in their trade with the West – from declining terms of trade (the 'Prebisch effect'), i.e. they had to export an ever larger volume of their raw materials and food to pay for a given volume of imports postulated in their plans. And they could do very little about it until they reached a reasonably viable industrial base, becoming less dependent on

[1] S. Albinowski, *Handel między krajami o różnych ustrojach* (Trade between Countries with Different Social Systems), Warsaw, KiW, 1968, p. 109.

imports of manufactures and more capable of exporting highly processed articles.

These policies were partly a product of dogmatic views on economic development and were partly imposed by conditions from outside. Under pre-Communist regimes most of these countries were predominantly agricultural and backward, and were greatly dependent on the advanced West for their exports of food and raw materials, their imports of manufactures and capital inflows. As a natural reaction, under Socialism they turned to 'balanced development', i.e. a rapid all-round industrialization and their own sources of raw materials. In this drive, it was thought that the Soviet model of self-sufficiency was not only desirable but also possible, even for the smaller Socialist countries.

There were also acute balance of payments problems, owing to the narrowly limited capacity to earn foreign exchange. Export industries were underdeveloped and there were prevalent sellers' markets which tended to curtail the availability of goods for export and magnified the (latent) demand for imports. At the same time Socialist countries were faced with discrimination in Capitalist markets in the form of import quotas, discriminatory tariff treatment, prohibitive anti-dumping procedures and strategic embargo – all largely instigated by the Cold War.

In effect, investments were scattered in a large number of industries, and in particular the exploitation of the new sources of raw materials involved heavy and alarmingly increasing capital outlays. As a result, Socialist countries were developing parallel economic structures and were suffering from similar shortages and surpluses. Moreover, bottlenecks began to appear more and more frequently, especially in the smaller countries, leading to widespread disruptions. It became perfectly clear by the late 1950s that continued autarkic policies were applying brakes to further economic development.

M. Kalecki, the first Socialist economist who placed the study of accelerated development on a systematic basis, came to the conclusion that a failure to expand foreign trade presents 'a barrier to economic growth', just as critical as shortages of capital or labour. A continued high rate creates increasing pressure on the balance of payments and 'the import-replacement investment is usually less gainful than investment outlays for expanding exports'.[1]

Foreign trade can, of course, play a strategic role in the intensification of economic growth. A greater participation in the international division of labour removes the need for a scattering and duplication of investment. Exporting goods in which a country has the greatest comparative advantage and instead importing those in which the country is least efficient, not only saves resources but also accelerates technological progress. The extension of markets also enables economies of scale to be made, which are substantial in modern complex industries. For a long time, Bulgaria appeared to show little enthusiasm for foreign trade, but recently the Bulgarian Premier and the First Secretary of the Communist Party, T. Zhivkov, stated bluntly:

> Bulgarian enterprises must be organically linked with the international division of labour and trade, because their exposure to foreign competition will compel them to catch up and keep abreast of the technical standards attained in the advanced countries. It will further prod them to specialize in the production of those goods in which they are most efficient and which can be sold in world markets.[2]

A Polish economist stressed the role of foreign trade in the intensification of economic growth:

> The main challenge to our economic policy is to tap intensive sources of growth. But a better utilization of production capacities, the increase in the effectiveness of investment, the acceleration of technological progress, the growth of labour productivity and the reduction of material costs are all dependent under our conditions not only on internal economic relations but also largely on foreign trade, without which no economy can be efficient enough.[3]

In the drive towards a greater participation in foreign trade, the Council for Mutual Economic Assistance (CMEA) has assumed an active role. Since the mid-1950s a number of organizations have

---

[1] M. Kalecki, *Zarys teorii wzrostu gospodarki socjalistycznej* (Outline of the Theory of Growth in a Socialist Economy), Warsaw, PWN, 2nd ed., 1968, pp. 56, 65.

[2] Quoted from: *Vunshna turgoviya* (Foreign Trade), Sofia, 4/1969, p. 7.

[3] B. Jaszczuk, ('Foreign Trade and the Intensification of Economic Development'), *Życie gospodarcze* (Economic Life), Warsaw, 17/3/1968, p. 1.

been established under its auspices for this purpose. Those most relevant are:

(i) The Permanent Commission for Foreign Trade (established in 1956 with its headquarters in Moscow).
(ii) The PC for Transport (1958, Warsaw).
(iii) The PC for Currency and Finance (1962, Moscow).
(iv) The PC for Standardization and the Institute for Standardization (both in 1962, East Berlin, Moscow).
(v) The International Bank for Economic Co-operation (1964, Moscow).
(vi) The International Investment Bank (1969, Moscow).

In 1961 the dogmatic support of autarky was formally abandoned in the important document, 'Basic Principles of the International Socialist Division of Labour'. This new thinking was further reinforced by the adoption by the member countries in 1967 of 'Effective Measures for the Perfecting of Specialization and Co-operation in Production'; they are practical rules specifying the obligations and rights of the partner countries in respect of delivery conditions, guarantees, penalties, etc.

Specialization amongst the member countries has been based on inter-governmental agreements going back to 1957, and they have been extended since then to practically all branches of production. Inter-product specialization mostly applies to raw materials. Thus Bulgaria concentrates on non-ferrous metals, Czechoslovakia on coal, the German Democratic Republic on potassium salts and brown coal, Hungary on bauxite and fruits, Poland on coal, metallurgical coke and sulphur, Romania on natural gas, manganese ore and timber; the USSR produces most of these raw materials and also supplies them to other CMEA countries.[1]

Intra-CMEA co-operation in manufacturing production has consisted so far mostly in intra-product specialization, based on differences in size, model, stage of processing or component parts. This form of specialization has been greatly facilitated by the increasing adoption of common technical standards since 1962. The greatest progress so far has been in machine-building,

[1] O. T. Bogomolov, *Teoriya i metodologiya mezhdunarodnogo razdeleniya truda* (The Theory and Methodology of the International Division of Labour), Moscow, Mysl, 1967, pp. 12–13.

chemicals, ferrous metallurgy, ball bearings, machine tools, transport equipment, radio and electronics. By 1970 the CMEA countries had adopted specialization agreements on 2,300 types of machinery and equipment, 2,300 types of bearings and 3,000 types of chemical products.[1] The proportions of the different types of machines and equipment affected by CMEA specialization agreements were as follows:[2]

Installations for the canning industry	11%
Installations for the chemical indusry	25%
Installations for the dairy industry	55%
Equipment for the power industry	70%
Oil-refining equipment	75%
Installations for ball-bearings production	90%

The share of the agreed specialized machinery and equipment in total exports of machinery and equipment in the participating CMEA countries in 1967 was as follows:[3]

Hungary	15%
Czechoslovakia	19%
GDR	26%
Poland	30%
USSR	37%
Bulgaria	41%

Ninety-five per cent of the CMEA countries' requirements of machinery and equipment is satisfied from domestic and other CMEA sources.[4] Socialist leaders often point out with pride that the intra-CMEA specialization and trade are 'horizontal', involving all stages of production, and not 'vertical' – typical of the Capitalist world where developed countries exchange their manufactures for raw materials supplied by underdeveloped nations.

[1] O. Bogomolov, ('The Theoretical Heritage of V. I. Lenin and the Economic Integration of the Socialist Nations'), *Mirovaya ekonomika i mezhdunarodnye otnosheniya* (World Economy and International Relations), Moscow, 4/1970, p. 57.

[2] *Ikonomicheski zhivot* (Economic Life), 16/10/1969, p. 8.

[3] G. Sorokin, ('International Division of Labour – An Important Factor in Economic Growth'), *Voprosy ekonomiki* (Problems of Economics), Moscow, 2/1970, p. 116.

[4] *Ekonomicheskie nauki* (Economic Studies), Moscow, 8/1968, p. 44.

There has also been considerable interest, especially amongst the smaller Socialist countries, in expanding trade with the Capitalist countries. The Polish Vice-Premier, P. Jaroszewicz, addressing a CMEA conference in Moscow in 1967, made it quite clear:

> The idea of autarky is alien to us, whether in application to one Socialist country or a group of them or even the Socialist bloc. We subscribe to the policy of peaceful co-existence, which in the economic sphere finds its expression in the development of solid trade links.[1]

This trend has been most pronounced since the early 1960s, since when trade with the Capitalist world has been increasing at a faster rate than intra-CMEA foreign trade.[2] The growth of trade with Capitalist nations had been facilitated in the last decade by the fading away of the Cold War, by agreements on scientific and technical co-operation, trade fairs, Western credits to Socialist countries and the economic aid extended by the latter to developing countries (for further details, see Chapter 15 B and C, pp. 304–22).

The role of foreign trade in a country's economy can be judged by five quantitative criteria: the share in world trade, the foreign trade turnover per head, the rate of growth of foreign trade, the income elasticity of imports and the share of foreign trade in national income. We shall examine the statistical evidence pertaining to the Socialist countries under consideration.

Taking the eight Socialist countries as a whole, their share in world trade increased from an all-time low (in peace-time) of 5 per cent in 1948 to 8 per cent in the mid-1950s and since then the proportion has settled at 10–11 per cent. This share is in fact higher now than it was before the Second World War (6·5 per cent in 1938), when all these countries except the USSR were under Capitalism.[3]

---

[1] Quoted from: S. Albinowski, op. cit., p. 92.

[2] Between 1962 and 1970 the share of intra-CMEA trade fell from 66 to 63%, whilst that of Capitalist countries rose from 28 to 32% of the CMEA countries' total foreign trade. In 1967 Capitalist countries claimed the following proportions of the individual CMEA countries' total foreign trade: Romania, 47%; Poland, 35%; the USSR, 32%; Czechoslovakia, 28%; the GDR, 26%; Hungary, 26%; and Bulgaria, 25%; in the case of Yugoslavia the proportion was 67%. Based on: United Nations *Monthly Bulletin of Statistics*, 6/1970, pp. xii–xiii; *Życie gospodarcze*, 3/11/1968, p. 11.

[3] Based on United Nations *Yearbook of International Trade Statistics*, New York (different issues), and *Monthly Bulletin of Statistics*, 6/1970, pp. xii–xiii.

TABLE 33 FOREIGN TRADE TURNOVER PER HEAD IN SOCIALIST
AND CAPITALIST COUNTRIES, 1953–1969
(At Current Prices, in US Dollars)*

YEAR	European Socialist Countries†	Capitalist Countries‡	WORLD§
1953	46	88	65
1960	83	116	85
1965	118	149	113
1968	140	183	137
1969	154	197	153
Index for 1969 1953 = 100	335	224	235

* Both exports and imports are valued f.o.b.
† Albania, Bulgaria, Czechoslovakia, the GDR, Hungary, Poland, Romania, the USSR (including Soviet Asia) and Yugoslavia.
‡ All countries except the nine Socialist countries, China, Cuba, the DPR of (North) Korea, Mongolia and the DR of (North) Vietnam.
§ Does not include inter-trade between China, the DPR of Korea, Mongolia and the DR of Vietnam.

Sources. Based on: United Nations sources: *Yearbook of International Trade Statistics, Monthly Bulletin of Statistics* and *Demographic Yearbook.*

The growth of the foreign trade turnover per head is shown in Table 33. In the Socialist countries between 1952 and 1970 it increased 3·4 times[1] – faster than in Capitalist countries (2·2 times) or in the world as a whole (2·4 times).[2] Nevertheless, the Socialist countries' figure is still low compared with the levels attained in the Capitalist world, particularly when comparisons are made with

[1] The increase works out to have been 3·6 (Yugoslavia omitted) when calculated from Socialist sources, e.g. Central Statistical Office of Poland, *Rozwój gospodarczy krajów RWPG 1950–1968* (Economic Development of the CMEA Countries 1950–1968), Warsaw, 1969, p. 113.
[2] In general, the figures for the Socialist countries understate the growth of foreign trade because the rise in their foreign trade prices has lagged behind that in Capitalist countries. In intra-CMEA foreign trade (representing about two-thirds of total CMEA foreign trade) constant average Capitalist prices over a selected past period have been used. Thus over the currency of the 1966–70 five-year plans the 1960–64 average world market prices were in use with certain adjustments; see Chapter 5 D, pp. 90–91. The periods chosen before 1966 were 1957–58 and 1957. By the same token, the rates of growth of the CMEA countries' foreign trade tend to be understated in comparison with the rates scored in the Capitalist world.

some of the most trade-oriented nations. This is illustrated by the *per capita* foreign trade in 1969 in US dollars (both exports and imports are valued f.o.b.):

European Socialist Countries		Selected Capitalist Countries	
GDR	$485	Belgium–Luxembourg	$1,905
Czechoslovakia	$455	Netherlands	$1,550
Bulgaria	$420	Switzerland	$1,510
Hungary	$330	United Kingdom	$ 620
Poland	$195	United States	$ 360
Yugoslavia	$170	Australia	$ 325
Romania	$170	Japan	$ 290
USSR	$ 90	India	$ 7

Source. Based on: United Nations *Monthly Bulletin of Statistics*, 7/1970, pp. 1–5, 114–15.

The rates of growth of foreign trade at current prices of the eight Socialist countries, according to their own sources, work out as follows (the rates for world trade as a whole are stated in brackets):

1951–60	12 (8)% p.a.
1961–65	8 (8)% p.a.
1966–69	9 (10) % p.a.

Sources. Rozwój gospodarczy krajów RWPG 1950–1968, op. cit., pp. 4, 16–43; *Gospodarka planowa* (Planned Economy), Warsaw, 4/1970, pp. 9, 15.

If we accept these rates,[1] there is certainly no evidence so far suggesting that the economic reforms have produced an accelerating effect on the growth of these countries' foreign trade. However, the rates of growth of national income since the reforms have also been lower than in the 1950s (cf. Table 3, p. 8). Consequently, it can be shown that since the early 1950s foreign trade in the eight Socialist countries has been *rising faster* than national income. A Polish economist, S. Albinowski, who recently carried out a study on the relative growth of national income and of imports, demonstrated that since 1951, taking five- (or four-) year

[1] It may be argued that the Socialist average rate for the 1950s appears unduly high for at least two reasons. Owing to the low absolute size of trade during the most frigid stage of the Cold War (1950–53), even *small absolute* subsequent increments represented high *percentage* increases. In addition, the Socialist foreign trade prices probably contained a greater upward bias before the adoption of world (Capitalist) prices in 1958 as a basis for intra-CMEA foreign trade.

periods in all the European CMEA countries (except Poland over
1951–55), the income elasticity of imports has been more than
unity.[1] Moreover, in all these countries except the USSR the
elasticity tended to increase at least up to the mid-1960s. According
to Albinowski's projection, over the period 1966–80 a unit increase
in national income will be associated with a 1·5 increase in Soviet
imports and with a 2·0 increase in the imports of the remaining
European CMEA countries as a whole (see Table 34 for details).

TABLE 34 INCOME ELASTICITY OF IMPORTS IN THE EUROPEAN
CMEA COUNTRIES, 1951–1980

COUNTRY	1951–55	1956–60	1961–64	1966–80*
Bulgaria	1·1	1·7	2·3	
Czechoslovakia	1·3	1·8	4·6	
GDR	1·7	1·9	2·0	
Hungary	1·9	2·2	2·4	2·0
Poland	0·8	1·2	1·7	
Romania	1·0	1·0	2·0	
USSR	1·7	1·5	1·4	1·5

* Projected.

Source. S. Albinowski, *Handel między krajami o różnych ustrojach* (Trade between
Countries with Different Social Systems), Warsaw, KiW, 1968, pp. 44, 276.

In effect, the share of foreign trade in most of these countries'
(material) national income about doubled between the early 1950s
and the late 1960s.[2]

At one stage, many Western economists, such as L. von Mises,
L. Robbins and J. Viner believed that Socialism must inevitably

[1] The income elasticity of imports is calculated as a ratio of the annual increase in imports to the annual increase in national income ($\Delta M : \Delta Y$). A ratio
of less than 1·0 over a period suggests an autarkic tendency, and a rising ratio
indicates increasing participation in the international division of labour. As
Socialist countries calculate their national income on the material basis, their
indices of the income elasticity of imports are not comparable with those for
Capitalist countries.
[2] In Bulgaria, from about 30 to 75%; in the GDR, from 25 to 70%; in
Hungary, from 25 to 70%; in Poland, from 30 to 45%; in Yugoslavia, from 25
to 40%; in Romania, from 20 to 35%; and in the USSR, from 8 to 10%.

lead to autarky because foreign trade introduced too much uncertainty into the process of planning.[1] The remarkable growth of Socialist foreign trade since the mid-1950s has proved these beliefs to be groundless. 'There is nothing inherent in the Socialist economy', it was concluded in a Polish study, 'necessitating autarky. In other words, a Socialist economy may be just as easily geared to the international division of labour as any other type of economy.'[2] Nevertheless, in spite of the considerable progress achieved so far, it must be realized that the share of foreign trade in the Socialist countries' national income is still low in comparison with advanced Capitalist economies. If their national income is brought to the Western basis, the share of the foreign trade turnover in the seven European Socialist countries (including Yugoslavia but excluding the USSR) as a whole in 1968 was about 45 per cent, and in the USSR, 8 per cent. The proportions for some of the most advanced Western countries in the same year were as follows: the European Economic Community, 72 per cent; the United Kingdom, 42 per cent; Australia, 36 per cent; Japan, 23 per cent; and the share for the USA was 10 per cent.[3]

B. INSTITUTIONAL REFORMS

The increased importance attached to the international division of labour and the recent reforms of internal economic relations have naturally affected the planning, organization and management of foreign trade. There are two apparently conflicting trends in foreign trade planning. On the one hand, foreign trade plans tend to be less prescriptive and detailed. Instead, they are laid down in broad categories mostly expressed in value (not physical) terms, and the entities engaging in foreign trade participate more actively in the preparation of such plans. Only those targets are compulsory

[1] See especially J. Viner, 'International Relations between State-Controlled National Economies', *Amer. Econ. Rev.*, Mar 1944, Supplement, pp. 315–29.
[2] Z. Kamecki, J. Sołdaczuk and W. Sierpiński, *Międzynarodowe stosunki ekonomiczne* (International Economic Relations), Warsaw, PWE, 1964, p. 504.
[3] The figures for the Western countries are based on *Monthly Bulletin of Statistics*, 4/1970, pp. 110–15, 184–8.

which are considered to be of key significance to the economy.[1]

On the other hand, the role of planning is increasing with the efforts to extend the international division of labour on the CMEA scale. There is already joint planning covering certain types of rolled metal sheets, pipes and other metallurgical products in short supply, some types of metal-cutting machine tools, container transport and electronic computers.[2] In 1970 the Secretary of CMEA, N. Faddeyev, predicted that the CMEA countries would sign a comprehensive Treaty on Joint Economic Planning which would cover periods of more than five years.[3]

Under the old system, the conduct of foreign trade was centrally and rigidly controlled in each Socialist country by the ministry of foreign trade, whose policy was carried out by a small number of foreign trade corporations. Each corporation was a large organization with a monopoly of exports and/or imports of prescribed categories of goods. The corporations did not trade at foreign-exchange equivalents. They sold exports at whatever prices they could obtain in foreign markets, but they paid internal prices to domestic producers. Similarly, for imported goods they charged the prices prevailing in the domestic market (or of their nearest substitutes). In effect, there was an almost complete insulation of domestic from foreign prices, which was made possible by large subsidies (mostly on exported goods) on the one hand, and by heavy turnover taxes (mostly on imports) on the other. This set-up was first developed in the USSR in the 1930s, was later adopted by other Socialist countries and in essence persisted till the early 1960s (the early 1950s in Yugoslavia).

Since that time, the foreign trade system has undergone considerable transformation in favour of a decentralization of the organization and management, a greater flexibility and a closer relation between production on the one hand and exports and imports on the other. The State foreign trade monopoly is no

---

[1] In Yugoslavia, central authorities no longer impose compulsory targets. In Bulgaria, Czechoslovakia and Hungary orientational indicators predominate. In the GDR, Poland, Romania and the USSR compulsory targets still play an important role, but their number has been substantially reduced (e.g. in the GDR by 1968 to 27).

[2] *Neues Deutschland* (New Germany), East Berlin, 30/5/1970, p. 6.

[3] *Izvestiya*, Moscow, 27/3/1970, p. 3.

longer vested exclusively in the ministry of foreign trade. Other economic ministries, branch associations and even industrial and commercial enterprises have also been conceded the right to manage or conduct foreign trade.[1]

The role of the ministry of foreign trade has been limited to the overall co-ordination of foreign trade. Typically, it now concentrates on the following responsibilities:

   (i) the formulation of foreign trade policy;
  (ii) the preparation, or rather co-ordination, of foreign trade plans;
 (iii) the negotiation of trade agreements and trade protocols;
 (iv) the licensing of exports and imports, and of the enterprises to engage in foreign trade;
  (v) the shaping of the financial instruments for the regulation of foreign trade;
 (vi) the conduct of market research relevant to foreign trade;
(vii) the promotion of the most efficient structure of foreign trade.

These responsibilities are now discharged mostly by relying on a flexible use of incentives and disincentives, rather than by issuing directives. Instead of being preoccupied with the insulation and protection of the economy from foreign markets, the ministries of foreign trade have become active organs of promoting international specialization, especially within the CMEA region.[2]

Many foreign trade corporations have been divided into smaller and more specialized entities, so that on the whole they are less unwieldy than they used to be. Thus up to the mid-1950s the foreign trade of the CMEA countries was conducted by 120

---

[1] This process has, naturally, gone farthest in Yugoslavia. The State foreign trade monopoly exercised by the Ministry of Foreign Trade and its foreign trade corporations began to be relaxed as early as 1952, when it was decided to issue licences to other enterprises to carry on foreign trade. Since 1966 any enterprise can engage in export without having to obtain a licence.

[2] Some Western writers on the subject deduce that the reforms are breaking down the State foreign trade monopoly, confusing it with the disintegration of the monopoly as exercised by the ministry of foreign trade. With the exception of Yugoslavia, these deductions are pure nonsense. Only State entities (and co-operatives in some cases) can engage in foreign trade, and they can do so only by being given permission by the State (usually the ministry of foreign trade). Foreign trade is still more tightly controlled than internal economic relations and is further reinforced by a strict exchange control.

K

monopolistic foreign trade corporations, but by 1970 their number was increased to 220 and in addition over 120 industrial and internal trading enterprises, industrial associations and even research institutes had the right of engaging in foreign trade directly.[1] In some countries (in Yugoslavia, and to a lesser extent in Hungary and Czechoslovakia) there are opportunities of exporting and importing a particular article through more than one entity, which provides a possibility of choice and enhances competition in foreign trade.

Some industrial associations and leading enterprises have established direct permanent representation, technical advice bureaux, guarantee offices and servicing and spare-parts stations in foreign markets, not only in Socialist but also in Capitalist countries.[2] Of all the European Socialist countries, the Soviet foreign trade set-up has been changed least (in addition to that in Albania). But even in the USSR in 1967 export councils were established to provide a closer link between the enterprises producing for export and the foreign trade corporations, to raise the quality and efficiency of exports.

So far CMEA has no supra-national authority. This set-up contrasts with the European Economic Community, whose success has been largely due to the fact that it has several supra-national bodies (such as the EEC Parliament, the Commission for the European Communities). A proposal to vest the CMEA Executive Council with supra-national powers was made in 1962, when it was vigorously launched by N. S. Khrushchev, but it failed owing to the stubborn opposition of Romania and other less developed member countries. This means that intra-CMEA specialization and trade co-operation have been based on the principle of unanimity, each member country being free not to participate in any

[1] In the late 1960s, the number of foreign trade corporations ranged from 25 in Romania to 43 in the USSR. In Bulgaria about one-half of foreign trade was conducted by associations of interested enterprises producing for export and those relying heavily on specialized imports. The number of entities (other than foreign trade corporations) which had the right of direct dealings in foreign markets was 70 in Hungary, 36 in Czechoslovakia and 8 in Poland. In the GDR most foreign trade corporations were acting as agents on behalf of the industrial associations so that the former were subordinate to the latter.

[2] e.g. the East German industrial associations and enterprises have established more than 170 such centres in 40 countries. *Gospodarka planowa* (Planned Economy), Warsaw, 7/1968, p. 60.

particular scheme.[1] Many Socialist leaders believe that when the member countries attain higher and more even levels of economic development, there will be less reluctance to hand over some supra-national powers to the Executive Council (or some other body).

C. FROM BILATERALISM TOWARDS MULTILATERALISM

Ever since the Second World War, Socialist countries have been noted for their preference for trading on a bilateral basis. This policy is aimed at an annual balancing of exports and imports with each country and moreover at ensuring the desired structure of trade. The main instrument of this policy is normally a bilateral trade agreement covering periods of two to six years, supplemented with more detailed annual trade protocols. A trade agreement usually specifies not only the total value of mutual trade but also the more or less detailed classes of goods to be exchanged, the method of payment, tariffs, the exchange of trade missions, arbitration, etc.

Like many other Socialist policies and practices, bilateralism has been partly adopted by choice and partly imposed by circumstances, but in each case it has represented a number of advantages to Socialist countries in the past. The balancing of trade with each partner country and trade agreements specifying the composition of exports and imports in advance facilitated economic planning of the traditional type, based on tight physical balances. In particular 'clearing settlements enabled central planners to keep their fingers on the pulse of the plan fulfilment processes'.[2]

The balancing of exports and imports with each country also reduced the need for currency transactions to the minimum. Owing to their limited export capacity (a small range of exportables, low quality, sellers' markets at home), poor marketing techniques and various forms of discrimination encountered in Capitalist markets,

---

[1] e.g. Romania has refused to participate in such important CMEA-wide co-operation schemes as the Organization for Co-operation in the Ball-Bearing Industry, Intermetal, Interchim and the International Investment Bank (see Chapter 13 D, p. 255).

[2] A. Wakar, *Handel zagraniczny w gospodarce socjalistycznej* (Foreign Trade in a Socialist Economy), Warsaw, PWN, 1968, p. 313.

Socialist countries have experienced great difficulties in earning enough foreign exchange, especially hard currencies. Consequently, in trade agreements or in actual trade deals these countries have often endeavoured to use the lever of imports to force their exports. In addition, bilateral trade agreements can be used as an instrument of foreign policy paving the way for political influence.

Bilateralism was probably inevitable in the past. Its peak of development was reached in the early 1950s, when it coincided with extremes reached in command planning and management and in the East–West cold warfare. As a Hungarian economist concluded:

> The bilateral system of trading of the early 1950s answered the existing needs of the Socialist countries, considering the nature of planning and political relations of the times. In those circumstances, bilateralism was historically and economically justified.[1]

However, many economists and political leaders alike soon came to recognize the disadvantages of bilateralism, even under Socialism.

Bilateral balancing of exports and imports with each country erodes the gains from international trade, because either export has to be reduced to the paying capacity of the weaker partner, or otherwise the exporting country has to accept payment in goods which it does not necessarily want. Furthermore, there are large administrative costs associated with the negotiation of trade agreements and protocols and the settlement of clearing accounts. The need for the multilateralization of trade and currency convertibility became obvious in the late 1950s, but its full significance has been grasped only since the early 1960s in the context of the intensification of economic growth. A Czechoslovak monetary expert expressed this need in a succinct way:

> The inconvertibility of currency under Socialism reduces the gains that can be derived from the international division of labour, insulates each national economy, shelters domestic industries from foreign competition, and so on. It makes international comparisons of prices impossible and it distorts the composition and direction of foreign trade.[2]

[1] I. Wiesel, ('Five Years of Existence of the International Bank for Economic Co-operation'), *Közgazdasági szemle* (Economic Review), Budapest, 5/1969, p. 538.

[2] R. Zukal, ('Currency Convertibility and External Economic Relations'), *Plánované hospodářství* (Planned Economy), Prague, 6/1968, p. 56.

The essence of multilateral trade is that exports are no longer limited by the exporting country's imports from the partner country. Exports are sold wherever they fetch the highest prices, and only those imports are purchased which are wanted – and in the cheapest market at that. As such, multilateralism provides a new source of economic growth – an intensive source *par excellence*.

The multilateralization of the Socialist countries' trade is without doubt the most complex problem of them all. It cuts across some of the most vital sinews of a Socialist economy, and its success necessitates far-reaching changes going to the very foundations of those economies. We shall now bring out the developments which are relevant towards the realization of this declared goal. Some of these developments are evolutionary background changes contributing to the creation of preconditions for multilateral trade, whilst others are specific steps taken in this direction.

(a) Rational Prices

The most basic precondition for multilateralism is the evolution of a rational price system. Only rational prices, i.e. those reflecting cost-preference conditions, can provide a solid basis for the maximization of the gains from trade in accordance with the principle of comparative advantage. Since 1957 the CMEA countries have been using Capitalist world market prices as a basis in their mutual trade. Internally, as a part of the general economic reforms, all the Socialist countries have embarked on far-reaching reforms of prices, especially of producers' prices (see Chapter 5).

Some attempts have also been made to bring producers' and retail prices into closer correspondence (see Chapter 12 C, pp. 221–6). In most Socialist countries (especially in Bulgaria, Czechoslovakia, the German Democratic Republic, Hungary and Yugoslavia), many prices relevant to foreign trade have been transferred to flexible categories, so that to some extent they can be influenced by current market conditions. At the same time, owing to the decentralization of planning and management, enterprises are now in a better position to respond to changing prices and demand.

There is a tendency for the enterprises producing for export to be paid in foreign-exchange equivalents (instead of the artificial insulated domestic prices). Similarly, there is a trend to price imports at their foreign-exchange equivalents, and not merely in line with the closest domestic substitutes. Thus direct links have been initiated (but with the exception of Yugoslavia, no more than that) between domestic and foreign prices.

(b) Exchange Rates

The efforts to rationalize price systems will not help the cause of multilateralism much until the exchange rates of the Socialist currencies are brought to such levels as will reflect their purchasing power in terms of internationally traded goods. Although some progress has been made in the last decade, Socialist currencies are still subject to multiple exchange rates, at practically all of which they are over-valued in relation to convertible currencies. This is shown in Table 35.

It can be seen that the official basic rates, at which the value of visible trade is recorded in official statistics, are furthest from equilibrium rates. So far, only Yugoslavia – by devaluation (in 1952, 1961, 1965 and 1971), the virtual discontinuation of multiple rates (since 1961), and a domestic monetary reform (in 1965) – has evolved near-equilibrium official exchange rates. She is also the only Socialist country to be a member of the International Monetary Fund (having joined it in 1949). In reality, with the qualified exception of Yugoslavia since 1961, the official basic rate has hardly ever been relevant in determining the flow of foreign trade, particularly since the introduction of the foreign trade efficiency calculations (see section D of this chapter). This rate has been periodically corrected by special coefficients to reflect more closely the prices in different markets, the degree of convertibility of different currencies, the conditions of payments, and above all to ensure a balance of payments equilibrium. Thus in effect the implicit exchange rates have in such cases been closer to equilibrium rates.

The implicit rate became explicit in Hungary in 1968, since when the most important rates of exchange affecting Hungarian exports have been:[1] US \$1·00 = 60·00 forints (compared with the official basic rate of \$1·00 = 11·74 forints), and 1·00 rouble = 40·00 forints (the official basic rate being 1·00 rouble = 13·10 forints);[2] note that by the official exchange rates the Soviet rouble is worth 12 per cent more than the US dollar, but in the new corrected exchange rates economic common sense has prevailed and the US dollar is rated as being worth 50 per cent more than the Soviet rouble.

Little progress has been made so far in other countries in evolving equilibrium, or even realistic, official exchange rates, but in the USSR multiple rates have been practically discontinued since 1961. The Czechoslovak economist mentioned before, R. Zukal, pointed out that the exchange rates will have to be set at such levels as to promote exports and restrain imports, i.e. amounting to substantial devaluation compared with the present official basic rates. He justifies it on the grounds of the continued shortages of many key commodities ('hard items'), especially of raw materials – the present unrealistic rates only encourage the extravagant use of these items, which further aggravates the shortages. Such realistic exchange rates would also be conducive to the accumulation of international liquidity reserves to support the convertibility of Socialist currencies.[3] The vice-chairman of the Polish State Planning Commission has recently put forward a proposal for the introduction of a uniform (non-multiple) exchange rate in intra-CMEA trade, to be based initially on the cost of living, as a step towards the gradual evolution of equilibrium rates in the future.[4] Such rates would be more indicative of retail

[1] According to the chairman of Hungary's Materials and Prices Commission (Béla Csikós-Nagy), the value of the Hungarian forint in relation to the US dollar differed depending on the basis of comparison. In 1970, in purchasing power \$1·00 was equivalent to 20 forints on the basis of consumer-goods prices, to 30 forints in tourist trade and to 56 forints in terms of producers' prices in the gross social product. See B. Csikós-Nagy, ('Features and Tasks of Price Policy'), *Pénzügyi szemle* (Financial Review), Budapest, 2/1970, p. 101.

[2] However, it appears that in application to imports for use in agriculture, the rates are 30–35% lower. In the same year the non-commercial ('tourist and financial') rate in relation to the US dollar was devalued from 23·48 to 30·00 forints. See *Ekonomista* (The Economist), Warsaw, no. 6, 1969, p. 1396.

[3] R. Zukal, op. cit., p. 57.

[4] J. Pajestka, ('Socialist Integration – Directions in the Development of Co-operation'), *Życie gospodarcze*, 9/6/1968, p. 11.

TABLE 35 EXCHANGE RATES OF SOCIALIST CURRENCIES
(Units of National Currency to US $1·00)

TYPE OF EXCHANGE RATE	BULGARIA (Leva)	CZECHOSLOVAKIA (Korunas)	GDR (DD Marks)	HUNGARY (Forints)	POLAND (Zlotys)	ROMANIA (Lei)	USSR (Roubles)	YUGOSLAVIA¶ (Dinars)
Official basic rate	1·17	7·20	2·22	11·74	4·00	6·00	0·90	12·50
Implicit non-commercial rate for the rouble area	0·70	8·70	2·88	11·81	13·75	7·00*	—	—
Non-commercial rates for hard-currency areas: ordinary rate	2·00	14·36	4·20†	30·00	24·00	18·00	—‡	—§
bonus rate¶	—	16·20	—	—	40·00	—	—	—
Rate on non-commercial remittances from hard-currency areas‖	—	55·00	6·50	30·00	72·00	—	5·00	—
Other legal rates**	n.a.	36·00††	n.a.	60·00‡‡	n.a.	n.a.	n.a.	13·75§§
Black-market rate	3·70	60·00	15·00	55·00	120·00	35·00	6·00	13·50

n.a. = not available.

* Average; the range of the rates with individual countries (including China) works out as from 2·16 to 12·84.

† Known as the 'Valuta Mark', applicable to all visible trade and non-commercial transactions with hard-currency areas.

‡ The tourist rate has been discontinued since January 1961 (revaluation of the rouble).

§ The tourist rate has been discontinued since February 1961.

¶ Applies to exchanged amounts exceeding $3·00 per day in Czechoslovakia and $50·00 in Poland.

‖ This rate is usually allowed to be negotiated freely between buyers and sellers. It fluctuates about 10% below and above the stated rates.

** Clearing rates are not listed here, but it is understood that there is a large number of these rates; those applicable to trade with Capitalist countries are further complicated by discounts (depreciation) when Socialist credit balances are sold in free markets.

†† The so-called 'travel dollar' for residents going to Capitalist countries.

‡‡ The foreign trade price coefficient applicable to visible transactions with hard-currency areas. The implicit rate for trade with the rouble area (40·00 forints to 1·00 rouble) works out as 36·04 forints to $1·00.

§§ Applicable to blocked accounts in Yugoslavia which can be spent only in Yugoslavia.

¶¶ In January 1971 Yugoslavia devalued her official basic rate of 12·50 dinars to 15·00 dinars to US $1·00 (i.e. by 20%)

Source. Compiled from Socialist and Western daily and periodical publications.

prices and thus would be closer to the present non-commercial ('tourist') rates, which are more realistic than the official basic rates.

The chairman of the Hungarian Materials and Price Commission, B. Csikós-Nagy, believes that equilibrium exchange rates will be evolved in the CMEA countries in two stages. At first there is a need for further perfection of financial instruments and market relations, to create solid foundations for realistic parity (official basic) rates. In the next stage, parity rates will be further readjusted to ensure a balance of payments equilibrium and the intensification of international specialization.[1] There have also been rumours in recent years that Bulgaria, Czechoslovakia, Hungary and Romania have expressed interest in joining the International Monetary Fund.

(c) Trade Agreements and Protocols

In contrast to previous practice, these have tended to become less specific – rather an expression of intention, especially in relation to Capitalist countries. Besides, more and more trade takes place outside the confines of agreements and protocols. With some Capitalist countries trade is no longer engaged in on the basis of agreements, and in many other cases where it is, bilateral balancing is not specified. For example, of the 162 trade agreements between the nine Socialist and eighteen Capitalist countries of Europe in the mid-1960s, only 67 (i.e. 40 per cent) specified bilateral clearing

[1] B. Csikós-Nagy, ('Foreign Exchange and Pricing Problems of Socialist Economic Integration'), *Gospodarka planowa*, 8/1969, p. 29.

payments.[1] Even in intra-CMEA foreign trade, above-quota trade is now not uncommon and it is often settled on a multilateral basis in convertible currencies (mostly in US dollars or sterling) or gold.[2] Some economists are in favour of extending the market mechanism to foreign trade and discontinuing trade agreements even in intra-CMEA trade.[3]

(d) The Access to Markets

On the one hand, many Capitalist nations (such as France, the Federal Republic of Germany, Italy, the Scandinavian countries, the United Kingdom) have been gradually relaxing and abolishing quotas on imports from the European Socialist countries, thus enabling the latter to earn more convertible foreign exchange.[4] Anti-dumping procedures, which previously had been commonly applied to counter any Socialist export promotion, are now more reasonably invoked. The access to Socialist markets has also been improving. Restrictions on business travel, on the opening of offices by foreign (including Western) firms and the exchange of trade missions have been largely lifted, even in the USSR. As economic planning is not as tight as it was in the past, unexpected purchases by foreign importers do not represent such a threat of disruption to plan fulfilment as before.

A closer relation has also been established between production and foreign trade, and many industrial enterprises can engage in foreign trade directly (not necessarily through the monopolistic foreign trade corporations), so that foreign traders can deal with such enterprises directly. The promotion of East–West trade through advertising across the disintegrating Iron (or Strategic)

[1] S. Albinowski, op. cit., p. 96.

[2] I. Dimov, ('The Place of Collective Foreign Exchange, or the Transferable Rouble, in the Development of Socialist Economic Integration'), *Finansi i kredit* (Finance and Credit), Sofia, 3/1970, p. 13.

[3] See, e.g., *Die Wirtschaft* (The Economy), East Berlin, 1/8/1968, Supplement, pp. 6–7; *Planovo stopanstvo* (Planned Economy), Sofia, 2/1969, pp. 23–4.

[4] A summary of the quantitative controls administered by Western European nations in the late 1960s on imports from the European Socialist countries can be found in United Nations *Economic Bulletin for Europe*, vol. 20, no. 1, Nov 1968, pp. 53–4. Further and more recent details are available in *The American Review of East–West Trade*, New York, 3/1969, p. 65, 12/1969, p. 40, and 1/1970, pp. 47, 50; *East–West Commerce*, London, 4/1969, p. 9, and 4/1970, pp. 2, 3.

Curtain has become a common feature.[1] Foreign competition is welcome in Bulgaria, Czechoslovakia, Hungary and Yugoslavia.[2]

(e) Buyers' Markets

Shortages are becoming less common in the Socialist countries as their economies are attaining greater capacities for production – quantitatively and qualitatively – and more experience has been gained in monetary and incomes policies. Some genuine efforts have been made in all these countries to develop export production not only for the needs of other CMEA countries but also for Capitalist markets. This is illustrated by Bulgarian communications equipment, Czechoslovak machinery and vehicles, East German office equipment, Hungarian pharmaceuticals, Polish machine tools, Romanian petrochemicals, Soviet oil and gas and Yugoslav ferro-alloys.

(f) Tariffs

Socialist interests in tariffs as an instrument of economic policy was first aroused in the late 1950s as a possible bargaining weapon in answer to the economic integration in Western Europe. But their possible role has been enhanced by the economic reforms since the early 1960s, as a tool for regulating imports in lieu of the former rigid quantitative controls.[3] In contrast to quotas and

---

[1] Some Socialist countries have established special corporations for this purpose. For example, Czechoslovakia – Rapid, the GDR – Interwerbung, Romania – Publicom. A good deal of advertising is also done directly by the chambers of foreign trade.

[2] As reported in 1969, only 2·6% of Yugoslav exports was subject to State controls and about 50% of imports was subject to foreign exchange quotas.

[3] Yugoslavia was the first Socialist country to embrace tariffs as the main weapon of foreign trade policy. Legislation for the introduction of protective tariffs was passed as early as 1949 but no tariff schedule was prepared at the time. In 1960 tariffs were introduced on parcel traffic affecting private individuals. On commercial imports tariffs were applied only in 1961, with *ad valorem* rates ranging from 0 to 60%. Thus tariffs began to replace quotas as one of the conditions which Yugoslavia had to meet for admission to full membership of GATT. In 1963 'free trade zones' were created at Rijeka, Khoper and Belgrade, and according to recent reports more are to be established at Bar, Ploce and Split. In 1965 the Customs Tariff Act was passed, constituting an important element of economic reforms. In 1967 she introduced anti-dumping duties. The average level of tariffs in different years was as follows: in 1962, 18·8%; in 1964,

prohibitions, tariffs do not interfere with the market mechanism as a system and they are consistent with the use of financial incentives and disincentives under the new economic model. Tariffs have been most actively used in recent years in Bulgaria, Hungary and Yugoslavia and to some extent also in Czechoslovakia. In these countries a flexible use of import duties is seen as a useful instrument for cushioning the impact of the gradual abolition of quantitative controls and the transition to equilibrium exchange rates.

The German Democratic Republic and the USSR administer tariffs, but they remain passive, reciprocating devices; in 1964 the USSR abolished tariffs on imports from developing countries. Poland and Romania have so far not introduced commercial tariff systems, but they administer duties on the parcels of private persons. A common external tariff for the CMEA grouping has been advocated by a number of Socialist economists,[1] but according to others it is not likely to eventuate in the near future.[2]

(g) Incentives in Foreign Trade

As a rule, profit has been accepted as the main, or only, criterion for judging the success of enterprises engaging in foreign trade, especially in export. It is therefore in their interest to buy in the cheapest and to sell in the most profitable markets (unless directed to the contrary). Moreover, export incentives have been strengthened to promote the earning of foreign exchange.[3] In all the

---

23·3%; in 1965, 12·0%; in 1966, 10·3%; and in 1968, 13·8%. See M. Savičević, 'Protective Tariffs and Other Measures of Protection of the National Economy', *Yugoslav Survey*, Belgrade, Feb 1970, pp. 55–62.

[1] e.g. P. Penkov, ('A New and Effective Tariff Policy'), *Vunshna turgoviya*, 4/1969, pp. 7–9.

[2] Z. Kamecki, ('Problems of the Economic Integration of the CMEA Countries'), *Gospodarka planowa*, 10/1968, p. 12.

[3] It is generally believed in the West that of all Socialist countries the USSR is least interested in expanding her exports, owing to her vast domestic resources and substantial gold production (see note 1, p. 285 below). Yet in 1968, the bonuses payable to enterprises for exports were raised from 1 to 3% of the value of machinery and equipment delivered, and from 0·2 to 0·6% in the case of other industrial products, raw materials and foodstuffs. In addition, special bonuses were introduced on deliveries of spare parts – 5% of the sale price. *Ekonomicheskaya gazeta* (Economic Gazette), Moscow, no. 3, Jan 1968, p. 31.

Socialist countries under consideration, most enterprises engaging in exports are now allowed to retain a portion of their foreign exchange earnings and make use of them outside bilateral channels to improve their production and marketing. Efforts are made to make production for export equally or more profitable than that for domestic use.

(h) International Commercial Co-operation

In contrast to the Cold War years of the 1950s, in the last decade the Socialist countries have shown considerable interest in joining international organizations relevant to commercial co-operation, and Capitalist countries are no longer as opposed as they were before. Yugoslavia was admitted to GATT as a full member in 1966 and Poland in the following year, Czechoslovakia being a foundation member. Bulgaria, Hungary and Romania have hinted that they may join, too. The Economic Commission for Europe has proved a most valuable meeting-ground for Eastern and Western European countries, and many solutions to East–West problems have been jointly worked out under the patient tutelage of the Committee on the Development of Trade.[1]

(i) The Transferability of the Socialist Balances Earned in Western Countries

Since 1957, the Secretariat of the Economic Commission for Europe has operated a multilateral clearing system (on a modest scale) in which most Eastern and Western European countries and some developing nations have been included, to ease Socialist payment problems. With the Cold War on the wane and the Socialist countries having proved valuable and reputable customers, many Western nations (particularly those within EEC and EFTA) have relaxed the transferability of Socialist trade surpluses, especially since the early 1960s. In a sense, multiangular trade and switch deals, where settlements are completed in circuits involving

[1] For further details, see J. Wilczynski, *The Economics and Politics of East–West Trade*, London, Macmillan, 1969, esp. pp. 361–89.

three or more countries, also contribute in small ways to the development of multilateralism.[1]

(j) International Reserves

To enable multilateralism to work on a solid basis, Socialist currencies would have to become convertible, for which one of the basic prerequisites is the accumulation and maintenance of reasonable reserves of gold or hard currencies. Socialist countries, with the partial exception of the USSR, have suffered from an acute pressure on their balance of payments, and this is likely to continue in the near future.

At present, only Yugoslavia regularly publishes her international liquidity reserves, as she is the only Socialist member country of the International Monetary Fund. Her reserves (of gold, convertible foreign exchange, the reserve position in IMF and special drawing rights) have increased remarkably since the early 1960s – from about $70m. to about $200m. in 1970.[2] Although Yugoslav reserves have increased substantially in recent years, they represent only 10–15 per cent of the country's annual import bill. The proportion in the case of Western countries is usually 25–40 per cent, by which token Yugoslavia's reserves should be $500m.–$800m. to support the convertibility of her currency. The growth of Yugoslavia's reserves will be aided in the near future by her improved capacity for gold production[3] and increasing inflows of foreign capital from Western countries (see Chapter 9 D, p. 163). The reserves (of gold and convertible foreign exchange)

---

[1] Some of the well-established multiangular channels include: Poland – Finland – the USSR; the GDR – the FRG – Denmark; Czechoslovakia – Japan – North Vietnam. Switch-dealing, whereby imports from a Socialist country in the form of (unwanted) counter-purchases are re-exported to other Capitalist countries, has been developed in recent years by some specialized banks in Amsterdam, London, Paris and Vienna. The possibility of such operations reduces the reluctance of Capitalist countries with hard currencies to accept unwanted imports from Socialist trade partners. For further details, see especially *The Economist*, 14/1/1967, pp. 143–4.

[2] *International Financial Statistics*, 9/1970, pp. 358–9.

[3] In the late 1960s, Yugoslavia produced about 2,500 kilogrammes of gold (worth $3m.) annually, or one-quarter of all gold mined in non-Socialist Europe. According to a recent survey, this output may double in the near future. See D. Milovanović, ('Prospects for the Production of Gold'), *Rudarski glasnik* (Mining Herald), Belgrade, Jan–Mar 1969, pp. 55–60.

of the Soviet Union are estimated to be $2,500m., or perhaps less, representing less than 25 per cent of Soviet annual imports.[1] The combined reserves of the remaining six Socialist countries (Bulgaria, Czechoslovakia, the German Democratic Republic, Hungary, Poland and Romania) are believed to be normally $800m. or less, sufficient to pay for no more than 5–10 per cent, or less, of their annual imports.

There is no lack of proposals – put forward in the CMEA countries, as well as in the West – for overcoming the problem of Socialist reserves. J. Pajestka (of Poland) has proposed the creation of a new 'Socialist currency' linked by 'realistic' exchange rates to domestic currencies and backed by the common monetary reserves and real resources of the CMEA countries. Z. Rurarz (also of Poland) has advocated that the pool of international reserves should consist not of gold but of 'hard' commodities on the CMEA scale, which could be purchased with a trade surplus earned with any country.[2] On the other hand, L. Ács (of Hungary) is in favour of a compromise – the reserves should consist of both gold and 'hard' items in common demand in Socialist as well as Capitalist countries.[3] Y. Shiryayev (of the USSR) thinks that multilateral investment schemes, financed out of a common fund, to develop joint

[1] The Socialist countries, other than Yugoslavia, publish no figures on either their reserves or their current gold production. But there are indications suggesting that the USSR produces about $150m. worth of gold annually (being the largest world producer after South Africa, but ahead of Canada, the USA and Australia). The USSR is normally an important seller of gold in the leading Capitalist financial centres (especially in London and Zürich) for Western hard currencies. The annual value of these sales in the last two decades works out at about $150m., but in the first half of the 1960s they averaged $350m. In recent years the search for additional gold deposits has been intensified, and apparently new gold fields have been discovered in the following districts: Armenia, Azerbaijan, Kamchatka, Kirgizia, the Kyzyl Kum desert, the Pamirs, Tadzhikistan, Tula, Tyumen, the Upper Bikin River, Vladimir, Voronezh and Yaroslav. One of these fields, at Muruntau (in the Kyzyl Kum desert), has been described by Soviet commentators as the 'Soviet Klondike'. For details, see, for example, Soviet News, Soviet Embassy in London, 30/1/1968, p. 63, and 12/3/1968, p. 140. It is difficult to say whether these announcements, which are eagerly circulated by the Soviets in the West, are genuine and herald a stepping up of Soviet gold production, or calculated propaganda to inspire confidence in the Soviet rouble.

[2] For further details see P. Bożyk, ('Economic Integration of the Socialist Countries'), Gospodarka planowa, 4/1969, pp. 43–51.

[3] L. Ács, A szocialista pénz elmélete (The Theory of Socialist Money), Budapest, KéJK, 1966, p. 299.

projects (especially to produce 'hard' commodities) in the CMEA region would provide a significant step forward towards multilateral payments.[1]

Some economists, in the Socialist as well as in Capitalist countries, look to the West for financial support. It is not without significance that the CMEA International Bank for Economic Cooperation (see p. 287–9 below) specifically provides, under Article 43 of its Charter, for the admission of Capitalist countries. J. Bognár (of Hungary) has gone further by suggesting the creation of an 'East–West Bank', and the late J. Vajda (of Hungary) an 'East–West Payments Union'; B. Csikós-Nagy (also of Hungary) maintains that the CMEA countries should establish a workable link with the monetary system in the Capitalist world and gradually open their domestic markets to Capitalist traders.[2]

This line of approach has also found support from such a shrewd American authority on Socialist countries as Z. Brzezinski, who a few years ago recommended that a special fund be set up by Western interests for underwriting joint East–West ventures.[3] Another American specialist on Socialist economies, H. W. Shaffer, proposed that the USA – which in 1950 contributed $350m. to the European Payments Union – might find it to her advantage after all to support the East European multilateral aspirations with a similar fund which might prove equally as successful as it did in Western Europe.[4] An interesting scheme has been put forward by the well-known French economist, M. Byé. He has proposed that the affluent Western countries should substantially step up their economic aid to developing nations in the form of untied grants and loans, so that the latter can increase their imports (to be paid for in convertible currencies) from the

---

[1] Y. Shiryayev ('Problems of Improving the System of Economic Cooperation amongst Socialist Countries under Modern Conditions'), *Ekonomicheskie nauki*, 6/1969, p. 46. Since that time, the CMEA countries (excluding Romania) have established the International Investment Bank for similar purposes.

[2] Reported in *Figyelö* (Economic Observer), Budapest, 6/11/1968, pp. 3–4.

[3] Z. Brzezinski, *Alternative to Partition*, New York, McGraw-Hill, 1965, pp. 162–7, 170.

[4] H. W. Shaffer, 'An East European Payments Union?', *East Europe*, 3/1966, pp. 14–21.

CMEA region.[1] Some Western economists, such as R. Triffin, R. McNamara (both of the USA), G. Carli (of Italy), are credited with being in favour of the CMEA countries joining IMF, or perhaps participating in some sort of joint East–West Monetary Fund.[2]

(k) Work under CMEA Permanent Commissions

Two Commissions – those for Economic Questions (established in 1958, with its headquarters in Moscow) and for Currency and Finance (1962, Moscow) – have been carrying on studies on the organization and systematization of intra-CMEA prices, payments and progress towards the multilateralization of the member countries' trade. In particular, efforts are being made to introduce a uniformity of principles and practices affecting the formation of prices – especially of such elements as labour costs, capital charges, depreciation rates, profit mark-ups and trade margins. It is also known that the Permanent Commission for Currency and Finance is working on methods of rationalizing the exchange rates of the member countries. On the recommendation of the same Commission in 1963, the member countries established the International Bank for Economic Co-operation, which we shall examine next.

(l) The International Bank for Economic Co-operation

The creation of IBEC, which began its operations in January 1964 (with its head office in Moscow), is the most direct step taken by the CMEA countries towards the multilateralization of their trade. Article 9 of IBEC's Charter states: 'The Bank shall organize and carry out multilateral settlements in transferable roubles in commercial and other operations.' Its initial capital is 300m. transferable roubles (about $335m. at the official exchange rate), consisting of the member countries' foreign exchange, hard currencies and gold.

[1] M. Byé, *Relations économiques internationales* (International Economic Relations), Paris, Dalloz, 2nd ed., 1965, esp. pp. 280–5.
[2] Reported in: Z. Królak, ('Socialist Integration – From Multiangular Clearing to Convertibility'), *Życie gospodarcze*, 14/7/1968, p. 7.

Each member country has a clearing account with IBEC into which all its payments are made. Member countries can use their trade surpluses for offsetting their deficits with some other member countries. The instrument of multilateral settlements is the 'transferable' (or 'clearing') rouble, which although divorced from the Soviet internal monetary system has the same 'gold backing' as the rouble in internal circulation (0·987412 grammes of fine gold). In fact it becomes transferable only if the transaction partners agree, so that so far it is neither convertible into gold or hard currencies, nor automatically transferable even in intra-CMEA payments.

Subject to the agreements, each country needs to balance its payments only with the group as a whole. Even this does not have to be done on an annual basis because the Bank extends credits.[1] These credits enable the exporting countries to receive transferable cash payments for exports exceeding those agreed upon in annual plans, and thus to make purchases immediately in other member countries. In 1968, the Bank decided to increase the rates of interest to induce borrowers to repay their credits on maturity and to speed up the turnover of the Bank's resources.[2] The value of payments handled by IBEC has been increasing most remarkably (from 22,900m. in 1964 to 57,200m. transferable roubles in 1969). The Bank has established business relations with about 130 banks in Capitalist countries. It carries out substantial operations in gold and convertible currencies (mostly US dollars, sterling, West German marks and French and Swiss francs); between 1965 and 1970 the amount of these operations increased from $3,000m. to $15,000m.[3] According to recent reports, which have apparently originated in Paris, the transferable rouble may soon find its way

---

[1] In 1968 they amounted to 2,000m. (compared with 1,500m. in 1964) transferable roubles, now representing 11–13% of the member countries' total payments carried out through the Bank. K. Nazarkin, 'The International Bank for Economic Co-operation Today', *Foreign Trade*, Moscow, 1/1970, p. 49.

[2] Even so, the interest rates are still very low: seasonal credits, from 1·5 to 2·5% a year; trade expansion credits, 1·5–2·5% p.a.; clearing credits, 2·0–3·0% p.a. Some credits are interest-free (in the mid-1960s they constituted about one-half of the total). The chairman of the Board of IBEC, K. Nazarkin, recently stressed that free credits should be discontinued and interest rates should be further increased. *Vunshna turgoviya*, 1/1969, p. 5; K. Nazarkin, op. cit., p. 50.

[3] *Ekonomicheskaya gazeta*, no. 25, June 1970, pp. 20–1.

into Western markets, as a move towards making it an international reserve currency.[1]

(m) Conclusions

Whether full multilateralism is compatible with Socialist central planning remains yet to be demonstrated in practice. The slow progress achieved so far is a legacy of the old policies dominated by autarkic and extensive considerations. These policies produced parallel economies in the CMEA region, where each country suffers from similar deficits and surpluses. A Soviet writer recently described the situation as follows:

It is rather disappointing that the available opportunities for the extension of trade on a multilateral basis are not fully utilized. The CMEA countries still continue to plan their foreign trade and ensure its balancing predominantly on a bilateral basis. It appears that the factors impeding the growth of multilateralism include the slow progress in specialization amongst the member countries, limited co-operation amongst enterprises and an insufficient production of hard items of required quality.[2]

So far IBEC has in fact been little more than a glorified bilateral clearing house. Only 2–3 per cent of intra-CMEA foreign trade was reported in 1969 as being settled on a multilateral basis.[3] It is doubtful if a uniformity of price-determination procedures can be evolved in the CMEA region without a freer operation of the market mechanism or a supra-national authority. If, for intra-CMEA foreign trade, these countries decide to adopt their own regional price system, divorced from world markets (see Chapter 5 D, pp. 92–5), the problem of the multilateralization of trade with the Capitalist world will be magnified. Some economists are still convinced that convertibility is a luxury that only highly developed countries can afford. The need to maintain large reserves, which essentially represent idle resources, coupled with instability, which is likely to be associated with multilateral trade, may only lead to a slowdown of both economic growth and the rise in the

---

[1] Reported in *The American Review of East–West Trade*, 1/1970, p. 12.
[2] V. Karpich, ('Development of Currency and Financial Relations among the CMEA Countries'), *Voprosy ekonomiki*, 7/1969, p. 104.
[3] I. Wiesel, op. cit., p. 538.

standard of living. These arguments are raised even in a country like Yugoslavia.[1]

The ultimate indication of multilateralism is the external and internal convertibility of currency. As yet, no Socialist currency, not even the Soviet rouble, in the possession of foreign or domestic holders is convertible into hard currencies. Nor is it freely convertible by foreign (and to some extent even domestic) holders into commodities in any CMEA country. So far the authorities in these countries have been interested more in improving their access to Western markets than in allowing Capitalist (or even other Socialist) traders the freedom of buying what, how much and when they want.

No doubt progress will continue to be made, but it will be slow. According to B. Csikós-Nagy, Hungary may achieve partial convertibility of the forint in about the mid-1970s, and a rational price system reflecting costs should be evolved by the late 1970s.[2] But it is uncertain at the time of writing whether these timings will in fact be realized. Other CMEA countries, except perhaps Czechoslovakia, the German Democratic Republic and the USSR, are likely to lag behind.

D. THE PROBLEM OF THE EFFICIENCY AND STRUCTURE OF FOREIGN TRADE

Up to about the mid-1950s, Socialist countries attached little importance to the efficiency of foreign trade. The accent was on extensive development, and foreign trade was essentially treated as a means of attaining a greater degree of self-sufficiency. But the increasing attention being given to the international division of labour as a source of growth, and the growing proportions of foreign trade in national income, brought the problem to the fore. It is not the size of foreign trade but the extent to which it saves domestic resources that makes it a source of intensive growth.

A Socialist centrally planned economy has no automatic mechan-

[1] e.g. I. Dvornik, ('Problems of the Convertibility of the Dinar'), *Finansije* (Finance), Belgrade, July–Aug 1969, esp. p. 380.

[2] B. Csikós-Nagy, *Pricing in Hungary*, London, Institute of Economic Affairs, 1968, pp. 33–4.

ism for ensuring the most gainful flow of foreign trade. The distorted domestic price structure, disequilibrium exchange rates and the insulation of domestic from foreign markets render the differentials between domestic and foreign prices largely meaningless. To overcome these inherent disabilities, two approaches have been followed – centrally managed foreign trade efficiency calculations, and the extension of the market mechanism to foreign trade.

Systematic studies of foreign trade efficiency were first introduced in the early 1950s in Czechoslovakia, Hungary and Poland, but soon other Socialist countries took them up as well. Although there have been national differences of methodology, scope and definitions, the following generalizations may be made. The studies have produced three types of indices to measure the foreign-exchange effectiveness of exports, imports and investment relevant to foreign trade. In these indices domestic costs are related to the receipts or expenditure of foreign exchange. The indices are further supplemented by the coefficients of the relative value of foreign currencies and the marginal exchange rate. More recently, econometric models of the overall efficiency of foreign trade have been devised (but nowhere fully applied in practice yet).

The indices and coefficients have been used in planning and in the current conduct of foreign trade in an endeavour to optimize the structure and direction of exports and (to a lesser extent) of imports, and to ensure the balance of payments equilibrium. The indices are applied to arrange potential exports, imports and relevant investments in descending order of foreign-exchange 'effectiveness'. The marginal (or 'limiting') exchange rate, fixed and adjusted periodically by the ministry of foreign trade (in consultation with the ministry of finance), indicates the least efficient exports or imports still allowed to achieve a balance of payments equilibrium.

So far, the efficiency analysis has been developed most in application to exports. An example of a formula to calculate the comparative effectiveness of export is given below:

$$nfeEx = \frac{C + K - M - X}{fP + fK - fM - fX};$$

nfeEx = the net foreign-exchange effectiveness of export;
C   = the cost of production (producers' or wholesale price) in domestic currency;
K   = domestic marketing costs in domestic currency;
M   = the value of imported components in domestic currency;
X   = the value of exportable components (which could earn foreign exchange in their own right) in domestic currency;
fP   = foreign price obtainable in foreign currency;
fK   = marketing costs incurred in foreign exchange;
fM = the value of imported components in foreign currency;
fX   = the value of exportable components in foreign currency.[1]

The efficiency calculations have not so far been applied to the same extent to imports as to exports. A Polish economist has formulated the following 'law of imports' applicable to the different stages of development of a Socialist economy. In the early stage, imports are limited to indispensable investment goods without which accelerated industrialization is impossible; at this stage, the import efficiency analysis is largely pointless. In the middle stage, the import effort is concentrated on machinery and equipment embodying the most advanced technology lacking in domestic production; as these imports are complementary rather than competitive, import efficiency studies are in fact more technical than economic. Only in the higher stages of economic development, when there is a solid basis for choice between domestic and foreign sources of supplies, are imports determined by comparative advantage and the efficiency analysis assumes its full significance. Most European Socialist countries are now in stage two, but all of them are steadily expanding what has come to be known as 'comparative' imports.[2] The indices used in the evaluation of import efficiency are similar to those used for exports.[3]

The success of enterprises engaging in foreign trade is now

[1] For further details and sources, see J. Wilczynski, op. cit., pp. 311–30.

[2] J. Kotyński, ('Foreign Trade and the Economic Growth of Romania'), in J. Sołdaczuk (ed.), *Handel zagraniczny a wzrost krajów RWPG* (Foreign Trade and Economic Growth of the CMEA Countries), Warsaw, PWE, 1969, p. 310.

[3] For examples of the indices of import efficiency, as well as of the efficiency of investment relevant to foreign trade, see J. Wilczynski, op. cit., pp. 318–22.

generally judged by profits. Where domestic prices do not reflect costs and where official exchange rates distort the relation of domestic to foreign currencies, *computational profit* is adopted as the basis for bonuses to the enterprise personnel. In Poland it has been calculated by the following formula:

$$cP = \Sigma F \cdot mRx - cCP = \text{max};$$

cP = computational profit;
ΣF = foreign-exchange proceeds;
mRx = the marginal exchange rate of export profitability;
cCp = computational prime cost in which adjustments are made for the varying rates of turnover taxes and the distorted valuation of the material components of foreign-exchange value.

More recently it appears that capital charges are also included in the cost of production. Where this is done, the formula becomes:

$$ncP = \Sigma F \cdot mRx - (cCp + qA) = \text{max};$$

ncP = net computational profit;
q = capital charge (it varies in different countries, and even in different branches of the economy; see Chapter 10 C, pp. 176-9);
A = the value of assets employed in production.[1]

Although foreign trade efficiency calculations have in practice been limited to a narrow framework, they nevertheless represent one of the most fascinating developments in Socialist economic thought and the conduct of foreign trade. This analysis has a promising future in view of the possibility of the application of modern advanced mathematical methods and high-memory computers. Highly sophisticated and complex, static as well as dynamic, models of the optimization of foreign trade have already been devised by such econometricians as J. Kornai, T. Liska and B. Martos of Hungary and W. Trzeciakowski of Poland.

At the same time, internal economic reforms and their extension

---

[1] Adapted from: W. Trzeciakowski, ('The Decentralized Mechanism of Economic Management from the Standpoint of Foreign Trade'), *Handel zagraniczny* (Foreign Trade), Warsaw, 3/1969, pp. 99-100.

to foreign trade are creating more favourable conditions for the improvement of the efficiency of exports and imports and relevant investments. These reforms include the decentralization of planning and management (see Chapter 4), the rationalization of costs and prices (Chapter 5), the reformulation and strengthening of material incentives to enterprises (Chapter 6) and to labour (Chapter 7), the acceleration of technological progress (Chapter 13), the development of closer links between production and foreign trade (Chapters 12 A, 14 B) and the measures adopted to extend multilateral settlements (Chapter 14 C).

Of particular importance are two developments – the progress made in linking domestic and foreign markets and the extension of competition. There is a tendency for foreign trade transactions to be settled domestically not at the distorted, insulated internal prices common in the past, but at foreign-exchange equivalents. Where this is done, enterprises producing for export, and those using imported components, are interested in selling in the most profitable markets and acquiring their imports from the cheapest sources. Institutionally, this is now workable because in many cases domestic industrial and some internal trading enterprises have been granted the right of direct dealings in foreign markets. Where this is not the case, the principle of co-responsibility is now widely applied, whereby domestic enterprises and foreign trade corporations are jointly responsible for production and marketing, and this is reinforced by joint participation in overall profits.

The gradual dismantling of the former tight insulation of domestic from foreign markets is also designed to introduce or strengthen competition in foreign trade as an instrument of efficiency discipline. The trend towards the discontinuation of export subsidies means that if enterprises producing for export are to survive, their production has to rise to world market standards with regard to costs, quality and conditions of delivery. However, with the exception of Yugoslavia, progress in the pruning of export subsidies has been slow.[1] The liberalization of access to domestic

---

[1] Hungary is about the most determined CMEA country to phase out subsidies on exports. In 1968 (the first year under the new system), 60% of her exports to Socialist countries and 70% of those to Capitalist countries required

markets in the form of competing imports also exerts a pressure towards cost reduction, improvements in quality, and the weakening of monopolies. The importance attached to this development is indicated by the statement recently made by a well-known Hungarian administrator and theoretical writer:

> Potential competition, that is, competition stimulated by the theoretical possibility of imports, assumes tremendous significance in the new economic mechanism. In recent years it has been found that imports have a stronger influence on the modernization of productive processes and on the improvement of quality than competition between domestic enterprises. We shall strive, therefore, as far as possible, to increase imports and participate in the international division of labour even in consumer goods.[1]

All the eight Socialist countries, even the German Democratic Republic, Romania and the USSR, have taken steps to extend at least partly the market mechanism to foreign trade. This extension has, of course, been advanced furthest in Yugoslavia, where the use of the indices of export and import efficiency has been discontinued since 1961; instead market forces have been enlisted almost exclusively to shape the most efficient flow of foreign trade. Hungary has embarked on a similar course, and some progress has been made along these lines in Bulgaria, Czechoslovakia and Poland.

Socialist countries have always attached a good deal of significance to the structure of foreign trade from the standpoint of value added. It has been widely accepted that a high or increasing proportion of manufactures, compared with primary products, in a country's exports is highly desirable, as it is indicative of large or increasing gains from trade. This view partly explains the early Socialist predilection for autarky, because these countries were reluctant to fit into the traditional international division of labour, whereby Socialist countries were expected to continue to be

---

subsidies, mostly ranging from 10 to 35% (but in some cases up to 100%). In 1970, 44% of her exports to Socialist, and 32% of those to Capitalist countries still had to be subsidized. B. Csikós-Nagy, ('Features and Tasks of the Price Policy'), *Pénzügyi szemle*, 2/1970, p. 96.

[1] B. Csikós-Nagy, *Pricing in Hungary*, London, Institute of Economic Affairs, 1968, p. 33.

TABLE 36 THE PROPORTION OF MANUFACTURES* IN THE
SOCIALIST COUNTRIES' FOREIGN TRADE ACCORDING TO REGIONS,
1957-58 AND 1967-68

SOCIALIST COUNTRIES'† EXPORTS TO OR IMPORTS FROM:	1957-58‡	1967-68‡
Exports to the Socialist countries†	56·2	70·9
Exports to developed countries§	35·8	41·1
Imports from developed countries	61·1	78·1
Exports to developing countries¶	71·1	70·7
Imports from developing countries	4·0	14·2
WORLD TRADE AS A WHOLE	51·7	62·4

* Based on United Nations *Standard International Trade Classification Revised*. Manufactures are taken as classes 5–8, i.e. chemicals, basic manufactures, machinery and transport equipment and miscellaneous manufactured articles. (The balance of the percentage in each case includes food, raw materials and fuels and unclassified items; SITC items 0–4, 9.)

† Socialist countries in this table include Albania, Bulgaria, Czechoslovakia, the GDR, Hungary, Poland, Romania and the USSR.

‡ Two-year annual averages. The valuation is at current prices in US dollars.

§ North America, Western Europe, Japan, Australia, New Zealand and South Africa.

¶ All Asia – except Japan, Mainland China, DPR of (North) Korea, Mongolia, and the DR of (North) Vietnam; all Africa – except South Africa; all Latin America.

Source. Based on United Nations *Monthly Bulletin of Statistics*, 3/1963, pp. xiv–xxix, and 3/1970, pp. xvi–xxxi.

exporters of raw materials and food to the industrialized West and to serve as a market for its manufactures.[1]

The proportion of manufactures in the Socialist countries' foreign trade before and since the recent reforms is shown in Table 36. It is evident that their increasing industrialization is reflected in the rapid growth of trade in manufactured goods

[1] Socialist countries cannot help but see the continuation of these policies even today. According to a Socialist source, this is exemplified by the discriminatory common external tariff applied by the European Economic Community to imports from Socialist (and other non-member) countries: on raw hides, skins, wool and cotton the duty is nil; on combed wool it is 3% *ad valorem*; on woollen yarn 5–10%; on leather 10–16%; on woollen carpets 32%. Quoted from S. Albinowski, op. cit., p. 157.

TABLE 37 THE PROPORTION OF MACHINERY, INSTALLATIONS
AND TRANSPORT EQUIPMENT IN THE CMEA COUNTRIES' TOTAL
EXPORTS, 1950–1967*

COUNTRY	1950	1955	1960	1965	1967
Bulgaria	0	3	14	25	26
Czechoslovakia	26	43	45	49	49
Hungary	23	30	38	33	31
Poland	8	13	28	34	36
Romania	4	6	17	18	19
USSR	16	22	21	23	21
CMEA Region	15	25	30	31	31

* In value percentages at current prices. No separate figures are available
for the GDR (owing to a different classification followed in that country), but
the total figures for the CMEA region include estimates for the GDR.

Sources. Gospodarka planowa, 7/1968, p. 19; Central Statistical Office of Poland,
Rozwój gospodarczy krajów RWPG 1950–1968 (Economic Development of the
CMEA Countries 1950–1968), Warsaw, 1969, p. 114.

amongst these countries – an increase from 56 to 71 per cent of
their total trade in a decade. These proportions are higher than
those in world trade in general. Manufactures also play a large part
in these countries' exports to the developing nations, but the share
has remained static at about 71 per cent.

It will also be noted that the Socialist countries import twice as
much in the way of manufactures from the West as they export to
it. These countries are greatly dissatisfied with this 'vertical' structure of trade because in their view it does not reflect the level of
Socialist industrialization already attained. The composition of
Socialist exports to the developed Capitalist countries rather indicates the ease of marketing primary products there and the discrimination against imports of Socialist manufactures.[1]

Of all exports, the proportion represented by machinery, installations and transport equipment is usually regarded as a good
indicator of the degree of industrialization and economic progress. According to Socialist sources, this proportion in the CMEA
region's exports as a whole doubled in the 1950s from 15 to 30 per

[1] Urszula Płowiec, ('Stages of Economic Growth and the Phases of the
Development of Polish Foreign Trade'), in J. Soldaczuk (ed.), op. cit., p. 82.

cent (see Table 37). However, since that time this growth has been arrested and the proportion has settled around 30–31 per cent, which appears to be slightly higher than the world average but lower than in the case of the developed Capitalist countries.[1]

This slowdown can be explained by the following causes. Since the basic industrialization has been laid down, most CMEA countries have displayed some reluctance in importing machinery and other industrial equipment from each other, and have instead been turning to the most developed Capitalist nations for items containing the most advanced technology. At the same time, owing to the varying quality of their machinery and equipment, poor marketing techniques and the discrimination encountered in many markets, Socialist countries have found it difficult to expand these exports to the Capitalist world, especially to the West. This is demonstrated in Table 38.

TABLE 38 SOCIALIST COUNTRIES' TRADE WITH THE WEST IN MACHINERY AND TRANSPORT EQUIPMENT, 1957–58 AND 1967–68*

SOCIALIST COUNTRIES':	1957–58	1967–68
Exports to the West:		
Value in US dollars	$360m.	$457m.
As a percentage of total exports to the West	9·4%	8·5%
Imports from the West:		
Value in US dollars	$765m.	$1,890m.
As a percentage of total imports from the West	21·9%	36·3%

* Socialist countries – as in Table 36; the West – developed Capitalist countries as in Table 36. The figures are two-year annual averages.
Source. As for Table 36, p. 296.

[1] A rough comparison is afforded by the percentages representing 'Machinery and Transport Equipment' in 1967 in total exports of the following: the world, 26%; all developed Capitalist countries, 33%; the European Economic Community, 34%; Japan, 37%; the USA, 40%; and the UK, 42%. The above United Nations classification, based on *SITC Revised* (Class 7), appears to cover a smaller range than the CMEA classification, 'Machinery, Installations and Transport Equipment'; the difference is estimated to be less than 5%. The figures given above are based on: United Nations *Monthly Bulletin of Statistics*, 3/1970, pp. xviii–xix, xxviii–xxix.

It may be observed that as a result of the growing cost-consciousness in the Socialist countries, the traditional views on the 'desirable' structure of foreign trade have been subjected to a critical reappraisal by some economists. Thus two East German writers[1] attacked the central theme in the well-known article written by the Soviet economist, I. Dudinskii,[2] that the rate of economic growth can be speeded up by increasing imports of raw materials and stepping up exports of manufactures. The essence of their argument is that foreign trade enhances economic growth not by the extent to which value is added to primary products through manufacturing processes, but by the extent to which foreign trade saves domestic resources. A country may enjoy special advantages in the production of some raw materials and be relatively inefficient in producing many industrial articles. In such a case, unless there is some other overriding reason, such a country would be advised to exchange primary products for manufactured goods, thereby saving its resources and thus increasing the rate of economic growth.[3]

For a long time, Socialist economists most emphatically rejected the validity of the theory of comparative costs, because its observance would mean perpetuating the traditional division of the world into industrialized and progressive economies on the one hand, and primary-producing, backward countries on the other. However, in recent years many writers have re-examined the theory in a new light, and they concede that the principle of comparative advantage is a valid guide even to Socialist foreign trade, provided that the partner countries have reached a reasonably advanced stage of economic development.[4]

[1] R. Koehler and K. Morgenstern, ('The Branch Structure of the National Economy, Branch Outlays and the Socialist International Division of Labour'), *Wirtschaftswissenschaft* (Economic Science), East Berlin, 1/1969, esp. pp. 73-5.
[2] I. Dudinskii, ('The Problem of Fuels and Raw Materials in CMEA Countries and Its Solution'), *Voprosy ekonomiki*, 4/1966, pp. 84-94.
[3] R. Koehler and K. Morgenstern, op. cit.
[4] This problem is examined in detail in J. Wilczynski, op. cit., pp. 69-74.

15 Socialist Reforms and the Capitalist World

A. REACTION TO SOCIALIST ECONOMIC REFORMS

As is well known, the economic reforms in the European Socialist countries have aroused a good deal of sensation, particularly in North America and Western Europe. Many cynics have taken delight in interpreting the reforms as an admission on the part of Socialism of its defects and an acknowledgement of the superiority of Capitalism by the adoption of several features of the rival system. Some, in their naïveté, have gone even further – depicting the reforms as a return to Capitalism. Alternatively, others have looked upon the reforms as evidence of strength in the sense that Socialist leaders have been able to rise above their ideological prejudices and have embarked upon the adaptation of the system to meet the challenge of the higher stages of economic development and the technological revolution.

On the whole, Socialist reforms have been received in the Capitalist world as a welcome development which has produced internal liberalization, and which can thus be interpreted as being conducive to more tolerant external policies vis-à-vis Capitalist countries. Some observers, recollecting the lively discussion in Western journals on market socialism in the 1930s, have hailed the reforms as a significant step in the evolution of an ideal social system – consisting in the elimination of the worst abuses of centralized command planning and the engrafting of the best features of the market economy. The new system also appears to be more acceptable to the developing nations, because if borrowings are made from it they involve less drastic departures from the existing social order. Believers in the 'convergence thesis' regard the reforms as an unmistakable reciprocating trend towards the ultimate coalescence of Socialism and Capitalism.

In the conviction of many Western specialists on Socialist economics (including this writer), the reforms have not yet provided a
satisfactory basis for a rapid and continued intensification of
economic growth. Some of the disabilities of the present system
derive from the fact that the reforms have not gone far enough
owing to the opposition of Party hard-liners and even local enterprise managers. Other weaknesses can probably never be removed
as long as loyalty to Marxism, the mono-party system of government and central planning prevail.

Bureaucracy and unwieldy economic administration are still
prevalent, especially in the German Democratic Republic, Poland,
Romania and the USSR, which hamper the freedom of initiative
on the part of enterprises and consumers. Price determination is
still largely subordinated to administrative decisions, and the price
systems in each country are still bedevilled with irrationalities.
The wide differentiation of prices (for essentially the same resource or product), interest rates and even capital charges is in
obvious conflict with the optimum distribution of resources and
products on a macroeconomic scale because it militates against the
equimarginal principle. A Czechoslovak economist as late as 1969
observed that 'we are not far from chaos and price anarchy'.[1]
Similarly, the chairman of the Polish State Planning Commission
complained in the same year that 'there is still no general price
theory in Socialist economics'.[2]

The system of material incentives to enterprises and to labour
is not yet strong enough to call forth the entrepreneurship and
effort present in the advanced Capitalist countries. This is indicated by the common reluctance of Socialist enterprises to make
full use of their recently acquired independence. The profit criterion has not been fully extended to agriculture and the
non-productive sphere.[3]

Banking and financial institutions are still too unsophisticated

---

[1] D. Ocka, ('Principles of Price Regulation'), *Hospodářské noviny* (Economic
News), Prague, 13/6/1969, p. 4.

[2] Quoted from: W. Dudziński, ('Prices – As They Are and As They Should
Be'), *Życie gospodarcze* (Economic Life), Warsaw, 29/5/1969, p. 3.

[3] It was reported in 1969 that in Poland there were 285,000 farms without
successors and 30,000 farms were economically hopeless. *Życie gospodarcze*,
21/9/1969, p. 9.

to answer all the needs of intensive growth. The institutional set-up remains essentially unchanged in Hungary, Romania and the USSR, and where it has been reformed, the degree of centralization has been increased in several respects – in contradiction to the general trend towards decentralization.

In spite of considerable improvements in the system of market supplies, sellers' markets still prevail for most goods as well as services, with continued adverse effects on production and distribution discipline. Although some progress has been made, competition is still weak. The continued presence of monopolistic suppliers, recurrent shortages, the generous social security and the clearly limited possibilities for private enrichment are all applying brakes on further progress.

No satisfactory price basis has yet been worked out for trade amongst Socialist countries, and bilateralism still dominates their trade. With the exception of Yugoslavia, the insulation of domestic from foreign markets still continues. No equilibrium exchange rates have been evolved yet and no Socialist currency yet approaches full convertibility (with the qualified exception of the Yugoslav dinar). Autarkic inclinations are still strong, particularly in the less developed countries, as reflected in continued import-replacement policies. The participation of these countries in world trade is still very small, considering their large share in the world's industrial output and national income.

The economic scene is still strongly dominated by the Communist Party, and the latter by its doctrinaire allegiance to Marxist ideas. In effect, some of the outstanding weaknesses of the Socialist economic system outlined above are tolerated because more drastic reforms would be ideologically unacceptable and politically unpalatable. In an appraisal of the reforms from the standpoint of the growth of productivity, Abram Bergson sees the emerging 'market socialism . . . as a successor not to capitalism but to centralist planning under socialism'.[1]

There is no doubt that the reforms represent a retreat in the march towards such Marxian goals as the elimination of the market mechanism, private enterprise and non-labour incomes (and costs),

[1] A. Bergson, 'Market Socialism Revisited', *J. Polit. Econ.*, Oct 1967, p. 670.

the abolition of money, and distribution according to needs. Now, the crux of the issue is whether the incorporation of Capitalist devices is regarded by the Socialist leadership as temporary or permanent. If they are treated as transitional on the road to Full Communism, do the leaders really believe that once the age of plenty is attained, these devices – which are essentially alien to ideal Communism – can be dispensed with and that the Communist cornucopia will be full and overflowing for ever? Half a century of transitioning in the USSR had demonstrated that Capitalist devices, instead of being gradually eliminated, had in fact to be strengthened. One wonders whether, as the Socialist economy becomes more complex and sophisticated, they may not prove more necessary. If, on the other hand, the elements of Capitalism are to be embraced as permanent organic features and carried into Full Communism, then the Socialist leaders might as well burn the works of Marx, Engels and the other founding fathers of the Communist ideology on a bonfire in Red Square in front of Lenin's Mausoleum!

B. SOCIALIST DEPENDENCE ON CAPITALIST COUNTRIES

Many Socialist leaders have traditionally cherished the dream of becoming economically independent of the Capitalist world, and they thought that as their countries became more developed the degree of their dependence would diminish. One of the repercussions of the reforms, hardly anticipated by the leaders, has been to make the Socialist economies in several respects more dependent on Capitalist countries – both developing and (especially) developed ones. The spheres of dependence include the increased need for imports of raw materials, equipment embodying advanced technology, industrial know-how, markets for Socialist manufactures, and the multilateralization of trade.

As is generally known, the Socialist countries, with the partial exception of the USSR, have been increasingly suffering from a deficit of several key raw materials. This is largely a reflection of the growing industrialization and the changing cost relationships between primary and manufactured products – a trend which no

L

doubt will continue in the future, even in the USSR. The requirements for raw materials are expanding rapidly, but investment and exploitation costs in extractive industries are heavy and are rising steeply (see Chapter 5 B, pp. 84–5).

Yet the CMEA countries have been reluctant to acknowledge this fact sufficiently in intra-CMEA trade prices, with the consequent tendency for raw materials to become 'hard items'. The increasing concern with comparative cost considerations (especially in the USSR, the chief supplier of raw materials to other CMEA countries) is making these countries turn to Capitalist sources of supply, particularly for such commodities as copper, cotton, fissionable materials, grains, hides, molybdenum, nickel, titanium, tungsten and wool. In contrast to the CMEA region, the prices of primary products in world Capitalist markets have tended to decline in relation to manufactures.

But of greatest interest to the Socialist countries under the new system is Western technology. In the 1950s, some Western economists (and many political leaders) attributed the high growth in the Socialist countries to the poaching of Western know-how. This is only partly true. The Socialist countries at that stage were mostly interested in quantitative additions of capital stock to their relatively unsophisticated economies, with a lesser concern for the latest technological refinements and efficiency.[1] However, under the new system the most modern Western industrial equipment and know-how have assumed unprecedented importance to the Socialist countries because they unquestionably provide major sources of intensive growth.

In their drive for imports from the West, the Socialist countries are now particularly interested in instruments, machinery and complete industrial plants incorporating the most advanced technology for the chemical industry, machine construction, vehicle-building, modern communications and electronic data-processing. Table 39 shows a select list of such imports in recent years. Other noteworthy items include acetylene hydrogenation plants, cellulose plants, computers (including third-generation models), data-

---

[1] The Socialist (especially Soviet) interest was mostly concentrated on the equipment and know-how of direct military application (where economic efficiency is of secondary consideration).

processing equipment, electron microscopes, flexible polyurethane moulding plants, high-speed film-processing equipment, hydro-level plate-straightening installations, multi-slide power presses, oscilloscopes, steel fabricating plants, thyristor-controlled silicon-plating rectifiers, and a wide variety of scientific instruments and apparatus.

Another form of assimilating Western technology is by means of the acquisition of licences. With the exception of Yugoslavia,[1] the Socialist countries' approach was rather haphazard up to the early 1960s. They either illicitly appropriated know-how without compensation,[2] or only occasionally purchased patents on a lump-sum (one-for-all) basis. However, since that time, transactions in industrial licences have been placed on a systematic basis. All CMEA countries have established specialized foreign trade corporations for this purpose (including the sale of licences to foreign parties).[3] Of all these countries Czechoslovakia, Poland, Romania and the USSR appear to be most interested in the acquisition of Western licences, and their purchases have increased substantially since the mid-1960s.[4]

Since the mid-1960s efforts have been made under the auspices of CMEA to co-ordinate the member countries' acquisition of licences from the West, and beginning in 1966 the CMEA

[1] Over the period 1954–64, Yugoslav enterprises concluded 341 agreements to utilize foreign industrial know-how – 24% of the total number with West German firms, 19% with Italian, 10% with French, 38% with other Capitalist firms and only 9% with enterprises in other Socialist countries. *East Europe*, 10/1965, p. 36.

[2] According to an American writer, this was mostly done by the USSR importing prototypes (one model of a particular piece of equipment) from the West, mostly for applications in the following industries: hydroelectricity, steel, precision tools, petroleum refining, oil drilling and coal mining. M. L. Harvey, *East–West Trade and United States Policy*, New York, National Assn of Manufacturers, 1966, pp. 30, 47.

[3] Bulgaria – Technoimpex, Czechoslovakia – Polytechna, the GDR – Limex, Hungary – Licencia, Poland – Polservice, Romania – Industrialimport, the USSR – Litsensintorg. In Yugoslavia enterprises can procure (and sell) licences directly.

[4] e.g. Poland up to 1960 purchased only 29 licences from the West and over the period 1961–65, 47 licences. In 1965 the four countries acquired 80 licences and the estimated number in the late 1960s was about twice as high. J. Metera, *Współpraca naukowo-techniczna krajów RWPG* (Scientific and Technical Co-operation amongst the CMEA Countries), Warsaw, PWE, 1969, pp. 45–6.

Permanent Commission for Scientific and Technical Research has been publishing an annual bulletin which includes a list of patents purchased by the member nations from Capitalist countries. In their quest for Western know-how, Socialist countries are mostly

TABLE 39 MAJOR SOCIALIST IMPORTS OF WESTERN EQUIPMENT EMBODYING ADVANCED TECHNOLOGY, 1968–1970*

IMPORTING SOCIALIST COUNTRY	DESCRIPTION, SOURCE AND VALUE OF THE IMPORT†
Bulgaria	Cold-rolled steel mill (Fr, $42·5m.); fertilizer producing complex (UK, £16m.); airborne communications equipment for navigation (US, $110,000).
Czechoslovakia	Urea plant (FRG and Ne, $6·9m.); plant for the manufacture of epichlorohydrin (Ne, $2·5m.); spectromatic equipment (Swi, $300,000); equipment for the production of sanitary pipeware (UK, £500,000); paraxylene plant (UK, £250,000).
GDR	Radiation analyser system (Swi, $50,000); high-density polythene plant (UK, £3·0m.); polycondensation and spinning plant (UK, £6·5m.); synthetic rubber plant (UK, £2·5m.); terephtalic acid plant (UK, £13m.); electron accelerator (US, $520,000).
Hungary	Special-purpose paper mill (Fi, $10·0m.); ring-twisting machines and double-twisting frames (Swi, $350,000); instrumentation for a super-phosphate ammonizing plant (UK, £150,000); tin and aluminium plate printing and lacquering lines (UK, £100,000).
Poland	Automatic electroplating plant (UK, £385,000); glass-fibre plant (UK, £2·5m.); matrix precision machine tools (UK, £200,000); marine automation installations (UK, £500,000); polythene plant (UK, £2·5m.); stainless steel blade manufacturing equipment (UK, £350,000); power presses and automation equipment for automotive industry (US, $3·0m.).

TABLE 39—*Continued*

IMPORTING SOCIALIST COUNTRY	DESCRIPTION, SOURCE AND VALUE OF THE IMPORT†
Romania	Industrial complex for the manufacture of refrigerators (Fr, $10m.); acid anhydride plant (FRG, $4m.); carbon electrode extrusion equipment (UK, £250,000); ethylene carbonate recovery plant (UK, £550,000); irrigation equipment (UK, £22m.); nuclear reactor and fuels (UK, £150,000); plant for the manufacture of fuel-injection equipment (UK, £1·om.).
USSR	Automated splint board finishing equipment (FRG, $5m.); brake-lining plant (FRG, $4m.); iron-ore pelletizing plant (Jap, $18m.); plant for the manufacture of air, oil and ventilator filters (Jap, $4m.); butadiene production complex (Jap and US, $25m.); automatic telephone equipment (Swe, $15m.); complete transfer lines for manufacturing vehicle engine components (UK, £2·5m.); electrolytic tinplate plant (UK, £4m.); polyester film plant (UK, £12·6m.); polythene plants (UK, £20m.); gear manufacturing equipment (US, $2·1m.).
Yugoslavia	Polyester fibre plant (FRG, $5m.); voice frequency terminal equipment for telecommunications (Swe, $1·2m.); aircraft hydraulic equipment (UK, £100,000); fertilizer plant (UK, £2·5m.); hot-strip rolling-mill equipment (UK, £1·om.).

* Including contracts signed during the period.

† In £ stg. and US dollars. Fi = Finland, Fr = France, FRG = the Federal Republic of Germany, Jap = Japan, Ne = the Netherlands, Swe = Sweden, Swi = Switzerland, UK = the United Kingdom, US = the United States.

Sources. Compiled from Socialist and Western daily and periodical publications.

interested in industrial processes which have been tested and applied by reputable firms, so that most licences are acquired from large, well-known concerns, especially in France, the Federal Republic of Germany and the United Kingdom. Examples of Western licences recently utilized in the Socialist countries are shown in Table 40.

The emphasis on the expansion of the technologically most dynamic industries and the growing awareness of costs are making the Socialist countries increasingly look to the Capitalist world as a market for their manufactures. Such industries have the greatest potential for the economies of scale, and these cannot be fully exhausted by relying merely on local and even the CMEA region markets. The evidence of this growing interest is found in the fact that all the Socialist countries have established special research institutes to study prices and economic fluctuations in the Capitalist world, and they are increasingly employing market research agencies in the West to guide their export effort.

It must be realized that the Socialist countries' capacity to export advanced equipment and licences has considerably improved in recent years, and continued improvement appears to be certain in the future. To illustrate, the following items have recently been exported to advanced Capitalist countries: equipment for casting with counter-pressure (by Bulgaria); ball-bearings plants, hydraulic jet looms (by Czechoslovakia); optical, precision and electronic instruments (by the GDR); complex electronic scoreboards, medical laboratories, numerically-controlled lathes (by Hungary); control and measuring apparatus, self-propelled caterpillar stone-breakers (by Poland); atomic reactors, giant turbine generators, hydrofoils, the world's largest civilian helicopters, jet aircraft (by the USSR); transformer stations and mining equipment (by Yugoslavia); computers and electronic data-processing equipment (by Bulgaria, Czechoslovakia, the GDR, the USSR); and ships (by Bulgaria, the GDR, Poland, the USSR and Yugoslavia). Czechoslovakia is now the fourth largest (after the USA, UK and the FRG) exporter of machine tools, which are used by such firms as General Electric, Krupp, the Pittsburgh Steel Foundry, Renault, Rolls-Royce, Siemens and Westinghouse.

It is not generally known that many Socialist countries have also become sellers of know-how to the West. For example, licences have been sold for the following applications:

Bulgaria: the high-current density refining of copper (to Italy, Japan and the USA); the automatic replacement of bobbins in spinning machines (Italy); protective coating for graphite electrodes (UK).

Czechoslovakia: spinning frames for spindleless mills (to Japan); vertical forging presses (Japan).

Hungary: the preparation of sorbitol for use in food-processing, pharmaceutical and textile industries (to the Netherlands).

Poland: a new blood-pressure-reducing medicine (to France); an accelerated cement-setting process (to the FRG); crank-shafts for locomotives, large corrugated rollers for high-power engines and ship engines (UK); high-accuracy, continuous isotope balances (USA).

USSR: an extrusion method for producing double-walled plastic tubes (to Austria); a new method of arc and steel tube welding (FRG); smelting by electrodes (Japan); the shaping of a self-forming, self-moving and self-hardening sand type of casting mould (Japan and UK); special-type welding equipment (Sweden); specialized surgical instruments (USA).[1]

The statistical evidence of the increased dependence of the Socialist countries on the Capitalist world can be found in trade figures. It is indicated by the proportions of the European CMEA countries' foreign trade claimed by developed and developing countries in selected three-year periods[2] (continued on p. 312).

---

[1] According to an East German source, in 1961 alone US firms acquired over 50 licences and in the third quarter of 1963, 19 licences from the USSR. K.-H. Domdey, ('Economic Aspects of Peaceful Co-existence'), *Aussenhandel* (Foreign Trade), East Berlin, 2/1964, pp. 32-5.

[2] i.e. the countries included are Bulgaria, Czechoslovakia, the GDR, Hungary, Poland, Romania and the USSR. Yugoslavia's trade has followed a trend of its own. Upon her expulsion from Cominform (in 1948), the share of the seven Socialist countries in her trade dropped from 53% over the period 1947-8 to less than 2% in the early 1950s. Since that time her trade with these countries has recovered substantially, but not to the previous level of importance. The percentage shares of the European CMEA group, the developed and the developing countries (in this order) in Yugoslavia's trade were as follows: over the period 1961-63, 23, 62 and 14; over the period 1967-69, 29, 59 and 11 (the balance of the trade in each case was with the remaining six Socialist countries: Albania, China (Mainland), Cuba, Mongolia, North Korea and North Vietnam).

TABLE 40 EXAMPLES OF WESTERN LICENCES USED BY SOCIALIST
ENTERPRISES, 1968–1970

WESTERN LICENSOR*	SOCIALIST LICENSEE†	THE NATURE OF THE KNOW-HOW
Burmeister & Wain (Den)	Uljanik (Yug)	Construction of ore/oil carriers
Bull General Electric (Fr)	Tesla Industrial Complex (Czech)	Manufacture of middle-range computers
Gutbrod (Fr)	Agrostroj (Czech)	Manufacture of small agricultural machinery
Promil (Fr)	Ejpovice Ore and Mineral Mines (Czech)	Manufacture of universal driers for food processing
Deutsche Babcock & Wilcox (FRG)	Ses Timace (Hung)	Manufacture of large steam boilers
Eckert und Ziegler (FRG)	Zywiec Machine Building Works (Pol)	Manufacture of extrusion equipment for rubber synthetics
Elba Etlingen (FRG)	Mostaren (Czech)	Manufacture of mobile concrete mixers
Industriewerke Karlsruhe (FRG)	Shipyard and Crane Works (Hung)	Construction of special transport containers
Siemens (FRG)	Zbrojovka (Czech)	Manufacture of teleprinters
Volkswagen (FRG)	Videaton Radio & TV Works (Hung)	Manufacture of car lighting switches
Fiat (It)	Togliattigrad Automobile Complex (USSR)	Construction of Fiat passenger cars
Stamicarbon (Ne)	Technoimport (Bulg)	Preparation of NPK fertilizers
Ericsson (Swe)	Budavax (Hung)	Manufacture of telephone equipment
Sibir (Swi)	Lehel Refrigerator Works (Hung)	Manufacture of absorption-type domestic refrigerators

TABLE 40—*Continued*

WESTERN LICENSOR*	SOCIALIST LICENSEE†	THE NATURE OF THE KNOW-HOW
Automotive Products Group (UK)	Avtopromimport (USSR)	Manufacture of Borg and Berg clutches for cars
Edwin Cooper (UK)	Machinoimport (USSR)	Production of chemicals used as lubricating-oil additives
English Electric (UK)	Ganz Electrical Works (Hung)	Manufacture of large transformers
International Computers and tabulators (UK)	Metronex (Pol)	Manufacture of computer-controlled fast printers
International Synthetic Rubber (UK)	Tekhmashimport (USSR)	Manufacture of high solids latex by pressure agglomeration process
Leyland (UK)	Mielec Transport Equipment Factory (Pol)	Manufacture of bus engines
Smith Industries (UK)	Polimex (Pol)	Manufacture of sparking plugs
Allis-Chalmers (US)	Litsesintorg (USSR)	Pelletizing of iron ore
Toledo Engineering Corporation (US)	Polimex (Pol)	Operation of glass-fibre furnaces

* Den = Denmark, Fr = France, FRG = the Federal Republic of Germany, It = Italy, Ne = the Netherlands, Swe = Sweden, Swi = Switzerland, UK = the United Kingdom, US = the United States.

† The Socialist licensee is often a foreign trade corporation which passes on the licence to one or more domestic enterprises and makes other necessary arrangements for the transfer of the know-how.

Sources. Compiled from Socialist and Western daily and periodical publications.

	1951–53	1961–63	1967–69
Developed countries	17%	21%	25%
Developing countries	3%	9%	9%
ALL CAPITALIST COUNTRIES	20%	30%	34%
in value terms	$2,380m.	$9,320m.	$16,520m.

Sources. Based on United Nations *Yearbook of International Trade Statistics* and *Monthly Bulletin of Statistics* (both exports and imports are valued f.o.b., and trade between the Federal Republic of Germany and the German Democratic Republic is treated as part of foreign trade).

The share of Capitalist countries is highest in the trade of Yugoslavia (70 per cent), Romania (50 per cent) and Poland (35 per cent), and lowest in that of Bulgaria (25 per cent), Hungary (27 per cent) and the GDR (30 per cent).

The role of the European CMEA countries in the Capitalist countries' foreign trade is much smaller, but it is of course growing. The figures below represent the percentage shares of the developed and developing Capitalist nations' total foreign trade absorbed by the CMEA region in the same periods:

	1951–53	1961–63	1967–69
Developed countries	2·0%	3·4%	3·5%
Developing countries	1·0%	4·8%	5·0%
ALL CAPITALIST COUNTRIES	1·7%	3·7%	3·8%
in value terms	$2,380m.	$9,320m.	$16,520m.

Sources. As for the preceding table.

The increasing specialization in the Socialist countries, enhanced by the reforms, is making the bilateral basis of trade more anachronistic than ever. A goal which is of vital interest to these countries is the multilateralization of their trade – as a means of increasing their gains from trade and a source of intensive growth. This process can be considerably facilitated by Capitalist nations, particularly those with convertible currencies such as the Group of Ten (Belgium, Canada, France, the Federal Republic of Germany, Italy, Japan, the Netherlands, Sweden, the United Kingdom and the USA). These nations play an important part in the Socialist countries' trade, and they could assist the latter countries to earn more convertible foreign exchange by further liberalization of quotas and the extension of MFN.

C. FROM ANTAGONISM TO CO-OPERATION

Up to the early 1960s, East–West economic relations were dominated by the Cold War. Socialist trade deals were often dictated more by 'carrot and stick' considerations than by sound economic calculation, especially with the uncommitted nations of the Third World. Many Socialist leaders, fascinated by Lenin's and Stalin's dicta on the collapse of Capitalism,[1] believed that limiting imports from Western countries would aggravate their unemployment and speed up their economic breakdown. Socialist countries often boycotted international organizations, claiming that the latter served the interests of Capitalist nations; and where they did attend international conferences, they often used them as platforms for Cold War propaganda.

Business and tourist travel, both into and out of the Socialist countries, was strictly controlled, and hardly any foreign firms were allowed permanent local representation. Socialist exports were sometimes dumped in Capitalist markets at cut prices, causing market disruption and uncertainty. Trade agreements and even signed contracts were broken on occasions. In trade contracts with Capitalist traders, clauses were usually inserted stipulating arbitration – in the case of possible litigation – in the Socialist country.

Western countries, of course, did not remain passive. In fact, the initiative usually rested on the Western side, because Socialist countries were much more dependent on trade with the West than vice versa. The main weapons of Western economic warfare were severe quantitative restrictions on imports from the Socialist countries, arbitrary anti-dumping measures, strict limitations on credits, and the strategic embargo on exports of not only

[1] V. I. Lenin, *Selected Works*, London, Lawrence & Wishart, vol. IX, p. 307; J. Stalin, *Economic Problems of Socialism in the USSR*, Moscow, FLPH, 1952, pp. 34–6.

military items but also industrial plants, machinery and licences if they embodied advanced technology. Western governments were usually less concerned with missed opportunities or losses to their own economies than with potential gains that might have accrued to the Socialist countries.[1]

The causes of the Cold War were complex and, in retrospect, there is little doubt that both Socialist and Capitalist countries – particularly the leading powers – must bear the blame for it.[2] But it is worth noting that the Socialist behaviour and methods used can be at least partly explained in terms of the old economic system, which roughly coincided with the Cold War.[3] Centralized directive planning and management provided the leadership with a powerful machine for manipulating trade (and aid) according to political needs.

The entities which were engaged in foreign economic relations had little independence and they could be issued with directive instructions to carry out transactions where profitability and efficiency were of secondary importance. As little significance was attached to intensive sources of growth, the consequent losses or missed gains from trade were not viewed with great concern. Furthermore, for a long time under the old system, foreign trade was regarded as being of residual importance. Capitalist markets were treated as reservoirs to absorb planners' errors, which were inevitable under tight central planning. Thus unexpected sales were not infrequently made in Capitalist countries as a result of sudden surpluses, or bottlenecks which could be overcome only by unscheduled imports, and the latter had to be paid for by whatever could be exported at short notice.

It did not take long for both Socialist and Western countries to

[1] For further details, see J. Wilczynski, *The Economics and Politics of East–West Trade*, London, Macmillan, 1969, pp. 138–90, 236–307.

[2] Space does not allow going further into this problem here, but there are several good studies available on the subject: N. Graebner (ed.), *The Cold War*, Boston, Heath, 1965; D. B. Heather, *The Cold War*, Oxford UP, 1965; C. O. Lerche, *The Cold War and After*, New York, Prentice-Hall, 1965; D. Rees, *The Age of Containment: The Cold War*, London, Macmillan, 1967; H. L. Trefousse (ed.), *The Cold War: A Book of Documents*, New York, Putnam, 1965.

[3] The Cold War is generally considered to cover the period from March 1946 (W. Churchill's speech at Fulton, USA) to August 1963 (the signing of the Nuclear Test Ban Treaty), or January 1967 (The Tripartite Agreement, signed by the UK, USA and the USSR, banning nuclear weapons in space).

find that the Cold War techniques were producing disappointing political results, incommensurate with the economic sacrifices. The Soviets declared the policy of peaceful co-existence in 1956 (also accepted by the other European Socialist countries), and the economic reforms since the early 1960s have further convinced most Western leaders and businessmen that the old militant Socialism was gradually being transformed into a more moderate system, not only internally but also in external relations.[1]

Increasing East–West co-operation in the economic field has been one of the most outstanding features of international relations in the last decade. The new economic system is more sensitive to the opportunities for growth afforded by the development of closer ties with the Capitalist world, particularly with the economically most advanced nations. The Socialist countries have adopted a more co-operative attitude to international organizations.

The GDR and the USSR acceded to the International Union for the Protection of Industrial Property in 1965 (so that all European Socialist countries except Albania are now members of the Union). Poland and Yugoslavia became full members of GATT in 1966 and 1967 respectively, and Hungary and Romania have recently applied for full membership too (Czechoslovakia is a foundation member). All the eight Socialist countries have also ratified the United Nations convention on the Recognition and Enforcement of Foreign Arbitral Awards of 1958 and the European Convention on International Commercial Arbitration of 1961. Some of them have also recently joined such international organizations relevant to economic co-operation as the Baltic and International Maritime Conference, the Food and Agriculture Organization, the International Exhibition Bureau, the International Fur Trade Federation, the International Lead and Zinc Study Group, the International Organization for Standardization, the International Wheat Council, the International Union of Official Travel Organizations, the Union of International Fairs and the World Power Conference.[2] The Socialist countries have also

[1] Many Western observers believe that China is recapitulating the stages traversed by the European Socialist countries, and that her adventurism and militancy will also moderate themselves once she enters higher stages of development and the threshold of affluence.

[2] For further details, see J. Wilczynski, op. cit., pp. 366–73.

liberalized the issue of passports and visas and foreign travel in general. They have agreed to foreign firms establishing permanent offices,[1] and they themselves have been doing the same in Capitalist countries.[2]

The Socialist interest in economic co-operation has met with a favourable, and more recently enthusiastic, reception in Western industrial and commercial circles. Socialist countries have proved to be reputable traders and the contracts they offer are usually large. They provide valuable markets for industries suffering from surplus capacity, especially the iron and steel, engineering, chemical, precision instruments and electronic industries. For example, the Soviet contract with Fiat for the construction of a passenger car complex at Togliattigrad is worth more than \$600m.; direct orders have been placed with some 200 Western firms, indirectly benefiting about 200 other suppliers in the West (over 140 in Italy alone, in addition to Fiat).[3] An American economist, Eliot Janeway, voicing the sentiments of many business interests in the USA, bluntly stated in 1969 that the expansion of trade with Socialist countries could prevent a recession in his country.[4]

Even Western governments, although cautious at first, have been increasingly well-disposed towards the removal of various forms of discrimination in trade with the European Socialist countries, especially since 1963. There has been a progressive liberalization of import quotas and currency transferability. Restrictions on credits have been largely lifted, and in fact most Western governments now extend guarantees on such credits for up to twenty years. Strategic embargo is no longer a

[1] e.g. it was reported recently that at least 22 big Western firms have opened permanent offices in Moscow (previously only some of them were allowed representation in hotel rooms), such as Fiat, ENI, Golodetz, Mitsubishi, Montecatini-Edison, Renault, Sifal, Sorice, Stemmler-Imox, and others. About 50 Japanese companies have established such offices throughout the USSR, they are staffed with Japanese personnel and they represent thousands of Japanese firms.

[2] Even setting up branches or agencies of their banks in such financial centres as Beirut (Bulgaria, USSR), Frankfurt a.M. (Yugoslavia), London (Bulgaria, Czechoslovakia, Hungary, USSR), Milan (USSR), Munich (Yugoslavia), New York (Yugoslavia), Paris (Hungary, USSR, Yugoslavia), Teheran (USSR), Trieste (Yugoslavia), Vienna (Yugoslavia) and Zürich (Hungary, USSR).

[3] Reported in *East–West Commerce*, 12/1968, p. 7.

[4] Reported in *The American Review of East-West Trade*, 12/1969, p. 10.

factor significantly impeding the growth of East–West trade.[1]

But the most direct form of economic co-operation is represented by joint East–West business ventures. Although they existed before the early 1960s, they were rare and were limited only to trading activities. However, since 1963 there has been a veritable proliferation of these partnerships, usually on the initiative of the Socialist countries, mostly concerned with production. The bases of co-operation vary according to circumstances. In some cases, one partner leases its licence, experts or special equipment to the other in exchange for a portion of the output so produced.

In other cases, there may be unilateral or bilateral sub-contracting for the production of agreed components and independent assembly of the final product. In still other cases, the lower stages of production may be undertaken by one partner and the higher stages by the other ('vertical co-production'). The partners may also co-operate in jointly constructing projects in third (usually developing) countries. Joint production is often associated with co-operation in marketing the final product, either separately in agreed areas or through a joint trading entity.

The countries most interested in these ventures are Bulgaria, Czechoslovakia, Hungary, Poland, Romania and Yugoslavia on the one side, and France, the Federal Republic of Germany, Italy, Japan, the Netherlands, Sweden and the United Kingdom on the other. According to a Socialist source, there were 'thousands' of direct co-operation agreements in force between the enterprises in the CMEA countries and Western Europe alone in the late 1960s.[2] Some of the most successful joint East–West business undertakings are listed in Table 41.

Although in most cases the co-operating partners remain separate entities, there is an increasing number of fully integrated enterprises with jointly contributed share capital and management. Their head offices are found mostly in Capitalist countries.

[1] The scope of the embargo was reduced in five major revisions (1954, 1957–58, 1962, 1964 and 1966). Sweden lifted the embargo altogether in 1968 and in 1969 a Japanese court declared the embargo illegal. In 1969 the US version of the embargo was further relaxed (in application to the European Socialist countries) to bring it in line with other NATO countries' practices.

[2] S. Albinowski, *Handel między krajami o różnych ustrojach* (Trade between Countries with Different Social Systems) Warsaw, KiW, 1968, p. 167.

TABLE 41 SELECTED EXAMPLES OF RECENT SOCIALIST–
CAPITALIST PRODUCTION AND MARKETING CO-OPERATION

CO-OPERATING ENTERPRISES Socialist–Capitalist*	THE NATURE OF CO-OPERATION
Machinoexport (Bulg)– Meringson Mij NV (Ne)	Marketing and servicing of Bulgarian and Dutch machinery
Machinoexport (Bulg)– Mecchaniche Gaetano Zocca (It)	Production and marketing of grinding equipment
Minerva Sewing Machine Works and Investa (both of Czech)– Necchi (It)	Production, marketing and servicing of sewing machines
Škoda (Czech)–Simmons Machine Tool Corp. (US)	Marketing of Czechoslovak machine tools in the USA
Slovak Power Supply (Czech)– Deutsche Babcock & Wilcox (FRG)	Production and marketing of large boilers
Technoexport (Czech)–Voëst (Austria)	Construction of engineering projects in third countries
Transporta (Czech)– International Combustion (UK)	Design, development and production of heavy engineering machinery in the UK
Building Industry Assn (Hung)–AB Byging (Swe)	Production of high-structure scaffolding
Budapest Chemical Works (Hung)–Stickstoffewerke (Austria)	Production of trichlor-fenoxi-acetone acid
Csepel Machine-Building Works (Hung)–Krupp (FRG)	Manufacture and marketing of numerically controlled lathes
Györ Waggon Works (Hung)– Renault (Fr)	Construction of diesel engines for Hungarian buses
Ikarus (Hung)–Berliet (Fr)	Production of bus chassis
Investa (Hung)–Sucker (FRG)	Production of slashing machines for the textile industry

TABLE 41—*Continued*

CO-OPERATING ENTERPRISES Socialist–Capitalist*	THE NATURE OF CO-OPERATION
Kobanya (Hung)–Siemens (FRG)	Production of ceramic condensers
Nikex Trading (Hung)– Geo W. King (UK)	Production of conveyor systems in Hungary
Red Star Dutra Tractor Works (Hung)–Munch-Hamiern (Norway)	Production and marketing of Hungarian tractors
Bydgoszcz Automated Machine Works (Pol)–Amtec (Fr)	Production and marketing of turning machines
Contexim (Pol)–Tsubane Coat (Jap)	Production and marketing of polyester and cotton-blended fabrics
Elbląg Mechanical Works (Pol)–Ateliers et Chantiers de Bretagne (Fr)	Production and marketing of cutting presses
Machine-Building Industry Assn (Pol)–Jones Cranes (UK)	Manufacture of caterpillar and wheel cranes
Metronex (Pol)–Racal Instruments (UK)	Marketing of Polish electronic manufactures
Polimex (Pol)–Walmsley (UK)	Construction of machinery for paper mills
Poręba Mechanical Works (Pol)–Waldrich Siegen (FRG)	Design, manufacture and marketing of precision lathes
Chimimport (Rom)–Ataka & Co (Jap)	Handling of business deals in chemicals between Romania and Japan
Chimimport (Rom)–Tennant Trading (UK)	Marketing of British and Romanian chemicals
Masinexport (Rom)–Ducati Meccanica (It)	Production of concrete mixers and irrigation pumps
Masinexport (Rom)–Isotta Fraschini (It)	Manufacture of automatic generator sets

M

TABLE 41—*Continued*

CO-OPERATING ENTERPRISES Socialist–Capitalist*	THE NATURE OF CO-OPERATION
Far Eastern Steamship Co. and Sovfrakht (both of the USSR)–Yamashita Shinnikon Steamship Co. and Azuma Shipping Co. (both of Jap)	Shipping in Pacific trade
Promsyryimport (USSR)–Voëst (Austria)–Italsider (It)	Construction of gas pipelines from the USSR to Austria and Italy
Soyuznefteksport (USSR)–Bunkering & Stevedoring Co. and Antoine Vloeberghs Co. (both of Belg)	Marketing of Soviet oil products in Belgium
Elektronska Industrija (Yug)–Kuba Imperial (FRG)	Manufacture of TV sets
Ina Oil Concern (Yug)–Farbwerke Hoechst (FRG)	Construction and operation of a polyester fibre plant in Yugoslavia
Interexport (Yug)–Volkswagen (FRG)	Production and marketing of Volkswagen cars in Yugoslavia
Jugolek (Yug)–Siemens (FRG)	Production of medical and dental apparatus and marketing in third countries
Litostroj (Yug)–Renault (Fr)	Production of components and assembly of Renault cars in Yugoslavia
Novi Sad Tractor Works (Yug)–Ford (US)	Assembly of tractors in Yugoslavia
Rade Končar (Yug)–Castor & Imel (It)	Manufacture of super-automatic washing machines

* For abbreviations of the countries used, see note 1, Table 40, p. 311.

Sources. Compiled from Socialist and Western daily and periodical publications.

Examples of such enterprises established in recent years are: Arcode (Romanian–British), Bumac International (Bulgarian–Australian), Bulitalia (Bulgarian–Italian), Cortez Mexico (Hungarian–Mexican), Indopol (Polish–Indian), IPH Calanda (Polish–Dutch), Koneala Norge Bill (Soviet–Norwegian), Konsumex (Hungarian–French), Nafta (B) (Soviet–Belgian), Nitibu (Bulgarian–Japanese), Richmond (Hungarian–British), Sigma Italiana (Czechoslovak–Italian), Stim-France (Czechoslovak–French) and Trade and Commissions Transactions Co. (Yugoslav–Austrian–West German). The variety of these arrangements shows that, given goodwill and understanding on both sides, Communists and Capitalists can co-operate to their mutual benefit.

Partnership with Capitalist firms obviously provides Socialist economies with opportunities for intensive growth. It enables them to obtain Western designs and processes, expert advice on technical and management problems and the use of sophisticated equipment – and all this paid for in output rather than in hard currencies. Socialist enterprises can also utilize their partners' marketing channels and techniques to establish their products in Capitalist markets. Thus this co-operation directly aids the Socialist countries in introducing new products, assimilating more efficient methods of production, achieving the economies of large-scale production, providing valuable extra employment opportunities (especially in Bulgaria, Poland, Romania and Yugoslavia) and in tapping new sources of foreign-exchange earnings. Benefits accruing to Capitalist partners derive mainly from a greater specialization, a reduction of overhead costs and idle capacity in their establishments and from lower labour costs and sheltered markets in Socialist countries.

It must be pointed out that in this co-operation drive, the Socialist countries (with the possible exception of Yugoslavia) are not seeking ordinary economic aid from the West. They treat East–West economic co-operation as being normal business propositions of mutual advantage. Their interest is centred on acquiring advanced Western technology and extending their markets in the Capitalist world – and not necessarily on capital inflows of one sort or another. The prevailing attitude was clearly summed up by a Polish economist:

East–West industrial co-operation does not have to involve a
flow of investment capital from Capitalist to Socialist countries,
especially in such forms as it assumes in underdeveloped areas.
Socialist countries are primarily interested in acquiring modern
technology, and not capital. The main constraint on Socialist
economic growth does not consist in the inability to provide
sufficient capital but in the slow growth of foreign trade and
productivity. Therefore, this co-operation must not lead to the
formation of colonies of Capitalist property – enclaves isolated
from our socioeconomic system and operating under rules of
their own.[1]

Co-operation between enterprises has often paved the way for
broader East–West co-operation between industrial associations,
chambers of commerce, research institutes and government departments. These channels have in many cases been formalized in
official or semi-official agreements on scientific, technical, economic
and even cultural co-operation.[2]

The cases of economic co-operation between Socialist and
Capitalist countries outlined above, although impressive, do not
necessarily prove that the two camps have forgotten their fundamental differences and that harmony will prevail in the future.
Each side has been preoccupied with its immediate advantages
rather than genuinely interested in lasting reconciliation. There are
still various forms of discrimination in East–West trade, such as
quantitative restrictions on imports as well as exports and the
refusal to accord preferential tariff treatment and the transferability
of foreign-exchange earnings.

Some of these measures are specifically designed against the

[1] H. Kierzkowski, ('East–West Industrial Co-operation'), *Ekonomista* (The
Economist), Warsaw, 1/1968, p. 70.
[2] The Socialist countries have signed such agreements with at least the follow-
ing Western countries: Bulgaria – with Belgium, Denmark, Finland, Italy, the
UK; Czechoslovakia – with Austria, Belgium, Denmark, France, Italy, the UK;
the German Democratic Republic – with Austria and Sweden; Hungary – with
Austria, France, the Federal Republic of Germany, the Netherlands, Norway,
Sweden, Switzerland and the UK; Poland – with Belgium, Denmark, France,
Italy, the Netherlands, Sweden, the UK and the USA; Romania – with Austria,
France, Greece, Italy, the Netherlands, Sweden, the UK and the USA; the
USSR – with Austria, Belgium, Canada, Denmark, Finland, France, the Federal
Republic of Germany, Italy, Japan, Switzerland the UK and the USA;
Yugoslavia – with France, the Federal Republic of Germany, Italy, the UK and
the USA.

countries from the other side, whilst others are a by-product of exclusive economic groupings (especially CMEA and EEC). There are still deep-rooted vested interests – in particular industrial-military complexes in the West and ideological fervour in the East – with a stake in East–West tension. East–West relations have always been marked by sudden changes in the political climate and there is no guarantee that the recent *détente* will not be followed by more cold (or hot) warfare.

D. PROSPECTIVE CAPACITY FOR GROWTH

In this concluding part of the book, we shall attempt to estimate the capacity of the Socialist countries for economic growth up to the year 2000. It may be reasonably assumed that intensive sources of growth will continue to receive the focus of attention from the authorities. In the last two decades of this century, they are likely to be responsible for some two-thirds of total growth in the region (compared with about a quarter in the past two decades).

But in most of these countries – Bulgaria, Poland, Romania, the USSR and Yugoslavia – extensive growth will still play an important part in the next ten to twenty years. It will do so particularly in industry, which is likely to continue benefiting from preferential allocations of investment, and from increases in employment (partly contributed by transfers of manpower from agriculture). Profiting from extensive as well as enhanced intensive sources, industrial production is certain to grow more rapidly than national income as a whole, probably by about a fifth.

Compared with the pre-reform period, the pace of economic development in the Socialist countries will be enhanced by the following intensive sources of growth:

(*a*) *A More Efficient Use of Labour*. Shortages and hoarding of manpower will be less prevalent which, together with a greater possibility of dismissal, should contribute to the improvement of work discipline. The link established between material incentives and enterprise profits, the increasing attention given to time and motion studies (using Western experience and techniques) and a more systematic transfer of manpower from less efficient to more efficient industries will contribute to a greater productivity of labour than in the past.

(b) *A Greater Effectiveness in the Use of Capital.* Capital charges, higher interest rates, flexibly applied depreciation allowances and the increased practice of self-financing will discourage extravagant demands for fixed and working capital, the concealment of idle capacity and unwarranted extensions of the construction periods of investment projects. Larger proportions of investment resources will be channelled into working equipment, rather than into factory buildings and infrastructure, so that the capital–output ratio may decrease, or at least stop rising. The discontinuation of quantitative targets and the system of incentives based on them will encourage a greater economy in the use of raw materials and components.

(c) *More Economical Patterns of the Utilization of Land.* The implicit or explicit application of differential rent will provide a restraining effect on the taking over of land for non-agricultural purposes. It should also contribute to the distribution of different grades of land to their most effective uses.

(d) *Efficiency-Oriented Price Structures.* Prices are more likely to be related to scarcity, i.e. efficiency, than to the redistributive or rigid centralized planning needs of the State. An extension of the operation of the market mechanism, or optimal planning, or perhaps both at the same time, will be enlisted in evolving such prices.

(e) *A Greater Capacity for Technological Progress.* This will be aided by more initiative allowed to enterprises and research establishments and by the special research and innovation mark-ups on costs. This system will be more conducive to structural changes in favour of the technologically most progressive industries.

(f) *Progress in International Specialization.* Foreign trade is likely to continue growing at a faster rate than national income. Gains from trade should be enhanced by closer links between domestic and foreign markets and by the extension of multilateral payments.

(g) *A Better Error-Correcting System.* Waste on the macro-economic scale, consequent upon the misallocation of resources and recurring bottlenecks common in the past, should be reduced in the future owing to the elimination of directive centralized planning based on incomplete and biased information. The substantial decentralization of management, the wider operation of the market mechanism, the improved system of incentives and the strengthening of cost accounting should all prevent some errors from being committed and minimize losses in cases where they do occur.

At the same time, the reforms have created new problems which, directly or indirectly, may inhibit the pace of growth. Some of these problems did not exist before, or they could have been tackled more effectively by the administrative machinery available in the past. Under the decentralized system, it will be more difficult to make concentrated drives along the highest growth points. Growth may be further impaired by conflicts produced by the existence of central planning side by side with the market mechanism.

Recent experience has shown that the freedom granted to enterprises to determine their own prices for some products has led to many abuses, especially in Czechoslovakia, Hungary and Yugoslavia. In fact even in the remaining countries, enterprises have tended to produce the most profitable articles to the exclusion of less profitable items, however indispensable they might be to the economy.[1] Moreover, as a Socialist economist put it, 'The price paid for abandoning directive planning and management is the release of the inflationary spiral'.[2] This is most apparent in Yugoslavia, where the reforms started earliest and have gone furthest.[3]

[1] See, e.g., V. Garbuzov, ('Economic Reforms and Financial Matters'), *Kommunist*, Moscow, 3/1968, p. 46.

[2] K. Kraus, ('Guided Economy'), *Życie gospodarcze*, 30/3/1969, p. 11.

[3] According to official Yugoslav statistics, between 1952 (when the reforms first began) and 1969, retail prices increased by 185% and the cost of living by 287%. The rate of inflation has been the higher, the greater the degree of liberalization. Thus the average annual increase in retail prices was 2% between 1952 and 1960, and 14% between 1964 and 1969; the average annual increases in the cost of living over the respective periods were 5 and 17%. The inflationary pressure has been more tightly suppressed so far in other Socialist countries, but according to Socialist sources the annual increase in the cost of living since the

The freer operation of the market mechanism appears to be generating or accentuating economic fluctuations.[1] Similarly, unemployment is no longer an exclusive feature of Capitalism.[2] Where buyers' markets are developing, piling-up stocks of unsaleable goods are making their appearance side by side with shortages of other commodities. So far, the new problems have appeared most strikingly in Yugoslavia, but they may reach a similar magnitude in other Socialist countries if reforms are pushed to the same extremes and no lessons are learned from the Yugoslav experience. It is not unlikely that the liberalization produced by the reforms may lead to an increasing criticism of the Communist Parties. There is little doubt that the official policies will be directed first of all at the preservation of Party power, even if in conflict with

---

reforms has been in the order of 1–2%. Based on: Central Statistical Office of Yugoslavia, *Statistički godišnjak Jugoslavije 1969* (Statistical Yearbook of Yugoslavia for 1969), Belgrade, 1969, p. 121; *Życie gospodarcze*, 7/4/1968, p. 3.

[1] Since the reforms of 1952, Yugoslavia has experienced at least four recessions (in 1956, 1962, 1965 and 1967), and a Hungarian economist pointed out that in recent years fluctuations in Hungary were greater than in some market economies. It appears that most Socialist countries (especially Czechoslovakia, Hungary, Poland, Yugoslavia), even before the recent reforms, have been developing 'investment cycles' (with troughs commonly experienced in the mid-1950s and early 1960s); the reasons given for these cycles include errors in medium-term forecasting, tight planning, indifference to technological progress, bureaucracy and alienation. However, many Socialist economists, such as L. Leontyev of the USSR (see reference below), deny the possibility of cyclical fluctuations in a Socialist planned economy. For further details, see A. Bródy, 'Methods of Analysis and Forecasting Applied in Hungary', *Acta oeconomica* (Economic Papers), Budapest, vol. 4, no. 3, 1969, pp. 299–314; N. Čobeljić and Radmila Stojanović, *The Theory of Investment Cycles in a Socialist Economy*, New York, IASP, 1968; J. Goldmann, 'Short- and Long-Term Variations in the Growth Rate and the Model of Functioning of a Socialist Economy', *Czechosl. Econ. Papers*, no. 5, 1965, pp. 35–46, and his 'Karl Marx, the Soviet Economists of the Twenties and Contemporary "Konjunkturforschung" in Socialist Economy', *Czechosl. Econ. Papers*, no. 11, 1969, pp. 43–50; R. Hutchings, 'Periodic Fluctuations in Soviet Industrial Growth Rates', *Soviet Studies*, Jan 1969, pp. 331–52; L. Leontyev, ('The Market Process in a Socialist Economy'), *Kommunist*, 3/1967, pp. 62–73, esp. p. 64; B. Mieczkowski, 'The Unstable Soviet-Bloc Economies', *East Europe*, 10/1967, pp. 2–7; H. Olsienkiewicz, 'Problems of Imbalance, Inflation and Cyclic Fluctuations in the Communist Economy', *Bulletin*, Munich, 8/1968, pp. 13–25; W. Przelaskowski, ('Estimating the Average Investment Cycle in Poland under Socialism'), *Gospodarka planowa* (Planned Economy), Warsaw, 8/1968, pp. 39–40.

[2] In Yugoslavia since the reforms, unemployment has oscillated around 6%, ranging from 2 to 10% of the work force. See Chapter 1 C, note 4, p. 18, and Chapter 8 A, note 1, p. 125.

economic efficiency. If social or political disorder ensues, economic growth will suffer the more.[1]

But there are also other factors, not directly associated with the reforms, which may inhibit growth. These include the declining rates of increase in employment, reductions in the hours of work, lagging agriculture, raw material deficits (in countries other than the USSR) and the difficulties which are likely to be experienced in expanding exports to Capitalist countries. Furthermore, as higher levels of *per capita* consumption are reached, both workers and the authorities will be more concerned with the costs, rather than the maximization, of growth.

It is probable that the Socialist economic system will continue to be improved and more reforms will follow in the future. As a greater insight is gained into the operation of the new system, more effective measures will be evolved to cope with new problems. The more liberal attitudes amongst the leaders, a greater flexibility in the institutional set-up and the determination to increase the performance of the Socialist economy in competition with Capitalism suggest that continued improvement is likely.

But all in all, it is fairly certain that the new sources of intensive growth will not be sufficient to compensate for the shrinkage of extensive sources and the fact that at higher levels of national income greater absolute increases in production are essential to maintain a given rate. Consequently, in the author's reasoned view, the high rates of growth of the 1950s will not be repeated in the future over a period (as distinct from occasional years), even when economic reforms are fully implemented.

Socialist views on the future rates of growth differ widely. According to some economists, 'the languishing growth curve'

[1] According to a prediction made by I. de Sola Pool in a paper presented in 1965 at the Conference of the American Academy on the Year 2000: 'Around 1980, there will be a major political crisis in the Soviet Union, marked by large-scale strikes, the publication of dissident periodicals, a temporary disruption of central control over some regions, and an open clash between the major sectors of the bureaucracy over questions of military policy and consumer goods. This will stop just short of revolution, though it will result in the effectual abolition of the Communist Party or its splitting up into more than one organization, the abolition of the *kolkhoz*, and so forth. During these events, the Soviet hold over Eastern Europe will be completely broken.' I. de Sola Pool, 'The International System in the Next Half Century', in *Toward the Year 2000*, D. Bell (ed.), Boston, Houghton Mifflin, 1968, p. 321.

(declining rates of growth in higher stages of economic development) will not apply to Socialist planned economies. It is claimed
that the Socialist State is in a position to control the major proportions in the economy, and moreover it can increasingly activate
intensive sources of growth.[1]

A well-known Soviet economist, S. P. Pervushin, recently
argued that a long-run annual rate of 10–12 per cent is feasible.[2]
This rate would be about twice as high as that expected for the
Capitalist world. However, some other economists believe that
the average Socialist rates will stabilize themselves at the level of
50–70 per cent above the expected rates for Capitalist countries[3]
(according to Socialist sources, the percentage in the 1950s was
on the average 80 per cent). Both these predictions are, in this
writer's view, too optimistic. In particular, Pervushin's 'feasible'
rate is obviously based on the assumption that the proportion of
national income reserved for investment is pushed close to the
limits of social endurance, thus providing an ample source of
extensive growth as in the 1950s.

As is well known, economic forecasting is a very ungrateful task.
First of all, the pitfalls associated with current or past estimates of
national income involving countries using different systems of
valuation are formidable enough, and the absence of equilibrium
exchange rates represents another hurdle. When it comes to forecasting, these problems are, of course, in many ways magnified.
Nevertheless, rather than concede 'it cannot be done', attempts are
made here to make predictions on the basis of the available data and
on what are thought to be 'reasonable' assumptions.

Even though the results produced in the following pages are
approximate, and the future can prove them to be either optimistic
or below the actual mark, they can still be considered as interesting
and useful for broad comparative purposes – and no more than
just that is aimed at in this discussion. To enhance the compar-

[1] E. Gorbunov, ('The Efficiency of Accumulation and Economic Growth'),
Kommunist, 8/1967, pp. 88–97; K. Łaski ('The Question of Economic Growth
in Socialist Countries'), *Nowe drogi* (New Paths), Warsaw, 1/1968, pp. 85–93.
[2] S. P. Pervushin, 'Production and Consumption at a New Stage', *Problems of
Economics*, Jan–Feb–Mar 1967, p. 11.
[3] J. Kleer, J. Zawadzki and J. Górski, *Socjalizm–Kapitalizm* (Socialism versus
Capitalism), Warsaw, KiW, 1967, p. 98.

ability with Capitalist countries, the Western concept of national
income is adhered to in the subsequent analysis, and furthermore
all values are expressed in US dollars at constant prices of 1970.
The figures produced in the four tables to follow are based on
low, medium and high projection variants up to the end of this
century, and in the last table extrapolation is carried beyond the
year 2000. The figures for the period after 1985 must, of course,
be regarded as merely reasoned 'guestimates'. An absence of
major wars and social upheavals is implicitly assumed.[1]

The most plausible Socialist annual rate of growth for the next
fifteen years is considered by this writer to be about 6 per cent for
the region as a whole. This rate would be about 20 per cent higher
than the expected rate for the Capitalist world. The less developed
Socialist countries (Bulgaria, Romania) will attain higher rates,
perhaps 7 per cent, whilst the more developed ones (Czechoslovakia, the German Democratic Republic, Hungary) will reach
about 5 per cent. In the last fifteen years of this century, all these
rates are likely to fall, perhaps by one-sixth. The estimated rates for
the next thirty years, with low, medium and high variants and
projections of national income for the years 1985 and 2000 for each
of the eight Socialist countries, are given in Table 42. For comparison, estimates and projections for the USA, the Capitalist
countries and the world are also included.

If we accept the predicted possible rates of growth for each
Socialist country for 1970–85 and 1986–2000 (columns 5 and 7 in
Table 42) and make comparisons with the actual rates recorded
over the period 1951–69 (column 2), it is apparent that no Socialist
country will repeat its past growth performance in the future – not
even by the high variant.[2] In contrast to the assertions made by

---

[1] To avoid a misleading impression of accuracy, the figures for national
income as given in Table 42 have been rounded to the nearest $10m., the national
income per head (in Table 44) to the nearest $10, for population (Table 43) to
the nearest 10,000. The rates of population increase have been rounded to the
nearest first decimal point and the variant rates of growth of national income
have been restricted to the multiples of 0·5%; in the latter case, however, overall
rates for the eight Socialist countries have been arrived at from the totals of
absolute figures. The rounding of the totals was not, of course, done in the
process of calculations but only after final figures have been extrapolated.

[2] Except perhaps Hungary (which over the period 1951–69, for a variety of
reasons, scored a relatively low rate) over the period 1970–85, but this is rather
unlikely.

TABLE 42 ESTIMATES AND PROJECTIONS OF THE GROWTH AND
SIZE OF NATIONAL INCOME,* 1950–2000
*In all Cases, the Size of National Income is Expressed in US $ Million
at Constant Prices of 1970†*

COUNTRY (1)	Average Annual Rate of Growth,‡ 1951–69 (2)	Estimated National Income in 1970§ ($m.) (3)	Projection Variant ¶ (4)	Possible Average Annual Rate of Growth, 1971–85 (5)	Projected National Income in 1985 ($m.) (6)	Possible Average Annual Rate of Growth, 1986–2000 (7)	Projected National Income in 2000 ($m.) (8)
Bulgaria	8·4	7,240	L	5·0	15,050	4·0	27,110
			M	6·5	18,620	5·5	41,570
			H	8·0	22,970	6·5	59,070
Czechoslovakia	6·3	26,810	L	3·0	41,770	3·0	65,070
			M	4·5	51,880	4·0	93,440
			H	6·0	64,250	5·0	133,570
GDR	7·3	32,500	L	3·0	50,630	3·0	78,890
			M	5·0	67,570	4·5	130,760
			H	6·5	83,580	6·0	200,310
Hungary	5·1	13,440	L	3·0	20,340	2·5	30,330
			M	4·5	26,010	3·5	43,580
			H	6·0	32,210	4·5	62,330
Poland	7·0	41,070	L	4·0	73,960	3·5	123,920
			M	5·5	91,690	4·5	177,440
			H	7·0	113,310	6·5	291,420
Romania	8·4	16,840	L	5·0	35,010	4·0	63,050
			M	6·5	43,310	5·5	96,690
			H	8·0	53,420	7·0	147,380
USSR	8·8	409,000	L	4·0	736,580	3·5	1,234,030
			M	6·0	980,190	5·0	2,037,740
			H	7·5	1,210,180	6·5	3,112,370
Yugoslavia	7·3	13,360	L	3·0	20,810	3·0	32,430
			M	5·5	29,830	5·0	62,000
			H	7·0	36,860	6·5	94,800
The EIGHT SOCIALIST COUNTRIES	8·2	560,260	L	3·9	994,150	3·4	1,654,830
			M	5·8	1,309,100	4·9	2,683,220
			H	7·3	1,616,780	6·4	4,101,250
USA	3·6	802,000	L	2·5	1,161,530	2·0	1,563,270
			M	4·0	1,444,350	3·5	2,419,790
			H	5·0	1,667,300	5·0	3,466,180
ALL CAPITALIST COUNTRIES	4·6	1,889,750	L	3·5	3,165,980	3·0	4,932,490
			M	4·5	3,657,190	4·0	6,586,370
			H	5·5	4,218,810	5·0	8,770,580
WORLD	5·3	2,555,000	L	4·0	4,601,400	3·5	7,708,920
			M	5·0	5,311,650	4·5	10,279,510
			H	6·0	6,123,190	5·5	13,669,840

* Except in column 2 in application to the Socialist countries over the period 1951–69, the
Western concept of national income is used throughout (i.e. net national product at factor cost).
† The price structure assumed for the Socialist countries is intermediate between that of the
USA and the USSR.

‡ The rate in application to the Socialist countries is based on the Socialist concept of national income (net material product at realized prices). This rate, based on official returns, has been derived from the averages calculated by the United Nations (*Yearbook of National Accounts Statistics 1968*, vol. II, p. 112) supplemented by the author.

§ The Soviet national income is taken as representing 51 % of the US national income in 1970. The national income figures of the other Socialist countries have then been arrived at by applying weights derived from a variety of Socialist and Western sources, adjusted by the author.

¶ L = low, M = medium (not necessarily a mean between 'low' and 'high'), H = high.

some Socialist economists, in the writer's view the 'languishing growth curve' applies to Socialist planned economies as well.

It may also be assumed that with higher levels of material well-being the pressure for more leisure time and the likely decline in authoritarianism, governments will be increasingly concerned with the social cost of excessively high growth. Progress being made in social cost-benefit analysis under Socialist conditions appears to support this speculation. A drive towards 'Full Communism', which is probable in the last two decades of this century, is also likely to slow down growth. It may be observed here that some of the economic performance in the future, particularly in respect of the suitability and quality of output, will not necessarily be reflected statistically in growth rates. In other words, future rates may appear low in comparison with the past Socialist figures because the latter were unduly influenced by the quantitative growth of material production, and the extreme price irrationalities added an upward bias.[1]

Another reason for the prospective slowdown of the growth of national income is the declining rate of population increase in the Socialist countries. The annual rate over the period 1950–70 for the eight Socialist countries was 1·3. But the medium rate for 1970–85 is expected to be 0·8, and for 1985–2000, 0·6; in fact in the case of Hungary, the growth of population in the last decade or two of this century is likely to be close to nil. The average annual birth rate in the region as a whole was 2·5 in the 1950s, 2·0 in the 1960s and is expected to fall to 1·7 or less in the future.[2]

---

[1] Because industrial production, which was growing fastest, was relatively over-priced in relation to the slowest-growing branches of material production (agriculture and trade) whilst the 'non-productive' sphere – which was neglected most in the whole economy – had no direct effect on growth rates (as it did not form part of material production).

[2] For a thorough study of this question, see J. Berent, 'Causes of Fertility Decline in Eastern Europe and the Soviet Union', *Population Studies*, Mar 1970, pp. 35–58, and July 1970, pp. 247–92.

TABLE 43 ACTUAL AND PROJECTED POPULATION GROWTH,
1950–2000

COUNTRY		RATES OF POPULATION INCREASE			POPULATION IN '000*		
	1950–70 (Actual)	1970–85 (Possible)†	1985–2000 (Possible)†		1970 (Actual)	1985 (Projected)†	2000 (Projected)†
Bulgaria	1·0	L 0·5 M 0·6 H 0·8	0·2 0·3 0·8	L M H	8,510	9,040 9,260 9,870	9,200 9,650 11,050
Czechoslovakia	0·8	L 0·2 M 0·3 H 0·7	n 0·2 0·6	L M H	14,470	14,890 15,180 16,250	14,900 15,550 17,850
GDR	0·3	L −0·1 M 0·1 H 0·5	n 0·3 0·7	L M H	17,110	16,900 17,400 18,360	17,000 18,250 20,300
Hungary	0·6	L 0·1 M 0·2 H 0·6	−0·2 0·0 0·5	L M H	10,340	10,490 10,750 11,430	10,200 10,750 12,250
Poland	1·4	L 0·6 M 0·8 H 1·1	0·3 0·4 0·6	L M H	32,860	35,940 37,030 38,720	37,600 39,350 42,350
Romania	1·3	L 0·7 M 0·9 H 1·4	0·6 0·9 1·5	L M H	20,300	22,540 23,430 25,020	24,650 26,560 31,250
USSR	1·5	L 0·7 M 0·9 H 1·3	0·5 0·7 1·1	L M H	242,870	268,650 278,200 294,100	289,600 309,900 346,700
Yugoslavia	1·4	L 0·6 M 0·9 H 1·2	0·4 0·6 1·0	L M H	20,550	22,500 23,400 24,700	23,700 25,800 28,700
THE EIGHT SOCIALIST COUNTRIES	1·3	L 0·6 M 0·8 H 1·2	0·4 0·6 1·1	L M H	367,010	400,950 414,650 438,450	426,850 455,800 510,450
USA	1·4	L 1·2 M 1·4 H 1·6	1·1 1·3 1·5	L M H	205,320	245,500 252,900 260,500	289,300 307,000 325,700
ALL CAPITALIST COUNTRIES	2·1	L 1·9 M 2·1 H 2·4	1·7 1·9 2·3	L M H	2,466,500	3,271,100 3,368,700 3,520,300	4,212,200 4,467,600 4,951,200
WORLD	1·9	L 1·8 M 2·0 H 2·3	1·5 1·8 2·2	L M H	3,630,000	4,743,000 4,885,000 5,106,000	5,930 000 6,384,000 7,076,000

n = negligible, less than 0·05.

* In the case of the Socialist countries other than Yugoslavia, negligible net emigration is assumed; if substantial emigration does take place in the future, the figures in the table are overstated to that extent.

† L = low, M = medium (not necessarily a mean between 'low' and 'high'). H = high.

Sources. The rates of population increase or/and projections are based on the following: Central Statistical Office of Poland, *Rozwój gospodarczy krajów RWPG 1950–1968* (Economic Development of the CMEA Countries 1950–1968), Warsaw, 1969, pp. 51–2; *Gospodarka planowa* (Planned Economy), Warsaw, 9/1969, p. 23; G. Baldwin, 'Projections of the Population of the Communist Countries of Eastern Europe, by Age and Sex: 1969–1990', and 'Projections of the Population of the USSR, by Age and Sex: 1969–1990', in *International Population Reports*, US Dept of Commerce, Dec 1969, Series P–91, nos. 18 and 19; United Nations, Population Division, *World Population Prospects 1965–1985 as Assessed in 1968*. Working Paper No. 30, Dec 1969. Adjustments have been made by the author to the data in these sources in the light of the latest evidence.

There has also been a slight decline in death rates from about 0·9 in the 1950s to 0·8 by 1970. This, together with the falling birth rate, is contributing to the 'ageing' of the population – with the consequent prospective decline in the proportion of population in the working-age bracket, and an increase in the old-age group and in the death rate (to perhaps 1·0 by the year 2000).

The rates of population increase, together with totals for each Socialist country for 1970, 1985 and 2000, are listed in Table 43. The predicted slower growth of Socialist population contrasts with the higher rates for Capitalist countries and the world as a whole. If the Socialist countries liberalize their restrictions on emigration, their working-age group and perhaps birth rate may be further adversely affected.

One of the big ambitions nurtured by Soviet leaders has always been to catch up with and surpass the production level of the United States – economically the largest and most developed Capitalist country. As many readers will recall, according to the Programme of the 22nd Congress of the Communist Party of the Soviet Union presented by N. S. Khrushchev in 1961, the USSR was to overtake the USA by 1970.[1]

This target has not, of course, been reached. According to this

[1] *The Road to Communism*, Documents of the 22nd Congress of the CPSU Moscow, FLPH, 1961, pp. 515, 524, 539.

writer's estimates, the Soviet national income in 1970 stood at 51 per cent of the US figure.[1] Nor is this goal likely to be achieved before the end of this century. If we accept the medium growth variants of national income in both countries continuing as in Table 42, the Soviet Union will overtake the United States in the year 2013.[2] It is, of course, possible that the actual rates of growth in the two countries may be different from the medium variants, in which case the Soviet dreams may come true earlier, later or never.[3] But even if they are realized, will this feat enthrone the Soviet economy supreme in the world scene?

Not necessarily, if the forecasts by some economists on the prospective growth of the Japanese economy prove correct. There are indications that Japan is likely to overtake the United States in steel output by the middle (or late) 1970s, and according to an

[1] The comparative studies carried out in the USA and the USSR in recent years placed the Soviet national income (or GNP) between 1962 and 1970 at from 31 to 64% of the US total: the International Bank for Reconstruction and Development, 31·3% (for the year 1967); H. Kahn and A. J. Wiener, 42·9% (1965); S. H. Cohn, 46·7% (1964); US Congress, Joint Economic Committee, 48·0% (1966); M. Boretsky, about 51% (1970); B. Vladimirov, 62% (1966); S. Strumilin, 62·8% (1962); the Central Statistical Office of the USSR, 63·6% (1968); it may be surprising to many (American as well as non-American) readers, but in 1970 the American magazine *Time* credited the USSR with a GNP of $600,000m. for 1969, or 64·4% of the US GNP in the same year. Sources (in the same order): IBRD, *World Bank Atlas*, Washington, 1969, p. 3; H. Kahn and A. J. Wiener, *The Year 2000*, New York, Macmillan, 1967, p. 159; S. H. Cohn, in US Congress, JEC, *New Directions in the Soviet Economy*, Washington, GPO, 1966, Part II-A, p. 109; US Congress, JEC, *Soviet Economic Performance 1966–67*, Washington, GPO, 1968, p. 16; M. Boretsky, in US Congress, JEC, *New Directions in the Soviet Economy*, p. 155; B. Vladimirov, in *Kommunist*, 1/1968, p. 41; S. Strumilin, in *Voprosy ekonomiki* (Problems of Economics), Moscow, 7/1963, p. 114; *Time*, 13/7/1970, p. 15.

[2] This prediction is less optimistic than that by some Soviet economists who, even with the benefit of the hindsight of the 22nd Party Congress Programme, forecast in the mid-1960s that the number of years needed would be fifteen to twenty. This writer's prediction, by the medium variants, is close to that made by a Polish economist, J. Zawadzki, who in 1967 estimated the number of years needed as between thirty and forty and who criticized the Soviet forecasts as unrealistic. See J. Kleer, J. Zawadzki and J. Górski, op. cit., p. 62.

[3] If the low variant of growth in the USA is combined with the high, medium and low variants in the USSR, the USA will be overtaken in 1985, 1991 or 2017 respectively; if the medium variant in the USA is paired with the high variant in the USSR, in 1992; if the high variant in the USA coincides with the high variant in the USSR, in 2008. The USSR will never overtake the USA if the US medium variant is matched with the low variant in the USSR, and the US high variant with the low and medium variants in the USSR.

American expert, H. Kahn, Japan may supplant the USA as the world's No. 1 economic power by the end of this century or early in the next.[1] It must be realized that over the last two decades Japan's rate of growth (9·5) was nearly three times as high as the US rate (3·6) and it was also higher than that scored by the USSR (8·8).[2]

The estimate of *per capita* income for 1970 and projections for 1985 and 2000 are presented in Table 44. As in preceding tables, figures for the USA, the Capitalist countries as a whole and for the world are also given. It will be noted that according to the estimate for 1970 the German Democratic Republic was rated as having the highest national income per head ($1,900), followed by Czechoslovakia ($1,850) and the USSR ($1,680), whilst Bulgaria (with $850), Romania ($830) and Yugoslavia ($650) were at the other end of the scale. The figures for Hungary ($1,300) and Poland ($1,250) were also below the region's average ($1,530). It can be observed that even the highest *per capita* income, in the German Democratic Republic, was less than half of the US level. However, the region's average of $1,530 was about twice as high as for the Capitalist countries taken together (i.e. underdeveloped areas included) – $770 – and compared even more favourably with the world average of $700.

Projections for the years 1985 and 2000 are based on the low, medium and high variants of national income divided by the medium population. To protect himself against all contingencies, the author was tempted to include results for low, medium and high population variants. However, at the risk of being proved wrong but in the interest of greater clarity, the low, medium and high national income figures were divided by medium population only in each case. Socialist leaders frequently like to refer to the process of 'the evening out of the economic levels amongst fraternal Socialist nations'. The achievement of this ideal implies that the growth of *per capita* income will have to be faster in the poorer than in the richer Socialist countries. If the same growth variant is assumed for all these countries, there is little hope of

[1] See, e.g., H. Kahn, *The Emerging Japanese Superstate*, Englewood Cliffs, Prentice-Hall, 1970.
[2] See Table 3, p. 8, and Table 42, p. 330.

TABLE 44 ESTIMATED AND PROJECTED NATIONAL INCOME PER
HEAD IN 1970, 1985 AND 2000
In US Dollars of 1970

COUNTRY	Estimate for 1970		Projections for:*	
			1985	2000
Bulgaria	850	L	1,630	2,810
		M	2,010	4,310
		H	2,480	6,120
Czechoslovakia	1,850	L	2,750	4,180
		M	3,420	6,010
		H	4,230	8,590
GDR	1,900	L	2,910	4,640
		M	3,880	7,160
		H	4,800	10,980
Hungary	1,300	L	1,890	2,820
		M	2,420	4,050
		H	3,000	5,800
Poland	1,250	L	2,000	3,150
		M	2,480	4,510
		H	3,060	7,410
Romania	830	L	1,490	2,380
		M	1,850	3,640
		H	2,280	5,550
USSR	1,680	L	2,650	3,980
		M	3,520	6,580
		H	4,350	10,400
Yugoslavia	650	L	890	1,260
		M	1,270	2,400
		H	1,580	3,670
THE EIGHT SOCIALIST COUNTRIES	1,530	L	2,400	3,630
		M	3,160	5,890
		H	3,900	9,000
USA	3,910	L	4,590	5,090
		M	5,710	7,880
		H	6,590	11,290

TABLE 44—*Continued*

COUNTRY	Estimate for 1970		Projections for:* 1985	2000
ALL		L	940	1,100
CAPITALIST	770	M	1,090	1,470
COUNTRIES		H	1,250	1,960
		L	940	1,210
WORLD	700	M	1,090	1,610
		H	1,250	2,140

* Low (L), medium (M), high (H) variants of national income divided by medium population. The Western concept of national income is used and constant prices of 1970 are assumed throughout.

Source. Derived from Tables 42 and 43.

equalization in this century. Even in the year 2000, the figure for the most prosperous country (the GDR) is expected to be nearly three times as high as for the least affluent (Yugoslavia). For the gap to be eliminated, the less developed Socialist countries would have to follow higher growth variants than the more developed ones. It is possible, however, that the gap within the CMEA group may be narrowed down by economic aid and some form of concessions to the poorer member nations.

Although the Socialist countries have on ideological grounds traditionally disparaged the 'American way of life', they have none the less cherished the vision of enjoying the 'American' standard of living. If the same patterns of growth and their continuation after the year 2000 are assumed as in Table 44, then the most affluent Socialist country, the German Democratic Republic, will reach the US *per capita* income of 1970 ($3,910) between 1981 and 1998, Czechoslovakia between 1983 and 1999 and the USSR between 1983 and 2001. On the other hand, Yugoslavia will attain this level some time during the first half of the next century. The details for each Socialist country, corresponding to the high, medium and low variants of the growth of national income, are set out in column 2 of Table 45.

TABLE 45 THE SOCIALIST COUNTRIES AND THE US NATIONAL
INCOME PER HEAD*

COUNTRY	When the US National Income per head of 1970 ($3,910) is projected to be reached			When the USA may be overtaken in National Income per head		
	H	M	L	H	M	L
Bulgaria	1993	1999	2010	2007	2021	2070
Czechoslovakia	1984	1989	1998	1997	2018	2105
GDR	1982	1986	1997	1991	2005	2118
Hungary	1992	1999	2014	2014	2053	never
Poland	1990	1997	2008	2002	2031	2103
Romania	1995	2002	2017	2010	2034	2137
USSR	1984	1988	2000	1993	2009	2115
Yugoslavia	2002	2012	2049	2022	2056	never

* To reduce the projections to manageable proportions, the figures are based
on the following assumed variants: (a) for the USA – medium variants of the
growth of national income and of population; (b) for the Socialist countries –
high (H), medium (M) and low (L) variants of the growth of national income and
the medium variant of the growth of population. Constant prices of 1970 are
assumed throughout.

Source. Derived from Tables 42 and 43 (on the assumption that the trends continue after the year 2000).

However, the aim postulated by Socialist leaders is not merely
to reach a given level of *per capita* income, but actually to surpass
the most prosperous Capitalist nations. This ambition is conditioned not only by the desire to create the promised cornucopia
for the masses but also to prove the superiority of Socialism as a
social system. If the Socialist growth rates continue to be higher
than in the most affluent Capitalist economies, this is not impossible. Still adhering to the same assumptions, some Socialist
countries (Czechoslovakia, the GDR and the USSR) may outstrip
the USA in the 1990s.

However, in the most likely case – medium growth variants of
national income (and population) in the Socialist countries as well
as in the USA – the overtaking may occur in the first six decades of
the next century. If the low variant of the growth of national in-

come is assumed for the Socialist countries, some of them (Hungary and Yugoslavia) will never make it. The complete list is given in column 3 of Table 45. These calculations are based on two convenient assumptions – that the rates of growth for the remaining three decades of this century are correct and that the trend continues after the year 2000. In particular, the latter assumption is a gross over-simplification which almost certainly favours the Socialist countries (especially in respect of population).

However, it may very well turn out that even if the United States is eclipsed, the Socialist countries may yet find – like weary travellers who realize that there is always another mountain between them and their destination – that their aim still exceeds their grasp and that an unexpected obstacle still bars the way. If Japan – with half the US or Soviet population – surpasses the US level of GNP by the year 2000 or soon after, as some forecasters claim, then the Socialist countries will be confronted with a challenge of a new dimension altogether.

But even if the Socialist countries do outstrip the wealthiest Capitalist nation in *per capita* income, will this prove the superiority of Socialism (or Communism) over Capitalism? As is well known, Socialist leaders have been, and still are, obsessed with reaching material production targets. Thus it has been repeated with pride time and again that the USSR is now the world's leading producer of coal, iron ore, cement, bricks, window glass, milk and butter, that in 1967 she topped the 100m. tons of steel-a-year mark, and that by 1975 she will exceed the US steel output.[1] According to a Polish economist, by 1980 the CMEA region's share in world agricultural output will rise to 29–38 per cent (compared with 20 per cent in 1960), in world industrial output to 36–39 per cent (30 per cent in 1960) and in world exports to 20 per cent (10 per cent in 1960).[2]

This writer has no intention of disputing the fact that the Soviets produce more window glass, bricks, milk, etc., than any other country in the world, and furthermore that all the promised targets

---

[1] See, e.g., I. Kuzminov, 'Superiority of Socialism', *International Affairs*, Moscow, 12/1967, p. 34; P. Alampiyev and Yu. Shiryayev, ('In Honour of the 20th Anniversary of the Council for Mutual Economic Assistance'), *Vop. ekon.*, 1/1969, pp. 47–57, esp. p. 48.

[2] S. Albinowski, op. cit., pp. 27, 47.

will be fulfilled by 1980 and so on. So what? Production per head has hardly ever been a reliable measure of either economic viability or the standard of living, even by present-day thinking.

But this indicator will be even less satisfactory in the future. In fact it may become obsolete in the context of the high levels of material welfare reached all round. It is likely that other criteria – of a qualitative nature – will be perfected and accepted as more closely reflecting economic progress and social welfare. Such prospective indicators may very well include the production and application of high-memory computers, lasers and masers, intermetallics and cermets, super-performance building materials and fibres, magnetohydrodynamic and thermionic appliances on the one hand,[1] and the physical and psychological work environment, social amenities, educational and cultural standards, personal freedom, harmony amongst different social groups and the amount and quality of leisure on the other. The Socialist countries have a greater potential for excelling in some of these fields than in others, but in any case they will have to prove themselves in reality, and perform better in many of these and similar respects than they have in the past.

[1] For the prospective technological developments in the next three to five decades, see the authoritative study by H. Kahn and A. J. Wiener, op. cit., esp. pp. 51–7.

Index of Names

Subject Index

Acceleration of economic development, 20, 44, 62, 129 ff., 165, 220, 239 ff.
Access to markets, 280–1, 294–5
Accumulation, 29–30, 165 ff., 219, 236. *See also* Investment
Advertising, 107, 209
Agriculture, 9, 12, 39, 76, 139–40, 189 ff., 201 ff., 339
Albania, 1, 101, 176, 272
Allocation of resources, 57, 62, 71 ff., 77, 82, 96, 156, 179, 183, 191, 301, 325
Artificial fertilizers, 206–7
Assets, 101, 131, 172
Autarky, 41, 187, 260, 261, 265, 268–9, 302

Banks, 144 ff.
  and incentives, 152
  central, 144, 146, 148 ff.
  centralization, 146 ff.
  diversification, 146
  function under the old system, 144 ff.
  new banks, 147
  reforms, 145 ff.
  relations with enterprises, 147 ff., 152 ff.
  savings, 149, 151
Bilateralism, 90, 273–4, 289
Bottlenecks, 5, 31, 34, 63, 154, 172, 230, 250, 260, 261, 314
Budgetary allocation of finance, 152, 159, 166
Bulgaria, 5, 6, 10, 12, 50, 88, 92, 113, 114, 121, 134, 150–1, 157, 177, 190, 194, 204, 207, 211,

218–19, 246, 249, 267, 268, 278, 297, 306, 308, 309, 317, 330, 332, 336, 338
Buyers' markets, 90, 97, 106, 107, 115, 173, 231, 232, 326

Capital charges, 42, 93, 104, 140, 176 ff., 179–80, 187, 324
Capital deepening and widening, 41, 131, 169
Capital–labour ratio, 131, 233, 235
Capital–output ratio, 219–20
CMEA, 2, 71, 85, 91 ff., 101, 127, 128, 163, 179, 187, 191, 192–3, 195, 198, 207, 208, 246, 252 ff., 253 n., 261 ff., 271, 272, 275, 287, 289, 297, 304, 305, 339
Cold War, 265, 267 n., 313, 315
Collective farms, 203 ff.
Comecon, *see* CMEA
Commercialization of economic relations, 40, 205, 232, 245, 258
Communist Party, 21, 54, 55, 62, 69, 128, 143, 241, 302, 326–7
Competition, 42, 58, 96, 106–7, 112, 200, 215, 231, 232, 295, 327
Computers, 40, 69 ff., 75, 82 n., 228, 239, 270, 293, 304
Concentration, 41, 186, 197, 199, 201, 211, 253
Consumer credit, 113, 149, 154 ff., 217, 223
Consumer durables, 113 ff., 149, 154 ff., 198
Consumer goods, 110, 197, 221, 228
Consumers' preferences, 77, 103, 104, 222, 227, 232